Swallow Summer

Charles R. Brown

University of Nebraska Press
Lincoln and London

The paper in this book meets the minimum require-
ments of American National Standard for Information
Sciences—Permanence of Paper for Printed Library
Materials, ANSI Z39.48-1984.

Library of Congress Cataloging-in-Publication Data

Brown, Charles Robert, 1958–
Swallow summer / Charles R. Brown
p.   cm.
"A Bision original"—P.
Includes index.   ISBN 0-8032-6145-4 (pbk.)
1. Hirundo pyrrhonota—Nebraska.   2. Social behavior
in animals.   3. Zoology—Field work.   I. Title.
QL696.P247B7624   1999
598.8′26—dc21   98-4551   CIP

One swallow does not make a summer.
—Aristotle, *Nicomachean Ethics*

Contents

Illustrations

Maps
following page xii

Plates
following page 125

following page 265

Preface

This is a book about why I love to do research. I have had two goals in mind while writing. The first has been to convey the challenges, thrills, and frustrations that come with studying wild animals in the field. Scientists often aren't very good at communicating what they do, and the public in general is unaware of the excitement that comes—often daily—to those of us fortunate enough to be involved in scientific discovery. I want to share that excitement. I have tried to make my story about research accessible to anyone with even a casual interest in natural history. This book describes research in one place on one species, but it could represent any time, any place, or any scientist who seeks to learn something new about things he or she loves.

My second goal in writing this book has been to tell the cliff swallow's story. This bird is one of the world's most fascinating creatures. It nests in enormous colonies, and its social life is a complex web of diverse traits, all associated in some way with its habit of forming groups. Some of these traits are shared by all social organisms, including humans. It's impossible to convey in sterile scientific language the true essence of these little birds: how competitive, cooperative, mean, insecure, and thoroughly social cliff swallows are. I want to share with others why they have intrigued me for so long.

Since this book is about both field biology and the cliff swallows themselves, I have intended it for several audiences. One consists of people who are interested in science, natural history, or birds but have no formal training in biology. I have tried to write as plainly as possible, without technical terms. Other readers I've had in mind are students who might be contemplating research, especially field research, and who might gain some guidance from my experiences. Professional ecologists and ornithologists might find this story at least entertaining, and perhaps they too will learn something new about these birds and their behavior. I hope most of all that anyone with even mild interest in what scientists do, or curiosity about what motivates some of us, will use this book to vicariously experience life in the field.

The research this book is based on was possible only because I received help from many people over a fourteen-year period. I am grateful to them all, but a few deserve special mention. Nearly forty students have come to the field with me as assistants over the years, and all have had their own stories. But none have been exposed as publicly as the three young women who figure so prominently in this book. They are special people whom I will never forget, and I thank them for their tireless efforts in the field and especially for allowing my "warts and all" description of their summer experience. I have changed their names in the text to spare them any embarrassment.

To the other members of the cast, I offer my thanks: Ted Burk, Joan Darling, Duane Dunwoody, Tony Joern, Dave Knight, Josef Kren, Diana Pilson, Ron Randall, Nanci Ross, and all the 1995 inhabitants of the Cedar Point Biological Station. I've generously been allowed use of Cedar Point's facilities by a succession of field station directors, but my research owes the most to John Janovy Jr., who originally invited me to come to Nebraska and has remained a friend and supporter. My research has been backed financially by a number of agencies and organizations, especially the National Science Foundation and the National Geographic Society. I was first encouraged to write this book by Christie Henry. The Ecological Society of America, Art Gingert, and the University of Chicago Press kindly allowed me to use copyrighted material. I thank James Lacy at the University of Nebraska–Lincoln's Center for Advanced Land Management Information Technologies, who produced the maps. Mary Bomberger Brown, Christie Henry, John Hoogland, John Janovy Jr., James Platz, and Bruce Rannala read the manuscript and gave me useful advice on ways to improve it. The most improvement, though, came from Alice Bennett, who copyedited the manuscript. I thank the staff at the University of Nebraska Press, whose efforts made the book a reality. I'll always be grateful to John Hoogland for suggesting I study cliff swallows in the first place. My parents, Raymond and Kathryn Brown, have always tolerated my rather esoteric interest in birds, which began at age eleven. Most of all I thank my wife, Mary Bomberger Brown. She's there on every page, standing behind me, beside me, or in front of me. Without her love and support, and her integral role in the research itself, there would have been no swallow summer.

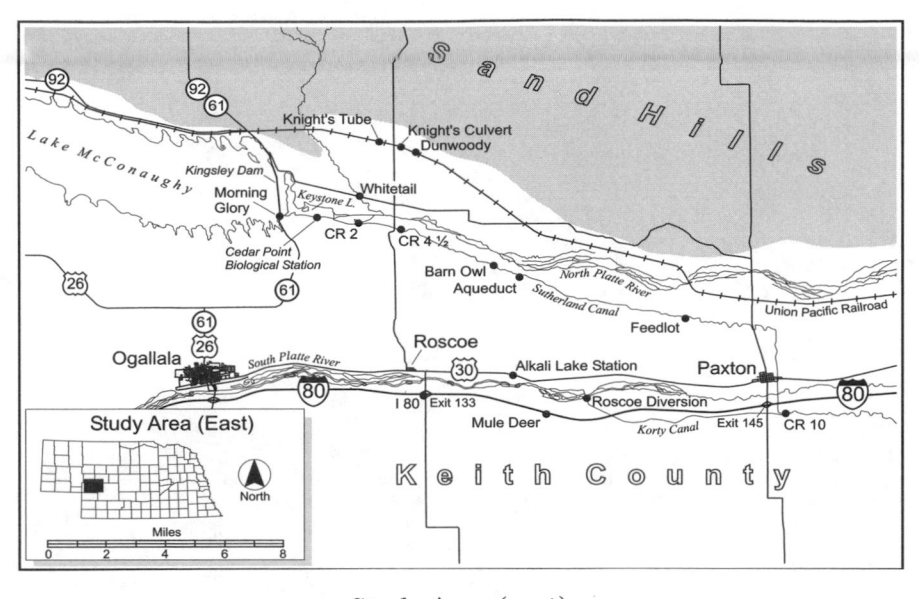

Study Area (east)

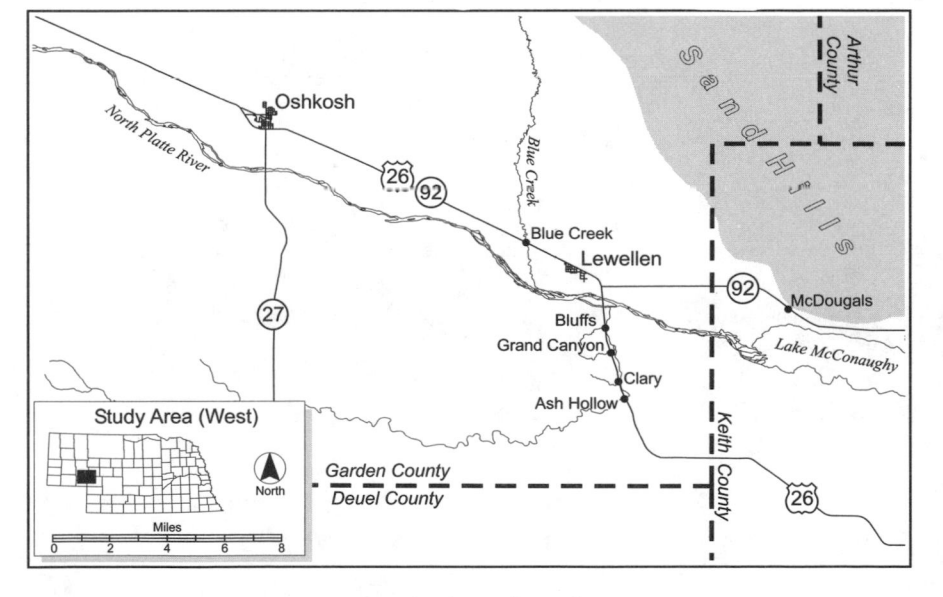

Study Area (west)

1

Beginnings

"I'm bound for Ogallala, honey."
"Where's that?"
"In Nebraska."
"What's there?"
        —Larry McMurtry, *Lonesome Dove*

May 8, 1995

Will the birds use Whitetail this year? I've asked myself this question daily for the past nine months, wondering whether the cliff swallows Mary and I study each year will return from South America and occupy the same small road culvert in Nebraska where we have studied them for fourteen summers. We'll soon know the answer, because the time has finally come to drive north and begin another swallow summer.

The friendly toll taker on the Cimarron Turnpike in Oklahoma notices the Nebraska license plate on the truck and asks where in Nebraska I'm from. Although right now we live in Tulsa, Oklahoma, we register one of our research vehicles in Nebraska, in part because local tags mean fewer hassles from lawmen when they see our truck parked beside a bridge or highway culvert where swallows live. Without thought, my immediate response is "Ogallala." Despite institutional affiliations over the past decade and a half that have led Mary and me to call Princeton, New Haven, Seattle, and Tulsa our academic-year "home" at various times, our real home is our research site near Ogallala. We've spent more time there—always during the summer— than in any other single place, reflecting the gypsy lifestyle of many field biologists whose research provides the only stability in their lives. To my surprise the toll taker replies that she lived in Ogallala for nine months and disapprovingly informs me that it's usually cold and windy up there. I smile and wonder if she's ever watched the cliff swallows of Ogallala. Probably not, because few people who don't explicitly look for them see the incredible natural history spectacle these birds present.

The toll taker stands between me and theft, rape, aggression, exploitation, parasitism, competition and cooperation, egotism and altruism. These words describe cliff swallow society, a world where conflict is the rule yet teamwork is essential for survival. I'm about to spend another summer living with these birds and asking some fundamental questions about the social life of animals. The answers might someday help us understand why all creatures that live together, humans included, generally act much the same. The traits I'm about to observe in cliff swallows are far from being unique to this bird, and perhaps this is why I've been able to sustain my fascination with the same research project for fifteen years. But right now I simply want to see the swallows again after the forced winter hiatus. I was too excited to sleep last night.

Mary and I are heading northwest to the Sand Hills country of western Nebraska, where we'll spend the summer under bridges and inside highway culverts along the Platte River. The cliff swallow's world is accessible to anyone willing to go under a bridge and observe. Travel to far-off, exotic lands is unnecessary. If you watch a cliff swallow colony, you will wonder why hundreds of birds cluster their gourd-shaped mud nests so tightly that they may use all the available space, while there are similar nesting places within sight where they could breed at lower densities. You will wonder why a bird so often tries to intrude into its neighbor's nest and why it will steal another bird's nesting material or destroy its eggs. You will marvel at the blood-sucking bedbugs and fleas that infest some of the nests and wonder why the birds would not spread out to escape these parasites. You will be surprised at the apparent altruism the swallows show when they find food during hard times and call to share their good luck with unrelated swallows that have not been as fortunate. You will wonder why some choose to live in a colony of over three thousand pairs, whereas others live with fewer than ten other birds.

The cliff swallow world is complex. After fourteen summers we are still far from understanding everything. Each year, though, we make progress, and the thrill and mystery of this year's discoveries fills me with growing anticipation as I pocket the toll taker's receipt and urge the aging truck westward.

The start of a summer's fieldwork is a time of excitement and anxiety, because each year is different. What challenge awaits us this summer? It may be the weather; unusual climatic conditions may prevent certain research or threaten the birds' survival. It may be the research itself; we may be asking different questions or using new methods that might fail. It may be the birds; for reasons unknown they may not conform to all our expectations and may confound what we plan to do. We never can just pick up where we left off.

As often happens with the start of a new field season, while I drive along I'm flooded with memories of this project's origins. One of the biggest challenges for an aspiring field researcher in animal behavior and ecology is finding an appropriate species to study. Everyone is taught that the animal should be common and accessible, easy to capture and mark, and that its biology should present interesting "problems" that would seem exciting to other scientists. Relatively few species meet all these criteria, and more than a few researchers end up tackling animals that are unsuitable for the questions being asked or whose biology contains no interesting problems. It's especially important for a graduate student to pick the right animal because the academic system rewards only results, and no rewards come to those who study boring species or ones that yield few data.

I was lucky in graduate school to choose the cliff swallow, *Petrochelidon pyrrhonota*, which fulfills all the classic criteria for the ideal study animal. I still wonder why no one had yet realized how fabulous this bird is: its social behavior was virtually unstudied as late as 1981. The decision to study cliff swallows—one that has dictated the course of my life and Mary's for the past fifteen years—was so obvious that it took me about five minutes to make.

In the early 1980s scientists were intensely interested in why animals form groups. In 1976 John Hoogland and Paul Sherman had published a paper on the advantages and disadvantages of group living in the colonial bank swallow. Their study illustrated that there were important costs to social life. For animals living close together these included, among others, a greater likelihood of contracting parasites and diseases, more competition for resources such as food and nesting materials, and increased probability of giving care to an unrelated baby. Living in a group is far from an unmitigated blessing, and if the costs are too severe, animals live solitarily.

John and Paul concluded that the main reason bank swallows lived colonially was to avoid predation. A group presented many "eyes" watching for potential predators. But there was a controversy about group living in bank swallows. At the same time John and Paul were studying bank swallows in Michigan, Steve Emlen and Natalie Demong were studying them in New York State. Steve and Natalie suggested that food was the key. By nesting together, bank swallows could use each other to find swarms of insect prey. When a bird was unsuccessful at finding food, it could go back to the colony, watch other birds returning with food, and follow those successful ones when they next left their nests.

In 1981, not long after I had selected Princeton for graduate school, John Hoogland, soon to be my adviser, suggested I reexamine coloniality using the cliff swallow, the only other highly colonial North American swallow. John had toyed with the idea of studying cliff swallows after completing the bank swallow project but ultimately decided to study prairie dogs, which he has been doing ever since. I suspect that John hoped a study of cliff swallows would support his side of the bank swallow controversy.

I had read John and Paul's bank swallow paper and had been especially impressed by their comparative approach, which measured differences among birds living in colonies of various sizes. Many people had studied colonial species per se, but almost all had focused on individuals within a single colony. Only by comparing birds in different-sized colonies could one determine what costs or benefits of social life were important. I knew that my study of cliff swallows would have to incorporate colonies of different sizes, and I would need a lot of colonies.

As a boyhood birder, I had seen cliff swallows. A small colony lived under a bridge not far from my home in Texas, and I would occasionally stop to view the birds and their unique gourd-shaped mud nests. The idea of studying cliff swallows was especially appealing to me because for years I had been watching purple martins—another kind of swallow—that nested in birdhouses in our backyard. My father had installed a martin house in the mistaken belief that martins control mosquitoes, a myth perpetuated by the manufacturers of the birdhouses. As soon as some martins moved in, I got hooked on birds and fell in love with swallows in particular.

For a successful field study you need three things: the right question, the right animal, and the right study site. I found the first two rather quickly, but locating a place to study cliff swallows was another matter.

As I cruise along the Cimarron Turnpike today, I notice cliff swallow colonies in culverts under the interstate. Whenever I see swallow colonies in new areas, I automatically start evaluating them as potential study sites—perhaps a legacy from the early years when I had to find a place to do my research. These colonies along the Cimarron occupy concrete box culverts. There are no access roads on either side of the highway, meaning one would have to stop on the interstate to reach the culverts. State patrolmen frown on researchers' pulling off on the shoulders of interstates to study swallows, and if the cops don't get you, a semi blasting by at seventy-five miles an hour will. After a few miles I see no more colonies. There are too few here for this area to be a legitimate study site—more confirmation that Mary and I have found the best of all places to study cliff swallows.

It seems obvious now that southwestern Nebraska is the clear choice for any research on cliff swallows, but that was not so apparent in the spring of 1981. My first choice of a study area was in southeastern Arizona. While in college, I had spent a summer as a "volunteer" at the American Museum of Natural History's Southwestern Research Station near Portal. In exchange for four hours a day of cleaning toilets, washing dishes, moving rocks, and digging up horehound, I had free room and board and an opportunity to explore the Chiricahua Mountains. The Chiricahuas are a paradise for birders, a region where eastern species meet western, Rocky Mountain birds meet Mexican ones. I spent that summer chasing exotic birds I had never seen before. Although I did not see a single cliff swallow in Arizona, which should have been telling, my first thought on deciding to study cliff swallows was to return to Arizona.

My letters asking several prominent ornithologists about locations of cliff swallow colonies kept turning up the name Steve Speich. Speich had studied cliff swallows extensively in the 1970s, working from Oregon, California, and Nevada south to Arizona and Sonora. I was told he would surely know the best locations. I finally tracked him down at his home in Washington State and asked him about colonies in Arizona. After listening to my description of the research I planned, Speich was skeptical that the Arizona colonies he had used—near Sonoita—would be appropriate. He suggested I check out the area around Minden, Nevada, where cliff swallows occurred in large numbers. To this day I have not visited Minden, so I don't know if that part of his advice was sound. But since I insisted I wanted to work in Arizona, he sent me photocopies of his maps showing the locations of colonies near Sonoita.

The Sonoita colonies are of Mexican cliff swallows. These birds tend to be slightly smaller and have chocolate brown forehead patches rather than the white ones characteristic of cliff swallows throughout most of North America. The unique feature of the birds' biology in southeastern Arizona is a close association between their nesting and the summer rains. In that region of the Southwest a true summer monsoon begins each year, typically extending from early to mid-July into August. The Mexican cliff swallows arrive in that area in May and June but usually delay breeding until the rains start.

The colony sites Speich had used, coincidentally, were near a biological field station. The Research Ranch, owned by the National Audubon Society, was a former cattle ranch near Elgin that had been donated for use as a research station. The presence of a field station there reaffirmed my naive belief that I had found the perfect study site, and I made arrangements for an immediate visit.

When I arrived at the Research Ranch in early July, I had hopes of collecting some data that summer. Breeding had started, and the cliff swallows were busily building nests. But among the twenty or so colony sites in the area, only two contained active colonies. Two colonies would not be enough for anything. I didn't know then that cliff swallows often skip a year or two in using a given colony site, and later Speich sent me some data showing that as many as five years could elapse before the birds returned to a colony site in Arizona.

And the area was infested with rattlesnakes. I watched the researchers at the Research Ranch go out into the grassland for their studies of sparrow communities covered to the knees with protective leggings. I was told to be careful because the Mojave and western diamondback rattlesnakes like to rest inside highway culverts to escape the heat of the day. Great!

Within a couple of days it was clear that the Sonoita area was not even close to being the place to study cliff swallows. I had a choice: I could wade through the rattlesnakes and try to collect some data, knowing that the area was ultimately unsuitable and that I would have to find another site the next year. Or I could try to find another study site that summer. A phone call to Hoogland convinced me the second option was the more palatable.

Fortunately, earlier that spring I had written to the directors of several biological field stations within the cliff swallow's range, asking if they had cliff swallows nearby. My summer at the Southwestern Research Station had shown the advantages of working out of a field station: its logistical support can be enormously helpful, and the camaraderie with other field biologists boosts your spirits during the long, and at times boring, grind of a field season. Some of the field station directors replied unequivocally that they had no cliff swallows, and others didn't seem to know whether they had any or not. But one reply stood out. It was from John Janovy Jr., director of the Cedar Point Biological Station in Nebraska. John said there were enough cliff swallows near Cedar Point for several dissertations. I'd never been to Nebraska, and the idea of working there hadn't seriously entered my mind.

I called Janovy from the Research Ranch. To this day I remember the conversation vividly, as he described the locations of colonies, even some on natural cliffs along the shore of a lake. Cliffs in Nebraska? But mostly I remember how strongly Janovy encouraged me to visit his station as soon as possible and see the birds firsthand. It was clear I would be most welcome there.

I exit the Cimarron Turnpike and head north on Interstate 35 into Kansas. At Salina the route turns west again. Kansas seems to stretch on interminably, made worse by a thirty-five mile an hour crosswind that tries to blow the truck off the highway. Mary is behind me in our second research vehicle, a much newer and more powerful pickup truck, and I hope she's having an easier time. In western Kansas the sky is vast, and you can see the weather develop all around you. There's a thunderstorm maybe five miles to the south. Based on our speed and trajectory and the typical path of these storms, I predict (correctly) that we'll skirt the edge of it. We may not be so lucky with the one to the northwest, however, because it lies between us and Cedar Point.

After a stop for gas in Russell, Kansas, where we're greeted by a billboard proudly proclaiming that we're in Bob Dole country, we resume our fight with the wind for another hour before turning north again for the final push into Nebraska.

The rain starts quickly and is intense. I have trouble seeing the road and focus on the taillights of a grain truck ahead of me. Prairie thunderstorms can be severe, and each summer we're caught outside in several. The wind is often violent, and tornadoes are common. Isolated thunderstorm cells like the one we're in right now often spawn tornadoes, but fortunately this storm is all rain. It pours on us for twenty miles before we reach the edge. Our battle with the elements has worn me out, and we're still two hours from Cedar Point.

The rainstorm we've just survived epitomizes this spring. After a mild winter, the past six weeks have been cold and rainy throughout the Great Plains. Flooding was rampant in the Tulsa area yesterday. I knew that spring had been cool in western Nebraska, but until now I had no idea how cool or how wet. It could be February from the way the trees look. Usually, by now the willows and cottonwoods have at least a fuzzy green haze covering them, but this year they're still bare twigs.

The western Great Plains are in the rain shadow of the Rocky Mountains, so this region is dry most of the year. Pacific storm fronts moving from the west strike the Rockies and dump much of their precipitation there. By the time they cross the mountains their moisture has been depleted, and they move several hundred miles to the east before acquiring enough wet Gulf air to become significant rainmakers again. Hence one finds that corn is grown in much wetter eastern Nebraska and Iowa; out here only short-grass prairie can thrive without irrigation.

This spring, though, rainfall has come in record amounts. Large upper-level low pressure systems have been stalling over the northern Great Plains and pulling in vast amounts of humid air from the south. The ground cover is verdant as I've never seen it. The greenness of the ground next to the bare trees is a strange juxtaposition, and I immediately know this is going to be a weird summer.

We narrowly miss another thunderstorm near McCook and finally reach North Platte. My growing excitement masks my weariness, because now we're in the study area. North Platte is on the eastern edge of our research site and is the only city of any size (population 23,000) within a half day's drive of Cedar Point. After hiding behind threatening clouds for the past three hours, the sun is now shining brightly and lights our way west to Cedar Point and our cliff swallows.

I'm not seeing swallows at the overpasses and culverts along the interstate, but I am seeing a lot of standing water. I figure this foreshadows some problems. Most of our study colonies are associated in one way or another with water. Water either flows under or through them or else abuts them. As water rises we have more trouble reaching the nests, and if it's too deep we can lose a colony for study entirely. With the heavy rain this spring, I start imagining all kinds of horrible scenarios.

I can't muse about high water for long, because the Ogallala exit is upon us. The drive from Tulsa has taken two hours longer than usual owing to the strong crosswinds and rain en route. Only about an hour of daylight remains, so we use our time efficiently by stopping in Ogallala for supper before continuing the nine miles to Cedar Point. The pizza restaurant we choose is only about two hundred yards from a cliff swallow colony.

This colony site is a tall, long highway bridge that spans the South Platte River, connecting Ogallala to its tourist-laden lifeline, Interstate 80. The birds use this site perennially. About a hundred birds are hovering under the bridge investigating nests. Aside from one or two flying near a culvert site we call McDonald's, these are the first cliff swallows we've seen in the study area today, and it's like reuniting with family.

But I immediately notice something different. In past years willow trees and cottonwood saplings choked the riverbed so completely that the trees nearly touched the top of the bridge and made parts of it unsuitable for cliff swallows. The brush under the bridge was so thick that we had long ago deleted this site—named simply Ogallala—from consideration as a research colony. In most years diversion of the South Platte for irrigation and recreation reduces the river to a trickle, allowing the woody growth to take over. But this year the brush under the bridge has disappeared. Maintenance crews have cleared a swath about fifty yards wide on each side of the bridge. The implication is clear: we can now reach this colony and band the birds here, provided the river isn't too deep from the spring rains and mountain runoff. Already here is something unexpected. Can it be that we'll learn what birds colonize Ogallala, a colony that has always frustrated me by attracting hundreds of cliff swallows each year but never letting us in on its secrets?

May 9

A northwest wind is blowing, and the day is gray and cold. Mary and I feel like ice cubes by the time we finish unloading the research equipment we didn't have time to deal with last night before it rained again. In western Nebraska the wind blows constantly. Coupled with cold or even just cool temperatures, the wind sweeping down out of the Canadian prairies can make life miserable even in June or July. Our research this summer will consist mostly of mist netting swallows, and the conventional wisdom is that you can't net birds when it's windy. Wind blows the fine-thread nets so that the flapping mesh is easily seen—and avoided—by birds. But out here we break all the rules of netting and sometimes set up nets in horrendously windy conditions. I often think of the irony inherent in our crafting a research project now based almost entirely on mist netting in one of the windiest parts of North America.

The weather today is in stark contrast to this time last year, when we arrived to temperatures in the eighties that continued day after day in one of the earliest springs on record. Cliff swallow breeding was at least a week ahead of "normal," and the entire summer was hot. Climatic variability is the rule in the western Great Plains and is one factor that makes fieldwork out here so challenging.

May 10

The sun has appeared this morning, and Mary and I strike out to scout a few of the cliff swallow colony sites close to Cedar Point. Birds should be around the active sites today. There's no point in trying to reconnoiter colony sites when the weather is bad, because the swallows will be away foraging and inactive sites can't be distinguished from ones the birds have chosen to use this year. It's an obvious lesson that I have to teach our newly arrived and gung-ho assistants every summer: nothing can be done when there are no cliff swallows at the colony sites.

One of the first sites we stop at is Aqueduct, still unoccupied by swallows. It's near a colony of great blue herons. The heron colony started two years ago as only three nests, but as we drive up today we are astounded to see twenty-five. The birds build bulky stick nests, and they've placed them in the tops of several cottonwood trees not far from the North Platte River. Their flimsy nests are balanced precariously in the treetops, and each summer at least one has blown down. Their vulnerability seems enhanced now because the trees have no leaves. Some herons are sitting in the nests, obviously incubating, and are not disturbed by our walking below them. The bare tree limbs make this heron colony noticeable, and I wonder if the birds can avoid being detected by the great horned owls that prowl this country. Horned owls are not reluctant to attack heron nests, and sometimes they even appropriate one and raise their own young there.

Speculating about predators reminds me that all colonial birds, whether cliff swallows or great blue herons, face similar problems. The increased conspicuousness of a bird colony, inherently unavoidable because of the sights, sounds, and smells of numerous animals concentrated in one place, is a beacon to predators. If predators gather at the colony, the risk for each colony resident can increase above what it would experience as a solitary. There must be advantages to colonial life that outweigh this cost, but with the herons those benefits are not obvious to me. Nesting trees are not limited—there are scores of similar cottonwoods along the river where the birds could spread out if they chose. Advantages associated with either avoiding predators or finding food—the old bank swallow debate revisited—must explain why herons cluster their nests.

As we drive from site to site along the Sutherland Canal, the lateness of the spring quickly becomes apparent. Relatively few cliff swallows are here yet, and the ones that are haven't gotten serious about nesting. Their extreme sociality is obvious even among these early pioneers; most of the birds have settled at only four colony sites in the immediate Cedar Point area. These colonies have sizable numbers of birds, whereas most of the remaining thirty or so bridges—which will undoubtedly attract swallows later—are still deserted. A cliff swallow's desire to be part of a group is overwhelming. I'd bet that many of the individuals now at the colonies migrated north in a group and may have even spent the winter together.

We know embarrassingly little about the cliff swallow's natural history during the nonbreeding season—close to ten months of each year. Whenever obvious migrants are seen, they're in flocks. In years when Mary and I arrived at Cedar Point in April before any cliff swallows had appeared, the first swallows always came as a group of up to fifty birds.

Most cliff swallows winter in southernmost Brazil, Uruguay, and northern and central Argentina. No one has studied them during the winter, but they likely inhabit grasslands, marshes, and agricultural areas. The birds from Nebraska commute thousands of miles to spend the winter in a region that is probably similar to the one where they breed. Other observations suggest that cliff swallows are nomadic in the winter. With no nesting to tie them to one spot, they're free to range widely in search of insects. Perhaps the same individuals stay together in these nomadic bands.

Although our survey today has included only a small fraction of the colony sites we'll study this summer, it's obvious that this is a late spring. Any serious research will be impossible for at least a week. This isn't disastrous; it means only that we (and the cliff swallows) will be here longer this summer than we originally planned. Mary and I are seasoned veterans of unpredictable Nebraska weather and can absorb this delay with grace. I enjoy a slow-starting season because it gives me time to watch the cliff swallows just for fun. For a little while I won't have to worry about sampling design, disturbance to the birds, or other concerns that intrude as soon as data collection begins. But I also know that our research assistants arrive in five days, and our chances of being able to start serious research by then are slim. The first law of having field assistants is to keep them busy, and that law will be violated as soon as this year's group arrives.

After supper we return to two of the active colonies to get a better estimate of the number of cliff swallows. When the birds first arrive, they spend considerable time searching for food away from their colonies, even in good weather. Consequently daytime censuses often underestimate colony size. Everybody shows up to sleep at the colony, however, so evening is the best time to see cliff swallows at this time of year.

As we sit in the truck, we watch the birds doing their mysterious massed roosting flights. In late afternoon the cliff swallows that have tentatively chosen to live at a particular site will gradually appear, seemingly from nowhere. Early in the season the birds may travel as far as ten miles from their colony while foraging during the day, but with the onset of evening they return and spend an hour or two foraging nearby in a loosely organized group that can be as small as ten birds or as large as three hundred. As the sun sets, the swallows begin to fly in a tighter and better coordinated flock, still well above the colony site. Before long the members of the group start flying close together, all twisting and turning at once and changing altitude in unison. The synchrony is incredible, as the group seems to become a single organism whirling overhead. No birds collide, though they fly only inches apart.

Gradually the dervishlike flock works its way lower until it's at the same altitude as the nests. Initially the entire group will pass under the bridge as one, no birds violating the group's integrity. After several passes underneath, individuals begin to break out of the group as it roars past, and these birds go straight into nests for the night. The flock maintains its synchrony even as more and more birds break off and enter nests. Only after it is almost too dark to see do the remaining birds cease their synchronized flying and look for vacant nests to sleep in. If there are more birds than nests, those that were last to break away will gradually depart to sleep in nearby trees. An entire hour may elapse from the time the birds stop foraging and begin to assemble until the first ones enter nests for the night, and minimally the rigmarole takes twenty minutes.

Cliff swallows invest considerable time and energy in this activity, at a time when the weather can be bad and food in short supply. Massed roosting flights are the rule for all colonies in April and early May, and they cease as the birds become better established at a site. Birds in the later-starting colonies don't perform these flights, but this summer is so delayed that it looks as if birds almost everywhere are still doing them.

The synchronized flying is such an unbelievable spectacle that Mary and I once again speculate on its function, a conversation we've had dozens of times over the years. Some birds are thought to fly in tightly coordinated groups to ward off predator attacks: if a hawk or falcon strikes a bird flying in such a group, the predator may unintentionally collide with other flock members and injure a vulnerable part of its own body such as its eyes. But there are few predators that attack cliff swallows in flight, especially at roosting time. If avoiding predators was the purpose of the massed flights, the birds should continue the behavior. Limiting it to early in the season doesn't make immediate sense to us.

For a long time we could get no further than this, but several years ago we realized that massed roosting flights might be a way the birds advertise their colony size. Cliff swallows have to choose a colony size each summer. Within our study area they may settle solitarily or in colonies that range anywhere from 2 to 3,700 nests. The choice determines how successful an individual will be at breeding. So how does a new arrival know how many swallows have already settled at a site early in the year? Many of the birds are out foraging during the day, and only at dusk when everybody comes back to sleep can colony size be accurately determined both by us and by the cliff swallows themselves. As the birds swirl together in a massed roosting flight, the colony size as of that day is obvious to all. If a new arrival is looking for a colony at least that large, it's in luck and can join. If a smaller colony is the goal, no time need be wasted there.

This explains how massed roosting flights could be beneficial to a nonresident seeking information on colony size. The ritual is also beneficial to the colony residents that perform it, for the same reason. Advertising colony size recruits uncommitted birds that may be looking for a breeding site. This increases colony size, to the presumed benefit of those already settled. We guess that birds do the massed flights while colony size is below some critical threshold, and that this advertising stops after enough birds have joined to reach the size most residents seek. Accurate assessment of colony size benefits everybody and explains why roosting flights occur early in the year when many colonies are small and need additional recruits. Often we see birds that are clearly not part of any roosting flight fly back and forth high overhead between two colonies while the colony residents perform their routine. It seems like a great chance for them to assess which colony may better meet their needs.

Mary and I always end our musings frustrated because we can come up with no feasible way to test the advertisement hypothesis. Fortunately, most of the cliff swallow behavior that is yet to come this summer is more understandable and more amenable to study.

We drive back in the dark, confident that we're in time to see everything this season. Despite the poor weather so far and the less than favorable long range weather forecasts, I'm having good vibes about the upcoming summer. The fun is just beginning.

2

Whitetail

How does one say . . . that Whitetail . . . rank[s] among
the most beautiful . . . most awe-inspiring sights of all the
earth? One simply says it, for it is true.
—John Janovy Jr., *Keith County Journal*

May 11

In past years Mary and I had begun netting and banding cliff swallows by this date, but that's out of the question today. Despite sunshine and moderately warm temperatures, the cliff swallows are spending little time at their colony sites. The birds must forage most of the day to replenish the fat reserves they've been relying on during the recent cold weather. Migratory birds like cliff swallows typically arrive on their breeding grounds with high levels of body fat, and these reserves can be used temporarily in lieu of food if the weather turns nasty and briefly reduces their supply of flying insects. Any day with warm weather must be used to refill the tank for the additional cold weather that might lie ahead.

Our plan today is to survey more colony sites to see whether they've been occupied this year, but we know before leaving Cedar Point that we're unlikely to get an accurate picture of site use because of the birds' foraging. However, we can still have a look at water levels. From the amount of standing water we see everywhere, I'll be surprised if our access to some colonies hasn't been curtailed by high water.

The first stop is the colony at Whitetail Creek. Despite the lateness of the spring, several hundred birds have already established residence. Whitetail is a culvert colony, under a county road just west of the tiny settlement of Keystone. At this small, inconspicuous concrete box under the highway, we've spent part or all of nearly every summer day for over a decade and made virtually all our discoveries about cliff swallow social behavior. Each field season begins and ends with a visit to Whitetail.

By the time I had abandoned my plan to study cliff swallows in Arizona in 1981 and had traveled to Cedar Point, it was mid-July and many of the birds had finished breeding. John Janovy showed me a few colonies on concrete irrigation structures, all situated over deep flowing water with the nests clearly inaccessible. We also toured colonies on highway bridges over the South Platte River, sites where nests would be accessible when the river was low but would require slogging into water, across sandbars, and through brush carrying twenty-foot extension ladders. I left Cedar Point that summer without seeing any colony site I considered ideal, but with so many cliff swallows there I figured I was bound to find some good colonies once I thoroughly searched Keith County the next year.

That first field season, Mary and I arrived at Cedar Point on a Sunday afternoon and immediately began looking for colonies. We especially sought highway culverts, because earlier that spring I had discovered how convenient they were as research sites. A few cliff swallows nested in a box culvert at Lake Texoma, not far from my parents' home in Texas. The culvert was no taller than I am, so we could reach the nests without ladders, and most important, mist nets could be placed across the narrow entrances, sealing the birds' flyway and letting us catch the colony residents. I didn't know much about cliff swallows then, but I did know we needed culvert colonies for our research to be successful.

Depending on the width of the stream flowing through it, a culvert may consist of several sections (or tunnels, as we call them), each about ten feet wide. Solid concrete walls separate the sections. The top and bottom are also concrete, giving the structure its box shape. Dirt is piled several feet thick on top. The outer sides of a culvert, extending beyond the entrance, usually flare out. Only paved highways typically warrant concrete box culverts; the road department usually puts steel cylinders under dirt roads.

From the picture windows in the main lodge at Cedar Point, you can look across Keystone Lake to the paved county road on the north side and on into the rugged Sand Hills beyond. That road was the obvious place to start looking, so Mary and I began our search there.

We drove out the west gate of Cedar Point and up the narrow dirt road leading to the top of the cedar-clad rocky bluffs that tower above the biological station. These outcroppings face north and represent the southern border of the North Platte valley, created as the river cut its course through the prairie tableland. Once we were on top of the bluffs, our route turned northwest over the three-mile-long Kingsley Dam, the second largest earthen dam in the world and one that creates the 35,000-acre Lake McConaughy. "Big Mac" is the dominant ecological and economic feature of southwestern Nebraska. The lake draws over sixty thousand visitors on a typical Independence Day or Labor Day weekend. Water is released from Big Mac through Kingsley Dam into the North Platte River.

Turning back east from the dam on the paved road leading toward Keystone on that gray May day that now seems so long ago, we began searching the roadsides for any evidence of a culvert—a flowing stream, standing water, or dry gully perpendicular to the road. The road passes through flat pastures that provide some of the best cattle-raising country in the Midwest. Whitetail was not hard to find, since the small stream passing through it is obvious to anyone who is looking. Whitetail Creek was named in the 1800s, apparently after a Sioux chief.

As soon as we pulled onto the grassy shoulder and walked down the embankment to stand beside the creek at the culvert entrance, I knew we had found the perfect study site. The culvert was head high, relatively short and thus well lit (so we could see inside from far back), only a short drive from Cedar Point, and—most important of all—full of old cliff swallow nests. The only problem was that no cliff swallows were there, but the site seemed so perfect that I guessed it was only a matter of days before the old nests would be reoccupied.

That was before we discovered that cliff swallow colony sites often are not used in any given year. Although I had seen that many of the Arizona colony sites were unused when I visited Sonoita, I initially assumed that irregular use of a site was unique to the Mexican variety of cliff swallows. For some reason it had not occurred to me that birds in Nebraska might follow the same pattern, even at a colony site like Whitetail that contained intact nests in good condition from the previous year. However, that was also before we knew much about the parasitic bedbugs that infest those old nests, often making them uninhabitable.

The next day we dutifully began numbering all the old nests at Whitetail. One great advantage of studying cliff swallows that breed on bridges and in highway culverts is that you can number the nests simply by writing with chalk on the concrete wall beside each nest. The long lives of the chalk marks—many dating from 1982 look as fresh in 1995 as the day we wrote them—reflect how well the bridge overhangs and culvert interiors keep the cliff swallow nests dry and protected from the elements. But numbering nests will not make the birds use a colony site if they are not so inclined, and Whitetail remained vacant with each passing day.

Fieldwork is often frustrating, but I have seldom been as frustrated as that first year when the birds ignored Whitetail. We would drive over there, park beside the road, and scan the surrounding pastures with binoculars. Haystacks, cattle, thunderheads, Cedar Point nestled on the bluffs in the far distance—but no cliff swallows.

On one visit we did see a couple of birds foraging overhead, and immediately I asked Laura, one of our research assistants, to spend the next morning watching the culvert. In those days I didn't know we could have simply visited in the evening to see if any swallows roosted at the site. Laura hunkered down beside a gigantic leadplant by the creek about fifty yards north of the culvert and started her vigil. Four hours later the word was that three or four birds flew through the culvert, stopped and briefly hovered in front of some nests for a few seconds, then disappeared. Sorry, Charles. Those birds probably determined rather quickly that the nests were too heavily infested with parasites, but it would be three more years before we would recognize that cliff swallows assessed nests this way.

I now realize that the birds' staying away from Whitetail that first summer was a piece of capricious good fortune. Had they used it, I probably would have focused considerable time on that one colony. But the first step needed to be a repeat of Hoogland and Sherman's bank swallow approach, comparing many colonies of different sizes. Without Whitetail that year, we began an exhaustive search of the region around Cedar Point for alternative sites. None was as ideal as Whitetail, but we found several where we could reach the nests. We spent that summer recording information on the timing of nest building and egg laying, the number of eggs laid, and nesting success at twelve colonies ranging in size from one nest to 1,600. To this day, 1982 remains the single year with the best data on reproductive success from the greatest range of colony sizes.

But more important, these boring data—collected by looking in each nest every second day throughout the summer—gave us our first glimpse of how fascinating cliff swallow social behavior can be.

For example, we knew after the first year that cliff swallows were brood parasites that is, they laid some of their eggs in the nests of other colony members. When our nest checks found two eggs appearing in one day, we knew two females had to have laid in the nest; no bird can lay two eggs a day. Virtually everything we've studied about cliff swallows in the subsequent decade has been guided by observations we made the first summer when we visited colonies of different sizes. For this we can thank the birds that avoided Whitetail that season.

Whitetail did not remain completely unused the first summer, however. One pair eventually moved into one of the old nests. This solitary pair was one of several such duos we find each year. What prompts a few independent, pioneer-spirited individuals to defy the powerful social attraction that defines a cliff swallow's very existence? Swallows that breed solitarily or in tiny aggregations face a very different social environment than the majority of birds that occupy much larger colonies. With no neighbors to speak of, these asocial individuals have no opportunity to learn from others where food might be; they can't form a mob to chase off a predator and perhaps do not even see the predator before it arrives; and they have no chance to find other nests in the colony that might serve as good foster homes for their parasitic eggs. Yet with fewer neighbors they also don't have to pay many of the costs of being social: more encounters with parasites, greater competition for food, nest sites, and mates, greater attraction of predators, and an increased risk of raising someone else's young, to name a few.

That first summer, I don't remember ever considering why colony size might vary, as we ran around with our extension ladders, wading in rivers and looking in nests. I only knew that I couldn't believe my good fortune in finding an area with so many different colony sizes for a repeat of Hoogland and Sherman's research. Heck, I had a much greater range of colony sizes than John and Paul had had with bank swallows. Few ecologists interested in colonial birds in the early 1980s had thought much about the basis for variation in colony size, although it was clear even then that it ranged widely within single populations of many species. Five years elapsed before Mary and I began to think seriously about why cliff swallow colonies come in so many sizes.

The single pair at Whitetail in 1982 maintained the site's status as "active" that year, if mostly in an official sense, and that was also the last year that Whitetail would contain a tiny colony.

The following summer we returned to Cedar Point with one objective: to watch cliff swallows. The past year we had collected a large amount of information on nesting biology but had done little actual observation of the birds' behavior. Hoogland was pleased with the start we had made, but he made it clear that we had to follow up on some of the tantalizing nest-check data (two eggs a day, for instance) by direct observation and verify what was happening.

When the next summer began, I initially hoped to use one of several colonies found on natural cliff sites along the shore of Lake McConaughy for our observations. We had discovered six such colonies the year before and had collected data from two. But the water's edge was directly below these nests, and they were not easy to reach. Deep water, uneven piles of submerged boulders, and the crumbling sandstone cliff where the nests were built made access treacherous. One of the colonies could be reached only by canoe. Mary and Karen, our assistant, paddled out to the site, hugging the coastline to avoid wind and rough water for the two-mile trip from the boat launch to the colony. They beached on the rocks below the nests, and Mary scaled a six-foot-high rocky shelf to come within head height of the nests. Karen stayed with the canoe and used a stick to hold off a prairie rattlesnake that lived below the nests and invariably put in an appearance. This sort of macho stuff was okay occasionally to check nests, but we needed a more accessible cliff site for the intensive observations we were planning.

Flooding ruled out using cliff colonies. The spring of 1983 was wet, with major snow runoff into the North Platte River from the Rocky Mountains, and Lake McConaughy reached a near record level. The overhanging ledges where the birds had built their nests the previous summer were all submerged.

Whitetail, however, lived up to its potential as the ideal study site we had sought the year before. In 1983 about 180 nests or nest fragments were occupied, and 165 of those eventually contained eggs. The colony size was perfect for making observations: there were enough birds for adequate sample sizes yet few enough that we could detect patterns in the birds' behavior. In later years we would observe much larger colonies, and the constant bedlam that characterizes such sites often makes it difficult to resolve what given individuals are doing. In large measure, many of our discoveries about parasitic egg laying and social foraging were possible only because Whitetail happened to be just the right size. We could not have designed a better colony for our research that season, and we spent all day every day at Whitetail, sitting and watching. We would return in later years to sit and watch some more, but the colony has never again been that ideal size. We would also come to appreciate how lucky we were to have a colony of that size when we needed it most, because colonies of one hundred to two hundred nests are not common in any given year. We owe the entire research project to those three hundred or so cliff swallows that decided to nest at Whitetail that summer.

Today there are already twice as many birds at Whitetail as in 1983, and the season has barely started. I wonder how many of the current residents are descendants of the 1983 crowd. Mary interrupts the reverie that overcomes me each time I come here to remind me we have other sites to check. Whitetail is my favorite place on earth, and it's always hard for me to leave.

We do a quick tour of colony sites from Cedar Point east to Paxton. After returning to Ogallala and stopping at the Dairy Queen for lunch, we check the South Platte River bridges at Brule and Big Springs and then return to Cedar Point by way of Ash Hollow at the western end of Lake McConaughy. It's a loop of about a hundred miles that contains most of our approximately one hundred "primary" colony sites. We looked at about forty today, and only half of them seem to have any birds. In more normal years, nest construction and repair of old nests would be in full swing by now, but at most sites the swallows are still mainly interested in feeding.

As I had guessed, the wet spring and consequent high water are going to present a problem. The water looks deep at the Roscoe and Big Springs bridges. At these sites last year, we started to catch birds with our "big nets": mist nets of twenty by forty feet that slide up and down twenty-foot poles on pulleys. The nets are placed across the sides of the bridges containing rows of active nests, and in a large colony they can capture over five hundred birds a day for banding. But nets this tall, even when the poles are braced by guy wires, are vulnerable to wind. Their vulnerability increases when the poles and guy wires are anchored in the soft, shifting sand of a flowing river. We had several near disasters last year when the stakes of the guy

wires were pulled out by the flowing water, causing the entire contraption to fall into the South Platte River. I came to loathe having to
set the nets over any water, even less than a foot deep, and the water
at Roscoe and Big Springs looks several feet deep. Mary consoles me
by reminding me that in a typical year the South Platte drops over
the summer, so perhaps we can still use the big nets in June or July.
After all, since spring is late the birds will probably be here longer
this summer.

When we get back to Cedar Point we encounter Josef for the first
time this year. Josef studies brown-headed cowbirds and red-winged
blackbirds, and he is the most skilled field ornithologist I have ever
known. He received a doctorate in zoology in Czechoslovakia during
the Communist era and came to America after the 1989 revolution
for further training at the University of Nebraska in Lincoln. Like
others of us, Josef fell in love with Cedar Point on his first visit. He's
spent the past three summers here. Energetic and hardworking, Josef
spends twelve to fourteen hours every day slogging through marshes
in chest waders or crawling on his stomach through dense stands of
poison ivy and wild roses, searching for nests of blackbirds, warblers,
vireos, buntings, and other small birds that serve as cowbird hosts.

Josef has moved into the "Mouse House," a 1930s farmhouse adjacent to the Cedar Point property that the field station leases to provide housing. I feel sorry for him because the house is about to fall in
and is heavily infested with mice. For seven summers Mary and I
and our assistants occupied it. But after live trapping fifty-three deer
mice in our kitchen in less than a month and having mice run across
the foot of our bed while we were in it, we decided enough was enough
and last year asked to be assigned to cleaner quarters. Mary insisted
we do something after she found mice giving birth in her folded underwear.

Josef is out in the front yard of the Mouse House setting up mist
nets, and he comes bounding over to the truck when we stop. I'm
curious to learn how the late spring is affecting his blackbirds and
cowbirds, and also to find out more about his extremely early sighting of cliff swallows almost a month ago.

We learn that Josef has been at Cedar Point for ten days, and that
there was still snow on the ground when he arrived. Another sign of
an unusual spring. In mid-April this year he came out to see how
many blackbirds had arrived, but he had to cut his visit short and
return to Lincoln because a blizzard was imminent. On that trip he

saw about fifty cliff swallows on the incredibly early date of April 13, five days before the birds had ever been reported. I would be skopti cal of the sighting if Josef weren't such a competent ornithologist. I wonder if those early birds survived the blizzard. Given the weather since then, it's hard to believe they're still alive.

Josef is upbeat because his blackbirds seem to be right on schedule despite the weather. We'll later learn that red-winged blackbirds were virtually the only species of plant or animal life in southwestern Nebraska that was not seriously delayed by this spring's weather.

My plan this afternoon is to do the first fumigation of the season at Whitetail, one of ten or so visits I'll make this summer to remove parasites from the nests. Fumigation is one of the few experiments we regularly perform in the field. By removing parasites from some colonies, we can compare the behavior and reproductive success of swallows living in the absence of parasites with those of birds nesting under natural parasite loads.

Cliff swallows are unusual among small land birds in having such a diverse and abundant parasite community associated with them. They harbor ectoparasitic ticks, swallow bugs, fleas, lice, blowflies, and mites and a multitude of endoparasitic cestodes, nematodes, trematodes, and protozoan blood parasites. Internal parasites can seldom be studied without killing large numbers of their hosts, so the cliff swallow's endoparasites are of little interest to us. However, ectoparasites like ticks and fleas live in the birds' nests and thus are much more amenable to study. The principal target of the fumigation is the swallow bug, a blood-sucking bedbug the size of a wood tick that is the most common cliff swallow ectoparasite in Nebraska.

Our fumigant is a potent insecticide called naled and is classified in the danger category by the *Farm Chemicals Handbook*. We use extreme caution in handling it. Fortunately, not much is needed to kill a swallow bug, and a dilute suspension in water is very effective. Before each application I mix up a batch that we carry to the colony site in plastic jugs. Then we pour the diluted naled into a garden sprayer and lightly mist the outsides of the existing nests and the nearby concrete wall where more nests may be built.

We haven't detected any adverse effects of fumigation on the cliff swallows themselves. Removing parasites benefits the birds in many ways, so we have less of an ethical dilemma than we might have if we were experimentally *increasing* their parasite loads. We fumigate only at Whitetail and leave all other sites untouched for comparison.

Today will also be the first time this year I have waded into the culvert at Whitetail. Whitetail Creek originates up in the Sand Hills about seven miles to the north. The headwaters are a remarkable place: miles and miles of level Sand Hills prairie suddenly drops, canyonlike, into a marsh where water comes bubbling up out of the ground like Jed Clampett's oil. Because the creek is spring fed its water level is constant each summer. In a state where all the major waterways are marked by dams, canals, and the politics of water use, it's comforting to know that Whitetail won't fluctuate in depth each year. Still, I feel some trepidation on wading in for the first time each summer, because the creek bottom might have shifted over the winter to create a hole, and I've never learned to swim.

Fumigation is a one-person job, so Mary stays at Cedar Point and allows me the honor. I load up the fumigant and gear, drive to Whitetail, and get into my hip waders, rubber gloves, and mask. At Whitetail we park on the shoulder of the road above the culvert. Our truck parked here is not unusual, because in Keith County vehicles are always parked along roads by water, generally while people are fishing. But clad in rubber waders, mask, and gloves and carrying a garden sprayer, I must look pretty weird to Joe Citizen driving by on his way to Big Mac for the weekend. I quickly walk down the highway embankment to the culvert entrance, where I'm far enough below the road not to be visible to passing cars.

I wade into the creek and gingerly feel my way forward one step at a time to avoid falling in a hole. To my relief I can tell that the creek bottom is much the same as it was last year. I notice two major changes, however. Whitetail consists of three tunnels: west, middle, and east. The middle tunnel, which typically contains most of the active nests, is usually the only one that has flowing water. The east tunnel has attracted birds at one end in recent years, but the creek had not been running through it. To my surprise, there are now swiftly moving channels in both the middle and east tunnels.

The middle is where most of the nests *were*. The other change I notice is that few of the mud nests remain from last year. Many have fallen during the winter, exposing bare sections of concrete wall inside the middle tunnel where nests are usually packed together in tiers five and six deep.

The falling of these nests is more interesting than the new water channel. Seeing some nests slough off is not surprising, because the nests at Whitetail often crumble and fall, sometimes during the same summer they are built and before the nestlings have fledged. The mud the birds use here is mostly sand gathered from the banks of the creek and does not adhere well. Nests made of sticky clay or other black silt can remain intact for years, and we know of nests at some colony sites that are at least fifteen years old. But at Whitetail the birds have no choice but to use the sandy soil, because little else is available within an economical flying distance. A negative consequence of stacking nests together in high density is that when one falls, it often pulls away the adjacent nests in a domino effect throughout the colony. This must have happened at Whitetail over the winter.

I begin spraying the nests and the remaining fragments, and I see a couple of opportunities. One is the chance to fumigate the colony more thoroughly than has been possible recently. I can soak the bare parts of the wall with fumigant to kill the bugs that hide in crevices. Many swallow bugs spend the winter not in the birds' nests but in cracks in the concrete or earthen substrate the nests are built on. This probably ensures that the bugs don't fall with a brittle and crumbling nest during the winter or get washed away with a nest during a winter storm. Then, when birds recolonize the site and start building new nests, the bugs move in.

There had been so many nests at Whitetail recently and they had been stacked so closely that it had become difficult to fumigate the site completely. I notice that the concrete wall is pockmarked with blackish crescents the diameter of a nest; the black marks look like paint. They are buildups of swallow bug feces deposited over the years by bugs that lived in the nests and escaped death by fumigation. The bare wall in the back of a nest serves as the swallow bugs' toilet, and I'm horrified to see how many bugs have managed to live here over the past several years despite our regular fumigation. I douse the black crescents, the surrounding wall, and the nests. There are no bugs visible today, but I'm sure they're there, hiding in cracks that will double as mausoleums for many after today's fumigation.

The other opportunity is to observe the way the loss of all these existing nests will influence how many cliff swallows decide to nest here this year. Several years ago Bill Shields, an ecologist studying barn swallows, proposed that swallow colonies form at "traditional aggregation" sites. He suggested that a bird's best cue to where it can nest successfully would be where old nests still exist. If a nest has remained intact from last year the site is probably safe, and odds are good that it can breed successfully there this year. The consequence is that birds congregate into colonies in the traditionally safe nesting sites. If this applies to cliff swallows, we might see fewer birds settle here this year, since the falling of so many nests over the winter would cast doubt on Whitetail's safety compared with other years.

I run out of fumigant before finishing all the nests. The unexpected opportunity to douse big chunks of the bare wall has taken more than I anticipated, and I'll have to mix another batch and return. I count all the nests that remain in the culvert: almost 550 are still intact or reasonably so. Whitetail last year had about 1,600 active nests. If the colony is to achieve that size, over a thousand pairs of birds will have to build nests from scratch. Nest building is a sizable commitment in energy and time, especially in colonies where nests are not in high density and there are few neighbors to share nest walls with. The extra time spent in nest building can delay the start of egg laying enough that the nest building birds breed substantially later in the summer than those that simply take over existing nests. There are many deleterious consequences of nesting late, so birds should avoid building nests from scratch if at all possible. A few birds here have started adding mud to nests, but so far they have only refurbished old ones—patching holes in the neck or sides—and no new nests have been started. As I'm crawling out of the creek I predict that this summer Whitetail will be substantially smaller than last year.

May 12

The morning dawns cool and misty courtesy of a low pressure system that arrived during the night. A foggy haze has enveloped Keystone Lake just below Cedar Point and obscures the rolling and unusually green Sand Hills to the north. Fog is rare in southwestern Nebraska— the wind is usually so strong that the air dries quickly. Today it is virtually calm, contributing to the London-like mist.

The cliff swallows will probably spend the day foraging. Mary and I decide to use this opportunity to try some house sparrow control at Whitetail. House sparrows are introduced pests, not protected by any laws. They were brought to North America from England in the mid-

1800s in the mistaken belief that they control cankerworms. Unlike most exotic species introduced into a new environment, which soon die out, house sparrows thrived in the New World. By the early 1900s they had spread from coast to coast at the expense of native species. House sparrows commonly nest in cavities and compete aggressively for nest sites with purple martins, bluebirds, tree swallows, and other hole-nesting birds.

The round, enclosed nest of a cliff swallow with its narrow entry provides a perfect "cavity" for a house sparrow, and sparrows will move into cliff swallow colonies and usurp the swallows' nests. The bigger colonies on bridges near towns have dozens of house sparrows. The sparrows stuff the swallow nests full of grass stems, making them unsuitable for further swallow use. An even bigger problem is that house sparrows destroy the eggs in several cliff swallow nests before selecting one as their own. A single male sparrow may clean out fifteen or twenty cliff swallow nests. The swallows seem strangely unwilling to defend their nests against house sparrows.

Seven or eight sparrows have moved into Whitetail over the winter during each of the past couple of years. Most are eventually eliminated during the summer—they get hit by cars speeding over the culvert or blunder into the nets we set for swallows. However, I'd like to get rid of some of them now, before they have a chance to destroy any cliff swallow eggs. In earlier years I spent hours sitting in the truck above the culvert with a pellet gun, trying to get a shot at the sparrows without hitting a passing car, but the wily sparrows refused to expose themselves. I finally gave up and resigned myself to catching them in nets over the course of the summer. If we could put up nets now, before our repeated visits to the colony make the sparrows even more wary, we might get lucky and catch several at once.

As soon as we arrive at Whitetail this morning, we know the sparrows have won a temporary stay of execution. The cliff swallows, contrary to expectation, are not away foraging. Several hundred are at the colony, many sitting inside their nests out of the mist, while others perch on a nearby power line looking wet and bedraggled. It must be too misty for them to forage, because it appears that virtually all the colony residents are here. Although it's cool this morning it isn't cold, and perhaps the birds aren't hungry enough to feed in the rain.

I'm reluctant to set a mist net for several reasons. It would flush many of the swallows out of their warm, dry nests, needlessly stressing them in this poor weather. Also, one has to be careful about disturbing them this early in the season because the disruption may cause some to leave the colony. The weather probably hasn't allowed many of these cliff swallows much chance to visit different colonies and make a "choice" of breeding site, and we don't want to alter their behavior. Besides, the weather is so bad at the moment that the sparrows are mostly just sitting in some bushes along a barbed wire fence south of the colony and aren't moving to and from the culvert enough for us to have any hope of catching them today.

We decide to sit and watch for a while. No birds are collecting mud, but the colony is surprisingly active for such lousy weather. Many swallows are going in and out of the culvert. Whenever one comes out, it usually makes a short arc to fly back in at the same entrance within a couple of seconds; though scores of birds are exiting the culvert, none are leaving the site. We call this behavior "swarming," and it's characteristic of cliff swallows investigating nest sites. Birds that do not have nests of their own constantly fly up to nests, get repelled by the owners inside, fly a short way out of the culvert, and then reenter to visit another nest. A bird may do this for hours, or it may leave the colony and travel to a nearby one to swarm there.

Many of the birds now at Whitetail probably lived here last year and in other years, and we'll confirm this later by catching them. Given the approximately 3,200 birds that were here last year, and assuming many of those return this summer, there'll undoubtedly be a lot of competition for the relatively few nests that survived the winter intact. Although we are sitting in the truck above the culvert and cannot see in from this vantage point, I'm sure the birds are already fighting viciously for those nests.

The birds on the power lines are preening and shaking the moisture out of their feathers. Nowhere is the essence of the cliff swallow better captured than by birds sitting on a power line. Despite plenty of wire space, they always crowd together so that only a few inches separate them. There may be twenty or thirty birds on three or four feet of wire while miles of adjacent wire are vacant. In all facets of their life, these creatures insist on being together. They also insist on confrontation. An incoming bird often attacks one already sitting on the wire and tries to knock it off its perch. Others light, sidle toward an adjacent bird, peck at it, and try to make it fly. If it's successful, the offender merely looks around with an innocent "Who, me?" attitude, then either flies away itself or goes after another bird nearby. There is no reason for this sort of aggression; the obvious conclusion is that these birds are just little shits to each other.

As we arrive back at Cedar Point, I hear cliff swallows overhead. Today is the first day this season I've seen more than a couple of them passing above the station. There are so many colonies near Cedar Point that on a typical summer day dozens of cliff swallows can be seen or heard foraging overhead at any time of the day, and sometimes hundreds or thousands appear over Keystone Lake. Usually the swallows are common here long before now, but this is clearly an atypical year.

My attention is drawn to the passing birds because they are giving "squeak" calls to signal to other members of their flock that they've found food. That these birds actively inform others about finding food is a remarkably cooperative act for animals that often do such rotten things to each other. Food calling represents a clear advantage of group living but still remains mysterious in many respects.

My interest in food calls goes back more than a decade. In spring 1982, as I was preparing for the first season of fieldwork, I learned that another graduate student, Philip Stoddard, was also studying cliff swallows. After some initial angst about competition, I talked to Philip and discovered that his primary interest was in how parent cliff swallows can recognize their own young by their voices. Each baby swallow develops a distinctive voice that its parents learn by repeatedly hearing it. By the time the young birds leave the nest, their parents can recognize them by sound. Philip and his graduate adviser, Mike Beecher, were working out the details of this story at the time, and their research had no overlap with mine. But Philip asked if I had ever heard the cliff swallow's food call, a vocalization he had encountered just a few times. When given by a forager returning to a colony, it seemed to mean food was available on the foraging grounds. If the birds lived in colonies primarily to enhance their ability to find food, a signal like the food call could be a critical part of their feeding strategy.

Sure enough, it didn't take long for Mary and me to hear the cliff swallows of Keith County giving food calls. The call is a distinctive high-pitched squeak, often given by birds foraging near Keystone Lake below Cedar Point. It seems to be used mostly in bad weather. When it is given, dozens of foraging birds fly toward the caller. Cliff swallows are one of only a few vertebrates that signal the location of food to others, so their food call is of major interest to behavioral biologists. But it has not proved easy to study.

In the early years of our research, we accumulated nothing more than anecdotal observations of food calling; calls occurred too rarely and unpredictably for us to study them. But in the spring of 1987 Marty, an undergraduate student, and I were discussing ideas for a research project that he could do in Nebraska. I mentioned the food call to him, and he got interested. Although I doubted that Marty was the person to study something as obscure and tricky as the rarely occurring food call, I finally agreed to let him try. If Marty could manage to record the call, he could do a series of playbacks to determine when and where the birds would respond to it and possibly infer the contexts in which food calling occurred. We loaded up a reel-to-reel tape recorder and parabolic microphone. On the drive across the country Mary and I kept thinking that something had better come of this, because the parabola was made out of some buteric-acid-based plastic and reeked with an odor like vomit!

I described the call to Marty and suggested he go down to the shore of Keystone Lake whenever it was cool and cloudy and run the tape recorder continuously in hopes that he might get lucky and record a squeak call. He went through reel after reel of magnetic tape without getting so much as a peep. I was not surprised at his lack of success, given how infrequently we had heard the call in the past.

After we had just about given up on studying food calls, one morning some cool and cloudy weather forced us to start late. About 9:00 I stepped out of the lab building to check on the weather, and barrages of squeak calls greeted me! I looked overhead, and directly above were at least a hundred foraging cliff swallows giving squeak calls almost constantly. I'd never heard anything like it.

As I ran up the hill toward the cabins to find Marty, I heard more squeak calls coming from other groups of birds. Hundreds of cliff swallows were giving hundreds of calls in some sort of calling frenzy. Within minutes we had managed to make several excellent recordings. To this day I've never heard a comparable bout of calling. That day apparently offered just the right combination of weather conditions and insect availability to stimulate food calls. The cliché about being in the right place at the right time applies nowhere more than to biological fieldwork.

After getting the local radio station to help him make taped copies of his recordings of calls, Marty began a systematic playback experiment. He broadcast a series of squeak calls from his car, parking at various distances from colonies of different sizes. Although cliff swallows would occasionally alter their flight to move toward the speaker, by and large they did not respond to the squeak call. By the end of that summer it was clear to us that the cliff swallows did not give squeak calls, or respond to tape recordings of them, around their colonies. This was in contrast to Philip's observations in Washington, where food calls seemed to be given by birds returning to a colony site. Marty had definitively shown that Nebraska birds do not food-call at the colonies, although after doing two hundred playbacks he was naturally discouraged—as are many beginning biologists—when his data demonstrated only the absence of a behavior.

Despite Marty's results, I was still convinced from our earlier observations that the squeak calls were associated in some way with food finding. If they were not used at the colonies, perhaps they were given on the foraging grounds. Furthermore, our earlier observations had been during bad weather, whereas Marty's playbacks had been done on warm and sunny days. The next summer we came prepared to present squeak calls to cliff swallows foraging away from their colonies and during bad weather.

Marty had graduated by then and gone off to spend a year as a bank teller before starting graduate school, and I knew that studying cliff swallow food calls in bad weather would be too uncertain for another student project. Mary and I decided to do the playback experiments ourselves, and we set up a "playback area" on the Cedar Point grounds. We found a rectangular grassy spot delineated on all four sides by rows of juniper trees. Many small insects rested in the grass and in the junipers during bad weather, and swallows cruised low over the grass and among the trees in search of them. By climbing onto a nearby bluff about fifty feet high, I could look down into the playback area and count all the swallows there. Mary sat in the middle and operated the tape recorder.

Playing back squeak calls brought a dramatic response. As soon as the calls were broadcast, from dozens to hundreds of birds converged on the playback area and swarmed around Mary and the tape recorder. Marty had seen nothing like this around the colonies the previous summer. The squeak call clearly attracted birds. We verified that it was specifically the squeak call the birds responded to and not just any cliff swallow sound. We broadcast recordings of the cliff swallow's general purpose *chur* call, which the birds use in many situations, and that caused no convergences.

We later determined that the squeak call was associated directly with food. As insectivores that feed only on flying insects, cliff swallows are not easy animals to give food to. But we noticed that the birds often follow horses and cows, feeding on the insects the livestock stir up. The birds do this especially in bad weather when food is scarce. So we mimicked a cow: we walked through tall grass, swatting the tops of the stems with a stick to flush insects. We found that the birds' squeak calls increased from three- to tenfold when insects were "provided" to them this way.

Eventually it became obvious that cliff swallows use squeak calls to alert any swallow within earshot to an insect swarm. The nearby foragers converge, and everybody shares in the find. The biggest problem, though, is explaining why a cliff swallow that finds food should announce its good luck. Almost certainly the callers and beneficiaries are not related to each other, so helping one's kin can be ruled out as an explanation. And evolutionary theory says an animal should not help unrelated individuals that ultimately compete with it to produce more offspring in the next generation.

The story with cliff swallows must be that callers also gain from sharing information on where food is. By alerting others to an insect swarm, perhaps the discoverer ensures that the insects' movements will be followed by the additional swallows now feeding on them. Most of these insect swarms are ephemeral and move unpredictably, and a single foraging bird might lose track of them. In this case both the caller and those recruited benefit.

Since the birds use their food calls only when they encounter food, Marty's results showing little response around the colony sites made sense: the birds do not forage near the colony and probably were not accustomed to hearing squeak calls there. But what still makes no sense to us is the use of food calls only during bad weather. Why share information on food only when insect availability is low? If a caller benefits from recruiting associates that can help it follow the insect swarm's movements in bad weather, there should be similar advantages in better weather. Yet we have never heard a food call given by foraging birds when the sky is clear or the temperature warmer than 70°. Why not?

As I look overhead at the calling birds, I guess that they must be using food calls a lot during this cool, wet spring. Today seems perfect for food calling: cloudy, cool, and not much wind to disrupt any insect swarm. But I notice that the morning mist has given way to a drizzle, and now it feels colder—a dank, penetrating cold. I look out across gray Keystone Lake and see hundreds of swallows foraging low over the water. Most are cliff swallows, but there are also some barn swallows, rough-winged swallows, bank swallows, and a few tree swallows. The birds are less than a foot above the water, chasing insects that fly up from the surface or picking them directly off the water.

These birds must be hard-pressed to find food. Cliff swallows normally feed high above the ground in well-defined groups, catching swarms of insects that are transported aloft by rising convection currents of warm air. When the birds abandon their high-altitude group foraging and descend to the water surface, it means food is dangerously scarce. I've seen the swallows spend two or three days constantly cruising across the lake surface, dawn to dusk, trying to find food. I figure they must be getting at least enough to sustain the energy requirements of flight but maybe not much more in weather like this.

May 13

I needn't get out of bed this morning to know that today will be a washout. The wind is howling, rattling the unlatched screen doors on the adjacent apartments in a cacophony that could wake the dead. Watching the flailing shadows cast on the bedroom wall by the junipers outside the window, I know the wind is over thirty miles an hour. We must be on the back side of the low pressure system that brought yesterday's clouds and mist.

As I step out the apartment door, the wind nearly knocks me over. Cedar Point can be an unpleasant place in a strong north wind, which comes roaring straight across the gently rolling and treeless Sand Hills, almost an unobstructed straight shot stretching a hundred miles from the South Dakota border. The wind blows across Keystone Lake, picking up a chill from the cold water that comes from the bottom of huge Big Mac behind the dam to the west, and slams smack into the field station perched midway up the bluffs on the south side of the valley. The surface of Keystone Lake, an eerie greenish slate gray, churns and tosses, swollen and broken with whitecaps and with waves up to two feet high. I'm surprised the day is sunny—rarely do lows bring sunshine in this part of the world—but there's a wind-driven chill in the air that the sun is unlikely to overcome.

I flick on the National Weather Service radio and hear them report an expected high of only 55° today, with wind gusts to forty miles an hour. I see no cliff swallows foraging over raging Keystone Lake, and I suspect that the birds are having a harder time finding food in this wind than in yesterday's mist. Any insect that tries to fly will get blown halfway to Kansas. I also imagine that a twenty-four-gram cliff swallow has trouble controlling its own flight in a forty mile an hour wind.

The wind has not abated by late afternoon when Mary and I drive into Ogallala to buy food. If anything, it feels worse. We pass Spillway, the colony site at the water release gates of Kingsley Dam. Not a cliff swallow is to be seen. The birds must be inside their nests out of the wind, but I wonder about the ones that don't have nests. Where do the nestless birds go in wind like this? The same for severe thunderstorms: Where do birds go that have no nests of their own? They vanish and reappear later, but we don't know where or how they ride out the storm. Perhaps this is the origin of the ancient legend that swallows bury themselves in the mud. Today is the second consecutive day of crummy weather, and I've begun to worry that some birds may starve unless things improve. It's a worry that will consume me repeatedly for the next several weeks.

When we reach Ogallala, we go to look at the water level in the South Platte River. My spirits lift when we see some cliff swallows foraging low over the riverbed, protected somewhat by its banks; at least some birds are finding food today. However, the river at the Ogallala bridge is higher than it was only two days ago, and this is not good news. There is still some exposed land in the riverbed under the bridge, but the channel looks wider and deeper. We may not be able after all to take advantage of the brush being cleared out so as to unlock the secrets of the Ogallala colony this year. The deeper water here also means that the more important Roscoe colony, eight miles to the east, is becoming less accessible by the minute. I'm depressed: the rivers are rising, the birds are behind schedule, the weather's bad, there's little we can do in the next few days, and our first research assistant is due to arrive day after tomorrow.

May 14

The wind finally stopped last night. Although it's still surprisingly chilly for a sunny day at this time of year, I know that today the cliff swallows can avert starvation. By midmorning nobody is foraging over Keystone Lake, so the birds must have moved to their more favored high-altitude feeding spots. I'm relieved, but I also know that again today most of the swallows won't be at the colony sites. The cool weather—a forecast high of only 60° this afternoon—that forces them to spend all day foraging will not help them advance in their breeding cycle.

Cedar Point will undergo a transformation today. Classes start tomorrow, and this afternoon the students and faculty will arrive. Most of the students are from the University of Nebraska, and during the next three weeks two courses will be taught—ornithology and botany. Biological stations like Cedar Point provide an opportunity to teach courses in the field, constantly exposing students to plants and animals in their natural habitats. Seeing these living organisms is a novel experience for most students and is the single best way to get kids excited about biology. Unfortunately, only a few schools offer such programs.

We can try again to catch the house sparrows at Whitetail. Because of the bad weather I didn't visit Whitetail yesterday, one of the few days all summer when I won't at least drive by the site. Whenever more than a day passes between visits, I get a vague, irrational fear that something might have happened to the colony. As if my presence for a few minutes a day makes any difference. I don't really know what it is I fear; Mary tells me it shows the hold Whitetail has over me.

When we arrive, there are no swallows at the colony. The sparrows—I count six—are lurking in the bushes along the creek. I figure this should be a good time to net them, because they seem more interested in going inside the culvert than they did two days ago. I put on waders and carry one end of the net across the creek in front of the culvert's south entrance, and Mary positions the net's other end on the bank. By leaving the north entrance open, we hope the sparrows will enter there and exit on the south side with the net. This is how we typically catch cliff swallows at culvert colonies.

We return to the truck and sit inside to wait. The net is below us, and we can't see it from the truck. Normally when we net at Whitetail we have to sit much closer, in case a bird gets into the low part of the net and sags into the water. But the house sparrows are so wary that we must hide in the truck to have any hope of catching them, and since there are no cliff swallows here this afternoon, we don't have to be too concerned about a sagging net. Should a sparrow drown, it will save me the unpleasant task of killing it.

The sparrows are in no hurry to go inside the culvert. Like the cliff swallows, they aren't far along in their breeding cycle and thus aren't very motivated to go into nests. The sparrows are mostly sitting in the brush along the creek not far from the net, the males "cheeping" to attract females or squabbling among themselves to impress the couple of females that are present.

As we sparrow watch, foraging cliff swallows continue to pass overhead. Most of them are high—specks in the sky—but a few come lower as if to check out what's happening at home. Mary says that—just like me—they keep coming back to make sure the culvert is still there.

After about an hour, the sparrows finally start to enter the culvert. Most of them have approached the net on the south side, and it appears that some are flying around it or over it to get inside the culvert. We wait a few more minutes until none are visible near the net. Four must have gone in, for I see only two remaining in the bushes. I decide to run down the opposite side of the highway embankment on the north end and try to startle them so they blunder into the net. Both swallows and sparrows can easily see the fine mesh of a mist net and are good at flying around it, but we've noticed that they sometimes panic at our sudden appearance and some will blunder into the net. I reach the north end and yell and wave my cap. One sparrow is already in the net, and another flies out of a nest and hits the net but wiggles out and escapes before I can reach it. There's no sign of the others. Well, one sparrow is better than none.

I return to the truck to resume the vigil. The disturbance has scattered the remaining five sparrows, and it's at least forty-five minutes before they reappear. They cautiously approach the colony site from the east, gradually moving closer along the barbed wire fence that parallels the road. They seem less interested in the culvert now and spend some time on the ground in the adjacent pasture looking for food.

An hour and a half later, two of them suddenly take off and fly toward some ranch buildings about a mile away. I watch them with binoculars but lose sight of them near some corrals. I figure that ranch is the source of Whitetail's sparrow problems. House sparrows thrive where there are buildings that provide nooks and crannies for nesting and roosting and livestock whose droppings, full of undigested seeds, provide food. The other three sparrows hesitate for a few minutes, as if weighing the cost of staying at the culvert with its potentially deadly net against the benefit of going to the ranch with its abundant food and safe places to roost. With a tacit "to hell with this," the three head for the ranch.

I look at Mary, and we know sparrow catching is over for today. They'll be back, though, more wary than before, and I feel a sense of failure. I had hoped to get more than one, and we won't have many more days this summer to waste netting sparrows. I'm relieved, however, that we didn't catch any swallows today; it's simply too early to be disturbing the birds. Although we can't know it as we drive away, our visit today will be the only time all summer that we set a net at Whitetail without catching at least a hundred cliff swallows.

3

Assistants

"Come, Watson, come! The game is afoot."
—Sir Arthur Conan Doyle, *The Adventure of the Abbey Grange*

May 15

The daily routine of life at the field station begins today. Forty students, two instructors, twenty researchers, and five Cedar Point staff members arrived yesterday for the first of three minisemesters that will extend for a total of thirteen weeks. That most of the students have never lived at a biological station before is obvious from the big hair, styling gel, designer outfits, and overpowering fragrance of shampoo and aftershave when they walk past.

This concentration of young adults at a summer school in the premier recreational spot for Nebraska and most of eastern Colorado presents all kinds of worries for Cedar Point administrators. When partying on the beach with beer is the default pastime for many field station residents and for most of the thousands of Lake McConaughy tourists, the potential for accidents is unlimited. The field station inaugurated this summer's session last night with a meeting for everyone in which John Janovy, on his second tour of duty as director, described the perils of alcohol and the costs of jumping over bonfires on the beach and driving too fast on slick, muddy roads.

The best aspect of field station life that starts today is meal service. A kitchen staff provides hot food three times a day. Mealtime is social time, with all station residents gathering to eat in the dining room of the main lodge. But each meal is served for only half an hour, and if you're late you don't eat. Since the cabins aren't equipped with kitchens, missing a meal means a nine-mile drive to McDonald's. The rigid mealtimes impose an orderly schedule on our summer activities, but I don't mind it in exchange for having someone else do the cooking and cleaning up. Cedar Point has a new cook this year, Dennis. He has a tough, thankless job delivering twenty-one meals a week for over sixty people.

The students who arrived yesterday are being treated to gorgeous weather. The 80° high today is the warmest of the season thus far, but it will be eighteen days before we see weather this warm again. Mary and I reconnoiter several of the colonies closest to Cedar Point this morning and decide against trying to net: the swallows are just not far enough along. Several more colony sites have become active in the past few days, although most of the nest building is occurring only at Whitetail and CR 4½.

Many of our colony sites along the Sutherland Canal, most of them under bridges that span it, are called canal road (CR) colonies. The sites are not numbered in sequence, however, and it takes our assistants a long time to learn which is which. CR 4½ is a relatively new bridge, installed two summers ago. Mary gave it its fractional name since it's between CR 4 and CR 5 and to prevent me from confusingly calling it CR 9, a number not yet used in our sequence. Last summer was the first time it had birds. About three hundred pairs nested then, but at least twice that number are there now and the season has hardly started.

Our decision not to try to net the newly arrived birds this morning ensures that this summer will be the first ever that Mary and I have not done some netting before our assistants arrived. Kathy, the first of this year's three, is due this afternoon.

Field assistants are almost as integral a part of this research as the cliff swallows. Mary and I have had assistants every year, and the number of students who've worked with us is now near forty. The names of each year's crew are etched in my mind. We often refer to a season by its assistants: so and so happened the Winnie-Laura-Veronica summer. You can't study cliff swallows without assistants. The birds are too numerous and do too much. A single person would be overwhelmed by the numbers of birds that get into the net at any one time. A single person cannot efficiently check the contents of so many nests; it would take too long and disturb a colony too much. A single person cannot watch enough birds to collect meaningful observational data, for the birds' behavior is so subtle yet fast paced that you can watch only a few nests at a time.

Many senior scientists rely on their graduate students for assistance. A professor will devise a research program, secure funds to support it, and recruit one or more graduate students interested in the subject to carry out the day-to-day research. The student's principal compensation is the advanced degree he or she earns, and the professor's name goes on the publications that result. This approach is most common in laboratory-based science that requires sophisticated and expensive equipment. But some ecologists and animal behaviorists also rely on their graduate students to conduct their research programs, to an extent many would not care to admit.

I've resisted this approach to the cliff swallow project. When I was in graduate school, the population biology program at Princeton was one of the few that specifically discouraged graduate students from working on their advisers' projects. We were expected to formulate questions, find the appropriate study animals, and carry out truly independent research, using our advisers only for advice. Some students floundered and would have been better off in a more structured research environment. But the independence expected led many of us to establish our own programs very early in our scientific careers. My training led me to a philosophy that graduate students should do their own projects, not mine.

But the main reason I don't turn over parts of the cliff swallow project to my graduate students is that I simply have too much fun studying the birds each summer, learning new things about them and just being near them. I would miss that if I became a project manager and delegated the thrill of discovery to students.

The assistants who help us study cliff swallows are undergraduates. Most of them are still in college, although a few have been recent graduates. Most have had no experience doing research; most have never held a living bird before. We train them to watch birds, check nests, net swallows, and record data. The training is intense but short, so most assistants are capable of working independently two or three weeks after they arrive.

In midwinter each year I mail advertisements for field assistants to various colleges and universities across the country. I try to find the best people regardless of where they go to school. The ads describe the hard work we expect of our assistants and explain that for this effort they will receive only their living expenses at Cedar Point. That we don't pay them a salary weeds out those motivated strictly by financial reasons, ensuring that our applicants—usually biology majors—are genuinely interested in learning how to conduct biological fieldwork. Some years I've been overwhelmed with inquiries, many from people at small colleges that provide few in-house opportunities for student research.

Trying to make the right selections based on their written applications and letters of recommendation is tough. The two most important traits I look for in potential assistants are a willingness to work hard and a cheerful ability to get along with others in the confines of a field station. These are often the hardest to judge in advance. For the most part I've been lucky in making the right choices. Most of our assistants have been excellent—some truly outstanding—and only a few have been mediocre. Those mediocre ones, though, dominate my memory at this time of year, because I have no idea what this year's group will be like. Nothing is more disruptive or emotionally draining than a bad assistant, who can mar an entire field season.

Most of our assistants learn a lot about themselves during a swallow summer. For some their initial interest in field biology is reaffirmed, and they go on to graduate school in behavioral ecology. Others get turned on by the intensity and intellectual highs afforded by research but decide to pursue other scientific disciplines: a few have become successful molecular biologists. But being a field assistant is also valuable for those who discover they are not interested in a career in scientific research. Better to spend eight weeks one summer learning that reality than devote a year or two to a frustrating graduate school experience.

Kathy is flying in to North Platte in late afternoon. I'll pick her up and check on some colony sites en route. We study colonies throughout the fifty-mile distance from Ogallala to North Platte, and I want to know which sites have been occupied. I also need to stop at an RV dealer in North Platte and have the camper shell on one of our trucks resealed. On the drive from Tulsa it leaked, and a computer we were carrying came dangerously close to getting soaked. Mary will stay at Cedar Point, and I ask her to save some supper for us in case Kathy's plane is late.

The route to North Platte goes through Roscoe, and I stop for another look at the bridge. The daily rise in the South Platte River is continuing: the water is higher than last time we checked. The South Platte is fed by snowmelt in the Rockies west of Denver, and we've heard that the snowpack in the mountains is 350 percent of its normal level. That means a lot of water is going to be coming down the river as soon as it gets warm enough to start the melt.

The cliff swallows at Roscoe are using the intact nests on the south end of the bridge. These nests were built last year and are directly above the deepest part of the river channel, where the water is probably up to my shoulders by now. I'm disappointed because I had expected the birds to move to the north end of the bridge this year. On large bridges like Roscoe, they frequently switch from one end to the other or one side to the other between seasons, probably to escape the ectoparasites in the nests used the previous summer. The birds' switching around gives each intact nest an intervening year of vacancy in which at least some of the parasites living there may die.

That the Roscoe birds have resettled in the same south-end nests as last year illustrates how risky it can be to generalize about the use of nest and colony sites. Their refusal to move to the opposite end is particularly frustrating this year, because the rising water still has not reached the north end, and at the moment we could set big nets in the riverbed there.

Standing on the bank watching the river flow under the occupied nests, I search for an explanation. The key must be that Roscoe is a new bridge. For years the bridge here was a narrow, rickety structure, part metal and part concrete. During the first summer we studied cliff swallows, Mary and I numbered the nests on the old bridge and used an extension ladder anchored in the river to reach them. Every time a tractor, semi, or heavy farm implement went across, the bridge vibrated wildly—enough to scare the crap out of whoever was fifteen feet up on the swaying ladder! The vibrations eventually knocked down most of the nests; the only ones that lasted the summer were those built near a leg of the bridge where the shaking was reduced. The colony that year proved virtually useless to us because of the extensive human-caused nest loss.

Two summers ago the road department constructed a new bridge next to the old one. The new one is a wide all-concrete structure of a style preferred by cliff swallows. Last year the birds moved onto it in large numbers: we counted about 550 nests. The old bridge usually had only about 50. The nests on the new bridge last year were all built from scratch, and since there were no swallow bugs on the virgin beams yet, parasite numbers were relatively small. The new bridge hasn't been in existence long enough for many bugs to have colonized it. Therefore, I tell myself, those old nests on the south end aren't too badly infested this summer, and the birds have reused them to save themselves the cost of building new nests at the north end.

The road department still hasn't torn down the old bridge; they've only closed it to traffic. Last year about forty pairs of cliff swallows persisted in nesting on it despite the new and safer bridge only a few feet away. I notice that some birds have again taken up residence on the old structure. Dumb birds, I think, but then I realize the old bridge doesn't shake any more because vehicles don't use it. Those swallows are probably doing okay there now.

I'm surprised, though, at the relatively few birds at Roscoe today. Counting birds on both bridges, there's only a small fraction of last year's total—maybe a hundred active nests. This must reflect the lateness of the spring. Some bridges of Roscoe's size and style contain two thousand nests or more, and we've been expecting Roscoe to get that large. The next two stops on my tour will be at similar bridges that annually contain thousands of cliff swallow nests.

I get on Interstate 80 and head east toward North Platte. I had planned to check the bridges at Sutherland, but I'm still musing about the birds at Roscoe and stewing about the water level and forget to turn off at the Sutherland exit. I'll stop on the way back with Kathy if we have time. At North Platte I take the easternmost exit, which leads to a big bridge over the South Platte that we call the Tire Colony. This site was given its ridiculous moniker a decade ago because we discovered it on a trip to North Platte to buy a new tire. A road sign proclaims that this part of the river is known as the Newberry Access, which would have been a more sensible name for the site. But once a colony is officially named and recorded in the data, to prevent confusion we never change names.

The Tire Colony bridge is all concrete and identical in style to the new one at Roscoe. It's among the largest bridges in the study area—about seven hundred feet long—and the nests are at least twenty feet above the riverbed. The site perennially contains between one thousand and three thousand cliff swallow nests, the latter among the largest colony sizes ever seen. Birds at the Tire Colony use all parts of the bridge, but in a given year they tend to concentrate on either the east or the west side. Today swallows are swarming at the intact nests on both sides, but they will probably determine that the side used last year is more infested with ectoparasites and start to avoid it. At least a thousand birds are here, and the colony will likely be quite large this summer.

A hundred or so birds are gathering mud for their nests along the riverbank, fluttering their wings above their backs and raising their tails as they stand in the mud and pick up globs in their bills. The ever-present need to be social is manifest among mud-gathering swallows: fifty birds crowd into a spot not over a square meter, brushing up against each other and refusing to land if they can't find a place in the crowd. There is similar mud all along the bank for miles in either direction, but the Tire Colony birds all gather it together in one small spot.

Not far away is another perennially large colony, Airport, which is my next stop. This site is a bridge over the North Platte River. Airport is almost within sight of the North Platte airfield and has the distinction of having contained the largest cliff swallow colony recorded anywhere in the world: 3,700 nests five years ago. This site often has more birds than the Tire Colony, although Airport's bridge is not as long and its beams are made of metal. Cliff swallows often avoid nesting on metal walls, but there's something about Airport's they like. Today there are fewer birds than at the Tire Colony, and none seem to be gathering mud. It's much too soon, however, to predict whether Airport or the Tire Colony will be bigger this summer.

Today the birds at Airport are concentrated on the east end, but they typically use the entire bridge. I've often wondered if the metal surface prevents ectoparasites from finding places to spend the winter, unlike concrete, which is usually full of little cracks and crevices where swallow bugs hide. The less hospitable metal environment might mean that bug numbers never get high, explaining why Airport is always large and all the nests are reused each season.

Airport and the Tire Colony are only about a mile and a half apart as the swallow flies. Each summer at least five thousand pairs of swallows live at these two closely spaced sites. Why are these colonies so big? Other bridges in the study area are nearly as spacious yet never have numbers close to this.

I don't know why the Tire Colony is so large: the surrounding habitat seems much the same as the colony sites at Ogallala, Roscoe, and all the other South Platte bridges. Airport, however, is clearly different. The river is wide on both sides of the bridge, and slow-moving shallows extend at least a mile upstream and downstream. As the summer wears on these shallows tend to become overgrown with aquatic vegetation. The amount of insect food this marsh provides must be exceptional and may explain why large cliff swallow colonies occur here. It takes a lot of insects to support 3,700 pairs of swallows, each with three or four nestlings to feed.

There's a similar marsh at another perennially large colony, Oshkosh, ninety miles to the west. The association between marsh and large colony at Airport and Oshkosh makes a nice story, but equally large colonies occur in areas without marshes. The second-largest colony recorded for cliff swallows—3,500 nests—was found about a mile from Cedar Point on the shore of Lake McConaughy, where there were no marshy feeding areas.

A major gap in our understanding of coloniality in general is knowing whether local resources like food determine how large a colony may be in a given place. Often we don't know what resources to measure. For cliff swallows, should we be measuring extent of marsh near the colony or some other index of resource availability? Might food, availability of mud for nests, number of parasites, size of bridge, or the local population of predators determine how many cliff swallows use a colony site? I wish we knew.

My colony tour ends after Airport, because the RV dealership is nearby. It takes an hour and a half for them to diagnose and repair the leak in the truck's camper shell. While I wait, I enjoy my last moments of freedom. When the assistants arrive, I'll be responsible for them: for keeping them busy, intellectually stimulated, and physically safe, and for trying to ensure that they enjoy their summer. They'll be living with Mary and me twenty-four hours a day, seven days a week. Unlike research projects back on campus, where assistants go home after an eight-hour day, ours don't vanish when the day's work is done. We still see them, eat with them, and interact with them until they leave eight weeks later. Most of our assistants are fabulous people, and Mary and I enjoy being with them. But this commitment of time to strangers makes me uneasy about not knowing each one better before they arrive. God, I hope Kathy is competent and easy to get along with. She's probably thinking the same about me.

I arrive at the airport in time to see Kathy's plane, a small twin-engine commuter craft, land. Only a handful of people get off, and I don't immediately see anyone I think is Kathy. I've never met her and know her only from telephone conversations. Eventually, though, I spot an anxious-looking young woman wandering around the airport lobby, and I introduce myself.

On the drive back we chat to get acquainted, sizing each other up. I describe the weather and the late spring, and Kathy says that the warm weather today is what she was expecting. Don't get used to it,

I advise her, because the forecast for tomorrow is not good. Kathy is asking intelligent questions about cliff swallows, but it's clear she hasn't read most of the literature I sent her. I mail each assistant a stack of cliff swallow papers and ask them to get familiar with the material before they arrive. Only a few ever find time to do so, and some never learn even the most basic facts about the birds. This used to frustrate the hell out of me, but I've gradually come to terms with it, because the students cheat only themselves. By not being prepared, they get less out of the research experience and can't place each daily observation we make in its broader context.

With Mary willing to save us some supper, we have time to stop at Sutherland. There are two colonies there, one on a big bridge over the main channel of the South Platte and another on a smaller bridge over a usually dry channel half a mile north of the main river. We walk down to the river under the bridge at Sutherland South, and I show Kathy her first cliff swallows. There are hundreds of birds, and they've been doing extensive nest construction, obvious from the wet mud on the outside of the nests. These birds are tame and don't seem alarmed by us, which means this colony is farther along than many of the others.

We drive up to Sutherland North and don't find much there. Maybe fifty birds are going into nests. This site will probably support a small colony this summer, in contrast to last year when several hundred nests were active. Many of last year's residents probably went down to Sutherland South. Kathy seems unimpressed by the significance and potential of observing a colony of four hundred nests, then driving just half a mile and seeing another of only twenty-five nests. I speak about it, but Kathy is exhausted, since she left home at 4:00 this morning.

We get back to Cedar Point in time for supper.

May 16

Like most assistants on their first day, Kathy is up early, brimming with enthusiasm when we meet her in the lodge for breakfast. Unfortunately, bad weather has returned. Once again the sky is overcast, a north wind is blowing, and the temperature is in the mid-fifties. But at least it's not raining. Swallows are feeding low over Keystone Lake, meaning everybody will probably be foraging away from the colony sites again.

I see no point in going anywhere, but Mary calls me aside and argues that I should take Kathy out for a while just to show her around. I reluctantly agree, because the worst scenario is for an eager field assistant to arrive and then just sit, which can quickly discourage young people who've never done this sort of work. I'm proud that our group works the hardest of any of the Cedar Point researchers, and Mary and I often use this to motivate our crew.

Kathy and I drive along the Sutherland Canal east of the station, and I point out colony sites as we come to them: Diversion Dam, IS 2, CR 1, CR 3, CR 2, IS 1, CR 4, CR 4½, CR 5, WB 5.48, Barn Owl, Aqueduct, CR 8, and Prairie Dog. Kathy listens intently and tries to memorize the names, but most of the bridges look alike, and it will be only after visiting each colony to net swallows that she and the other assistants will learn them. Kathy will discover the nuances and personalities of each site and indeed of the birds that occupy them.

Only a handful of cliff swallows are at each of the active colony sites, swarming around the nests, but even these few are more than I expected to see. Hundreds of birds are foraging low over the canal, protected from the wind by the ten-foot banks. These birds will spend all day cruising up and down the canal, logging who knows how many miles, and often passing under the bridges. They don't seem to stop or pause when they shoot past, but they must be aware of the colony sites. Perhaps foraging over the canal in bad weather serves a secondary purpose of making the birds familiar with the colony sites where they might want to settle.

I'm encouraged when we get to Aqueduct, for birds are there for the first time this year. The site would be more aptly named the Flume, because it's a gigantic concrete flume on legs through which the canal spans a small canyon. The nests are attached underneath it in long rows. Except when the rare flash flood comes down the canyon, there's always dry sand below the structure, so it's ideal for big nets.

Aqueduct has been occupied by the birds every summer since we began our research, varying from a low of 150 nests to a high of 670. That high was last year, and I've been concerned that we will see a large parasite legacy from last summer. If so, the colony could be either smaller or unused this season. It would be a blow to us for this site not to be occupied. I'm heartened by the fifty or so birds swarming under the middle and east sections of the structure. Normally the birds nest on all the sections, however, and I wonder why no one is interested in the west end. In two days we'll find out why.

Our tour ends at Whitetail. More cliff swallows are going into the culvert than at any of the other sites. Some are even gathering mud despite the crummy weather. This tells me the birds are gradually getting settled, and I think we can start catching and banding them as soon as the weather improves. Kathy, like most people when they first see Whitetail, has trouble believing that this one small culvert—invisible from where we sit in the truck—can contain thousands of birds. Her mouth drops open in disbelief when I quite seriously tell her that we'll be trying to catch all of them this summer.

To keep her occupied this afternoon, I encourage Kathy to attend the ornithology class lecture. I also suggest that she and the other assistants read the manuscript of our forthcoming book, *Coloniality in the Cliff Swallow*. Not only will it give her background on the project, it's long enough to keep her busy for a while. Sure enough, when I walk down to the lab building this evening, she's there reading the book. Anyone who spends her evening like this is clearly going to be intellectually engaged in the research this summer. My initial impression is that Kathy will be a good assistant, and now I can focus my anxiety on the two others who have yet to arrive.

May 17

I'm awakened before dawn by the sound of heavy rain and know immediately that we can't start netting. By breakfast the rain has stopped, but a strong north wind makes an already chilly 51° feel like 40°. I'm apologetic when I tell Kathy that the weather won't allow us to do anything again this morning. My frustration is growing quickly. Although the cold and cloudy weather is predicted to break tomorrow, we still have to endure today, waiting and trying to stay warm.

Tonight Annie, our second research assistant, arrives. Mary and I are due to meet her Greyhound bus in Ogallala at 9:30. We know a bit more about Annie than about our other assistants this year. Back home several months ago, we spent a day bird-watching with her. Although inexperienced, she had an infectious enthusiasm for birds and a cheerful sense of humor. I have no idea if she can learn to handle swallows or record data, but she seems to have the right sort of disposition for fieldwork. I'm not quite as nervous about her.

Even though I'm not sure the birds are far enough along yet to keep two assistants busy, I welcome Annie's arrival because she'll be a soul mate for Kathy. They'll live together in addition to working together every day, and the two of them can commiserate about the weather and the idle time. Most of our assistants each year become good friends.

Annie isn't on the 9:30 bus. No one gets off at the Ogallala station, and Mary and I verify with the driver—who looks just like Art Garfunkel—that he has no Ogallala passengers. We tell him Annie was to connect through Denver, and he says that the bus terminal there was in chaos tonight. Heavy snowfall in the mountains west of Denver caused an avalanche on Interstate 70 earlier today, delaying incoming buses for hours and scrambling many connections. (Great. All that snow will be headed our way as water down the ever rising South Platte.) He said a bus might be following within an hour, and another will reach Ogallala at 2:00 A.M. We wait for the next bus, which also has no Ogallala passengers. We give up and decide to return to Cedar Point and trust Annie to call if she ever gets here.

I don't expect to be awakened until at least 2:00, but Annie's call comes closer to midnight. She's in Ogallala, so I get dressed and drive back to town. She's still revved up from her journey, talking constantly, and can't believe how cold it is. The bus's last stop was somewhere in eastern Colorado, and the ground there was still covered with snow. Annie is clad in the shorts she was wearing when she left home. She tells me she owns only one pair of long pants, and she forgot to pack her tennis shoes. Her feet are going to get cold in sandals.

By 1:30 we've toted her bags up to the cabin she'll be sharing with Kathy, and I've given Annie a brief tour of the main lodge. The night sky has cleared. With no city lights anywhere near, the Milky Way is brilliant in the cold night air. Walking back to our apartment I don't feel the chill because the clear sky means that tomorrow the weather will finally allow us to collect some data.

May 18

Annie misses breakfast, and I'm not surprised. She was on the bus for almost twenty-four hours, and last night I told her to sleep in this morning. I want her alert when she starts handling birds for the first time. The day is perfect for netting: sunny and no wind. The good weather is supposed to hold for a couple of days.

Mary and I decide to start netting at Spillway. We often use this site to train assistants because birds are easy to catch there yet we never get overwhelmed with large numbers. If any birds will tolerate being netted today, it'll be the ones at Spillway. That was where Josef first saw cliff swallows on April 13.

There are two distinct parts to the colony at Spillway. Hundreds of nests are under the metal housing of a crane that's part of the Kingsley hydroelectric power plant. These nests are the highest off the ground of any in the study area: the crane housing must be at least fifty feet high. No terrestrial predator can reach it, so these must be among the safest of all cliff swallow nests. The swallows perennially occupy the housing, perhaps because the metal, as at Airport, doesn't allow parasites to survive the winter.

The second part of Spillway consists of a long concrete retaining wall that borders the water release channel for the dam. In an emergency, such as a rise in the lake's level that threatens to wash out the dam, water will flow through a massive concrete funnel under Kingsley Dam. The water would spill out beside the power plant, and the retaining wall is meant to direct it into Lake Ogallala. There's an overhang along the top of the retaining wall under which the swallow nests are built in long rows. The public has access to the top of the retaining wall, or at least to about two-thirds of it, with a protective railing installed along its edge. This is a popular fishing spot, and the convenient layout means we can walk directly above the nests and drop our net onto the birds from above. So many people fish here that the cliff swallows become very tolerant of people with long poles sitting or walking above their nests, making our job of catching them easier.

We load up our equipment and drive to Spillway, which is only about a mile and a half from the station. I'm relieved to see cliff swallows swarming at the nests along the retaining wall and no fishermen. Although the presence of "fishers," as we call them, around a colony site is undeniably useful in taming the birds, having spectators when we're working is a major distraction. Fishers usually approach us and want to know what we're doing. Most are just curious, but having to reply to them breaks our concentration and often causes errors in data recording, especially among our assistants, who start to think about the conversation and not about the band number or the sex of the bird in hand. I'm usually curt with spectators and say as little as possible; if we seem weird enough, maybe they'll go away. At first our assistants think I'm terribly rude, but before long most start to imitate my style, especially after they've messed up the data while conversing. Spillway is among the worst places for fishers, and we won't work there on weekends or holidays. But with the cold weather, few locals have been doing any fishing yet this spring, so we may have a temporary respite.

We unload and set up on top of the retaining wall. Spillway is a "drop net" site, meaning we catch the swallows by fastening each end of an eighteen-foot-long mist net to a ten-foot pole made of metal conduit and, with one person holding each pole, quickly flipping the net over the guardrail and stretching it in front of the nests. The net is usually two or three feet from the nests, close enough that the birds become entangled when they flush out of their nests in response to the sudden disturbance. We pull the net back up within seconds of the birds' hitting it and carry it away, anchoring the poles in buckets of dirt while we extract the birds.

The number of birds caught depends on their nesting stage. When birds spend a lot of time sitting in the nests, as during egg laying and incubation, we can catch many of them in a single drop; seventy-three at one time is our record. But once eggs hatch and the parents start to spend a lot of time foraging, we catch relatively few cliff swallows by drop netting. We have to resort to other netting methods then, and some colonies like Spillway are configured so that drop netting is the only option. We have to make sure we thoroughly sample these sites before the eggs hatch.

The success of drop netting also depends on the number and density of the nests. Colonies where many nests are stacked close together with only a narrow flyway for the birds (like the small bridges over the canal) are the best for drop netting. If a colony is small and nests are spread out, drop netting is inefficient and usually yields few birds. Some of the most frustrating days I've spent in the field have been at big bridges like Roscoe where nests are scattered and there are wide open spaces that let the birds fly around the drop net or in the opposite direction. Spillway has only a double row of nests stacked under the ledge of the retaining wall and thus is not a dense colony, but because the birds have no option of flying away from the net (they'd smack into the concrete wall behind them), we can do well here.

On our first day each year, before we've established a routine, we invariably forget some major piece of equipment. Today it's our lawn chairs. We get kidded by other Cedar Point biologists for sitting down so much, but chairs are essential. It's very awkward to try to process a bird, remove and open bands, or record data while standing up. Sitting also makes us less conspicuous to the cliff swallows and helps calm them down after each drop. Fortunately, Spillway is close to Cedar Point, so I drive back to get the chairs. While I'm gone, Mary shows Kathy the intricacies of unfolding and untangling a mist net and attaching it to the poles.

A mist net is made of thin thread that's supposed to be so hard to see it's like mist. The net mesh is usually rather small, since most nets are used to catch small songbirds, and on ours it's about a square inch. Each net has five thicker cords running through it that support it and give it shape, and the mesh is anchored to these cross-cords like a basket. Loops at the ends of each cross-string attach the sides of the net to the poles. In shady areas out of the wind mist nets can be hard to see, both for people and for birds. But we generally use them in more obvious situations, often just sticking them in the birds' way in full view, and many cliff swallows get caught despite seeing the net.

When I return, Mary and I do the first drop of the year. We catch seven cliff swallows. With that drop, our mark-recapture project enters its fourteenth season, and I'm thrilled by the sight of those birds in the net. We show Kathy how to remove them, and she begins the slow business of learning to handle and process birds. We demonstrate how to open bands and insert them into the banding pliers and explain how we tell the sex of the birds. Male and female cliff swallows have identical plumage, so we have to "feel them up." Males have a hard protuberance caused by a swelling of the seminal vesicles during the breeding season. Mary says it feels like an "outie" belly button. Females lack this hard knot. Later in the season females will lose feathers on the lower breast and belly to create a brood patch, a region of warm bare skin to press against the eggs. Sexing is the most difficult task for most assistants, and we constantly check their determinations to ensure accuracy.

Mary and I both discuss with Kathy the importance of proper data recording, and I try to make the point that the one thing I won't tolerate is sloppy record keeping. All our data are written directly on paper; I've never trusted computerized ways of recording data in the field. Too many things might go wrong electronically, and once a bird flies away there's no way to recover its information. But mistakes or omissions often can't be corrected even if you have a paper record.

It's frustrating to watch Kathy fumble with the bands and unsuccessfully try to remove a bird from the net. All assistants start out slow, and Kathy's no exception. She has large hands and seems clumsy, lacking the fine motor coordination needed for handling small birds. Several years ago one of our assistants killed the first bird she touched by holding it incorrectly and inadvertently suffocating it. Mary and I always tell our new assistants this story, as much for our own benefit as for theirs, to remind us to watch them like hawks. I quickly get impatient at the slow pace, but training Kathy will ultimately yield more birds this summer, and Mary patiently repeats the steps.

One of the first seven birds we caught was already banded. The prefix of its band number tells us it was banded last year. We wonder where it lived last summer, because it wasn't here—no birds used the retaining wall at Spillway in 1994. But we won't know any more about it until sometime this fall when Mary enters all of this year's data into the computer. Each of the 73,400 or so birds we've banded thus far has its own computerized history, so we can tell when we caught it, its age, what colonies it has occupied over the years, its weight, how many parasites it had, and a variety of other facts. I get excited each time we encounter a banded bird, which will happen thousands of times this summer, because each recapture means we'll know more history for that individual.

Spillway, however, isn't a particularly band-rich site. The swallows are erratic in their use of the nests on the retaining wall from year to year, and even when the wall is used we seldom band more than a few hundred because the nests are so spread out. That means most of the birds encountered at Spillway in a given year are unbanded. We'll later visit other sites such as Whitetail and some of the canal bridges where well over half of the colony residents have been banded in an earlier year. Although capturing unbanded birds is important—the ratio of marked to unmarked animals is a critical part of any mark-recapture study—the unbanded cliff swallows are not too exciting at the time we catch them.

We continue to get small catches of three to six birds. The swallows flush from their nests whenever we drop the net over the side, but they quickly return once we move away. They probably haven't experienced people on top of the retaining wall this summer, but they're tame nevertheless. The birds at each colony site generally act the same each year, and the Spillway birds are always cooperative.

We ask Kathy to handle one of the poles on each drop, and Mary and I alternate with the other. Drop netting is a simple procedure, but it takes assistants a long time to learn to do it correctly. The critical aspect is keeping the net taut—by maintaining the proper spacing between the two poles—at the moment it's flipped over. If the two persons are too close together, the net will sag in the middle and snag on the guardrail or bridge parapet when it's dropped over. This will both prevent catching any birds and tear up the net. I emphasize the correct technique to each assistant by having them follow behind me or Mary as we do some drops, but many never really learn it. Kathy keeps following too close, making the net too saggy to drop over. If Kathy leads, when I try to reduce the sag by moving away from her, she feels the tug on the net and moves in my direction. More sag. Another integral part of the procedure is inserting the pole firmly in the dirt-filled bucket when we move back to process the birds. If a pole isn't secured well, it may fall while we're extracting the swallows and kill or injure a bird. Many assistants get so excited by a net full of birds that in their dash back to the buckets they often forget to anchor the poles firmly.

By midmorning the nice weather has brought out three fishers. One is fishing from the top of the far end of the retaining wall, and he ignores us. He must be a regular who already knows what we're doing. The other two, an elderly couple, are clearly newcomers, and from what I can overhear they've never fished here and wonder if anything is "hitting." Initially they keep their distance, but the man keeps watching us. He soon strolls by, pretending to be looking for a fishing spot. After a while he gets up his nerve and approaches us. I know what's coming.

"I sure am curious. What are you guys catching?"

"Birds."

"Birds?"

"Cliff swallows. They build mud nests under the ledge."

"Sure are a lot of them here. What are you doing with them?"

At this point, I've often toyed with the idea of replying, "We are doing mark-recapture sampling to generate maximum-likelihood estimates of survivorship as a function of group size to understand the adaptive significance of avian coloniality and the selective pressures that promote it." That probably wouldn't go over too well, so instead

I quit talking and try to act preoccupied. Kathy is too busy concentrating on not messing up the data to say anything. Mary rides to the rescue, explaining briefly about bands and netting. He leaves after a few minutes, and I pray that he doesn't bring his wife over. But soon they drive off, and no more fishers bother us.

Our netting is productive until an employee of the power company appears. Workers are servicing one of the hydroplant's turbines and must move the crane to a new position. Soon the entire crane and its housing starts moving slowly along its track. All avian hell breaks loose as the birds are alarmed by the noise and movement. They follow their nests as the structure moves, and some sit inside them during the ride. The birds on the retaining wall join in, and at least a thousand swallows are swirling above and around the crane housing, poop falling like rain.

I point out to Kathy that the response of the retaining wall birds to an alarm on the crane housing is significant because this social interaction between the two groups of birds means they belong to a single "colony," even though they're physically separated. Often, neighboring groups of cliff swallow nests may be slightly apart—for example, on an irregular cliff face or on parallel highway bridges. When are the separate groups also separate colonies? We let the birds tell us: if they interact with each other, such as responding simultaneously to a predator or disturbance or foraging together, they're functionally the same colony. If they seldom interact, they're separate colonies.

The disruption seems to have caused many of the swallows on the retaining wall to lose interest in the nests, and after a few minutes most of the birds in the colony have left to feed. We see and hear them high overhead. We start catching even fewer birds per drop—often only one or none.

A half hour later the crane is moved back to its resting position, and once again the cliff swallows freak out. But they're undeterred and really don't care if the structure moves periodically. Several years ago the power company decided it didn't want swallow nests on the crane housing and rigged up a hose to wash off the nests. Every day the company turned on the spray, soaking the nesting regions. The cliff swallows persisted, however, and even though some nests were washed away, they found portions of the housing that the spray missed and built nests there in large numbers. The power company finally gave up and hasn't harassed the birds lately. The workers were probably unaware that they were violating federal law by interfering with the nesting attempts of a protected migratory songbird.

We end up with fifty-five birds for the morning, of which seven were recaptures from previous years. It's not a bad start, considering the site and that we were training Kathy. We return to Cedar Point for lunch and a rendezvous with Annie. Lunchtime is usually when Mary and I must decide what colonies to visit in the afternoon. Weather is too variable in the western Great Plains for us to plan ahead reliably for more than about half a day. Since the wind usually increases during the day, we tend to visit the more wind-tolerant colony sites in the afternoons. Our decision about where to go must also reflect the relative amount of capture effort needed at various sites and which ones require more sampling at a particular time.

Today the wind is still light, meaning we could set up the big nets this afternoon. We decide to try Aqueduct after lunch, since Kathy and I saw birds there two days ago. We load up the nets, and the four of us head east along the canal. Despite the beautiful weather, there aren't many birds around any of the colonies. I'm surprised to see some of the active ones—even big CR 4½—completely vacant. But the weather has been so bad lately that the swallows probably need a good day like this to feed.

There are no birds at Aqueduct. As we sit in the truck looking at the vacant flume, suddenly a great horned owl flies out from under the west end, where it had been sitting on a crossbeam of one of the support legs. The huge bird disappears in the canyon to the south. I wonder if this owl has decided to use Aqueduct as a day roost. If so, its presence might discourage the cliff swallows from nesting here this summer, and immediately I speculate that the owl was the reason the birds weren't interested in the west end two days ago. I also wonder if the owl has attacked the great blue heron colony in the nearby trees. Maybe it was attracted by the conspicuous herons and then found the flume with its shady roosting place. The herons appear to have stayed, but the owl could be a problem for both them and the cliff swallows. Horned owls are massive, fearless predators, and nothing's safe from them.

With no birds to catch at Aqueduct, we decide to drive on to the colony at Paxton—another big net site—and have a look at the river there. I don't know its status or the water situation in that stretch of the South Platte River. We continue down the canal and pass more colony sites: CR 8, Prairie Dog, WB 9.94, CR 7, 11.09, Pigpen, Feed-lot, and CR 6. We leave the canal road when we reach the paved county road north of Paxton and head south into town.

Paxton is a community of about three hundred people, famous mostly for Ole's Big Game Bar and Lounge. The inside of this bar is adorned with mounted heads of several hundred African and North American mammals, including elephants, giraffes, lions, and a complete polar bear with a seal in its paws. Ole, the former owner, shot these (and many more) on safaris all over the world in the forties, fifties, and sixties. Except for the polar bear, which is enclosed in a huge glass case, the mounts are exposed to touching by bar patrons. They're dusty, dingy, and reek of cigarettes and beer. Ole's is a major tourist attraction, and I usually show it to our assistants sometime during the summer. Most are revolted. We don't stop today: we'll wait for Judy, our third assistant, to arrive before paying our annual visit.

The Paxton colony is on a large bridge that spans the South Platte River south of town. We discover that the road department has cleared the brush from alongside this bridge, as it did at Ogallala. Paxton is usually a large colony: about 950 nests last year. The birds tend to concentrate each summer in particular sections of the bridge, making it easier to catch them. I notice far less water here than at Roscoe or Ogallala. This is typical; the power company has a diversion dam across the South Platte upstream, midway between here and Roscoe. That dam holds water in the river and diverts much of it into another canal. Surprisingly, many cliff swallows are here this afternoon, going into nests on the east side of the bridge above the channel and the adjacent exposed land. Mary and I agree that we should try to catch them.

We tote the big nets and lawn chairs down into the riverbed, descending a steep six-foot embankment. The bottom of the river is clean, soft sand, and Mary and the assistants wade in it barefoot. I'm more of a sissy and don't like to wade without shoes on. I strap on waders and discover a thick, sticky mudfield on the far side of the channel. Mary and the assistants are reluctant to wade through the mud barefoot, but we have only one other pair of waders with us. The solution is for Mary, Kathy, and Annie to take turns using them to cross the mudfield to a dry sandbar fifty yards away. I ferry the empty waders from the sandbar to the river after each of them completes the crossing. Annie is the last to cross, and the waders fit her the most poorly. Her feet are so small that they keep pulling out of the boots and soon she gets completely mired in the sticky mud. She can't move, and I have to help by grabbing her lower thighs and pulling up on her legs. Eventually we get her across, to the laughter of everyone. Why is someone stuck in the mud so funny?

Despite our flailing around and the inordinate amount of time we've taken to get across the mud, the cliff swallows are still busy at their nests and have ignored us. Mary and I demonstrate how to erect a big net. The nets we will use today are forty-two feet long, and we'll put them fifteen feet high, just high enough to cover the entrances to the birds' nests but low enough to allow them room to fly in over the top. We usually catch cliff swallows coming out, so a net must allow the birds room to reach the nests. The poles are in five-foot sections that fit together, and the top of each is anchored by two guy wires attached to stakes driven into the ground. We pull the net up and down using another rope that threads through a screw eye on the top of each pole. Unless we're overcome by tangled ropes, these nets can be set up and taken down in ten minutes or so. They were developed for netting forest canopy birds and are ideal for catching swallows on tall bridges, at least when the wind is light.

We set up two nets, which don't cover the entire span of active nests but will be enough for today given the greenness of our assistants. With a set net you wait for the birds to hit it and get caught, and at a colony like Paxton the wait is usually not long. The birds take a few minutes to get used to it but soon start going over the top to reach their nests. Before long, the nets start filling up.

Mary works with Kathy and I work with Annie, showing them how to figure out where the bird is within the net and how to back it out by pushing the net off it. Annie is more adept and catches on quickly. Within a few minutes she's removed her first bird without any help. We start getting so many birds that Mary and Kathy go back to the sandbar and process them while Annie and I remove more from the nets. Kathy focuses on recording and handling bands, and after a while I have her and Annie switch duties. I can already tell that Annie's strong suit will not be recording. She talks too much and seems to have trouble concentrating on the record keeping. Other conversation distracts her. I want each assistant to develop an equal aptitude for each task, which increases our flexibility when we later split up into multiple teams. I hope my initial impression that Kathy is poor at handling birds and Annie is poor at recording proves false.

We net for a couple of hours and catch 106 birds before we have to quit to make it back for supper. Paxton, like Spillway, is not full of previously banded birds. It's not one of our primary study colonies, and we net here only two or three times a summer. Last year we caught a total of 616 birds at Paxton over the season, which, based on the number of active nests, was only 32 percent of the total residents. We recaught some of those birds today, and we expect to catch more on return visits.

Little do we now know how valuable the data from the Paxton training session will be.

May 19

Given our success yesterday at Paxton, we decide to return for a full day. The morning begins sunny and still, like yesterday, but there's a chance of thunderstorms. We'll have to be careful, because the last thing we want is to be caught in a thunderstorm with the big nets up. There's no way they can withstand storm winds. The poles would also make nice lightning rods.

Although the quickest route to Paxton is the interstate, I want to go back down the canal to see if the owl is still at Aqueduct. Sure enough, when we stop it flies out from under the west end. Clearly it's using the site as a roost. No cliff swallows are visible when we arrive, but as soon as the owl flies off, about fifty appear and begin swarming around the nests on the east side—as far as they can get from where the owl sits. I bet the owl is the reason Aqueduct still seems to be attracting only ephemeral interest from cliff swallows.

We set the big nets again on the east side of the Paxton bridge but across a portion of the colony not netted yesterday. This should ensure that we catch mostly "new" birds. Over the summer, at most sites we try to net birds from each portion of the colony and return later to sample parts previously done. Comprehensive netting from throughout the colony gives us the chance, theoretically, to capture any bird present. Recaptures of birds banded earlier in the season confirm that individuals either have remained at the same site all year or have moved between colonies. Our selection of where to net at a colony each day reflects the trade-offs in getting these different kinds of data, given the constraints of a limited field season and a relatively few visits to each colony site.

The swallows are active at their nests this morning, and some have been nest building. We start catching many, and we divide the labor: Mary and one assistant process birds while I help the other one extract them from the net. Annie naturally leans toward net duty, and perhaps in response Kathy seems more interested in recording. Mary tries to have Kathy gain some experience in processing birds—placing the band on them, weighing them, and sexing them—but we're catching so many that there's no time. We're filling up the holding bags quickly, sometimes twenty birds to each mesh sack where we put birds we remove from the net until we can process them. Mary has to work as fast as she can. Kathy is doing a good job of keeping up with the recording and seems to be mastering it.

By noon we've caught 115 cliff swallows, and we close the nets briefly to eat lunch. I'm becoming concerned by the clouds. When we started this morning the sky was clear. By midmorning thunder-heads—white, puffy, anvil-shaped cumulonimbus clouds—were build-ing rapidly. Thunderheads are common on summer afternoons in the western Great Plains, but such rapid development this early in the day means some unstable air is moving in.

A rainstorm has already formed north of here, but from down here in the riverbed with my view partly blocked by the bridge, I can't judge its distance or the direction of its movement. Storms in this part of the country usually move west to east or southwest to north-east, so one to the north shouldn't pose any risk. The sky to the west, though filled with smaller cumulonimbus clouds, still looks benign. But I'm anxious whenever we have the big nets up and the sky starts to cloud over. Getting caught in a thunderstorm would wreck the nets, which cost three hundred dollars each, and we'd have to make a trip back to Tulsa for replacement materials and waste more time assembling new ones.

The wind has also intensified, blowing west to east, and the closed nets are billowing badly. With the wind and the disappearance of the sun a chill has returned to the air, and we put on jackets. Annie elected not to wear her one pair of long pants today, and now she's cold in her shorts. Mary suggests she put on some waders for warmth. We sit on the sand in the riverbed eating our picnic lunch—What do people passing over the bridge think?—but before we're finished the rain starts.

We move our chairs and gear to a dry spot under the bridge, sit-ting in a section where no swallows are nesting. I can tell that the storm to the north isn't playing by the rules and appears to be moving southeast. Its edge is skirting us now, giving us wind and heavy rain. The nets are soaked but will be okay as long as they don't blow over. At least they're closed, so they catch less wind. We huddle under the bridge like trolls and watch the storm move east of us. It's building by the minute, and lightning has started. Frequent thunderbolts spurt out of its dark bluish posterior, and we can see sheets of intense rain on the leading edge of the clouds. But it's moving away and is no longer a threat to us; the rain soon diminishes. A miss, but close: the storm was probably only two or three miles away at its nearest point.

During the rain most of the cliff swallows in the colony came back to their warm, dry nests. They joined us in sitting and watching the storm pass. Now many of them are milling around high above the river, acting excited. We raise the nets again, but the birds seem more interested in flying overhead; no one is coming home. The air is cooler now, and my guess is that we won't be catching much more unless the weather improves.

We're distracted somewhat by Annie, who's uncomfortable because she hasn't urinated since we left Cedar Point this morning. We learn that she's never "gone to the bathroom" outside and has been holding it all day. The rest of us find this almost unbelievable, but even when Mary offers her some instruction, she insists she just can't do it outside. I point out a gas station past the south end of the bridge near the interstate exit and suggest that she go there. To reach the gas station she has to cross a swampy marsh that spans a secondary river channel.

Annie puts on some waders and sets off. A half hour passes by the time she crosses the swamp, attends to her business at the gas station, and returns. On the way back she steps in a hole in the swamp, her foot pulls out of the poorly fitting waders, the wader leg fills up with muddy black ooze, and her leg, hands, and arms are caked with smelly slime. But she seems not to mind since she's finally gotten some relief. It won't be the last time this summer that Annie has excretory adventures in the field.

In early afternoon we notice another thunderstorm building to the south. Since the other one was moving to the southeast, this one shouldn't affect us. But often these storms build so fast and expand over such a large area that you can get clobbered by a growing storm even when it's moving in another direction. That may be happening now, so we decide to take down one of the nets. We're less vulnerable with only one net up; four people can dismantle a single big net quickly. We move fast and have one net down and bundled for transport in ten minutes flat.

Ultimately this storm moves south and doesn't hit us. I'm frustrated that we overreacted by taking a net down. These prairie storms are unpredictable, however, and it's best to not take chances. Besides, captures have fallen off since the first storm passed. Many of the cliff swallows have left to feed, and I guess they anticipate the change in weather that's forecast for tomorrow.

When we finally quit for the day, we've caught 173 birds. By netting a different part of the colony, we mostly avoided duplicating yesterday's captures; only 4 of today's birds were caught yesterday. That gives us 275 total birds from Paxton over the past two days, an excellent start here. As I wade across the river channel behind Mary and the assistants on the way to the truck, I think what a wonderful colony Paxton is and how much more we'll be able to do here this summer. I don't realize that the snowpack in the Rockies has other plans for Paxton.

May 20

Back to wet, cloudy, cool weather. The past two days have whetted Kathy's and Annie's appetites for fieldwork, and they're very disappointed at breakfast when I announce we can't go out. Their eagerness is a good sign. Clearly they won't mind long hours if the weather will ever allow them.

Light rain falls most of the morning, but it isn't heavy enough to prevent the cliff swallows from foraging. The cloudy skies and 50° temperature have again forced many birds to fly low over the surface of Keystone Lake, the only place any insects are active. After lunch Mary and I walk down to the diversion dam at the east end of the lake. From there we can gaze down the canal and the North Platte River, and we see thousands of swallows feeding low over the canal and river. The steady rain has stopped and now it's just a light drizzle, but the temperature has risen only five degrees since dawn. Another stressful day for the birds—and for us.

In midafternoon Annie and Kathy drop by our apartment. In part to stave off their boredom, Mary had offered to show them how we record the banding data in the computer, and Kathy wants to see a map of the study area to orient herself. Mary types in the band numbers of several of the previously banded birds we caught at Paxton, and their histories are displayed on the screen. The birds we look up were first banded last year, so their histories are short. Most were at Paxton last year; one was from Sutherland, ten miles to the east down the river. Mary retrieves the records for our two oldest cliff swallows. These birds were banded as nestlings in our first field season of 1982 and last recaught as eleven-year-olds in 1993. Though neither was found last year, these two birds are the oldest cliff swallows reported anywhere.

I point out the tremendous amount of information we have for old birds like these and for all the birds that have been caught repeatedly over several years. Whenever we miss catching a bird in a given year, we have a gap in that individual's history. Was the bird nesting at a local colony but we just didn't catch it? Had it temporarily emigrated out of our study area and bred somewhere else? Or didn't it breed anywhere that summer?

Kathy listens intently and is beginning to understand why we seek to catch as many birds as possible. Annie, however, seems less interested in why we're catching swallows and spends most of the time gazing around the apartment. I marvel at the attitude of many of our assistants, who come to Nebraska, work their butts off for us, and enjoy the experience but never seem to care why they're doing this or what the data reveal.

At supper Kathy announces that she's arranged to meet a fellow tonight who has a motorcycle for sale. He'll pick her up at Cedar Point and take her to town to look at it. She's been considering buying a motorcycle to ride back home at the end of the field season and saw this one advertised in a local newspaper. I'm not sure how smart it would be for her to ride a motorcycle halfway across the country alone, but more immediately I'm not sure how smart it is for her to go off in a car with some guy we know nothing about except that he lives somewhere in an Ogallala trailer park and is named Roy. I'm partly relieved when Annie decides to go with her, and later Mary prevails on Doug, the teaching assistant for the botany course, to accompany them. Doug knows a bit about motorcycles and, more important, is a former Marine. I doubt anything will happen to them with him along, but Mary and I leave the dining room after supper still a little anxious about their rendezvous with this stranger.

I guess this is what it's like to be a parent.

May 21

The time has come to net at Whitetail. Although we'd prefer to have Annie and Kathy a bit more experienced before trying a site where we sometimes catch over a hundred cliff swallows an hour, we can't delay any longer. Whitetail is where we mark and recapture birds at frequent intervals throughout the summer, enabling us to estimate daily immigration and emigration rates. Since Whitetail was among the first sites occupied this year, it's time we began netting if we're going to have a complete seasonal record of bird movement.

We're relieved to see Kathy and Annie alive and well at breakfast, having survived their trip to look at Roy's motorcycle. They describe him as indeed a creepy character, and they were glad Doug escorted them. Kathy loved the motorcycle. She asks me if purchasing it for the trip back home would be a legitimate research expense on the grant she got to come and study swallows. I reply that it probably would be if she sold it as soon as she got home and returned the proceeds to the granting agency. I don't think that's what she wants to hear, because keeping it permanently is her implicit goal.

The morning has started out cloudy and cool, and the assistants dread hearing me announce that we'll be grounded again. But the low pressure system is rapidly moving east into Illinois, and the forecast is for the clouds to break in midmorning. I decide we'll try Whitetail, though many of its residents will be away feeding.

As expected, we find that only birds owning existing nests seem to be here, and not all of them are around. I don't expect to catch many because in bad weather the swallows are often less tolerant of disturbance. Yet a slow morning would gradually introduce the assistants to the rapid pace that will be the norm here later.

Mary and I put the net on the south end, covering the middle tunnel as we did when we tried to catch house sparrows a week ago. Since our intent now is to capture swallows, we have to set up our lawn chairs on the creek bank so that the net will be in constant view. At Whitetail we're much closer to the birds; when removing birds from the net I'm only a few feet from the nests, so we must be sensitive to the disturbance we cause. I emphasize to Kathy and Annie that they must keep their voices low and avoid sudden movements. The single facet of fieldwork that our assistants each year are most oblivious to is the effect the sight and sound of humans may have on the birds' behavior. Cliff swallows are amazingly tame and tolerant animals, but our proximity here strains their ability to cope.

The procedure for netting Whitetail is for me to stay at the net and remove the birds while the others process on the bank. Once the assistants gain experience, we'll normally have three people here— me at the net and two assistants processing—while Mary takes the third assistant to another colony site. Either Mary or I always tend the net here, not only because we can remove birds faster but also because we can be quieter and cause less disturbance.

I anticipate a long wait this morning while the birds adjust to us, especially given the cool and cloudy morning. They surprise me, how- ever; the swallows return to their nests quickly after we place the net, and we start catching birds a few minutes later. We decide to have Annie and Kathy handle the processing. Mary will sit by them, verify their sexings, and oversee them. It's not long, though, before we're overwhelmed with birds and Mary also has to begin process- ing, while recording for herself. Whitetail usually stretches our per- sonnel to the maximum.

Although perhaps only a third of the residents are here this morn- ing, we're catching birds at a steady pace. The swallows are incred- ibly cooperative on this first day of netting. I'm standing at the net watching birds go in and out of their nests only six feet away. My guess is that egg laying has started, and the birds present are the ones with eggs.

There's been little new nest construction here this season. Only a few days this past week have been warm enough for nest building, not enough time for the swallows to make much progress. Either that or the traditional aggregation hypothesis indeed holds and many of the birds simply have no intention of building new nests at White- tail this year.

Kathy and Annie work intently and concentrate well all morning. They keep up with my delivery of birds from the net, but they're still slow. Mostly it's Mary's separate processing at twice their speed that keeps us caught up. I put several birds in each holding bag, and when a bag is full either I climb out of the creek or one of the processors comes to the bank and takes it from me. Kathy and Annie switch off between processing and recording, but clearly Annie is the better processor. Kathy is still clumsy at holding birds and is slow in at- taching the band and getting each bird into and out of the small cloth bag in which it's weighed with a spring scale. She doesn't seem to be improving, but Annie is becoming faster with each bird she does. The forecast break in the clouds at midmorning never comes, and by lunch-time we've caught about 150 birds. Not bad for lousy weather like this, but slow by Whitetail standards.

During our return to Cedar Point for lunch, the clouds finally do lift—quickly. By the time we get back to Whitetail about 1:00, the sky has gone from gray to almost clear blue in less than an hour. Even when we net at Whitetail for an entire day, we always take the net down at lunchtime. This keeps us from having to worry about the net and about any birds accidentally caught while we're back at the station eating, and it gives the birds an hour or so of undisturbed time in the middle of the day. A midday break is especially important later in the summer when the swallows are feeding young and are more disrupted by our presence.

With the arrival of sunshine, the colony is transformed. At least two thousand birds have shown up, going in and out of both the middle and east tunnels. All the nestless birds have returned from foraging, and many have started collecting mud. The swallows are working on nests throughout the colony, and large numbers are starting new nests in both tunnels. Hundreds of birds are putting blobs of mud on the walls in the east tunnel, which so far has never had more than about two hundred active nests. I figure that many of these birds are doing their first nest construction of the summer.

We start catching cliff swallows like crazy now that we have a moderate south wind. The net billows rather obviously, but that doesn't keep us from catching birds. Almost all the birds enter the culvert on the north side (into the wind), and when they fly through the tunnels and exit to the south (again into the wind) they encoun-ter the net. They find little space to maneuver around it. Swallows crash into the net faster than I can extract them, and the many cap-tures soon swamp Mary and the assistants. I tell Annie to process and Kathy to record until further notice; there's no time now to ac-commodate Kathy's slowness at handling birds.

The holding bags keep filling up, and throughout the afternoon a couple of full bags are always waiting. We organize them in order so no group of birds has to wait longer than others. At first Annie and Kathy were aghast at how often birds were hitting the net and stared at it exclaiming, "Oh, my God." But soon the sight of a full net be-comes commonplace, and they focus on processing without even looking at the net. This is Whitetail at its finest and is why most assistants come to dread netting here. But I love it!

The swallow activity continues unabated all afternoon. At about 4:45 I close the net so we can finish our backlog before quitting time. I also want to look in some nests. The assistants sigh with relief as I pull the net loops together; Kathy and Annie have been sitting in lawn chairs for three and a half hours processing birds nonstop, not getting up once. For Mary and me it's just another day at the office, but they look a bit frazzled.

I look in some nests toward the south end, inserting a small dental mirror through each nest's neck. By shining a penlight onto the mirror, I can see what's in the dark nest interior. Many nests are empty, but some have one or two eggs. Very few have complete clutches of three or four eggs. As I suspected, laying has just started. Usually, by this date well over half of the nests contain full clutches. The colony today is ten days behind where it would be in a more typical season.

By the time I emerge from the culvert, all the birds have been processed, and the count is over 300 for the afternoon alone. With this morning's haul, we end up with 467 birds for the day. Annie and Kathy have trouble believing my claim that we can do over 700 a day at Whitetail. They'll discover otherwise.

Everybody is tired but in good spirits by the time we return to Cedar Point—it's amazing how fatiguing it can be to handle that many small birds. A beautiful afternoon, lots of data (over half of our catch consisted of birds banded in earlier years), and good work by our assistants. Before supper Kathy celebrates by swimming round-trip across Keystone Lake with its 40° water—the first person I've ever known to do that.

At sunset Mary and I walk over the diversion dam to a beaver marsh on the far side. The marsh has started its spring green-up. Teal float on the water, red-winged blackbirds chatter in the willows, and cliff swallows forage overhead. The sky is mottled pink and blue with high, wispy cirrus clouds. We revel in what seems like a perfect evening. But far to the northwest, barely visible above the horizon, is a darker gray cloud bank. We pay no attention to it because we can't know that it heralds the start tomorrow of the single worst week we have ever spent in the field.

4

Weather Woes

A large area of rain continued to spin north and west across . . . the Nebraska panhandle during the afternoon . . . and by 3 P.M. thunderstorms had blown up over a good portion of central Nebraska with several reports of large hail.

—National Weather Service radio, North Platte, May 27, 1995

May 22

Another low pressure system arrived during the night, bringing more cold, cloudy weather. Much of the problem appears to be an upper-level jet stream that has dipped unusually far south over the Rockies and has stayed put for the past six weeks. Until the jet stream moves we can expect no improvement, and conditions for our research will be marginal at best. I can't recall another season with such frequent spring storms.

At breakfast Annie and Kathy are expecting to go out, but we can't net today. The temperature is much cooler this morning, 49° at 7:00. Netting would stress the swallows too seriously in cold weather like this. Some are foraging low over Keystone Lake, the traditional signal of hard times. The occasional breaks in the clouds that now reveal muted sunshine are supposed to give way to fully overcast skies before noon.

This morning I'd like to have a look at our colony sites in the Ash Hollow area in Garden County. It's been over a week since we visited those sites, and it was too early in the season then to determine their status. We've had so little good weather in the meantime that I haven't had a chance to go back. If we could get over there before the weather takes its turn for the worse, we could salvage this day. I ask Kathy and Annie if they want to come with me, and they are eager. Though we'll just be looking at sites, it beats sitting around in their cold cabin.

Mary's seen it all before, many times, so she stays home in our heated apartment.

The Garden County colonies are about thirty miles away, and we leave right after breakfast. We go across Kingsley Dam and turn west to drive along the north side of Lake McConaughy to Ash Hollow at the far western end of the lake. The north side of Big Mac is dotted with public beaches operated by the state parks commission and some private marinas. These offer only a few points of access, however, and most of the lakeshore is unpopulated and undeveloped. Cabins and trailer parks are clustered in spots along the highway, most facing south toward the lakefront.

The sky is darkening as we drive. Any hint of sunshine has disappeared by the time we're halfway down the lake, and the wind is blowing strongly from the north. I'm sure the residents of the colonies where we're headed have had to leave to forage. I now doubt we'll be able to determine anything about site use this morning, but since we're halfway there we'll complete the tour.

The first colony site we come to is McDougals, a culvert under the highway just east of the Keith–Garden County line. Its name comes from a bar and dance hall not far from the site. This culvert is one of the most inconspicuous of all those we study, and there's no ready landmark to signal that we're approaching it. It's a tall, dry, single-tunnel culvert that connects pastures for cattle. I slow down as we approach the bar and start looking for the culvert. The land is rolling short-grass Sand Hills prairie, rather heavily grazed, and it all looks the same.

Soon I spot it and pull over on the shoulder, which along this section of the highway is narrow and inclines steeply. I can barely park the truck out of the road's travel lane. No birds are visible. I walk to the edge of the culvert, standing on the highway embankment above the entrance. I yell and try to flush out any cliff swallows that might be in there, but none appear. I'm almost knocked over by the wind. Damn, it's cold. I'm not sure the birds could hear me with all the wind, but it doesn't look like any are here. Whether McDougals is really active and everybody's just away feeding, I can't say.

We proceed west across the county line and turn south near the town of Lewellen. We're now past the end of the lake, and almost immediately we cross two bridges over separate channels of the North Platte River. The lake begins along the river a few miles to the east.

The bridges at Lewellen usually contain colonies, and a few cliff swallows are flying over the more northerly of the two bridges. The river here is bordered by dense vegetation, and there are islands covered with extensive sedges, grasses, and willows. In many respects these sites resemble Airport with its marsh and abundant food. But the Lewellen colonies have recently been nothing like Airport in size— fewer than a hundred nests. The association between large colonies and a marshy habitat certainly breaks down here, underscoring how little we understand about how ecology determines group size in cliff swallows.

I don't stop at the Lewellen bridges because they're not netting sites for us. The water is always too deep to reach them from below, and the colonies are too small and the nests too spread out to drop-net them effectively. Just beyond Lewellen South is a colony called Bluffs. It's named for some massive outcroppings along the edge of the North Platte River valley visible less than a mile away, but the colony is in a culvert. Although it's another inconspicuous one, I readily locate it because it's near the little Ash Hollow cemetery where Oregon Trail pioneers were buried. I pull off to the side of the road and ask Annie to get out and clap her hands to flush any residents out of the culvert. Twelve cliff swallows fly out one side, into the wind. This means Bluffs is active, although in this weather the numbers don't mean much. Bluffs is an important site for us because it's an easily accessible small colony.

One of our goals this summer is to assess the feasibility of collecting blood samples for studies of parentage in cliff swallows. We hope to use DNA fingerprinting to determine precisely how often swallow broods contain nestlings unrelated to either the mother or the father. We know that brood parasitism—laying eggs in neighbors' nests—occurs often in these birds, so babies may not be related to their putative parents. So far the only way we can measure the frequency of parasitism is by checking the sequence in which eggs are laid in nests. As an indirect method, nest checks alone often underestimate the true extent of parasitic egg laying.

We also know that female cliff swallows at times copulate with males they are not paired with. If any of these extrapair matings are successful, some nestlings' biological fathers are not the male owners of the nests where the young are raised. There's no way to accurately measure the frequency of these events without comparing DNA profiles of nestlings with those of their presumed mothers and fathers. The technology is the same that's used to establish suspects' identity in court cases.

Biochemical analyses of this sort are expensive, and at present we don't have the grant money to do them. If we have the appropriate colonies this summer, however, we could collect blood samples from nestlings and their parents and store them until the money comes through. Bluffs would be good to use for this because we want to begin with a small colony. Mary and I need to decide soon whether we're going to pursue this project this summer. My reluctance comes from not wanting to invest time now in collecting samples when the funding for analyzing them is uncertain. Our predicament is all too common in field biology today, when money for basic research is in such short supply and the success rate of grant applications so low that planning ahead in a coherent manner is virtually impossible.

The next colony site is Grand Canyon, another highway culvert. Its name is a sarcastic reference to a steep-sided ditch that runs through it, cut by the road department for drainage. This culvert, although present for years, was first occupied by cliff swallows only last summer. Parasite numbers should still be low at this new site, so I wouldn't be surprised to see the birds return this year. But no swallows fly out when we stop.

Just down the road is Clary, named for a local landowner. I walk down the highway embankment to flush out any colony residents, and three cliff swallows leave the culvert when I clap. I'm surprised that fewer birds are here than at Bluffs, because Clary is usually much larger. The weather is so bad, though, that I must be cautious in concluding anything.

The final stop is the culvert at Ash Hollow, named after both the adjacent state park and the creek that flows through the culvert whenever a thunderstorm dumps rain to the west. This site isn't used every year, and my prediction is that it won't be active this summer. When we first discovered Ash Hollow in the mid-1980s, for a while it exhibited a consistent pattern of being occupied in even-numbered years and unused in odd-numbered years. Over short periods, other colony sites have shown similar patterns. This makes a nice story, suggesting that the birds regularly skip years to allow the parasitic bugs to die off in the intervening summer.

Yet as is often the case, what we initially thought was a pattern broke down: the birds decided to use Ash Hollow in odd-numbered 1989. The following year they were back, and since then the traditional use in only even-numbered years has resumed. Although it still seems likely that the birds' attempts to avoid parasites at least partly explain alternate-year site use, other factors are surely involved. Could this year be a repeat of 1989? Nobody flies out when Annie gets out and shouts, but who knows in weather like this?

We head back to Cedar Point, this time circling around the less-developed south side of Lake McConaughy, having seen a measly total of fifteen birds at our study colonies in Garden County. The trip has been a complete waste of time and gas, because in this miserable weather we can conclude virtually nothing from what we saw.

By midafternoon drizzle has started, and almost a thousand cliff swallows are foraging over Keystone Lake.

May 23

The cliff swallows are just trying to survive, and we're just sitting. Last night the temperature sank to 40°, and it never exceeds 50° today. Gray clouds continuously cover the sky. At breakfast and again at lunch, Annie and Kathy ask if we can go out, but they seem to anticipate my reply that there's nothing we can do in this weather. The morning is so cold and raw that I see no birds foraging over Keystone Lake. Those with nests must be holed up at the colonies, but where those without nests go keeps haunting me. Some birds return to feed over the lake by midafternoon, and a few are flying around the junipers and Cedar Point buildings, although the temperature has risen only three degrees since this morning.

The weather forecast just before noon offered some hope for a slight improvement. I report that to Kathy and Annie at lunch, and their spirits momentarily lift. I don't tell them that by this evening the forecast has been altered: continued cloudy with highs in the low to mid-fifties for the next three days.

I can't believe this.

May 24

In weather like this, the last thing Mary and I need is another assistant. Nevertheless Judy, our third one, arrives today. She's coming by bus and is due in Ogallala about noon.

We don't see Kathy and Annie at breakfast. Last night was one of only two or three times all summer when I was so certain that the next day's weather would be too bad to work that I told the assistants they could skip breakfast and sleep late if they wanted. In their unheated cabin, staying in bed covered with sleeping bags and blankets is the only way to keep warm. Many of the students were complaining yesterday about the cold and about having no place to go to get warm. Mary and I are almost embarrassed to admit to anyone that our apartment has a motel-style heater that makes it quite cozy.

The weather at breakfast is largely unchanged from yesterday. Cliff swallows continue to forage low over the surface of Keystone Lake and the North Platte River. I would again be seriously concerned about the birds' starting to starve if it weren't for a weather forecast predicting a break in the clouds this afternoon. Although temperatures this morning are still in the low fifties, the wind has stopped, so the day feels warmer than the past two. By the time I leave for town to meet Judy, the sun is actually shining through breaks in the cloud cover. My spirits lift because at least the swallows should have an easier time finding food.

Those spirits sink again when I get to Ogallala. The bus stop is at a gas station along the interstate less than a hundred yards from the Ogallala bridge. As I cross the bridge and drive into the gas station parking lot, I'm aghast at the amount of water in the South Platte. The riverbed is full of churning, muddy water that must be at least eight feet deep. There are no sandbars visible anywhere in the river, and many of the cottonwoods that had become established in the perennially dry riverbed in better times are now half submerged in the flow. I can't recall ever seeing this much water in the South Platte.

My attention is riveted on the river while I wait for Judy's bus. Exactly on time, a Greyhound pulls in. Only one person gets off, and I figure that must be Judy. I haven't met her before and accepted her as an assistant based on her impressive résumé. I introduce myself, and we load her bags into the truck. Driving back to Cedar Point, I can already tell that Judy is quiet and shy. We've had several assistants like that over the years, and they're tough to read. Most have been excellent workers, and later I realized that they greatly enjoyed their summer. But at the time they don't reveal much. You can't tell when they're upset, or bored, or having a good time. I also wonder how the group dynamics among the assistants will change once a third one enters the picture. Judy and Kathy seem more alike: quiet, reserved, studious. Annie is loud and boisterous.

We get to Cedar Point as the kitchen staff is putting away the lunch, but Mary has saved us a plate of tacos. I give Judy the afternoon off to unpack and get settled, but the rest of us are going netting because the sun has stayed out. For everyone's sanity we need to try to collect some data. Mary and I argue about whether we're ready to split into separate teams. I think we are, but she believes Kathy and Annie need more experience drop netting before we split up. Since the weather is marginal and Annie has yet to see how we dropnet, I reluctantly agree that we should stay together.

We figure our best bet this afternoon will be CR 4½. Its large size should ensure that some birds will be present, and we need to get started netting there. On the drive down the Sutherland Canal, I don't like what I see. No cliff swallows are at any of the colony sites we know are active between Cedar Point and CR 4½. The birds have obviously gone high to forage in this break in the weather—which will prove temporary. Seeing no birds at colony sites during a partly sunny afternoon on this late date is creepy and a little frightening. For some reason it strikes me that this is what the canal would look like if the cliff swallow became extinct, which fortunately is not likely.

Some birds are at CR 4½, but just a fraction of its residents. Only a couple of hundred birds seem to be here, although the colony probably contains the equivalent of seven hundred active nests. The swallows present this afternoon seem to be going into nests and staying for a while, so these are probably the ones that have started laying eggs. They're tolerant of us, and we start setting up our net on the edge of the dirt road that parallels the canal.

CR 4½ is a small one-lane bridge installed by the power company to provide the local rancher a connection between his pastures divided by the canal. We've never seen anything but cattle and horses cross it. The former wooden bridge had become rotten and decrepit, and two years ago the power company replaced it with a concrete one. Cliff swallows had never nested on the wooden bridge, perhaps because their mud nests don't adhere well to wood. The new bridge has steel legs that support a series of parallel concrete beams and a concrete top. The birds nest mostly under the bridge on the inner beams, out of our sight and that of potential predators. A few nests have been built on the outer beams, but nests on the more exposed beams of these small canal bridges often fail; they aren't well protected from rain and the strong winds that come roaring down the canal.

By the time we've shown Annie how to unbag and set up a drop net, I can sense a change in the weather. The sky above us is partly sunny, but there are darker, more uniformly gray clouds to the west, and I see no breaks in them. Mary and I demonstrate drop netting for Annie, and we catch eight birds on the first drop. Annie and I do the next one, and we have the usual problem with too much sag in the net. Our net hangs up on a bolt sticking out of the bridge's guardrail. We don't catch anything.

Be patient, I tell myself.

The birds are taking longer to come back to the bridge after each drop, and fewer and fewer seem to be returning, probably because of the deteriorating weather. Within half an hour of our arrival, the sky has clouded over and no breaks are visible on any horizon. With the sun hidden it becomes decidedly colder. Another twenty minutes pass, during which several drops yield one bird. We have a total of thirty-five, and in this weather we won't be getting any more.

The vision of all that water in the South Platte this morning has stuck with me all day. The question dominating my thoughts since then concerns Paxton: Is the river as high there as at Ogallala? I had counted on Paxton this year. There's still time this afternoon to go find out.

We pack up at CR 4½ and head to Paxton by the canal road. The colony sites we pass are all deserted, and the day is back to being gray, cold, and dismal. The only good news along the canal is that we don't see the great horned owl at Aqueduct, but of course no cliff swallows are there either. I don't know where the swallows are feeding. It seems too cold for them to be high, but none are foraging low over the canal.

At Paxton we're greeted by a sight I've never experienced in fourteen years. The entire six-hundred-foot-wide riverbed is full of rapidly flowing, very deep water. The sandbar where we sat in our lawn chairs to process birds five days ago is under at least six feet of water. The marsh where Annie fell in a hole on her way to the bathroom has vanished, completely covered with water. There's no longer a distinct river channel; the entire river from bank to bank is a rapid current. As at Ogallala, many of the cottonwoods that had invaded the riverbed are half or more submerged.

Any more netting here is out of the question. There's so much water in the river now that I doubt we'll be able to do anything else at Paxton all summer. Things will only get worse when the snowmelt in the Rockies starts. The bridge is too wide and exposed for drop netting to be effective. It looks as if the birds we caught here last week will be the extent of our sampling at Paxton this summer. This is a real blow, because there are previously banded birds here. For most of them we'll have a year gap in their history of colony use.

To cause this big a rise in the river, the power company must have opened the gates on its diversion dam upstream between here and Roscoe. The South Platte had evidently been rising to the point that it could no longer be held behind the dam, and the canal where South Platte water is diverted must be full. I shudder thinking of what might have happened had the power company decided to open the gates last week when we were here with the big nets. I doubt we could have gotten the nets down before the riverbed was flooded.

We return from Paxton on the interstate and exit at Roscoe. To no one's surprise, the water at Roscoe is as deep as that at Paxton and Ogallala—maybe even deeper. This is a serious situation for us: it means none of our colony sites along the South Platte are accessible for netting. With the status of Aqueduct uncertain because of the roosting owl, we have no colony sites anywhere in the study area— except Whitetail—where we can catch large numbers of cliff swallows.

At suppertime I sit in the dining room wearing a sweater and coat, staring out over gray, cold, and swallowless Keystone Lake.

May 25

The weather forecast last night was not encouraging, so we're surprised to awaken to a mostly sunny sky. The assistants are eager to get started.

Mary and I discuss today's destination. She's still unsure about splitting up into two teams, but with five people we almost have to. Five people at a single site, unless it's Whitetail, is not effective use of personnel. Group dynamics are such that three assistants working together invariably lose their concentration. Each focuses best when working alone with me. I sometimes worry that I intimidate them for reasons I don't understand or intend, because many of them are clearly more relaxed when working with Mary. They perennially go to her for counsel on problems with boyfriends and parents, on course selections for next semester, and on what to do with their life.

The code for a morning spent counseling assistants is when I ask Mary how things went and part of her reply is that "the doctor was in."

We also need to split up today to increase the data we can collect. We decide that Mary and Kathy will net at CR 2, one of the canal bridges, and I'll take Judy and Annie to IS 2 at the east end of Keystone Lake.

IS 2 stands for irrigation structure 2. The birds there build nests under a concrete walkway above the gates of the diversion dam that release water into the North Platte River. Only about a three-foot clearance separates the overhang and the lake surface, and sometimes it's less depending on the water level of Keystone Lake. IS 2 is among the easiest sites to net. The birds can fly out of their nests in only one direction, and the low clearance means their entire flyway can be covered with a drop net. People fish at IS 2 almost constantly, and the regular presence of fishers ensures that the cliff swallows there are always tame.

When we arrive today we see no fishers and precious few cliff swallows. We set up on the diversion dam above the walkway, and eventually a few birds appear and start swarming at the nests. The colony is usually small and certainly is so far this year. Annie and I demonstrate drop netting for Judy, and we catch thirteen on the first drop. I begin Judy's training, showing her how to disentangle birds, handle bands, and record data. She extracts her second bird without help—a natural bird netter. After she records the first data, it's also clear that she will be an excellent recorder. Her neatly written numbers look like type.

I won't have to worry about Judy.

IS 2 can be a beautiful place to spend a day if the weather's nice. We sit on top of the diversion dam, with Keystone Lake stretching out below us to the west toward big Kingsley Dam on the horizon. On a calm and sunny day the dark blue lake water sparkles, its tranquil surface disrupted only by the wakes of swimming loons, eared grebes, Canada geese, and beavers. The sky is vast, and the lake reflects white, puffy summertime clouds. On the other side of the dam, to the east, is the floodplain with cottonwoods lining the riverbanks and the river rippling over rows of small boulders that create miniwaterfalls. Turkey vultures quarter overhead as they soar above the cottonwoods, which serve as an evening roost for up to two hundred of them. Avocets and willets wade in the shallow river water, and white pelicans float near the ripples, cooperatively hunting for fish.

But this is not such an idyllic day. The wind is increasing, and we're cold. The diversion dam is elevated and exposed, and we can net here only when it's still. Clouds are increasing, and periodically they block the sun. Annie and Judy didn't bring enough clothes this morning despite my admonitions, and they must be miserable in shorts. The net is billowing and threatens to blow over if we don't keep the buckets weighted down with big rocks.

By 9:30 we've caught twenty-nine cliff swallows, and once again it looks as if weather will terminate our day. The sun has vanished behind thick, gray clouds that have spread uniformly as far as we can see. The swallows have left the colony. A group of several hundred have begun foraging low over the ripples in the river to the east, and I imagine many other birds are feeding low over the canal.

Back to more of the same.

Judy and Annie are still too newly arrived to complain, but they're immensely relieved when I announce we'll pack up. They sprint back to the truck to get thawed out. I fire up the heater, and we drive down the canal to look for Mary and Kathy.

I can't imagine that Mary and Kathy have had any better luck this morning than we did, and when we get to CR 2 there are no cliff swallows and no researchers. We continue down the road and soon see their truck at CR 4½. We hold back a short distance: they're moving out onto the bridge to do a drop. We watch as about ten birds fly out from underneath, but none get in the net.

They caught twenty-five at CR 2 before the clouds arrived and the birds left. Mary decided to go try at CR 4½ since it's larger, but that's been futile too. They've caught only six here, and nothing on the past five drops.

It's time to go back to Cedar Point.

We've caught a total of sixty birds today. Our goal is to average three hundred a day, including the days we're off because of bad weather. That means we need six hundred or more on some days. An average of three hundred birds daily over a sixty-day netting season would give us eighteen thousand captures for the summer. Some years we've exceeded that, but I don't even want to contemplate how minuscule our daily average has been so far this year.

The nice weather earlier this morning must have been an aberration, because the rest of the day is gray and cold and heavy rain falls after dark. Over the past couple of days I've been seeing markedly fewer cliff swallows in general. Few birds seem to be passing overhead at Cedar Point, and fewer seem to be feeding over the lake and canal than might be expected in this weather. Have many of the birds temporarily suspended their interest in breeding, perhaps wandering widely in search of food as they do in the winter?

We're not the only field biologists being screwed up by this weather. Mary and I eat and commiserate each day with Diana, an evolutionary ecologist. Diana is in the first year of a research project on sunflowers. She's interested in why some sunflowers develop resistance to being eaten by herbivorous insects whereas others tolerate being munched on. She's done a series of experimental crosses and has planted hundreds of seeds in a plot on the Cedar Point grounds not far from where we played back the cliff swallow food calls. Diana and her field assistant, Nanci, were here when we arrived this spring, spending day after day huddled on the ground planting seeds in their plot while a north wind howled and the afternoon temperatures hovered in the low forties.

Diana is concerned because few of her seeds have germinated yet. It's probably the cold weather, but she doesn't know what to expect, since this is her first field season. No one knows when sunflowers out here normally germinate, but growth of all local plants is obviously retarded this spring. The weather has made this a bad year to be starting any sort of new research. Diana is also concerned that maybe her seeds needed to be scarified before being planted. Natural abrasions on the outer seed coat that usually occur through mechanical contact with the soil during seed dispersal enhance germination in some plants. Her seeds, however, came out of a laboratory and went directly into the ground. She now has Nanci scraping some seeds with a file, just in case replanting proves necessary. It must take incredible patience even in the best of times to sit and wait for seeds to germinate, and it must be doubly frustrating during cold weather like this, especially when you aren't sure your seeds will ever sprout.

The weather has also been hard on grasshoppers. This evening Tony, a grasshopper ecologist, showed me some data he'd just received on soil temperatures. These readings were taken at a site up in the Sand Hills just north of Cedar Point. The mean soil temperature for this April was over seventeen degrees cooler than the long-term average. Cold spring soil means no grasshopper eggs will hatch. Tony is apprehensive because he thinks this cold weather may have killed off a large fraction of the eggs laid last year. Populations later this summer could be so low that he won't find enough grasshoppers to conduct his research.

Tony's not the only one concerned by cold dirt. If this has happened with grasshoppers, it may have happened with many other kinds of insects that lay eggs in the soil, including the ones cliff swallows feed on. Now I start to worry that insect populations will be so low this summer that our birds may starve, or not have enough food to breed, even if the weather eventually improves. Maybe that's why I'm not seeing many birds around now. Can this get any worse?

This afternoon Mary was in town and went past the bridge. The water in the river is still rising.

May 26

At breakfast Josef brings bad news. Yesterday he saw three dead cliff swallows floating near the shore on the far side of Keystone Lake. Starvation must have started.

Josef's report brings flashbacks to 1992. Until this year, that season had been the coldest and most stressful for the birds. Spring began warmer than normal and stayed that way until mid-May. The cliff swallows began breeding earlier than usual, and most had eggs and some had babies when a spell of severely cold weather set in on May 25. For three days afternoon highs were in the lower forties and nighttime lows dipped below freezing. We awoke on the morning of May 27, 1992, to see a dusting of snow on the grass, car windshields, and rooftops. The thousands of cliff swallows in the study area probably found virtually no food during that time. A few tried to feed over the lake and canal, but most just holed up in their nests.

Three or four days without food can have serious consequences for small birds with a metabolism as high as the cliff swallow's. On May 28 Doug the botanist was the first to report birds in trouble—several were weakly flopping around on the road leading into the station. We went out that evening and started finding dozens of dead birds.

Spillway was particularly hard hit. My graduate student, Bruce, and I found almost a hundred dead or dying swallows along the retaining wall, floating in the water underneath it, in the adjacent parking lot and campground, and under the crane housing. Many were already dead; others were so weak that death was imminent. Two black-billed magpies were feeding on the moribund swallows, walking up, pecking them to finish them off, then tearing off bits of meat before moving on to the next one.

That same evening Mary found more dead birds floating in Keystone Lake along the edge of the diversion dam near IS 2. She used a fisher's net to scoop the corpses out of the water, and almost all the birds she found were banded.

Our survey that evening had been too limited for us to know the extent of the mortality. I knew we were losing birds, and if the next day's weather didn't improve we'd lose more. Bruce tried to cheer me up by pointing out the scientific opportunities this mortality event offered. Assuming some birds survived, we could examine whether certain individuals had been at an advantage or a disadvantage in times of severe food deprivation. Perhaps we would find that mostly small birds were killed; if so, the population might have experienced almost overnight a shift toward larger body size. Selective mortality demonstrates natural selection in action. My concern, though, was losing hundreds of banded birds whose histories of colony use we had started to chart.

The cold weather did not break until midmorning of the next day, May 29. When the sun finally came out and the survivors were able to feed, we surveyed fifteen colony sites to estimate mortality. At ten of the fifteen we found casualties—only a handful at most sites, but enough to know that mortality had occurred. Later it became apparent that some colonies had been reduced by as much as half during the cold weather. Of all the sites we censused, Spillway had the highest losses. It was also the largest colony we surveyed.

Surprisingly, the overall effect on the cliff swallow population as a whole did not seem very great that summer. With a few exceptions such as Spillway, colony sizes at most sites later rebounded to near normal. All the babies that had hatched before May 25 succumbed, but eggs seemed to be unaffected. The rest of that season stayed unusually cool, and July was the coldest on record. It was a tough summer for the birds, but in retrospect perhaps the most interesting of any year of our research.

It was interesting in part because the cold weather of 1992 changed our view about the advantages of social foraging. Until that time we had assumed that living in a group always enhanced a cliff swallow's ability to find food, and the bigger the colony the better. We had found that birds with more neighbors could more quickly locate some that knew where food was at that moment. This enhanced their foraging efficiency by not requiring them to spend time searching for food alone. Bigger colonies meant more birds active on the foraging grounds at any given time, increasing the chances that food would be found by others and its whereabouts revealed by food calls.

This view was supported by another mortality event that occurred four years earlier. It was less severe: the only dead birds we found were in colonies smaller than one hundred nests. Only the small colonies were reduced; the larger ones increased, meaning cliff swallows moved into them to live during the bad weather. This reinforced our assumption that finding food was always easier in larger colonies.

We did not see this pattern in 1992. The two smallest colonies we surveyed had no fatalities and showed either an increase in colony size or no change during the bad weather. Mortality was spread over colonies ranging from thirty to one thousand nests, and the colony most affected was Spillway, the largest. In that season there was no advantage to being in a large colony, and there may have been a cost. Perhaps thousands of birds at a site caused heavy localized competition for the scarce insect food. Whatever the reason, it caused us to reevaluate our "understanding" of the food-related advantages of larger colonies.

We've had two spells of cold weather that showed contradictory mortality patterns. Unfortunately, we need more such events to know if either of the first two was anomalous. Josef's observation of dead birds suggests we might soon get a chance to revisit this issue.

The day has begun cloudy and cool, as usual, and it rains until midmorning. When it stops, Mary and I walk down to the diversion dam to look for casualties. Large numbers of cliff swallows are feeding low over Keystone Lake, the canal, and the North Platte River. That's encouraging.

Also encouraging is that the feeding birds still seem vigorous. None are sitting on the lakeshore acting weak and pitiful. Foragers cruise back and forth and have the energy to squabble occasionally, one bird briefly chasing another, or two coming together in flight for an altercation. We see some chimney swifts fly over, however, and they are not looking good. Swifts, like swallows, are aerially feeding insectivores and highly susceptible to cold snaps that reduce insect availability. Swifts normally fly with rapid wingbeats and seldom soar. They look like flying cigars with long skinny wings that arch slightly backward from the body. The swifts today are trying to soar for protracted periods—sometimes several seconds—and look very awkward. I've watched chimney swifts all my life, but I've never seen them fly like this, obviously trying to reduce the energy expended in flight. These swifts are probably close to starvation and will die if warmer temperatures don't arrive soon. Fortunately I don't see any similar flight alteration by the foraging cliff swallows. I guess they're not in as bad shape as the swifts—yet.

We walk along the diversion dam and look for dead birds in the same places we found them in 1992. We don't see any. On the far side of the lake we inspect the line of debris deposited on the shoreline by waves. That's where any dead birds in the lake will eventually wash up. None are found; even those Josef saw seem to have vanished, probably carried off by scavengers. The only conclusion can be that so far there hasn't been much cliff swallow mortality.

By noon lighter patches of gray sky are showing, and the weather forecast is calling for partial sunshine by midafternoon. I've gone from feeling frustrated by the weather and the idle time to hoping all our marked birds don't die. I celebrate each hour of precious sunshine when the birds can find food.

When the sun finally breaks through in the early afternoon, Mary and I decide to check some colonies, in part to relieve our boredom, but also because I want to go to Whitetail. It's been a couple of days since I last drove by there, and my standard fears that something may have happened to the colony are back. These fears are a little less irrational today, given the heavy rain of last night. Occasionally intense downpours in the Sand Hills to the north fill Whitetail Creek to flood stage, and high water sweeps through the culvert. So far these floods haven't been high enough to wash out any nests. Still, I get uneasy when we get a lot of rain in a short time. Pools of water are standing in the cultivated fields just north of Keystone Lake, and earlier today geese and pelicans were swimming in these temporary ponds several hundred yards from the lake. Mary assures me Whitetail is fine, but I want to go look anyway.

The colonies along the canal are deserted, and no cliff swallows are to be seen anywhere. The birds must have moved to high-altitude foraging, a sign that times are getting better. We arrive at Whitetail, and I walk down to the culvert entrance to assess the water. I'm relieved: the level of the creek hasn't changed despite the heavy rainfall. Only a few swallows fly out of the culvert in response to me; everybody else is away foraging.

The canal road was muddy, slick, and treacherous, and twice we almost slid into the canal on the way to Whitetail. To avoid a repeat, we return to Cedar Point across Kingsley Dam. At the southern end of the dam is the colony called Morning Glory. At this site the birds nest on two gigantic towerlike structures that protrude from the lake. The farther one looks like a grain elevator on legs and controls the normal water release through the dam. The more massive structure closer to the dam is the circular funnel that water would flow through in an emergency. The funnel is shaped like a morning glory's flower, and both structures are collectively termed the Morning Glory by locals. The outlet tower and funnel are connected by a metal catwalk, and cliff swallows nest under the catwalk, the outlet tower, and the funnel.

Morning Glory is always a large colony, sometimes reaching 3,500 nests, and like Whitetail it's among the first occupied each spring. Unfortunately it's completely inaccessible to us. The power company tightly controls access to the top of the Morning Glory. We haven't tried to get permission to net there, primarily because none of us are eager to drop-net from a narrow, flimsy catwalk seventy-five feet above the lake.

As we pass Morning Glory I notice a road-killed cliff swallow on the shoulder of the road. We frequently encounter birds killed by cars along roads, especially given the cliff swallow's propensity to nest in highway culverts and on bridges. If it's fresh and not damaged, I may be able to save it as a museum specimen. We screech to a stop at a pull-off on top of the dam, and I walk back along the narrow shoulder to find the bird.

Dodging speeding cars and semis, I finally locate the carcass. It's too mangled to save, but the stop was worthwhile: the bird is banded. I run back to the truck carrying the bloody corpse by a wingtip. On reaching the safety of the truck, I remove the band. We have so many marked birds in the population that roadkills often prove to be banded, and we stop for each one.

Picking up dead birds always reminds me of the summer Marty was here studying food calls. On one of his first days in the field, at Whitetail, I announced I was going to look for deadheads. He stared at me in amazement, thinking a Grateful Dead concert was to be held nearby and the group's fans must be on the way! But he confessed he couldn't imagine why I would have cared, especially when we were at Whitetail, or why I'd be looking for the group's followers in the grass along the roadside. Marty didn't realize that "deadhead" is my term for road-killed cliff swallows.

The banded deadhead today, we'll later learn, was first marked last summer at Whitetail, and this year it had obviously been at Morning Glory. Scavenging roadkills is about the only way we can know when a bird decides to live at this intractable site.

I had promised to report to the assistants on our colony check, so I go looking for them when we get back to Cedar Point. I find them playing horseshoes in front of the main lodge. They'd been hoping we'd find enough birds at the colonies to permit netting this afternoon, and they seem crushed when I tell them the colony sites are deserted. I've never seen assistants so depressed. They're feeling useless, compounded because most of the other residents their age either are taking classes and have been able to stay engaged in their coursework or, like Diana's assistant Nanci, are working on research projects that don't require constant good weather. Nanci can cut scars in seeds in any kind of weather, even at night. Kathy, Annie, and Judy have woebegone faces that implore me to do something, anything, to break their boredom. This is a price I pay for selecting bright, highly motivated assistants who aren't used to just sitting around.

I emphasize again that there's nothing we can do if the birds aren't at the colony sites; we just have to wait for better weather no matter how boring it may be. This is a part of doing fieldwork, which they came here to learn about. But the assistants' mental state is becoming serious and will only get worse if the bad weather continues. Yesterday Kathy and Annie began working in the Cedar Point kitchen to help pass the time, and Dennis can keep them busy washing dishes and cutting up vegetables. But that's hardly what they came to Nebraska for, and their romantic notions about biological fieldwork have been destroyed by this weather.

I decide we need to get them doing something, even if it's a waste of time. I announce that after supper we'll try to net at CR 1, only about a mile away. They perk up immediately, though I tell them not to expect to catch much. CR 1 is the first canal bridge past the diversion dam and has concrete sides that extend above head height. We have to stand on stepladders to drop the net over, and it's one of the most challenging places to drop-net. At least we can practice with the ladders, which will make life easier there later.

By supper the clouds have returned, and we're treated to another dark and gloomy evening. Diana sees us loading the truck after supper and, given the weather, is surprised that we're going out. I tell her we're going to practice dropping a net over an empty bridge and that I don't expect to catch a single swallow. She laughs, but since she also has to keep an assistant busy, she understands our predicament.

We arrive at CR 1 and, to no one's surprise, there are no birds. As we set up the net, I start noticing cliff swallows overhead. Several hundred birds in a loose group are gradually coming lower and getting better organized. Because the birds may be about to go under the bridge, we wait to demonstrate the netting method.

Before long the swallows have started to mass together in a typical synchronized roosting flight and are making passes over the top of the bridge. I'm floored: this is nearly two weeks later than we've ever seen massed roosting flights. The birds must be even farther behind in their breeding cycle than I'd imagined. If they're doing this to advertise the colony's size to potential newcomers, the colony must still be smaller than these birds would prefer, probably because many cliff swallows aren't here yet or haven't had a chance to choose a colony. Mary and I marvel at this demonstration of the lateness of the season and explain to the assistants why we think the birds do these roosting flights. They're more impressed, though, when I look overhead and exclaim, "Look at all those bands!" CR 1 is typically one of our most band-rich sites, and many of the birds caught here each year are from previous years. I can't wait to get my hands on them.

The swallows don't swirl overhead as long as earlier in the season, and after ten or fifteen minutes they start going into the nests. There's still plenty of daylight, so we decide to see if we can catch any of them. Mary and I tell the assistants to watch, and we do a drop. We each carry a two-foot stepladder in one hand and a net pole in the other. Walking out onto the bridge, we lean the ladders against the tall concrete side of the bridge, trying not to bang them against the concrete and flush the birds out from under us. Once the ladders are positioned, we climb to the top rung and drop the net over, stretching our arms as far down as we can and holding onto the very bottom of the poles. This gets the net low enough to fall between the bridge and the canal surface. Once birds hit it, we pull it back up (sometimes difficult when we're grasping only the end of a ten-foot pole and thirty or forty birds are in the net), climb down the ladders, pick them up, and walk back to the road. But this time we're also carrying a net full of birds and trying to walk back as quickly as possible before they escape.

The assistants ask why we don't just leave the ladders on the bridge. There are two reasons. The narrow bridge is such a tight fit for cars (mostly driven by fishers on their way to the diversion dam) that one might brush against the ladders. Second, during the first season we netted here Mary left the ladders on the bridge between drops. She and an assistant were so absorbed in processing birds that they didn't notice a fisher who decided to help himself to the ladders. Mary just happened to look up and saw him walking away with them. Mary ran after him down the canal road, yelling, waving her arms, and gesturing to him to stop, and he finally gave up the ladders. Since then we always move them after each drop.

To our surprise, we catch six birds on the first drop. I feel bad disturbing them when the weather has been so stressful, but again to our surprise, we find that these birds have nearly normal body weight for this time of year. Obviously they've been finding more food this week than I had imagined. That discovery tempers my reluctance to disturb them today, and we start a series of drops, each assistant in turn handling one of the poles. It's clear that Annie and Judy are too short to be effective here; even on the ladder, they have trouble reaching far enough to get the net down. It appears that Kathy will get full-time duty at CR 1.

By dusk we've caught forty-five birds, and we quit to give the swallows time to get settled back in their nests for the night. We hadn't expected to catch anything, so this is a welcome mental boost to us all. The assistants are feeling much better, and I can't remember ever being so happy to have caught a paltry forty-five birds! But as we expected, the cliff swallows are amazingly far behind in their breeding: only one of the birds we caught had the beginnings of a brood patch. In some summers babies have hatched by now.

As we walk back to the apartment in the rapidly fading light, Mary spots a poorwill sitting on a rock by the road. It periodically flies up to hawk insects and then returns to the same perch. A nocturnal bird that reminds me of a frog, it has an enormous head and mouth, huge eyes, and stiff bristles around its mouth. Poorwills are members of the goatsucker family that also includes nighthawks and the closely related whip-poor-will, and they are noteworthy as one of the few species of birds that do a form of hibernation. During bad weather they enter torpor, slowing their metabolism to a fraction of normal. This enables them to endure stressful times, and in some areas it may obviate the need to migrate to warmer winter climates. I wonder if this bird has just come out of hibernation. At night we often hear the poorwills' plaintive "poor will" call repeated over and over, and they probably breed on the cedar-clad bluffs around the field station. This bird is clearly finding insects even on this rather cool and cloudy night, an encouraging observation.

What is not encouraging is the National Weather Service forecast we hear when we return to the apartment.

May 27

The nightmare has worsened today. A howling north wind, pouring rain, 51° temperatures all day, and severe thunderstorms just to the east of us make this perhaps the worst single day I have ever spent in the field.

The morale boost from last night has worn off by breakfast, and the assistants are again seriously depressed. I feel particularly bad for Judy. Since she arrived three days ago, she's spent a total of about two and a half hours actually doing anything. Everyone at Cedar Point is cold, wet, and miserable, and I've never known such collective malaise among the field station inhabitants. No cliff swallows are feeding over Keystone Lake, and with this wind and rain I doubt any are foraging anywhere. I worry again about starvation.

Until today I had been trying to use the idle time productively by doing some writing, but suddenly I'm also overcome by frustration and depression. We've been sitting around almost constantly since this field season started, and I can't concentrate on paperwork any more. Usually when I start to feel like this, I drive over to Whitetail. Even if no birds are there, just being near it helps me regain my composure and sense of priorities. But today the roads have turned to muck with the rain, and it would be dangerous to try to go anywhere. We're held captive at Cedar Point.

Mary is also feeling the stress. Next week she'll be leaving for a weeklong bicycle ride across Nebraska. The ride is an organized event and over six hundred people participate. It's become a tradition for Mary to do it each summer, an opportunity to renew old friendships and simply relax. The ride comes at a poor time during the field season, however, and she feels guilty each year when she leaves. She doesn't feel as bad if our assistants are well trained, because her absence has less effect on the research project. But Kathy, Annie, and Judy have had only minimal experience netting and processing birds, and they're a long way from being able to work solo. I can foresee a long week while Mary's gone.

The rain finally stops at suppertime, but the wind continues to howl and the temperature has stayed in the low fifties all day. I guess we should be grateful it didn't fall into the forties. All we do these days, it seems, is go over to the lodge, eat, come back to our apartment, and wait until we can go eat again.

Tomorrow has got to be better.

May 28

Last night I told the assistants they could stay in bed this morning. At least until lunch, Mary and I won't have to see them and repeat our standard laments about the weather. The day has improved some already, though, because the rain is gone and the wind seems to be dropping by the minute. Gray clouds remain, but the forecast is for good weather tomorrow.

We drive over to Whitetail to verify that no flooding resulted from yesterday's rain. None has. Staring into the culvert, I'm struck by how little progress the birds have made on their nests since we netted here a week ago. The new nests that were started that day look unchanged. All week long the bad weather has forced the swallows to spend all their daylight hours foraging. Never during our study has an entire week in late May passed without any cliff swallow nest construction.

En route to and from Whitetail we see large numbers of swallows foraging over the river and canal. They're hanging on and seem surprisingly vigorous considering the weather yesterday. I'm continually surprised at the toughness of these little birds. Natural selection has crafted a remarkably rugged animal, able to exploit an aerial insectivore's niche in a highly variable, and at times harsh, climate. It seems that only occasionally, such as in 1992, do environmental extremes exceed the cliff swallow's tolerance limits. These rare events give natural selection an opportunity to fine-tune some more.

Over time, individuals who can survive periodic bouts of cold have been favored, and they have left more descendants. Mortality events, like that in 1992, have probably been repeated countless times, perhaps in response to colder weather each time. Cold spells have gradually transformed the ancestral cliff swallow—which presumably originated in the tropics, where most swallows live—into a hardy survivor whose range now extends past the Arctic Circle.

This sort of perspective makes me realize that my worries about the birds this spring have probably been unfounded. Natural selection has ensured that the birds today can cope, by long ago getting rid of the ones that couldn't.

I tell Judy, Annie, and Kathy to be ready to go to CR 1 this evening. We'll try to repeat our after-dinner success from two days ago. Mary and I decide, however, that five people would be overkill, so I'll make a quick trip to Garden County to check the status of those colony sites. The two visits we've already made this season were uninformative, and it appears that the only way to know what's happening at those sites will be to go at dusk when I can see how many cliff swallows—if any—return to the culverts to roost.

All of us assemble after supper except Annie. We wait some more, and still she doesn't appear. Each passing minute is costing us birds we could be catching, because I'm sure the swallows are back at the colonies by now and we have only about two hours until dark. I'm irritated and walk back up to the lodge to look for her. I find her talking to a young man in the dining room, oblivious to time. She doesn't own a watch. Annie seems to be spending more and more time with this fellow, and I wonder if she'll be the first assistant this year to develop a summer romance. I urge her to get down to the truck quickly before Mary and the others leave.

As I drive west along the southern side of Lake McConaughy this evening, I sense that this long, frustrating week is nearing an end. The favorable weather forecast for tomorrow has put me in a good mood, and I'm feeling better by the minute as I drive along, drinking in the beautiful sky. The wind has died, and the western horizon is clear. To the east, gigantic puffy white cumulonimbus clouds reflect the late afternoon light in brilliant shades of gold and pink. The high cloud tops are snow white, jutting up thousands of feet like Andean peaks, with shafts of yellow and red alpenglow streaming down their sides. The flat bases are gray, and my entire imaginary mountain range is surrounded by soft blue sky. On the ground, the fields that stretch to each horizon are lush green wheat or amber hay, with hardly a tree or building anywhere in sight. I've been so depressed this week that I'd forgotten these spectacles, usually so commonplace here in the summer. All the frustration and all the hassles are worth it for an evening like this.

God, I'm lucky I can come here each summer.

My spirits stay high when I reach Ash Hollow and Clary. Both colonies are active, and I'm pleased to see almost two hundred birds at Ash Hollow. The pattern of its not being used in odd-numbered years is not holding this summer. We had seen nothing here on the two previous visits, an illustration of the futility of trying to collect information on site use when the weather's bad. Over a hundred birds are at Clary, up from the three we saw here a few days ago in bad weather.

Birds at both Ash Hollow and Clary are gathering mud this evening. I'm surprised they have energy for nest building after such a long period of poor foraging conditions. Perhaps they're getting desperate to start breeding.

On down the road I pass Grand Canyon, which has no birds, and then come to Bluffs. Twelve to fifteen cliff swallows are flying overhead or preening on nearby wires. Bluffs remains small, as we observed earlier, and I'm reminded again that Mary and I soon need to decide if we're going to use Bluffs for the parentage studies. We haven't thought much more about it this week, given everyone's depression over the weather.

My final stop is McDougals, where I see one bird go into the culvert. This is fantastic; we might have a solitary pair here! Solitaries don't occur often, especially at accessible culvert sites. Of course it's still possible—even probable—that more birds will move in before the summer is over. I cross my fingers that this "colony" doesn't change in size.

I end my tour knowing that the Garden County colonies are healthy. With McDougals and Bluffs we'll have two wonderful small colonies. We'll have to net at both Clary and Ash Hollow. I'm pleased by having these four active sites, but I also feel some pressure in adding more colonies to our list of places that must be netted. We've had such limited time for netting this spring that we've hardly touched any of the sites on our list. An overwhelming amount of fieldwork needs to be done if the weather will ever allow it.

I rendezvous with Mary and the assistants at CR 1 just as the sun is setting. They're shutting down after a productive evening, catching seventy-eight birds. Spirits are high, and everyone senses that a change in our fortunes is imminent. The air has a different feel to it.

It feels as if the summer is finally going to start.

5

Catching Birds

To tell you all in simple words:
I make my living catching birds.
The moment they attract my eye
I spread my net and in they fly.
—Wolfgang Amadeus Mozart, *The Magic Flute*

May 29

Sunshine streaming through the apartment window wakes me early. It's been over a week since a day began sunny and calm, and the optimism of last night continues this morning. The weather is perfect for netting. Walking over to the lodge at breakfast, I pause along the top of a hill to gaze at the Sand Hills beyond Keystone Lake. The wet spring has made the prairies much greener than usual, and the bright morning sun accentuates the lushness. The air feels fresh, and I breathe in the wonderful aroma of the woods that surround us here. No matter where I am, the odor of cedar immediately transports me back to Cedar Point and these magnificent views of the Sand Hills. Mixed with the smell of cedar comes the faint whiff of bacon cooking in the kitchen.

I can't enjoy this moment for long, though, because I must decide where we should net. A day like this presents many dilemmas. In some respects such great weather is exasperating because there are so many colonies we won't have time to visit today. But this is better than the frustration of last week, and at breakfast we're greeted by Kathy, Annie, and Judy, up early, in good spirits, and eager to catch birds.

Mary and I decide to visit CR 4½ and CR 2 this morning. I'd love to go back to Whitetail today, but my rational mind knows that sampling other sites is the better call, especially since we had one good day at Whitetail last week.

With the weather the best it's been in ten days, I'm eager to see how many cliff swallows are at the colony sites. Annie, Judy, and I load up in one truck, the blue one nicknamed Woodrow, and head down the canal to CR 4½. Mary and Kathy are using the white truck, which Mary calls the *Valdez* because it seems as long as a super-tanker—an extended cab plus a full eight-foot bed—and has such an unwieldy turning radius. When we arrive at CR 4½, we find at least a thousand swallows. This is more than I've ever seen at this site, and I know immediately that we'll have a good morning.

The sunshine seems to have put the birds in a good mood too. Most of them are busily gathering mud for their nests. They're swarming under the bridge, and many are clinging to the outer beams, working on nests at various stages. The air is full of birds—everywhere in all directions there are scores of flying swallows. The racket they're making with their calls, though nothing like the noise at Whitetail, is enough to draw the full attention of anyone (or any predator) within at least a hundred yards.

The swallows are getting their mud in a farmyard just north of the bridge. A couple of windmills in a maze of corrals feed small metal water tanks where horses and cattle drink. Water leaks out, creating a small mudhole by each tank. Dozens of swallows from here and nearby CR 4 are constantly streaming back and forth between the mudholes and the bridges.

We park the truck along the side of the canal road just west of the bridge and set up our lawn chairs and drop net. After we set up, I notice that the streams of mud-gathering birds are going just over our heads. Besides their inadvertently dropping mud on us, this could cause another problem. The mud gatherers in flight may notice us and alarm-call before we can get on top of the bridge with our net. Alarm calls flush the colony residents from their nests, meaning we'll come up with an empty net. But today the swallows seem oblivious to us, and we hear no alarm calls by the mud collectors. They seem intent on using this good weather to further their nest building.

We start a series of drops, and what seems like hundreds of birds flush from under the bridge each time we flip the net over. Still being rookies, Annie and Judy haven't mastered getting just the right tension on the net for maximum effectiveness. But they're making progress, and we catch as many birds as we can handle. Our first few drops yield between twenty and forty birds each, and getting them out of the tangled net is what limits our rate.

The double-flip nature of drop netting means it can be extremely difficult to figure out what "pocket" a bird is in. A bird will look hopelessly wrapped up in the fine mesh with no conceivable way to remove it, and sometimes ten or fifteen will all be wrapped up together. My experience and the patience I've learned over the years enable me to extract each one, but Annie and Judy get frustrated because they can't diagnose many of the tangles. I tell them to keep trying. It took Mary and me several summers to get skilled at taking birds out of drop nets, and I feel that I still improve each year. Mary's the best at drop netting, able to remove two birds to my one.

The swallows quickly return to their nests and mud gathering after each drop. Since each drop takes less than a minute, the total time the colony is disturbed—especially when the birds come back immediately—is minimal. One major advantage of drop netting is that it's never as traumatic or disruptive to a colony as setting a net and waiting for birds to fly into it. The swallows in large colonies like CR 4½, especially early in the season, always seem to cooperate, mostly because they're not as wary as the birds in small colonies. Perhaps it's safety in numbers: you don't have to worry as much about predators (or bird netters) in a big colony where the odds are somebody else will spot an approaching predator and give the alarm. And if a predator attacks, most likely somebody else will be the victim.

We spend the entire morning constantly removing birds from the net and processing them. We speed through the birds with me banding and sexing each one, Annie weighing it, and Judy recording the data. By lunchtime we've done only eight or nine drops, yet we've caught 206 swallows, over half of them birds banded in earlier years. I wonder where these birds are from, especially those from two or more years ago before the concrete bridge here was built.

By quitting time I'm exhausted by the tension of handling that many small birds. All facets of our netting operation require intense concentration, to avoid injuring or killing birds or screwing up the data. We had no such events this morning, and I can finally relax when we close the net and pack our gear. Although we've had a good morning here, redeploying our forces for the afternoon is in order. Birds at most colonies become aware of us after we've done a series of drops; they hear us as we walk onto the bridge and flush out in response. Even the cooperative swallows at CR 4½ were finally starting to flush before we could drop. We need to let them forget about us for a while.

When we reach CR 2, Mary and Kathy are packing up. They had a good morning too, getting 125 birds. CR 2 is a smaller colony than CR 4½ and much tougher to net. The residents of this bridge are invariably uncooperative, and to get over a hundred in a morning is a major accomplishment. More than three-fourths of the birds they caught were banded in an earlier year. Each summer CR 2 is loaded with past-year birds, and many are old ones that we know a lot about. Mary thinks the swallows at CR 2 are relatively far along in their nesting, since most of the females they caught had well-developed brood patches. Although it's a little surprising that the birds could have progressed much given the wretched weather of late, earlier nesting is characteristic of colonies with older birds. These colonies are often more successful in raising young, since they escape the parasite infestations that increase later in the summer.

After lunch we decide to use the good weather to tackle perhaps the toughest of all the colonies. This site is another canal bridge of the same general style as CR 1, meaning it has tall walls where we must use ladders. These walls are even taller than CR 1's—seven feet or so, and to drop the net low enough we have to stand on tiptoe on the top of the ladder and reach down so far that we can hold the net pole only by its tip. The difficulty of netting here is compounded because the birds at this bridge are always skittish and unwilling to serve as study animals in any way! Mary thinks it's a bad call to go there today, because those birds will just be the usual little brats and we'll end up wasting the good weather. But I want to try it at least this once when we won't have to battle the elements too. If we can't catch anything there today with no wind, we won't go back. Besides, this site—named Prairie Dog—always has a lot of banded birds.

I decide to take Kathy, our tallest assistant—an essential attribute at Prairie Dog—and Judy. Mary and Annie head to another canal bridge, a site called Barn Owl. We drive the ten miles or so down the canal road to Prairie Dog, passing many of the other colonies. The cliff swallows are home this afternoon, but I'm struck by how small most of the colonies still seem to be. When we get to Aqueduct, we look for the resident owl. It's not there, but neither are any cliff swallows.

Prairie Dog is only about a mile and a half from Aqueduct, and I wonder if many of the usual Aqueduct residents have moved there to escape the owl. If we can catch some banded birds today, we'll know. We stop along the canal road just west of the bridge. Kathy and Judy ask why it's called Prairie Dog, and I explain that when we discovered this site eleven years ago there was a small colony of black tailed prairie dogs in a pasture just south of the bridge. The prairie dogs are long gone, probably shot or poisoned by the landowner, who grazes Black Angus cattle there. An animal with fascinating social behavior, the prairie dog is wrongly considered a pest by ranchers throughout most of the West and has been widely exterminated in most areas except protected national parks and refuges. That any would even try to settle here was remarkable.

The stretch of the canal containing Prairie Dog is mostly deserted, and cars seldom pass by. Few fishers appear along this part of the canal, so the birds aren't used to people and don't cope well with being netted. I know today will be no different, because the whole colony flushes from under the bridge as soon as we step out of the truck. But Prairie Dog is one colony that's not smaller than normal now; there must be at least a thousand birds here. This reinforces my suspicion that the Aqueduct birds have settled at this site.

We sit and wait for the swallows to calm down. The birds swirl overhead, alarm-calling at us. While we wait, I carry the ladders out onto the bridge and lean them against the concrete wall a net's distance apart. This place is so desolate that we don't have to worry about anyone's snitching them. The top of the bridge invariably contains pools of liquid cow crap, formed when rainwater collects in a low spot on the bridge and dissolves the droppings of cattle that cross it. We have to wear rubber boots, adding the element of climbing the ladders in oversized galoshes to the routine here.

When the birds finally return to their nests, Kathy and I do the first drop. Most of the swallows flush out before we reach the ladders, even though I always think the tall walls of the bridge *should* block our approach from the sight of the birds at bridge level. Yet at a colony this large, there are always so many birds passing overhead that some are bound to see us from high above. Their quick detection illustrates again one antipredator advantage of colonial life.

Kathy has difficulty scaling the wall and getting the net over. She had mastered the similar procedure at CR 1, but this wall is more massive. We catch only two birds on the first drop, and I know it's going to be a long afternoon. Judy tries the next drop with me, but she's too short to reach the top of the wall even when on the ladder. Kathy and I begin a series of drops, having to wait ten to fifteen minutes after each one for the birds to calm down. They usually flush out before we get there, and we end up with only five or six birds each time. The effort is worth it, however, because almost half of our catch is banded from earlier years. Kathy gradually becomes more graceful at climbing the ladder, but it still remains a challenge for both of us to drop the net low enough to cover the birds' flyway.

Although netting here is hard work, we're getting enough birds to keep going, especially considering all the banded ones. Occasionally, if we do enough drops, we'll manage to sneak up on the birds and get the net over before they flush, resulting in a large haul. We come close a couple of times, but they barely beat us with their flush. I tell Kathy to walk as quietly as possible and try not to roll pebbles under her boots, which makes a scratching sound on the concrete bridge that signals our approach to the birds underneath. Mary and I have occasionally resorted to sweeping the tops of bridges! Once, Kathy and I manage to get the net over as they're flushing, and we end up with fifteen or twenty birds. Later we quietly creep out onto the bridge, stooping low and trying to carry the net poles as horizontally as possible to reduce their conspicuousness. We reach the ladders. The birds remain under the bridge. I make it to the top of my ladder, and the birds still haven't flushed. We'll get them now, I gloat. I wait for Kathy to climb her ladder, which seems like an eternity, and still the birds haven't flushed. As we start to drop the net over, Kathy accidentally clangs her pole against the top of the concrete wall. Whoosh— everybody's out immediately, and we catch two birds. That was our one shot at surprising them, and we never come close again.

As quitting time approaches, I ask Judy to count our captures, and I'm surprised to hear that we've caught ninety-five this afternoon. I say that one hundred sounds a lot better than ninety-five, so we vow not to leave until we get five more. By now the birds have been disturbed so often that many of them have said the hell with this and have left to go forage. It takes another seven drops to get five more birds for an even hundred.

On the drive back we see about twenty birds investigating nests at Aqueduct and no owl. That the site might still become active this summer reinforces my feeling of success for today. At suppertime Mary reports that she and Annie also had a good afternoon, catching 126 birds at Barn Owl. I'm pumped up by the day's accomplishments and feel we should go out again after supper. The crew seems more than willing, so as soon as we gulp down our tuna noodle casserole the five of us head to nearby CR 1.

Usually we regard CR 1 as a pain in the ass with its tall walls that require ladders, but after an afternoon at Prairie Dog, netting here seems like a snap to Kathy and me. The birds at CR 1 are cooperative, returning to their nests quickly and not flushing until the net is dropped over. I silently thank all the fishers whose presence has acclimated these cliff swallows to people. In barely an hour and a half we catch another hundred birds, with far less grief than at Prairie Dog.

By dusk we have a total catch of about 670 birds, a good day by any standard and a welcome antidote to the frustration of the past week. I'm exhausted by the day's fieldwork, but the assistants are still wired. They clamor for a trip to town to get ice cream at the Dairy Queen. There isn't much nightly entertainment at the field station for most of the students, aside from playing cards in the lodge or going to the beach to drink beer. I try to defer the outing to another night but finally acquiesce, deciding at Mary's urging that it might be a useful way to reward the good effort the assistants put in today. Our best day in the field yet this summer ends on a raucous note, with Annie yakking uncontrollably on the trip to town and all of us singing along to her tape of Neil Diamond's greatest hits.

May 30

I had decided yesterday that we would net at Whitetail today, and I refuse to be deterred by cloudy skies and 54°.

The colony is teeming when we arrive. Thousands of birds are going in and out of the tunnels, and many are collecting mud. The air is full of cliff swallows. I'm surprised by the heavy activity, given the weather.

We notice the wind is out of the north, meaning air traffic control is reversed from the last time we netted here. The swallows are mostly entering the culvert on the south end and exiting on the north, into the wind. Each second dozens of birds enter and leave the culvert. If we're to have any luck, we'll have to set our net on the north end. I'm less than thrilled by this prospect and explain to Annie, Judy, and Kathy that the Whitetail birds typically react very differently to nets placed on the south and north ends. On the south end the birds seem not to mind the net and settle down quickly once it's set. That's where we've had our record-setting days. But on the north side all hell breaks loose whenever we put up a net. The swallows usually stay agitated, fewer are willing to enter the culvert, and captures are reduced. I can see no obvious reason for the difference in the birds' behavior, but it's this way every year.

Another problem is that the creek bank on the north end is overgrown by stands of tall leadplants so there's no good place to sit and process birds. We usually sit inside the dry west tunnel of the culvert, largely out of sight of the birds. The west tunnel has no active nests, and cliff swallows rarely enter it. The inside of the tunnel is probably ten degrees cooler than outside, which makes for pleasant working conditions in the July heat, but today, with the air temperature in the mid-fifties, it will be cold and damp down there. I already know the assistants didn't bring enough clothes this morning.

They set up the lawn chairs inside the culvert while Mary and I set the net so that it covers mostly the middle tunnel. But I see we need a longer net that can also cover the entrance to the east tunnel. As predicted, the cliff swallows don't care for the net or for our being here. The whole colony takes off, and a gigantic smokelike cloud of probably three thousand birds swirls overhead, giving barrages of *pew* calls. *Pew* is the cliff swallows' alarm call, and they never show any hesitancy in using it to convey their displeasure at us.

The five us of sit in the dark, dank culvert waiting for the birds to return. The assistants are shivering, and it's unpleasant enough to make even Mary and me uncomfortable. Everybody is focusing on trying to stay warm, and idle conversation has stopped. Clad only in shorts, Annie's legs are covered with goose bumps and turning blue. She's so cold that soon Mary has to send her back to the truck to put on some waders for warmth. Her emergence from the culvert further inflames the passionate disapproval of the cliff swallows. We keep waiting.

Mary temporarily distracts the assistants from how cold they are by pointing out the "blood vessel things" in the dirt under their chairs. The floor of the west tunnel is crisscrossed with scores of thin, tubelike tracks that look like the veins that bulge under the skin on the backs of people's hands. We have no idea what sort of organism makes them—probably worms of some sort—and the assistants nervously shift in their seats and start checking the ground near their feet more often.

Eventually some cliff swallows return to the culvert, but at least half of the birds that were here when we arrived have left the area entirely, probably to feed. This may be more a response to the darkening clouds and increasingly cold north wind than to our net. The ones still here are likely the ones with complete nests and eggs. We catch birds at a steady pace, but nothing like the last time when we were on the south end. Mary and the assistants divide up into teams of two for processing, although four people aren't needed here today. It's too late in the morning and the weather's getting too bad to redeploy, however, so we stick it out.

By noon we've caught 198 birds, a surprisingly good haul considering the weather, and an illustration of how good Whitetail can be even on a subpar day. Another unexplained characteristic of north-end netting at Whitetail each year is a higher percentage of previously banded birds among the captures. The pattern holds again: we have a higher proportion of past-year birds than when we did the south end ten days ago. This compensates us in part for the frustration of netting on this side, but I wish I knew why we see this difference. Netting should yield a random sample of the colony no matter where you net, unless the birds aren't randomly distributed within it. Could it be that the north end is better for some reason and older birds that are more likely to have already been banded preferentially settle there? Perhaps, but I can see no compelling reason why one end of a concrete culvert would be superior to the other.

It's raining hard by the time we get back to Cedar Point for lunch, and the forecast calls for continued rain this afternoon. The assistants are bummed out by my announcement that we're grounded again, but by now they understand there's nothing we can do when it rains. Mary and I decide to use the time for some truck repair. Recently the blue truck has been sounding like it has a hole in its muffler, so we go to town to have it looked at. The garages in Ogallala are accommodating and usually try to help you right away. We stop at a tire dealer who also does mufflers, and sure enough, they're willing to look at the truck this afternoon. I think of mechanics in big cities, who often require an appointment two or three days in advance.

Soon the problem is diagnosed as a rusted-out pipe that connects the catalytic converter to the muffler. The tire dealer has no replacement in stock, and he begins calling the auto parts stores in town — all three of them. He eventually finds one, and we wait for the parts man to deliver it. I browse among the piles of gigantic tractor tires for sale. Some of these tires cost over a thousand dollars each. While we wait, two farmers come in looking for used tractor tires. Little wonder, given the price of new ones. The tire dealer has none, and these poor guys seem to be in a bad way. They need replacement tires for spring planting (if their fields ever dry out) but can't afford new ones. The tire dealer assures them they're unlikely to find any in western Nebraska but says they could try going to Denver. I feel fortunate that all I need is a thirty-five-dollar exhaust pipe. I'm reminded too of the problems we share with these farmers (besides being broke!): we're both completely dependent on the erratic Nebraska weather for success in our different endeavors.

May 31

The time has come for a day at The Deer.

This means we'll net at the colony called Mule Deer, our most infamous site. Mary says it's the worst place on the planet and long ago announced that she's through doing The Deer. Each winter when the time comes to recruit assistants, she reminds me I'd better find some if I want any help at The Deer the next summer.

Mule Deer is a culvert under Interstate 80 about five miles from Roscoe. It consists of two separate culverts, a long one under the interstate and a much shorter one under a dirt access road that parallels the highway. Between the two culverts is a low spot that collects water and supports a swamp full of cattails. These culverts serve as drainage ditches for adjacent pastures and contain flowing water only when rain floods the fields. The rest of the time Mule Deer holds stagnant water that's sometimes two and a half feet deep.

The long culvert under the interstate represents the essence of Mule Deer. Being so long, it's dark and foreboding, full of cobwebs, and in the middle it can be hard to read nest numbers on the wall without a flashlight. The mud underneath the water is extraordinarily sticky and gooey, and several assistants over the years have fallen into it. The cold, dark standing water has a slimy film, and the culvert smells of swamp, mildew, and rot. Invariably there are dead things floating in the water: swallows, ducks, sparrows, rodents, rabbits, snakes, turtles, frogs, crayfish, and many things too far gone to recognize. Usually the corpses are bloated and discolored, and one gets the sense that they met a really bad end. Mary tells the assistants she half expects a hand to reach up out of the muddy water and grab her. Tumbleweeds blow into the culvert, so wading also involves fighting your way through the dry, brittle, thorny brush. On damp days, condensation drips from the ceiling.

And no one who's been to Mule Deer can forget running the gauntlet of blood-sucking insects. Vast swarms of mosquitoes rest on the standing water waiting to flush up in clouds. The biting flies widely known as deerflies—an appropriate name at this site—live in the grass outside the culvert.

Yet I love this place. Mule Deer is where we have learned the most about cliff swallow life in small colonies. It's always a small colony— the largest was 140 nests eight years ago—averaging about 40 nests each season. Unlike many small colonies, which are not regularly occupied, Mule Deer has been used every year since we discovered it eleven years ago. This regularity means it's the one small colony we can count on each summer. Data gathered there have figured prominently in all our analyses of how colony size affects swallow biology. The site's foulness is a small price to pay for this insight.

For days Mary has been scaring the assistants with embellished tales of Mule Deer's horrors, so Kathy and Judy look enormously relieved when I tell them Annie will be going with me today. I choose Annie in part because it's already apparent that she works best when paired with me. That she gets along better with men than with women will become obvious later in the summer, but she also has a positive attitude and enough sense of humor to endure unpleasant conditions, so she should be able to handle The Deer.

Annie and I pack a lunch because netting at Mule Deer usually takes all day. It requires a set net, so we waste a lot of time waiting for the birds to adjust to the net's presence. Mary, Kathy, and Judy will net along the canal.

Annie asks why we call the site Mule Deer. On the day we discovered this colony, our assistant Laurie spotted a mule deer in the pasture south of the interstate. Though deer are common in southwestern Nebraska and in most places seeing them is routine, I couldn't come up with any other obvious name for the colony, so we honored Laurie's observation of the deer. In all the years since, I've seen a deer there exactly once.

Mule Deer consists of two separate colonies. The shorter culvert we refer to as Mule Deer North, and the long, dark tunnel under the interstate is Mule Deer South. Although the culverts are separated by only eighty feet, the birds living in them are functionally different colonies. The birds in the north culvert don't interact with the ones in the south; surprisingly, they don't feed together or respond to predators simultaneously. In some years we've even considered the birds nesting at the opposite ends of Mule Deer South to be separate colonies because they didn't interact. I'm unsure what the nest distribution in Mule Deer South is today, but it doesn't appear that the north culvert we're sitting on has any active nests. We can focus our netting on the culvert under the interstate.

Netting at small colonies like Mule Deer takes considerable patience. The more suspicious nature of cliff swallows nesting in small colonies usually forces us to wait for long periods while they come to terms with the net. Netting is complicated here because the same birds don't use both ends of the culvert, unlike the situation at Whitetail, where they enter one end and exit from the other depending on the wind. Both the length of this culvert and the busy traffic on the interstate that dissuades birds from flying across the highway apparently prevent the colony residents from realizing they can reach their nests from the other side. Since the swallows enter and exit the same end, we have to set our net farther out from the edge of the culvert to give them room to reach their nests. We catch them when they fly out.

We wade through the long tunnel, carrying our net poles and nets. Revulsion contorts Annie's face as she starts to make her way through the tunnel, but she doggedly follows me. I tell her to walk slowly so she doesn't fall and to please keep from getting stuck in the ooze on the bottom. This water is not the kind you want to splash on your skin, and I'm not eager to have to pull her out. She seems more concerned about snakes, but I assure her there are probably only dead ones here. The water is deeper than normal—not surprising given the wet spring—and makes walking even slower. This gives us more time to enjoy Mule Deer's charms. So far the only dead things I'm seeing are two very bloated barn swallows floating in the water. They probably succumbed to the cold weather this spring. But this is Mule Deer, so who knows what really happened to them.

We finally make it to the far end. We have to clear some brush, mostly tumbleweeds blown in over the winter, so the lower part of the net won't snag. Because the swallows here are a challenge to catch, I've decided to use "low-visibility" nets. These nets are made of thinner nylon thread and are much harder to see, both for us and for the swallows, and consequently are more effective at catching birds. Unfortunately the thinner net tears easily, especially if it catches on twigs or grass. Our low-visibility nets are full of holes and have been mended so often with thicker thread that they're probably not as invisible to the birds as they once were. But we continue to nurse them through season after season, because net makers no longer manufacture them.

We slog back through the culvert and set a second low-visibility net on the close end. It appears that most of the active nests are toward the far end of the culvert. The nests here are built out of the slimy ooze from the swamp between the two culverts, and once the mud is dry these nests are like concrete. Many of the nests at Mule Deer are at least eleven years old, here when we discovered the colony. Generations of swallows have been raised in the same nests by many different parents.

The only place to sit and wait here is in the truck. If we are visible in any way, the cliff swallows will see us and spend all day circling over our heads, alarm-calling and not going to their nests. A day inside the truck can be brutal in the heat of late June or July, but today it's pleasant. From our vantage point we can see most of the close net but can't see the far net at all. That means we'll have to wade through the long tunnel at regular intervals to check the other net. We watch the cliff swallows on the other side of the highway swirling above the far net, trying to decide whether to fly in over it. Only a few swallows are attempting to enter on this side. I'll look in the nests later to get a precise count of how many might be active, but from the birds I'm seeing I'd judge that the colony probably consists of forty-five to fifty nests.

It'll be a slow day.

After forty-five minutes some cliff swallows finally start flying into the culvert through the open space between the net and the entrance. We begin our routine that will last all day. About every twenty-five minutes I walk down to the culvert, wade through it to the far end, and remove netted birds. If this were later in the summer and Annie were more experienced, we'd take turns making the trip. But it still takes Annie a long time to extract the badly tangled birds, so I handle the far net. She removes whatever is in the close net, which isn't much, and she's glad to do it since it doesn't require wading through the long, dark tunnel.

As I expected, the low-visibility nets work great. Despite the swallows' wariness, by noon we've caught twenty-three birds, ten of them banded in a previous year. None of the past-year bands are very "old," however, which is a bit surprising. One of the discoveries from our swallow banding is that small colonies like Mule Deer consist of disproportionately more older cliff swallows than do large colonies. We seldom find yearlings or second-year birds in a colony this small. Most of our oldest birds have been in little colonies like Mule Deer.

Cliff swallows often start their breeding careers in large colonies where, as inexperienced yearlings, they have access to more information on food. In big colonies, at least a few birds will always know the location of an insect swarm and may signal its presence with food calls. Large colonies also provide better vigilance against predators, probably important for naive first-year birds. But as a cliff swallow gets older and more experienced at finding food and avoiding predators, it may have less use for the bedlam of a large colony and especially may want to avoid its costs—such as more parasites. We believe this is why many cliff swallows switch to small colonies like Mule Deer as they get older.

We don't know the ages of the banded birds we're catching today. Most of them were banded as adults in a recent year, and thus they were of unknown age then. Only birds we first band as nestlings or fledglings can be aged precisely when caught later, and we won't know whether we had any like this today until we look them up on the computer. Still, each time I go to the net I'm consumed by the anticipation of what might be there and the expectation that we'll get an obviously old band.

With all the idle time between net checks, sitting in the truck at Mule Deer provides abundant opportunity for conversation, or "philosophizing" as I call it. It's often a good chance to dispense advice on career planning and educational strategies or to describe misadventures of past workers as a subtle way of underscoring unacceptable conduct. Usually the conversation gets around to how I got started doing this in the first place. Annie is amazed that Mary and I have studied cliff swallows so long.

"I don't see how anyone can study something for fourteen years. Haven't you learned everything by now?"

"No, far from it. There's so much we still don't know about these birds that I could spend the rest of my life studying them. I probably will."

"But don't you ever get bored? Want to do something different?"

"Not me. Maybe some people would. But I'm so fascinated by this one kind of bird that I want to learn everything. Some people aren't cut out for long-term studies, and they probably would get bored, which is fine. My principal talent seems to be that I can keep coming here year after year, doing the same thing."

Annie's questions start me thinking, wondering if coming to Mule Deer every summer for over a decade is something that can really be called a talent! Some, like Mary, might argue that it's a sickness. I start to remember the dozens of people who've occupied Annie's seat beside me over the years: Laurie, a great assistant who discovered Mule Deer with me; Sheryl, the graduate student who came to Nebraska to try—unsuccessfully—to revive her sagging interest in biological research; Jerri, one of my favorite assistants who conducted her own study of barn swallows at Mule Deer; Marty, who introduced me to the joys of Jim Croce music while sitting here; Craig, who pounded the omnipresent deerflies with a rubber mallet; Linda, the most promising first-year graduate student I've ever known, who also studied barn swallows here; Winnie, the most intense, hardest-working assistant we've ever had, who was later to do a major analysis of our banding data; and others who've come and gone.

After we eat our lunch of turkey croissant sandwiches, the sun starts to make both of us drowsy, and Annie falls asleep. Captures have started to slow down, as they always do here in the afternoon. On some net checks, we're getting either no cliff swallows or only ones caught earlier today. However, we keep getting other species, principally barn swallows and house sparrows. Barn swallows have built nests throughout the long culvert, and this is the largest colony of them I've ever seen. Close relatives of the cliff swallow, barn swallows are similar in appearance and habits. They build mud nests on a vertical wall like cliff swallows, but the nest of the more forked-tailed barn swallow is an open cup, not domed over into a narrow entrance. Perhaps the biggest difference between the two species, though, is that barn swallows live in much smaller colonies, usually five nests or fewer. They often nest solitarily under a porch awning or inside a barn or shed. But at Mule Deer, over thirty barn swallow nests have been active in some years. I can't tell how many are active today, but barn swallows frequently go in and out of Mule Deer South, and by lunchtime we've caught nine.

The personalities of the two species differ like night and day. When we start removing the birds from the holding bag in the truck to band and weigh them, the cliff swallows are aggressive and climb as close as possible to the top of the bag. They constantly wiggle and try to escape, showing no fear of anything, including us. The barn swallows cower in the bottom of the bag and seem too timid to try to escape even if the top is left open. This difference is also reflected in the culvert. Cliff swallows routinely take over barn swallow nests, evicting the rightful owners. Barn swallows avoid the sections of the culvert with long rows of cliff swallow nests and retreat to parts of the wall that the cliff swallows don't want, usually the darker interior regions.

After lunch the local landowner drives by. This rancher owns the pasture on the other side of the access road that stretches at least a mile from the road north to the South Platte River. We see him each time we come here, and he usually acknowledges our presence with a grim-faced wave. I imagine he doesn't approve of people who come here and mess around in that filthy culvert, but we're not on his land so he doesn't harass us. There must be a hundred Black Angus cattle in the pasture, and before long three pickups with horse trailers appear. The rancher and his helpers unload and saddle four horses and head out into the pasture through a gate not far from where we're parked. They're obviously rounding up the cattle to move them or perhaps brand the calves. Eventually the herd is chivied toward the gate and out onto the dirt road. As they pass, we're surrounded by a sea of black cows. The herd and the cowboys soon disappear down the road. An excited Annie has never seen anything like this back home, and she takes fifteen or twenty pictures of the cows and the Wrangler-clad cowboys.

As the afternoon wears on, I start seeing rain showers on the horizon. These showers don't cover large areas, although the rain looks intense. One is off to the south of us and another to the north. They seem to be moving straight east, so these won't hit us, but after a while I notice another one due west of us. It's obviously moving this way. This one seems so localized that I figure we can just temporarily close the nets and resume netting when the rain passes. When the storm is about three miles away, I go down to remove any birds and close the nets. However, either I misjudged the storm's distance or it's moving like a mother, because it starts pouring before I can get back to the truck.

Annie and I sit in the truck, watching it rain. The closed nets—now just loosely twisted ropes—no longer obstruct the culvert entrances, so the swallows can go home if they want. The heavy rain makes a racket hitting the cab of the truck. I wonder briefly if it might be hailing but decide it's just big raindrops. As has often been the case this summer, the rain has no thunder or lightning with it and not much wind.

Finally the rain stops and I reopen the nets, mostly to let them dry off before we take them down. Captures have declined, and I don't figure we'll get much more. I'm right. We catch only seven more cliff swallows after the rainstorm.

As quitting time approaches, I tell Annie we need to check nests and take down the nets, so she should prepare to go back into the culvert. I wade through and look in each nest to determine if it has eggs or other signs of being active. Annie follows, writing down what I call out. It's a task from hell trying to check cliff swallow nests alone, because both hands are occupied by the dental mirror and penlight used to look in the nests. Nowhere do I rely on assistants more than during nest checking. The check reveals forty-four cliff swallow nests I'd consider active, but these birds aren't far along, having barely begun egg laying.

Our total catch for the day stands at forty-seven cliff swallows and seventeen barn swallows. This is an excellent start, since we got over half of the colony on this first try. Annie feels she's now among an elite set of people who've done a day at The Deer. It wasn't so bad, she proudly says as we drive away, after I tell her I'll probably bring Kathy or Judy next time.

At dusk I want to go to Aqueduct. Seeing birds swarming there two days ago has aroused my curiosity. Mary joins me, and we drive down the canal. En route, we see cliff swallows swarming at two wooden bridges. Of dozens of wooden canal bridges, these two are the only ones that regularly attract nesting swallows, for reasons we don't understand. Add two more sites to the list of places to net.

About ninety birds are at Aqueduct. We're surprised to see them going through their synchronized flying before finally bedding down. Watching them transports me back three weeks. This is the latest date I've *ever* seen cliff swallows do these flights. I wonder if the

Aqueduct birds are advertising for more colony recruits. Probably, because ninety birds is only a fraction of the number that normally live here. We see no owl, but by now it's probably gone off on its nightly hunt.

Things still look mighty tentative at Aqueduct.

On the way back we meet the assistants and Doug coming back from an evening canoe ride on Keystone Lake. I joke with them that we went back out to catch more birds. Annie comments that by now she knows me well enough that she wouldn't doubt it!

June 1

Led mostly by Annie, the assistants have been talking for days about trying to break the single-day record for number of birds caught. The record is 963, set by five of us on June 27, 1992. I'm skeptical that we can ever duplicate that effort, but if we're going to make a run at it this summer, today might be the day. The weather is perfect this morning and is supposed to stay that way. Whitetail, with its thousands of swallows, beckons.

Any attempt to set a record would require three of us at Whitetail all day and the other two drop netting at other large colonies where big numbers can be racked up. I'm still not convinced, however, that the assistants are experienced enough to try to do Whitetail with only two processors. Mary and I decide that all of us should go to Whitetail this morning.

As usual, Whitetail is teeming with birds when we arrive. Many colony residents are gathering mud, and perhaps a thousand are carrying mud into the east tunnel. More birds are here than the last time we visited, and as we approach the culvert entrance to set the net, the thousands of alarm calls from birds flushing out of their nests in waves make it hard to hear anything else. Today I've decided to try a longer, thirty-foot net, which will completely cover both the middle and east tunnels. A longer net may mean a lot more captures, perhaps overwhelming our ability to process them quickly, so it's with trepidation that Mary and I stretch out the long net on the favored south end. I feel that the pieces are coming together, if not for an attempt on the record, at least for catching hundreds of birds today.

With the good weather and us on the south side, the cliff swallows' activity is hardly interrupted. Nest building and the heavy bird traffic in and out of the culvert continue despite our presence. I wonder again why the birds allow this on the south end but not on the north. The long net is indeed effective, and I'm pleased that we catch many of the east tunnel residents we'd been missing. The assistants are more skilled and faster than on our first session here, but it's Mary's efforts that keep the processing on track. By noon we've caught about 360 birds, and over 40 percent of them have been banded in an earlier year.

During the lunch break, the assistants are still talking about trying for a single-day record. That would require another 600 birds this afternoon, which seems unobtainable even if we split up. In part to maintain their enthusiasm, I suggest that we focus instead on setting the single-day record for Whitetail. I don't admit that I can't remember what that record is, but for some reason the number 690 sticks in my head. If we could attain that today, I'd be more than satisfied.

We return to Whitetail and set the long net again. Captures begin with the same frequency, and I'm overjoyed by how many birds from the east tunnel we keep catching. When possible, I squat down by the net to watch the activity inside that tunnel. Hundreds of birds are starting nests from scratch. Many have put just a few blobs of mud on the bare wall, and these birds cling to the concrete like bats. Each of these little spots of mud will grow into a nest if the birds keep at it. In parts of the tunnel there's a long horizontal mud shelf that sticks out from the wall about an inch. This results whenever scores of birds start building side by side at the same time. It's almost as if they cooperate to build this continuous mud shelf, which gives each bird a place to perch while it works. Gradually, full nests will grow from the shelf at intervals equal to the distance a bird can defend while perching on its own spot on the shelf. After the first nests are completed, later birds will fill in around them, building their nests along the sides of existing nests or offset below or above the gap between two nests. If the colony is large enough, eventually a honeycomb pattern of nests may form, almost like the cells of a wasp or bee colony.

The cliff swallows in the east tunnel are also using some artificial plaster nests that hang there. These were installed two years ago by my graduate student Bruce, who spent three summers in Nebraska studying the parasitic swallow bug. Bruce used the bugs to develop and test various theories about the genetic structure of populations.

They're ideal for such studies, because they're restricted to isolated areas (swallow colonies), move between areas only rarely (when a swallow carries them from one colony to another), and may decline drastically or go extinct in a local area (when the swallows abandon a colony site for several years). Consequently the bugs in one colony may be descended from only a few immigrants or survivors of a population crash. There may be differences in the genetic composition of bug communities in different colonies that are separated by only a few miles.

For Bruce to estimate gene flow of bugs, he needed to know how often the cliff swallows introduced bugs from one colony into another. This is not an easy problem, because you usually can't tell if a cliff swallow is carrying bugs hidden in its feathers. Even if you see one carrying bugs, you don't know where it got them or if that bird is moving between colonies. So Bruce and I devised an artificial nest experiment. The idea was to erect plaster nests in a fumigated colony where there were no existing swallow bugs. Periodically we would remove each plaster nest from the wall, place its contents (eggs or babies) in an identical nest that would immediately go back onto the wall, and then examine the first nest for bugs and count how many had been introduced since the last check. Because the rest of the colony would be fumigated, any bugs appearing in the plaster nests would be ones the birds brought in from other colonies. Thus we could calculate a rate of bug immigration to the site. This experiment required only that the swallows use our artificial nests.

There was some basis for our hopes that the birds would cooperate. Cliff swallows in California in the 1950s used plaster nests that biologists had erected to make the birds easier to study. They were also known to have used artificial nests more recently in Oklahoma and Massachusetts, and during our second year in Nebraska we installed several plaster nests in the middle tunnel at Whitetail. We had hoped to use them to study how the degree of nest completeness affected the swallows' fighting for nests when they first arrived at a colony. But the birds would have no part of the fake nests and completely ignored them for two summers. For some reason that's still not clear, in the third year they finally decided to occupy them, and they've used the original plaster nests in the middle tunnel every year since.

Bruce made one latex mold for his nests, because he wanted them all to look identical. This would enable him to substitute one nest for

another during the nest checks without worrying that small differences in nest shape would confuse the birds that were given replace
ments. He installed about thirty plaster nests in the east tunnel at
Whitetail and at two smaller culvert colonies, McDonald's and Cemetery. We monitored the nests regularly throughout that season, but
the cliff swallows refused to cooperate. All that ever occupied the
plaster nests at Whitetail were spiders. House sparrows moved in at
Cemetery and McDonald's. So much for our experiment.

The plaster nests were unused again last year, and I didn't expect
any action this summer. I've often wondered if the long row of identical nests was the problem. In nature no two cliff swallow nests look
exactly alike—there are always slight differences in shape and size.
Perhaps the lack of variation among Bruce's nests confused the birds
because they couldn't recognize their own among the other twenty-
nine. Thus I'm surprised to see cliff swallows going into the fake nests
today; some are even adding blobs of mud to the plaster entrances.
Perhaps the huge size of the colony this summer is partly responsible for the birds' sudden interest in the fake nests, or maybe it just
takes a couple of years for them to "cure" and become suitable. Someone should still do the experiment to determine bug immigration rates,
but at the moment we have our hands full with the netting.

I can't watch the birds in the east tunnel or even think about them
for long, because swallows keep hitting the net. After about an hour,
captures stabilize at a steady rate, and I wonder aloud if two people
might be able to handle the processing. The assistants are eager to
try, which would permit Mary and one of them to go elsewhere.
Beating the 963-bird record is still their goal. Mary and I decide that
she and Judy will go to CR 4½, which is the largest colony nearby
and the one where the most birds can be caught. They drive away,
leaving me with no vehicle, a thirty-foot net full of birds, and two
rookie field assistants. Was this wise?

As soon as Mary and Judy leave, we start catching birds faster.
It's almost as if the birds know there are now fewer of us and do their
best to swamp us. Annie and Kathy work intensely and process birds
quickly, but the swallows keep plowing into the net, and I'm rapidly
filling all our bird holding bags. They soon have three full bags waiting and remain backlogged the rest of the afternoon.

For over three hours Annie and Kathy stay hunched over in their
lawn chairs, doing nothing but banding, weighing, and sexing cliff

swallows. They barely look up, usually just shooting a quick glance toward the net to see how many more birds are waiting. Annie moves her lawn chair so she can't see the net; she doesn't want to know how many more birds are coming. Each time I emerge from the creek to give them another full bag of birds, they groan and redouble their efforts.

Yet to their credit, they maintain a sufficient pace that I don't have to close the net before quitting time. At 5:00 I finally shut the net, giving us time to finish the final bags before Mary returns. After the last bird is finished, Annie and Kathy collapse in their chairs, exhausted and mentally drained. Kathy can barely summon the strength to tally up the count: she and Annie alone did 315 birds this afternoon. I tell them I'm proud of them. For these relatively inexperienced assistants, doing over 300 birds in an afternoon without any screw-ups in the data and band recording and with no deaths or injuries among the birds is truly an impressive achievement. Their shoulders are so tense from the stress that they can hardly move, but they're pleased with their effort.

With the net down and all the birds processed, I too can finally relax and enjoy this beautiful day. The brilliant blue sky is studded with puffy white clouds that stretch in all directions across the vast sky. The warm afternoon sun feels terrific after so much cold weather this spring. I stand on the creek bank and watch the swallows streaming in and out of the culvert, oblivious to our presence and now with no net to disturb them. I'm awed by the serenity of the scene even though the culvert echoes with the calls of thousands of cliff swallows. There can be no place on earth as wonderful as Whitetail at this moment.

Mary and Judy soon appear. They drop-netted 101 birds at CR 4½ in just a couple of hours. The daily count is quickly computed: 809 birds for the day, with 708 of those coming from Whitetail. I'm surprised that the assistants have enough energy left to suggest going out after supper to try for the record. But I point out that 100 is about all we can get in the daylight remaining after supper, and we'd need over 150 to approach the record. I emphasize that today's haul is the second highest daily total I can remember from any year, and to attain second-best is a major accomplishment. I'm sure that 708 is a new record for Whitetail.

Driving back, they ask how we caught 963 in one day. At that time it hardly dawned on us that we had set a record. We caught 674 at

Whitetail, 214 in half a day at CR 1 (which at the time was a drop-netting record), 58 at CR 2, and 17 at Keystone. We could have exceeded a thousand birds that day had we specifically tried to set a record. The total was all the more remarkable given that one team had a slow afternoon, getting only 75 birds from two colonies where big numbers weren't possible. I also remember being so exhausted that evening that we barely had the energy to eat.

June 2

Today we go west. Our plan is to spend the day at two of the colonies in Garden County on the western edge of our study area. I'm excited because these colonies are among my favorites and have yielded a lot of data over the years. Moreover, the weather is again gorgeous, a beautiful day to be alive in western Nebraska.

The colonies we're destined for today are Clary and Ash Hollow. This summer is one of the few when both have been active, a convenient situation for us because we can net at both on the same visit using two teams. We decide that Kathy and I will do Ash Hollow while Mary and the others visit Clary. Today will also be the first time the assistants will work solo. After lunch Mary will leave Annie and Judy at Clary and return to Cedar Point to prepare for her bicycle ride, which begins tomorrow. We've got to find out if they can handle netting alone.

The Garden County colonies are a half-hour drive away, and I'm eager to get going. However, only Judy is at breakfast with Mary and me. Annie and Kathy are late getting to the lodge and come in looking tired and sleepy just as the kitchen staff begins dismantling breakfast. We have to pack lunches since we'll be gone all day, and Mary asks what kind of sandwiches, soda, and fruit they want. In some years the cook has made our lunches, but this year Dennis yields to Mary and lets her assemble them from the designated lunch food. She generally tells me not to expect the sack lunch to be the highlight of our day, since it usually consists of a soggy sandwich, greasy potato chips, a sugary soda, and limp fruit.

I leave Mary to deal with the lunches while I get our gear ready. I have everything loaded, but no one shows up. Ten minutes go by and still no one. Ten more minutes pass, and finally Mary and the assistants appear with a cooler full of lunches. Mary takes me aside and laments that she had too much help; the assistants converged on her in the kitchen, each one wanting something different and making suggestions, and it turned into a mob scene. Also, all the lunches are packed in one cooler because that's all the kitchen had, but we'll be in two separate groups, so we have to get a second cooler from the lab and split the lunches. We don't have enough ice for two coolers, so someone has to go back to the lodge to get more. People start pawing through the wrapped sandwiches, trying to figure out whose is whose. It's another five minutes before we get the lunches separated, and ten more before Kathy returns with the ice. I'm getting agitated, frustrated, and about ready to climb the walls. It's been almost an hour since breakfast, and we're getting our latest start this year on a morning when we have to drive all the way to Garden County.

My growing impatience will later have an unfortunate consequence.

We finally depart, taking both trucks so Mary will have one to come back in after lunch. Making our late departure even later, I have to stop for gas in the blue truck. We pull into a convenience store and bait shop at the south end of Kingsley Dam to fill up. When I go in to pay with a credit card, I encounter an obviously new employee who has no idea how to operate the automatic on-line credit card machine. She fumbles around for five minutes before finally phoning Jim, the owner, to ask how to do it. I suspect she might have better luck if she'd focus less on smoking a cigarette and more on the instructions that are pasted right beside the machine. It takes ten minutes to get the gas paid for. I tell myself it'll be midmorning before we ever get to Garden County.

Kathy and I start the long loop around Lake McConaughy to the Ash Hollow area at the western end. Considering how this day has gone since breakfast, I half expect the weather to turn bad, but it stays sunny and calm. We first head to Clary to rendezvous with Mary and the others. Since we haven't netted the Garden County colonies this summer and don't know the distribution of nests there, Mary has asked me to stop at Clary and help her decide on net placement. I don't mind doing this, but it will delay me and Kathy even more in getting to Ash Hollow.

We take the faster route along the south side of the lake. In half an hour we reach Ash Hollow, a region of eroded, north-facing canyons where the higher prairie tableland abuts the North Platte River valley. These canyons are like those around Cedar Point, covered with stands of cedar on their northerly slopes, but they're noteworthy because for the most part they're undeveloped and protected by a state park. The landscape is rugged and seems more arid than the Cedar Point area only thirty miles to the east.

The Ash Hollow region consists of about six square miles containing canyons, outcroppings, and hills. With its extensive topographic relief, it reminds me of Wyoming or New Mexico. Most of the land is preserved within the state park except for scattered private holdings by ranchers. One such rancher was Oren Clary, whose grandfather originally homesteaded the region in the 1800s. Today the Clary family maintains a cattle ranch there.

Kathy and I pass over the culvert containing the Ash Hollow colony and go another two-thirds of a mile to Clary. Mary, Judy, and Annie are unloading the truck parked above the culvert. It can't be seen from the road and requires traipsing down a steep embankment to reach either end. The birds are already in a state of alarm, a couple of hundred swirling overhead giving barrages of *pew* calls. They don't like us here.

When I was at Clary five days ago, the birds seemed mostly interested in the east end, and I figure that's where we'll need to put the net. But I'll go down and have a look first. There should be fresh mud on the active nests, telling us which nests are being used. I put on some rubber boots because Clary is always full of crap. The culvert drains a canyon to the west, and standing water collects within the culvert and liquefies the cow manure that accumulates there. Slimy neon green algae grow on the surface of the poop in long, ropelike shapes. The liquid crud extends out from the culvert on the east side, creating a "mud" hole where the cliff swallows collect their nest building material. The nests here are built of cow shit.

I enter the east end of the culvert, and Kathy comes with me. Mary and the others have hauled their gear into a small sandy arroyo about fifty yards to the west, where they'll sit to process birds. Their processing area is a beautiful spot, with overhanging cottonwood and cedar branches to shade them and hide them from the cliff swallows flying overhead. It looks like a place where pioneers would have camped 150 years ago. Having such a nice place to sit between net checks compensates for having to enter the culvert.

This place smells like a sewer, and the mud is much stickier than that at Mule Deer. It bubbles and gurgles with each step, and it's probably doing some wicked microbiology. Pulling each foot up while walking causes a loud burping sound, probably like what the cows made when they deposited the stuff.

Walking through, I remember the first summer we worked here, when Clary was perhaps the most disgusting it's ever been. That season we came here often, doing observations of color-marked birds at their nests, nest checks, and the first fumigation experiment. The crap was so deep that we'd sink at least a foot and a half whenever we stood in the culvert, so I couldn't reach the nests to look in them. We built a wooden box for me to stand on. But the box wasn't very stable (perhaps reflecting my carpentry skills), and if someone didn't hold it, it would tip over and I'd fall into the muck. Fortunately our assistant, Rachel, had some enormous chest waders. She'd sit in the shit clad in the waders to hold the box upright. We owed our success at Clary that season in large part to Rachel's heroic efforts. That same summer John Hoogland came to visit, and I took him to Clary. He put on Rachel's waders and promptly fell over in the crap while trying to walk in the culvert. John hasn't been back to the study area since.

I see Annie approaching through the west entrance. The extreme west end of the culvert is usually dry, and Annie has no trouble walking for the first twenty feet or so. Suddenly she hits the sticky stuff, and her progress abruptly stops. I'm reminded of a similar situation with John Janovy, who came to Clary eleven years ago to film cliff swallows. The Nebraska educational television network was making a film version of Janovy's book *Keith County Journal*. It has a chapter on swallows, and he wanted to be filmed walking through a culvert while hundreds of birds flushed out in front of him. Clary was chosen as the set. I told Janovy the culvert was full of muck and he'd need waders. Naw, he replied, he could just use his regular work boots. The film crew set up on the east end, and in came Janovy from the west entrance. He hit the shit and stopped dead in his tracks, as Annie just did. His cowboy boots were probably ruined, because not long afterward a worn-out pair was nailed to a fence post at Cedar Point. The segment of John wading in the manure survived the editing and was included in the film.

I look around to see if there are any spadefoot toads in the bubbly "mud." If there are, they'll bring back bad memories. Nine years ago several toads—spadefoots, I was told—lived in the culvert at Clary. They had a loud, snoring call, and I had never heard toads like that anywhere. Deb, our assistant that year, mentioned them to one of the graduate students at Cedar Point. He wanted to see them, claiming they might be a new record for the area. Without consulting me,

Deb took him to Clary one evening at dusk. They traipsed down into the culvert just as the swallows were trying to get to bed, causing a major colony disruption. At the time we were using Clary for studies of brood parasitism, and as soon as I heard about it, I knew our research that season was ruined. If the swallows are flushed out of their nests at dark, they get disoriented and can't find their way back. Eggs will get chilled without anyone to sit on them.

Deb immediately realized she'd committed a major blunder, and they grabbed one toad and quickly got out of the culvert. I was so mad at her—madder than I've ever been at anyone in my life—that I couldn't sleep that night. One student saw the livid state I was in and went running to Mary, pleading with her to get to me before I got to Deb. The next morning I had to go sit at Whitetail for several hours to calm down before I could even speak to Deb. It turned out no harm was done to the birds; all of them apparently got back home. But the consequences could have been catastrophic.

I don't hear any toads today. They haven't been back since Deb's year, which is fine with me.

Kathy and Annie are grossed out by the interior of the culvert and wonder why we don't just walk over the road to get from the processing area to the east side. I explain that walking through the culvert flushes birds out of their nests and will increase captures in the net we're going to put on the east end. Get used to it, I tell Annie.

As I had guessed, most of the active nests are near the east end of the culvert. Kathy and I hurriedly stretch out the net, but we're having a problem anchoring the poles. The ground is rock hard. We fill two of the plastic drop-netting buckets and put the poles in them. A net anchored this way is never very stable, and one of the buckets is on badly uneven ground. Kathy digs out a depression in the hard sand and sets the bucket there to level it. The other one looks okay. I suggest to Mary that she set another net on the west end to get any of the stragglers that may exit that way.

Cattle use the culvert here to reach a water tank on the east side of the highway, but we're relieved not to see any around today. Several years ago Mary was netting here and looked up to see a cow and calf come strolling through the culvert. She had visions of them walking through the net, with the mesh wrapped around their heads and entangled birds dangling off them. She sprinted to the culvert, her heart in her throat, but found the net was untouched. The cow and calf must somehow have daintily walked through the two- or three-foot open space below it. Cows can be graceful when they want to.

It takes forever to get everything organized at Clary, but finally Kathy and I leave and return to the Ash Hollow culvert down the road. Ash Hollow is a larger culvert than Clary, consisting of six parallel tunnels. The birds here tend to be more spread out and consequently harder to net. Fortunately there's no Clary-style "mud" because Ash Hollow is always dry.

We go down to the culvert to see how the nests are distributed. Although the birds have used all six tunnels at various times, for some reason they prefer the second one from the south. That tunnel always has the most active nests, usually three or four times as many as any of the others. This year is no exception. There's no obvious reason for the preference. It looks as if there might be as many as three hundred birds here, all alarm-calling at us.

With the birds spread between four tunnels, I decide we'll use two nets. One is the thirty-footer we'd used so successfully at Whitetail. We string it across the west entrance of two and a half tunnels and cover the others with a regular eighteen-footer. The wind is surprisingly strong here and is billowing the nets back toward the culvert entrance. I wonder if we'll have any luck.

We set up our chairs under some cottonwoods along the edge of a sandy arroyo west of the culvert. The swallows here are wary and usually won't calm down when we're in plain sight, but we're far enough away and well enough shielded by the cottonwood trunks and overhead branches that the birds can't see us; they forget about us as soon as we sit down.

With the east end of the culvert open, the birds immediately start returning to their nests. Many are exiting on the west side, and within a few minutes ten or twelve birds are in the net. We go to extract them, and I'm surprised that our presence doesn't seem to deter them from entering the east end. As we stand at the net, more birds keep hitting it. Sometimes they crash into it only inches from where we're working on a bird already entangled. These guys are bold, and a south-westerly wind seems to be funneling them all out this direction despite our standing here.

I notice that Kathy is still clumsy at removing birds. She seems afraid to hold them firmly enough to prevent them from escaping when she untangles them. This is alarming because by now she should be relatively adept at taking birds out of set nets. She probably won't get any better this summer.

By noon we've caught exactly a hundred birds, and at this pace we don't have time to stop to eat. I'm surprised, however, that only about a third of our birds are previously banded. The Garden County colonies are notoriously band-rich sites in most years; sometimes over three-fourths of the residents at Clary have been marked in earlier seasons. Where are the many unbanded birds we're getting today coming from?

Almost exactly at noon, I notice a change in the wind direction. The wind has swung around to the southeast. Rather suddenly, captures diminish. The cliff swallows now seem to be both entering and exiting the east end, away from our nets. Nebraska wind can be unpredictable, so we decide to wait to see if it will stay southeasterly. We use the lull to eat our sack lunches, and it feels good to relax after a couple of hours of constantly processing birds.

As I eat my turkey sandwich, I gaze at the beautiful surroundings and enjoy this splendid day. Ash Hollow is one of our most scenic sites. The sandy arroyo in front of us snakes its way back up into the hilly pastures to the west. Directly opposite us on the other side of the arroyo is a massive bluff covered with blooming yuccas. The yuccas are in full flower, with pale yellow flower spikes sticking straight up a foot or more above the base of the plant. The wet spring has been good for yuccas, and I've never seen so many flowering at once. On the other side of the highway, more rolling hills dot the horizon to the east. This is a rugged, tough land, and the swallows that live here seem somehow different from those closer to Cedar Point. It must be easier to be a cliff swallow over near Cedar Point, where the pastures seem more lush, the insects more abundant, and the bodies of water more numerous.

In the tree overhead, I hear a squeaky call and look up to see an American kestrel sitting on a dead branch. I'd been hearing that call all morning, but I hadn't had time to look for its source. The kestrel, also known as a sparrow hawk, must have a nest in this tree. Although kestrels occasionally prey on cliff swallows, the Ash Hollow birds seem to ignore this one and its mate, which also appears from time to time. The kestrels, mostly interested in courting each other, also seem to ignore the swallows.

As I look at the kestrels above me, my thoughts are drawn to the cottonwood tree itself. The four or five cottonwoods clustered here are massive, with trunks at least eleven feet around. How long have these trees stood here? How many swallow colonies have come and gone in the nearby culvert while these stately cottonwoods looked on? How many generations of cliff swallows have been raised here during their lifetimes? Whenever I sit under these huge trees, I think of a romantic scene in John Wayne's classic movie *The Alamo*, where Davy Crockett and his fictional lover, Flaca, bidding a bittersweet farewell before the final battle, stand under giant trees and speculate that Adam and Eve must have met under trees like these.

I doubt that the Ash Hollow trees date back to the beginning of humanity, but I bet they were here, at least as saplings, when Oregon Trail pioneers passed through this area. Settlers in the mid-1800s, headed for a new life in Oregon or California, followed the South Platte River through western Nebraska to the present-day location of Big Springs. There they headed north to the North Platte River and followed it into Wyoming. The most popular descent into the North Platte valley was here at Ash Hollow. Just to the southwest of where Kathy and I sit is Windlass Hill. The pioneers selected this slope as the safest to traverse with wagons and rigged a rope and windlass system to get their wagons down the hill. The wagon ruts supposedly can still be seen etched in the hillside, although the marks look more like eroded gullies to me. The crossing at Ash Hollow was a major event in the immigrants' journey, and more than one wagon and human life were lost in the treacherous descent of these canyons. Once they got all the wagons down the hill, each wagon train would camp below—perhaps near where we sit—to recuperate. A cemetery just down the road contains dead from Oregon Trail expeditions, probably victims of cholera.

The popularity of Ash Hollow as a crossing for immigrants led indirectly to the first reported observations of cliff swallows in this area. In the mid-nineteenth century, naturalists associated with the United States Army passed through Ash Hollow and recorded cliff swallows in their journals. At intervals the army sent cavalry columns along the Oregon Trail to deter Indian attacks and to scout routes. The surgeons assigned to these cavalry detachments were often naturalists who kept detailed notes on plants and animals they encountered. Some collected specimens and sent them back to eastern museums and universities.

The first published report of cliff swallows from this area dated from June 1845, when a young lieutenant named J. Henry Carleton passed through Ash Hollow on an army expedition to South Pass, Wyoming, the important portal through the Rockies that made northerly travel to the West Coast possible in the mid-1800s. Carleton reported cliff swallows on bluffs along the North Platte River just west of here. The birds still occasionally use those same sites. Fourteen years later George Suckley, a surgeon with another cavalry expedition, also described cliff swallows at Ash Hollow. These Garden County birds seem somehow more special when we know that their ancestors, from their nests high atop these bluffs, watched the colonizing of the American West.

Carleton's journal reported grizzly bear tracks along a creek at Ash Hollow. Possibly the dry arroyo where we're sitting today was a real creek in 1845, and this very place probably was where Carleton's party saw the bear tracks. I can close my eyes and envision camping under these trees a century and a half ago. The land doesn't seem that much different today, other than the nearby road and culvert. I half expect a bear to come ambling down the arroyo or a pack of wolves to come over the crest of the nearby bluff.

By 1:00 it's clear that the wind is going to stay southeasterly, and we're not catching squat in the nets on the west side. I decide we'll try a net on the east end. We set it and return to our cottonwoods to wait for the birds. A net on the east end is something novel, and it takes the birds a long time to begin returning to the culvert.

While we're waiting, Mary stops on her way back to Cedar Point. She's left Annie and Judy at Clary for their first solo. They had a busy morning, catching sixty-four birds. But Mary brings sad news. They had a casualty this morning, the first of the summer. It happened right after I left. A bunch of birds came into the culvert, then suddenly all exited at once so that several dozen hit the net simultaneously. The wallop knocked over one of the net poles set in a bucket—the one I thought would be okay without our digging a depression in the sand. The pole hit a bird caught in the net and killed it instantly. Mary says it could have been a lot worse considering that the net fell over while full of birds. She got the pole more firmly anchored by digging a hole for it.

I feel terrible because it was my fault. I was in such a dither over our late start and in such a hurry to get to Ash Hollow that I wasn't as careful as I should have been when I set the net. That's what happens when you don't concentrate. We have an incredibly low fatality rate considering the vast number of birds we handle each year—usually losing about one bird in every four thousand we handle—but I still feel awful when it happens. I feel even worse because this death was preventable.

Mary is also amused by Annie, who's apparently had a difficult day. The closest thing to a restroom near Clary is a ravine full of bull snake burrows where cows peer over the top of an overhanging chokecherry bush to watch while one squats. Mary calls it the ladies' lounge. Annie was in such distress that she finally had to summon her courage and "go" outside for, I guess, the first time in her life. She first asked Mary if she could use a lawn chair by spreading the webbing apart to make a toilet seat! When Mary vetoed that idea, Annie asked for instruction on the proper stance in the absence of anything to sit on. Mary's instructions must have neglected some crucial aspect, because Annie peed in her boot. Only she will be wearing those particular boots for the rest of the summer.

Urination in the field has been a problem for many of our assistants. Most have been female, and the mechanics are far more inconvenient for women. Some just never went, sometimes for the better part of a day. The strangest, though, was one of our assistants last year. This young woman spent the summer deathly afraid of snakes, even though nonpoisonous bull snakes are the only ones we commonly encounter. She insisted on peeing on the road by the truck even if it meant being seen by passersby. Several times local ranchers drove by and exchanged waves with her while she was squatting on the road with her pants down. I had assumed that she preferred to pee in such exposed places because of snakes, but she later confided to Mary that she avoided grassy areas because she was afraid grasshoppers would get in her underpants.

After Mary leaves, we settle into our afternoon routine. The Ash Hollow birds aren't coping well with the net on the east end. Some of them mill around it, and others seem to have left to go feed. Periodically a foraging group passes high overhead, only specks in the blue sky. We catch birds, but at only a fraction of the morning's pace. Each time I go to retrieve birds the disturbance flushes everybody, and it takes twenty minutes for them to return to the colony.

Waiting between net checks provides more idle time to enjoy the landscape, yuccas, and kestrels. Kathy takes out her sketch pad and starts drawing the giant cottonwoods. She's a talented artist and often does quick sketches in the field. I glance at her sketch of the cottonwoods before knowing what it is and ask if she's drawing a bird in the net. She seems a bit exasperated with my one-track mind and replies that there *are* things in the world besides cliff swallows!

Although we've probably had 30 birds in the net this afternoon, most of them have been repeat captures of birds from earlier today. By quitting time we've caught only 16 new birds, making a total of 116 for the day. I do a quick nest count and find 108 active nests. It looked like more birds than that were here this morning, so possibly some haven't started nests yet or were visitors still hunting for a colony.

We pack up and head to Clary to pick up Judy and Annie. They're still netting when we arrive. They seem to have done well on their first solo and had no problems. They've caught only thirty-eight birds since noon, but the small catch was a good thing the first time they worked alone. One bird was badly tangled by its tongue. Cliff swallows have a triangular tongue with sharp edges, and frequently the net mesh gets wrapped around it. Usually the assistants leave these cases to Mary or me. Annie and Judy are proud of themselves for freeing today's tongue tangle without help.

We drive back to Cedar Point, satisfied with our day. We're off to a good start at both of the Garden County colonies. I can't really enjoy today's success, though, because I know that Mary leaves tomorrow. With her gone, for me the most challenging week of the summer is about to begin.

The cliff swallow, one of the most social birds in North America, is distinguished by its white forehead patch and square tail (from Charles R. Brown and Mary Bomberger Brown, *Coloniality in the Cliff Swallow* [Chicago: University of Chicago Press, 1996], © 1996 by The University of Chicago; reprinted with permission).

Cliff swallows massing for a roosting flight at dusk.

Cedar Point Biological Station, nestled on a hillside overlooking
Keystone Lake and the Nebraska Sand Hills.

Swallow nests in the middle tunnel at Whitetail—in a typical year—
stacked in tiers six and seven nests deep.

Cliff swallows tangled in the mesh of a mist net.

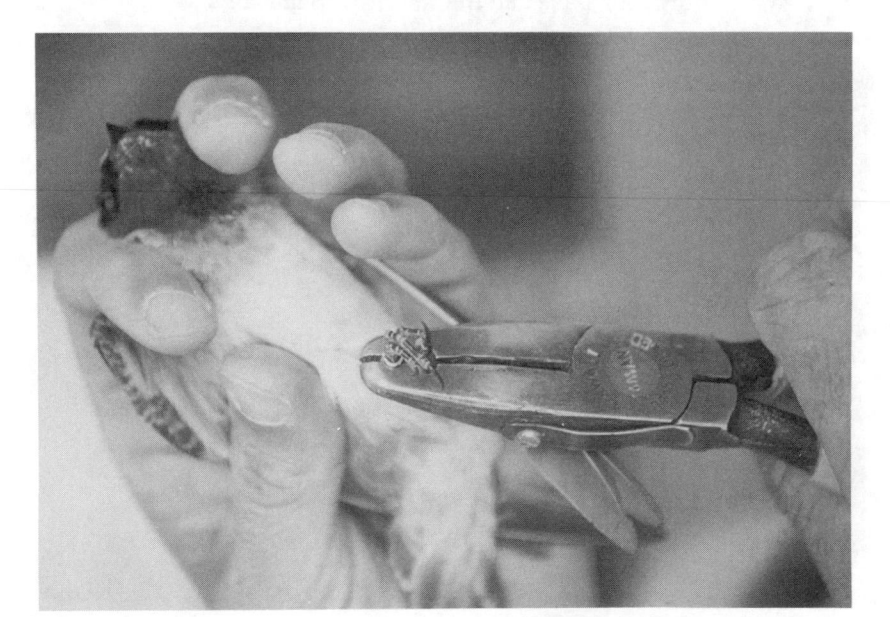

Each bird caught is banded on its leg with a numbered metal ring.

Catching eleven birds on this drop at CR 4 ½ is a victory in bad weather.

Down in the dark, dank west tunnel at Whitetail: watch out for the "blood vessel things."

The long culvert under the interstate known as Mule Deer.

Cliff swallows gathering mud for their nests (from Charles R. Brown and Mary Bomberger Brown, *Coloniality in the Cliff Swallow* [Chicago: University of Chicago Press, 1996], © 1996 by The University of Chicago; reprinted with permission).

The swallow nests under CR 2 are packed together in high density, covering almost all available space (from Charles R. Brown and Mary Bomberger Brown, *Coloniality in the Cliff Swallow* [Chicago: University of Chicago Press, 1996], © 1996 by The University of Chicago; reprinted with permission).

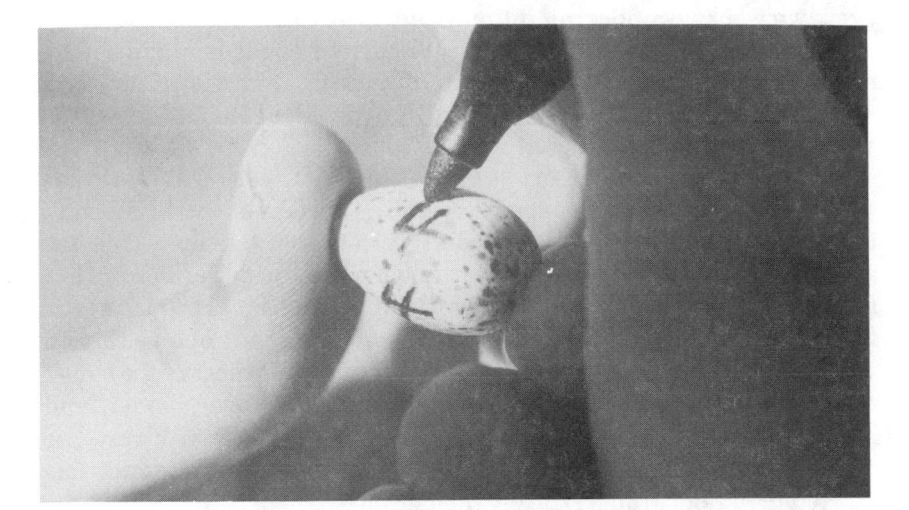

Cliff swallow eggs are numbered to study the birds' moving eggs between nests.

6

The Week She's Gone

*Had even Job, whose troubles have received such wide
publicity, ever had anything on this scale to cope with?*
—P. G. Wodehouse, *Cocktail Time*

June 3

I've dreaded this day ever since we arrived at Cedar Point last
month. This afternoon I'll take Mary to the town of Crawford, about
150 miles northwest of here, where her bike ride begins tomorrow.
The ride will end a week later in Omaha at the other end of the state.
In the interim, it'll be just me and the assistants.

Although I don't expect to catch much because it's again cloudy, cool,
and windy, I've been thinking about Roscoe and its high water for
over two weeks, wondering if there's any way to drop-net there. This
morning we'll try to find out. Mary is excited about her trip as she
spends the morning doing some final packing, but the dreary day
seems to have put Kathy, Annie, and Judy in a bad mood. I'm not too
enthusiastic this morning either.

Arriving at the Roscoe bridge, I see that the river level continues
to set new records. The space between the bottom of the bridge and
the water surface is shockingly small, perhaps only six feet. This has
greatly reduced the birds' flyway under their nests, and I have a
momentary surge of optimism that the high water might work in our
favor. The tall Roscoe bridge is normally an extremely open site, and
when there's hardly any water in the river (which is most of the time),
the cliff swallows have considerable space to fly over, under, and
around our nets. I wouldn't be so optimistic, however, if I were the
farmer who owns the field directly north of the river. The water has
started to break through the earthen levee between the river and the
adjacent farmland. Pools of standing water are already appearing,

and it looks like the entire field will flood if the river rises another foot.

Last year, when the South Platte was its typical trickle, we set big nets in the riverbed under the bridge and caught 745 cliff swallows here. I'm assuming that many of those birds will be back this year, and I desperately want to catch them. The assistants are a bit bemused by my determination to drop-net at this site, which seems prohibitively difficult. Why don't we just go to some place like CR 4½ if you want to catch birds? Annie wonders. They haven't yet appreciated the importance of sampling *all* the colonies in the study area if we're to conclude anything about survival and colony choice in our cliff swallow population as a whole.

We set up our chairs and net along the roadside at the south end of the bridge. There's no levee on this side, and the floodplain is completely submerged. The elevated road embankment is all that keeps us out of the water. The floodwaters extend at least a hundred yards to the south and threaten some abandoned buildings. I'd be more inclined to marvel at this high water if it weren't so damn cold. The overcast sky and increasing wind are making this a very unpleasant day. The assistants are cold and subdued, and I have to tell them everything to do. Fill up that bucket. Put the chairs here. Get the tape. Where are the bird bags? For reasons I don't understand, initiative always seems to drop when all the assistants work together. I guess each one has a clearer sense of personal responsibility when part of a smaller team. At any rate, I'm reminded of another reason I'm dreading this coming week: without Mary, all of us will be working together more frequently, and I'll have to be bossy.

The Roscoe bridge is a long one—394 feet to be exact—almost five times the length of sites like CR 4½. Consequently the birds' nests are more spread out. To have any luck at catching them, we should use a forty-two-foot drop net here. A piddly little eighteen-footer covers so small an area that you can't expect to get much. But a forty-two-footer catches an incredible amount of wind (in addition to birds at times), and getting it over the side of a bridge and back up can be almost impossible if a strong wind is blowing. It's too windy today to use a long drop net, so we'll see what we can do with a standard one.

A more significant problem may be a lack of birds. Cliff swallows are going in some of the active nests near the south end, but there's not much activity in the colony. Roscoe looks much smaller than last year. The colony probably hasn't grown since I first stopped here the day Kathy arrived, almost three weeks ago.

We start a series of drops. Our net covers hardly any space on this big bridge, and as expected we get very little. Few birds even fly out when we drop the net. It feels as if we walk forever to get far enough out on the bridge to reach the part with active nests. At intervals cars and trucks speed by, and I have to be certain the road is completely clear in both directions before we walk onto the bridge. After about an hour and at least twenty drops, we have only eighteen birds.

I know it's time to quit when a car pulls up and parks opposite us. A woman and two little boys about age ten get out, and the kids run out on the bridge and start throwing rocks in the water below. They're locals and are as shocked as I am about the amount of water in the river. We catch our last bird while they're out on the bridge, and I hear the momma tell her kids that those people are catching the birds to keep them from drowning. Okay. She seems to sincerely believe that, which is one I haven't heard before. The assistants are amused, and that seems to break the funk they've been in all morning.

I'm depressed that our attempt has failed, though I tell myself part of the problem was the lousy weather. We must come back when there's less wind and we can use the longer net. Annie, Judy, and Kathy make it clear that they don't like this place and wouldn't care if they never come back. We return to Cedar Point with little to show for our morning. At least the weather's so bad that I can legitimately give the assistants the rest of the day off while I take Mary to Crawford.

After lunch we drive northwest up the North Platte valley. Our route along the river is following the footsteps of the Oregon Trail pioneers. We pass the place west of Lewellen where J. Henry Carleton stopped to observe cliff swallows. The wet spring has made the river valley more lush than I've ever seen it. Dark green grass fills the floodplain where in a normal year it's a faded greenish brown. Many of the fields are carpeted with brilliant pink mustard. Southwestern Nebraska is not known for its wildflowers, but this year there are colorful ones everywhere. The mustard flowers are so numerous that entire fields are raspberry colored, and the sight is so striking I can barely keep my eyes on the road. Along the shoulder of the highway are thousands of little blue flax flowers, making me think of Texas bluebonnets from my childhood.

Our wildflower panorama is interrupted when we get to the town of Oshkosh. South of town is a big bridge over the North Platte River that annually contains thousands of swallow nests. Oshkosh is the westernmost colony that we study. We stop briefly at the bridge to verify that the colony is active. It is, although I knew it would be because this site is always used. The real purpose of the stop is to see where the birds are on the bridge. I'm planning to net here while Mary's gone. The birds are concentrated on the south end, again no big surprise, since they were on the north end last summer. This site shows a nice yearly alternation between the two ends, and for once this summer some birds are meeting our expectations.

We continue our journey up the valley. West of Oshkosh we pass some moderate-sized bluffs on the north side of the road, some close to the highway. We don't get this far west very often, and I scan the nearby outcroppings for evidence of cliff swallow nests. I've never seen a swallow colony on a cliff on the north side of the valley, but I'm sure they nest (or have nested) on some of these bluffs. The buttes and sculptured hills we pass look like something out of a John Wayne movie and Monument Valley. I drift back into the Old West, helped along by soundtrack music from *Lonesome Dove*, *The Commancheros*, and *Rio Grande* that emanates from the truck's cassette player.

For a while this beautiful drive preempts my thoughts of the hellish upcoming week without Mary.

At the town of Bridgeport we turn due north. We've been seeing cliff swallows at almost all the bridges and culverts since we left Lewellen, but soon there are no more birds. Going north quickly takes us out of the North Platte valley and into the vast, desolate Sand Hills. The horizon undulates with the irregular humps of the grass-covered sand dunes; it's a misconception that Nebraska is a flat prairie. Wide open is an apt description, with no trees anywhere except those planted around the few buildings or settlements. There are culverts under the highway we're on, yet they contain no swallow colonies. It's weird: cliff swallows are everywhere in the North Platte valley, but as soon as we enter the Sand Hills there are none.

We won't see any more swallows until we get to the next river valley, the Niobrara, eighty miles to the north. Although the birds have adapted to nesting on man-made structures like bridges, their distribution is still like that in Carleton's day. They confine themselves to the river valleys with their historical nesting sites on bluffs created by erosion from the rivers. They could move away from the river valleys and use culverts and bridges in other areas, but so far they've chosen not to. Why not? Cliff swallows surely don't have a gene that tells them not to leave the Platte River.

We crest a small hill as we approach the town of Alliance, a community of a few thousand people that grew up along the Union Pacific Railroad and the only settlement for miles in any direction. Below us we can see the town, but the scenery above us is what's impressive. The weather has been unsettled all day, and we ran into a heavy shower near Oshkosh. At Alliance, we have spectacular views of the most enormous thunderheads I've ever seen. All around us in every direction, massive anvil-shaped clouds extend thousands of feet into the sky. They're so tightly packed that we're surrounded by a wall of towering clouds; I imagine this is what the eye wall of a hurricane looks like. The background sky is dozens of different shades of blue and gray, punctuated with the puffy white and menacing gray of the thunderheads. The beauty of this scene is overpowering; only on the Great Plains can you see weather like this.

These clouds also make us a little anxious because they herald some nasty weather. You don't get thunderhead development like this unless the air is very unstable. Thunderstorms are a certainty, if not here, then farther to the east later today. Mary will be sleeping in a tent this week, so we hope these clouds don't become thunderstorms. But they're all around us, and the odds of escaping a storm aren't good.

Crawford is in the northwestern corner of Nebraska, a region known as the Pine Ridge. Very un-Nebraska-like, this area is the southern boundary of the Black Hills biome to the north. Ponderosa pine forests cover large areas, and the terrain is hilly and rugged. The Pine Ridge seems wetter than the rest of the state, although the contrast is diminished this summer because the entire state has had so much rain. The Niobrara River lies along the southern edge of the Pine Ridge, and we see cliff swallow colonies on bridges over the river's various channels. But as soon as we leave the Niobrara valley and climb into the higher country, the birds vanish again. There's something about those river valleys.

We finally reach Crawford and look for the local high school, directed by posters picturing a bicycle wheel that are tacked to road signs and light poles. Hundreds of cyclists have descended on this small town, and many of the locals are standing out in their yards looking astounded. The organized bike ride—imaginatively known as BRAN or Bicycle Ride across Nebraska—annually attracts six hundred riders from across the state and other parts of the country. Add several hundred more support personnel and family members of the riders, and the entourage outnumbers the population of many of the small towns along the route.

Each day the riders do between forty and a hundred miles. This year they're going west to east along the northern edge of the state. The organizers haul the baggage in a semitrailer that the riders themselves load and unload each day. The organizers also provide "sags"— vehicles that patrol the route and pick up riders who either have mechanical problems or are tired out. Mary is proud that she's never needed a sag in all her years of doing the ride.

Most of the riders sleep in tents each night at a communal camp, usually at the high school in the town where the day's ride ends. We find the Crawford high school, and the first order of business is to erect Mary's tent on the football field, among several hundred already there. The weather looks decent here at the moment, but the sky to the south is dark and stormy. If a thunderstorm or tornado threatens during the ride, the local sheriff announces it over a loudspeaker, wakes everybody in their tents, and makes them all evacuate to the high school gym. This has happened to Mary several times. From the looks of that sky, I wouldn't be surprised if she's sleeping on the gym floor tonight.

Mary has a cadre of friends she rides with, and she's been looking forward to this week for months, training daily since January. The bicycle ride is her one week of real vacation time. I try to be as supportive as possible, but I must admit I can't see the fun in pedaling a bicycle a hundred miles a day in the Nebraska wind and then curling up in a cold tent on the hard ground. What I mainly stew about, though, is that the ride is during the field season, especially now when our assistants are so inexperienced.

After Mary and I eat our spaghetti supper, cooked and served by the High School Music Boosters, it's time for me to head back to Cedar Point. It's at least a three-hour drive, and it may be stormy on the way. I don't want to leave, but I wish Mary good luck, tell her to be careful, kiss her good-bye, and point the *Valdez* southward. I drive alone in the dark, still meeting cars bound for Crawford with bicycles strapped on. This coming week without Mary will seem strange to me because she's been part of the swallow research for so long.

The winter before my first field season, Mary was the first person who responded to my advertisement for research assistants. She was just finishing her master's degree at the University of Nebraska and had seen me when I visited Cedar Point looking for a study site. On that visit John Janovy had asked me to give a seminar. I talked about the research on swallow vocalizations I had done as an undergraduate. Mary was in the audience and remembered that I mostly played a lot of boring tape recordings of swallow calls. She sat and picked paint off a bench during my rather dreadful seminar. She also remembered that I wore leather-soled shoes that squeaked whenever I walked across the lodge. I stood out because everybody else at Cedar Point was wearing tennis shoes. Yet despite my loud shoes and bad seminar, she called me and signed on as my first research assistant during the inaugural swallow summer. John Hoogland advised me against taking Mary as an assistant because, as a graduate student, she might try to "take over." I doubt, though, that John or I thought she'd "take over" to the extent that she'd still be studying cliff swallows fourteen years later. I'm often kidded that I married her because she was too good a biologist to lose and she married me because the research project was too good to lose.

Many factors have contributed to the long duration of my swallow research, but no factor has been more crucial than Mary's participation. Not many spouses would sacrifice as Mary has to make sure the research goes on each year. She gets sick and tired of living at Cedar Point, getting bird shit all over her, and seldom reaping any financial reward. Yet she keeps doing it because she believes the research is important and she enjoys working with the cliff swallows. And it's not just during the summer that Mary devotes herself to this project. She does it year-round, spending the academic year entering data in the computer or extracting information from our enormous computer files for analysis. I consider myself a lucky man for several reasons, but the biggest is having Mary as my wife.

We'll soon discover if I can hold things together without her this next week.

As soon as I leave the Pine Ridge heavy rain starts, making the road hard to see. There's occasional lightning, but mostly it's just rain. I hate driving at night in the rain, and I have to concentrate on the road and go slower than I'd like. I keep thinking it will let up, but it pours constantly until I'm about thirty miles from Cedar Point. At that point the road looks so dry that it probably hasn't rained at all in this area. I'm listening to the radio, KOGA out of Ogallala, and I hear that flood warnings have been posted for the South Platte River east to Roscoe. The rain I've just come through has apparently been stationary today over the Lodgepole Creek area to the west, and this region drains into the South Platte. Combined with the snowmelt and more rain in Colorado, they're expecting the worst flooding in thirty years along the South Platte. All the scenarios about losing many of our study colonies—nightmares I'd put out of my mind during the good weather of the past couple of days—come thundering back.

I arrive at Cedar Point and go to bed without worrying about what we'll do tomorrow. I defer to the morning thinking about how I'm going to use three green assistants effectively and keep them busy this next week without Mary and with high water everywhere.

June 4

This weekend falls between class sessions at Cedar Point. The ornithology and botany courses ended two days ago, and the next three—behavioral ecology, ichthyology, and invertebrate zoology—start tomorrow. Most of the students have cleared out for the weekend. The station has been quiet and peaceful since the classes ended. The problem for us, though, is that Dennis was also given the weekend off, so no meals are being prepared for the researchers who are still here. We've had to scrounge around in the kitchen for food. These "intersession" weekends when we must waste a lot of time fending for ourselves reinforce that having meals prepared for us is a major advantage of doing research at Cedar Point.

The assistants and I have plenty of time this morning to cook our own breakfast because the weather is bad. The incredible clouds we observed yesterday near Alliance indeed heralded the arrival of some turbulent air, and this morning thunderheads surround Cedar Point. The wind is strong, with periodic bouts of heavy rain. Kathy spends the morning in the lodge drawing some wildflowers she picked yesterday at Roscoe and put in a beer bottle. But Annie and Judy don't have anything to occupy them, and after being idle most of yesterday too, they're slipping back into the weather-related malaise that afflicted us so badly a week ago.

By lunch a weather pattern seems to have developed in which isolated showers pass over us, then abate as they move off to the east. The sun breaks through temporarily, only to be replaced within an hour by another rainstorm. The sky is full of thunderheads even when the sun's shining. But the assistants notice another break in the rain right after lunch and start nagging me about going out. It's against my better judgment given the weather, but I give in and decide we'll go to CR 4.

CR 4 is a canal bridge within sight of CR 4½, although it's a separate colony because the birds from the two sites don't interact. Some years CR 4 is one of the largest colonies in the study area, but this summer only a handful of birds live there. Being over the canal, CR 4 can only be drop-netted. Any small colony is frustrating to try to drop-net, because the birds usually are wary and fly around the net. Two years ago, however, we discovered that we can sometimes use two drop nets simultaneously at small colonies, to great effect. Two pairs of people carry drop nets out onto the bridge and in unison drop nets over both sides. If a bridge is relatively small like CR 4, this seals off the available flyway, and many of the colony residents can be caught. That is, they can be caught *if* we can get out onto the bridge before one of them detects us and *if* the nets are dropped over synchronously. When one net goes slightly before the other, the birds have a split second's warning to exit the other side before the second net drops.

We drive the three miles down the muddy, slick, and dangerous canal road to CR 4. Even as we set up our two drop nets, however, I can see the next rain squall approaching from the southwest. I tell the assistants to hurry, and they quickly fill the buckets and stretch out the nets.

The birds at CR 4 are incubating, and thus not many are flying around. This could bode well for us. I explain the double-net procedure to the assistants, but before we can do our first drop the wind gusts hit. The nets are billowing badly, but we run out on the bridge and try our drop anyway. In strong wind the folds (or "baskets") of a net often blow together, collapsing and reducing the net's surface area. That happens to Kathy and Judy's net, and they catch nothing. Annie and I catch seven birds in our net, although others blew out in the high wind under the bridge. The net's mesh gets pulled tight in a wind and not much hangs down for a bird to get entangled in; cliff swallows often just bounce out of a net when it's windy.

We try two more drops, but with the steadily worsening wind we get only five more birds. I barely get the last birds out before the rain starts. I knew we shouldn't have tried to net, and we're lucky not to have hurt a bird. Strong wind sometimes blows the net so badly it twists around a bird's neck before we can get it out. But still the exercise had some use, because it's obvious that the CR 4 birds can be caught if we have the right weather conditions. I look forward to better days ahead.

Meals by Dennis resume at supper. Most of the students and faculty for the new classes arrived during the afternoon. While everyone is enjoying cold-cut sandwiches, John Janovy repeats his orientation and welcoming speech for the new arrivals. When he gets to the part about the perils of alcohol, he spies Kathy's flowers in the beer bottle vase. He holds the bottle up as an example of a major transgression and announces that the owner should claim the flowers and find a new vase. Kathy blushes and says nothing. I guess her sketch is finished, because after the meeting Janovy trashes the unclaimed flowers and the beer bottle.

All day the radio has been broadcasting South Platte flood warnings, and someone at supper had heard that the river is out of its banks at Paxton and threatening the town. The embankment for the railroad tracks at the edge of town is supposedly all that's keeping the water out. I decide to go have a look after supper and invite the assistants to come with me. Judy and Kathy are eager to go, but Annie is more interested in socializing with her new boyfriend.

En route to Paxton, we go down the canal road to have another look at Aqueduct. On reaching the colony site, I see Josef and Ted, the instructor for the behavioral ecology class. Josef is now employed as Ted's teaching assistant. I had mentioned to Ted earlier that there was a great blue heron colony in the cottonwoods, and they've come down to have a look. They were hoping to have their class conduct observations on the herons. But Ted and Josef have bad news: all the heron nests have been deserted. That damn owl. Ted and Josef saw two great horned owls in the trees when they drove up; they must have attacked the heron nests. This certainly doesn't bode well for any swallows at Aqueduct, and I see none. Josef and Ted haven't seen any either.

When we get to Paxton, we find that the rumors about the flood are greatly exaggerated. Several fields north of the river and south of the town are flooded and look more like big lakes. I've certainly never seen anything like this here. We drive over the bridge, and the river itself is an ugly, muddy torrent that's much higher than the last time we were here, which I wouldn't have believed was possible. But no water is threatening the town; nothing's even close to the railroad tracks.

Even though Annie isn't with us, I decide we have time to stop and see Ole's Big Game Bar. Judy and Kathy are aghast: at least two hundred stuffed animal heads are hanging on the walls, everything from big animals like giraffes, elephants, bison, and moose to warthogs and little dik-diks. The bar is packed with tourists from the interstate, many of them families here for supper, but there are also a fair number of what look like smelly old locals. Judy and Kathy take a quick tour through the dense cigarette smoke and are ready to leave. A little bit of Ole's goes a long way. I see the guest book as we walk out, a book generally full of laudatory comments such as "amazing" or "enjoyed it tremendously." I'm always tempted to write something like what Marty penned when he visited: that it was "a tragic monument to one man's excesses." How many more animals must Ole have shot that weren't stuffed?

I've survived the first day of Mary's absence, and I wonder if she's experiencing this same unsettled weather. I hope not, but I won't know until she calls me, which will be only when she has access to a phone in the small towns along her route. I'm surprised when she calls later in the evening from the high school gym in Rushville. Her first day went well, although she rode in rain during the afternoon. She's calling between sets of a "talent showcase" put on by the Rushville locals to entertain the BRAN riders. The first performer was a cowboy poet singing and reciting paeans to the Old West, and the second one was a gospel duet best described as loud.

It's this that she's giving up a week of cliff swallow research for?

June 5

Overnight the weather has taken a major turn for the better. The day dawns sunny and calm, suddenly a perfect day for netting after two miserable ones. The stormy weather has moved east, and I hope Mary's not riding into it.

This morning we'll try two colonies where we haven't yet netted this summer. I'll leave Judy and Annie at IS 1 while Kathy and I net at a small colony on the diversion dam just a mile from Cedar Point. Annie seems tired and subdued this morning. Her nocturnal carousing with the Cedar Point students is beginning to show. My guess is that she's not going to bed until 2:00 or 3:00 A.M. That's just not enough sleep.

IS 1, irrigation structure 1, consists of a concrete diversion gate along the canal that's normally open but is designed to be closed if necessary to divert water. Should an emergency arise, this gate can stop the canal's flow, shunting the water down an adjacent ravine into the North Platte River. The structure provides a nice concrete overhang for cliff swallows. The birds at IS 1 are tame, perhaps because of the many fishers who stand on the overhang or along the nearby canal bank. The architecture of the site makes it easy to walk quickly up to the overhang and flip a drop net over instantly. It will be a good place for the assistants to work alone.

This summer I've estimated about two hundred active nests at IS 1. It's one of the few colony sites that has shown regular alternate-year use over the past decade. It's active in odd-numbered years and deserted in even-numbered ones. In the seasons it's unused, birds sometimes settle briefly but leave after a few days. If this were the only colony we studied, we'd probably devise a nice story about how the birds always alternate seasons in using a colony to let the ecto-parasites die off in the interim. The problem, of course, is that many sites don't show this consistent pattern.

I help Annie and Judy get set up and do the first drop with them. We get sixteen birds on the first try, suggesting they'll be busy here this morning. But the numbers should be manageable. Annie is in such a disagreeable funk that I'd like to take her with me, but Kathy is so slow at removing birds that it would be unwise to leave her here. I tell myself that despite her mood swings, Annie is a capable bird handler. They'll be okay, Judy assures me. I tell them I'll be just a mile and a half down the canal if they need me.

Kathy and I go to the colony called Diversion Dam. It's in the middle of the Keystone diversion dam where water is released downstream into the North Platte River. A concrete and metal catwalk spans the gates, and the birds nest on the support beams underneath it. Although unused last season, Diversion Dam is usually active, varying between ten and seventy nests.

We haul our gear across the dam from the parking area at the southern end. Vehicles aren't allowed on top of the dam, so netting involves a lot of toting. The swallows mostly enter their nests from the west side of the dam, and a drop net fits nicely in the flyway space on that side. On the east side, the big river gates obstruct the birds' flight path except for a narrow slit of open space directly above the gates. The birds seldom fly through the slit, so despite its small size, Diversion Dam can be an easy site to net when everybody's going out the open west side.

With the lack of wind, I'm anticipating a good morning. Although only about thirty nests are here now, I'm expecting to catch a large fraction of the colony, especially since the birds are incubating and thus easiest to catch. We sit on the dam, waiting for them to calm down before we try a drop. This is the kind of beautiful day I dreamed of ten days ago when we were freezing to death at the other end of the dam at IS 2: a glassy water surface, brilliant blue sky, soporific sun, and two white pelicans steaming along on the water directly in front of us.

Boy, am I wrong about the birds here! We start dropping our net, and to my complete surprise the swallows expertly avoid the net. Whenever we do a drop, they fly out the narrow slit on the east side. I've occasionally seen birds do this, but never before have so many eluded us this way. After half an hour and at least a dozen drops, we've caught three birds.

This is an ideal day for netting at Diversion Dam, and I have trouble believing our lack of success. I tell myself this is typical for the week Mary's gone. After another twenty minutes and no more birds, I finally decide we can't continue to waste this beautiful day. "Let's go try Roscoe," I suggest to Kathy. We need light wind to use a long drop net there, and a perfect day like this should tell us once and for all if it's possible to get anything at Roscoe this summer.

We haul everything back to the truck, only to realize I didn't bring the long drop net with us. More frustration. Fortunately Cedar Point's only a mile away, so we head back to the field station to get it.

We go on to Roscoe with a stop first at IS 1 to check on Annie and Judy. They have a net full of birds when we drive up, and I help them clear it. Their netting has gone smoothly but slowly; they've had a few badly tangled birds that took a while to remove. Annie's disposition hasn't improved, and she's complaining about not having her skin lotion. She suffers from dry skin, and I guess she's itching. She's making a big deal about her legs. She asks if she can walk back to get her skin cream, but I tell her we're at least two and a half miles from

Cedar Point. I suggest she just use some of Judy's suntan lotion. To my relief, Judy seems to be in total control and again assures me they're okay.

At Roscoe, Kathy and I set up the long net and repeat our attempts from two days ago to drop-net the residents. To my disappointment we have no better luck, despite the longer net and markedly better weather. The biggest problem is a fundamental one: not enough birds live here. The colony is much smaller than last year, and the birds are spread out on this monstrous bridge. Even a forty-two-foot net yields only one bird per drop, if any. The problem is magnified because the swallows here are little shits. They alarm-call at us before we can get into position to drop the net, and at least half of the colony flushes.

After a while it's painfully clear that netting at Roscoe this year is not meant to be. We quit after catching only sixteen birds. The only consolation is knowing that weather isn't the problem. Coming back here can be ruled out. I hope we'll find many of last year's Roscoe residents at other colonies this summer so we can maintain their colony-use histories. Obviously they're somewhere else this year.

Kathy and I drive back to IS 1. We've been floundering around all morning, with a grand total of nineteen birds in perhaps the best weather we've had all summer. I'm more disturbed about our bombing out at Diversion Dam, because it's critical that we sample the birds at that small colony. I'm frustrated by not having Mary here to discuss the situation.

When we get back to IS 1 and I announce that we'll all spend the rest of the morning there, Annie suddenly perks up and reverts to her cheerful self. It dawns on me that her earlier behavior may have reflected anxiety at being left alone to net. She desperately doesn't want to screw up and will maintain that obsession all summer. People react to stress in different ways. But this week's far from over, and I'm almost certainly going to need Annie to work without me again. Perhaps the next time won't be so hard for her.

The morning is salvaged when we end up with a total of 120 birds at IS 1.

The assistants are happy when we go to Whitetail this afternoon. I'm tired of messing around and want to catch birds. That we do. A light south wind allows us to net on our favored south end of the culvert. The assistants do three-person processing, which today means that

Annie bands and sexes the birds, Judy weighs them, and Kathy records the data. Having three people process is a faster and less exhausting way to do large numbers of birds. We end up with nearly 360 birds for the afternoon: maximum effort.

Annie announces at the end of the day that Whitetail is her favorite site because we're always busy. She's the first assistant I've ever had who liked Whitetail best.

June 6

The good weather is supposed to hold today, meaning it's time to try Oshkosh. Normally a two-person team goes to Oshkosh, but today I'll take everybody. More people will increase our haul, and I'm not eager to leave two assistants unsupervised somewhere else for an entire day. Oshkosh is forty-three miles away and an all-day trip.

Without Mary, last night I asked Dennis if he could make our sack lunches for today, and he said he would. I figured this would reduce the mob scene in the kitchen. Departure time comes, however, and there are no lunches. I guess Dennis forgot. Kathy and Annie make them, but once again we get a late start. We haven't had much luck getting away on time on our Garden County trips this year.

As we drive west around the lake, I tell the assistants that Oshkosh has become one of my least favorite sites. It's a big bridge like Roscoe, and drop netting there is hard work, requiring frequent trips out onto the bridge while we try to avoid the heavy car and truck traffic. But the primary reason I dislike this site is a game warden who lives in Oshkosh. I don't think this guy approves of us, and he sometimes harasses us.

Banding birds requires both federal and state permits. I make sure mine are always in order and carry them with me whenever we're netting. A stipulation of the Nebraska permit is that one must notify the "conservation officer"—the game warden—before conducting any scientific work in an area. For the colonies around Cedar Point, this notification consists of going into the game and parks office and telling the secretary that we're back for another summer of swallow banding. Whenever the game wardens assigned to Ogallala see us netting, they just wave. When we started netting at Oshkosh in 1989, I didn't know there was another game warden based there, because the town has no game and parks office.

Netting at Oshkosh is a conspicuous activity, because we're along-side a major highway that leads into town. We invariably attract spectators, and frequently passersby will call the game warden to report that we're doing terrible things to small birds. That happened on our first trip. The local game warden came tearing out to confront us, proudly displaying his badge and his authority. I explained who we were and what we were doing and said we had checked in with the Ogallala office. This was Bubba's territory, though, and he was clearly ticked off that I hadn't called him in advance. The guy looked like the quintessential redneck sheriff who throws out-of-town tourists in jail for some minor infraction without thinking twice. He eventually left us alone, but several times he'd slowly drive by, staring at us. I don't think he's ever forgiven me for assuming that the Ogallala office had jurisdiction over "his" bridge.

The next year, on my first trip to Oshkosh to check the colony's status I looked up Bubba. Without a formal game commission office in Oshkosh, I went to the courthouse, asking if anyone knew this guy. It didn't take long to find a good ol' boy who did, and he directed me to a motel out on the highway. I guess Bubba manages the motel when he's not tracking down deer poachers and bird banders. I stopped in to tell him we'd be netting at Oshkosh that summer. He wasn't too warm about it, but at least he didn't confront us later when we came to net. He'd just drive by while we were at the bridge, giving us the visual third degree.

A couple of years ago I stopped as usual to check in with him, telling him we'd be netting at Oshkosh in about a week. He said fine, and after five years he seemed to be getting a bit more friendly. It didn't last. The next time we came to net, we'd been there a few hours when Bubba came driving up, stern faced. Assistant Mike and I had a net full of badly tangled birds, and dealing with this guy was the last thing we needed.

"Have you guys got permits for that?" he demanded as soon as he got out of his pickup.

"Yes, we do. Do you want to see them?"

"I sure do."

Mike kept working on the birds while I handed over the permits. Bubba acted as if he'd never seen a banding permit before, reading the fine print on the back instead of the relevant information on the front. Or perhaps he was trying to find some loophole to arrest us on.

"Okay, but I keep having trouble with you guys not checking in with me. You're supposed to notify the officer in charge."

"I did, a week ago at the motel."

Bubba looked puzzled, then it dawned on him that I *had* spoken with him. He loosened up a little, saying he'd forgotten. I think he was out of sorts because he'd been over near Lake McConaughy when he got the predictable call from some citizen complaining about us, and he had to drive all the way back to Oshkosh to confront us.

The first order of business today is to stop and see Bubba. We pull up at the motel, but I don't see his truck. I go into the office and talk to an elderly woman—his mother I guess—and ask her to tell him we'll be at the bridge. She writes it down, and I give her a business card with my name. I leave and walk back to our truck. Before we drive off, I see Bubba's truck pull in. He gets out, limping so badly he can hardly walk. I return to the motel to see him, but the woman meets me and tells me she gave him the information and it's better not to disturb him. I don't know what's wrong with him, but he doesn't look in any shape to hassle us today.

I'm surprised when an hour later he drives past us at the bridge. I'm relieved when he just waves and goes on. We don't see him again.

We set up on the south end of the bridge where the swallows are concentrated. On one side the nests are stacked nine and ten deep on the outer beam. This section of the Oshkosh colony has the highest density of nests I've ever seen on a bridge. The nests are usually spread out in long rows on big bridges like this, and active nests on other parts of this bridge are in single rows as expected. But the extreme nest clustering on the southeast end indicates there must be active benefits of nesting close to each other; otherwise the cliff swallows should spread out and occupy the parts of the bridge that have few nests or none. The costs of dense nesting, especially parasite transmission, seem too great unless the birds are gaining some advantage from nesting so close together. That advantage concerns food finding, though it's still too early in the summer for us to observe how the birds benefit in this way.

We'll catch a lot of birds when we drop a net over the southeast end. Kathy and I do the first drop, and I warn her to expect a massive rush of birds. The net will be heavy, so she must take care not to let it slip out of her hands. My recurring nightmare is that someday someone will lose their grip on a net pole when we've dropped it over and the net's full of birds. It hasn't happened yet, but if and when it does, it'll probably be the week Mary's gone. We pull up after our first drop with a "black net"—so many birds in the brown-mesh net that it looks solid black. I'm glad all the assistants are here to help.

We start racking up big numbers. We're successful mostly because the birds don't alarm-call at us as we move out onto the bridge. Partly this is because cliff swallows at big colonies just naturally aren't as wary, but it's also because the birds are near the end of the bridge so we don't have to walk out very far before we're over them. It's a different story when the birds are concentrated in the middle of the bridge and we have to walk fifty yards in the open to get to them. The morning passes quickly and pleasantly, and we're not bothered by any spectators, a rarity here. One year we had so large an audience I should have sold tickets.

On one foray to the bridge, I notice a road-killed cliff swallow. It's still reasonably intact and is lying on its breast, its back and orange rump patch facing up. I see other cliff swallows fly down and try to copulate with the deadhead. We can add necrophilia to this species' list of charming personality traits. This isn't the first time I've seen cliff swallows do this; the bright orange rump sticking up seems to be all the stimulus these birds need. In fifteen minutes I count at least ten birds that attempt copulations before a cattle truck roars past and its wake blows the corpse into a drainage grate.

That copulations would be directed toward a dead bird is perhaps not surprising, since these birds are well known for their tendency to copulate with any swallow that's available. Cliff swallows engage in extrapair copulations, meaning birds of both sexes copulate with others they aren't paired with and with which they don't share a nest. When females go to a mudhole to gather mud, males that don't have mates or nests of their own hang out there and often try to forcibly copulate with the unescorted females. Sometimes females don't resist, suggesting that extrapair copulations are to their advantage. The precise nature of that advantage isn't known; perhaps the philandering females have lousy mates. Even males that have nests and mates will try to get a little on the side when they go to the mudhole, ostensibly to get mud for their nests. Mud gathering early in the season sometimes resembles an orgy, with copulating birds flapping around in the mud, some trying it forcibly, others more willingly, while others gather mud or just stand and watch.

When cliff swallows collect mud, they flutter their wings above their backs and also elevate their tails. People have speculated about why they do this, some suggesting that it helps keep mud off their wings and tails. But this doesn't seem too likely, because cliff swallows never get muddy unless another bird attacks them and knocks them into the mud. Wing fluttering remained mysterious until Canadian biologist Rob Butler suggested that the swallows flutter their wings above their backs to prevent birds from pouncing on them from above and trying to copulate. Butler put out stuffed models of birds, some with wings folded and others with wings extended. He found that copulations were directed mostly at the models that did not have extended wings.

We repeated Butler's experiments with the same result. Wing fluttering deters extrapair copulation attempts. Our birds copulated so often and so violently with the closed-wing models that they eventually ripped the head off one of them. Then they kept copulating with the headless model! I guess this is one reason I'm not surprised to see them doing it to a deadhead.

The consequence of these frequent extrapair copulations is that a male is sometimes not related to the offspring in his nest. That's why we want to do the DNA fingerprinting study, to figure out just how often the extrapair copulations are successful. It's surprising that a male cliff swallow doesn't escort his mate when she leaves the nest, to keep himself from being cuckolded. But perhaps guarding the nest is more important. An unattended nest is an inviting target for a neighboring female that may slip in and lay a parasitic egg for the absent "hosts" to care for. If a male allows his nest to be parasitized, he almost certainly will not be the father of the parasitic offspring. It's better, I guess, to guard your nest and take your chances that your mate will be faithful. Even if she isn't, you can still try to dilute any foreign sperm she may have picked up. Male cliff swallows do this by frequently copulating with their mates and filling them with prodigious amounts of their own sperm.

Colonial life is full of risks and opportunities.

After lunch it starts to get hot. The temperature must be close to 90°, and it seems worse by the side of this asphalt road, which reflects heat. We work quickly to remove birds from the net and process them before they overheat. On one drop, however, we have a casualty. The tangled mesh twists around a bird's neck before we can get the net back to the processing area. It's our second casualty of the summer, and again I feel terrible. This one was unavoidable, though, because the bird happened to be in the fold of the net that twisted when we pulled it up. Accidents like this happen two or three times a summer.

In midafternoon Kathy and Annie announce that there's a problem with the data. Somehow either a band was lost or a bird was banded and its data weren't recorded. The consequence is uncertainty about the information recorded for ten birds. I always emphasize that whoever is recording must check each band as she takes it off the string to be sure its number matches what's being written down, and the recorder must be certain that the processor gives her the data on a bird before releasing it. Kathy had a mental lapse, and now we don't know for sure the sexes or weights of the past ten birds. We also don't know whether one of the ten bands in that sequence was in fact put on a bird or was lost.

I'm annoyed, and the assistants know it. We all paw through the grass and sand under the chairs, looking for a lost band. When we don't find one after fifteen minutes we reluctantly conclude that a bird got banded and nothing was written down on it. Kathy feels bad and twice tells me she's sorry. I'm not in a forgiving mood, though, because I don't want it to happen again. The only way to resolve this problem is to try to recapture some of those birds and verify their band numbers and sexes.

Our afternoon comes to a close sooner than I'd hoped. We run out of bands. I brought three hundred, and we've caught about 350 birds, about 50 of them banded in earlier years. We don't net at this colony often, and for that reason—plus its location on the edge of the study area—we don't get many past-year birds. The principal reason we come here is to look for birds dispersing from the colonies near Cedar Point and to see if any Oshkosh birds in turn disperse to the sites near Cedar Point.

We return to Cedar Point by way of Ogallala. Annie wants to stop in town to buy candy. She's addicted to Twizzlers—long, rubbery cherry-flavored twists. I've seen her eat half a pound of these things in just a few minutes. Twizzlers are about all she does eat.

The electronic sign on the Ogallala bank said it was 98° this afternoon. Heat like this often generates thunderstorms, and tonight is no exception. By suppertime the western sky has clouded over, and dark storm clouds are gathering. A tornado watch has been issued for most of southwestern Nebraska. At dusk I step out on the veranda of the apartment building, where Tony and Diana are watching the clouds swirl overhead. The entire sky is menacing, and what's most scary are scores of pendulous mammatiform clouds protruding from the developing storm's underbelly directly overhead. These bulging gray lumps often spawn tornadoes in storms like this.

We keep watching the clouds, and before long Tony points out that the mammatiform clouds are moving in different directions. That's a precursor to funnel formation, and the three of us stand transfixed by this atmospheric spectacle. I wouldn't be surprised to see a tornado. Cloud-to-cloud lightning is increasing, and off in the Sand Hills to the north lightning bolts are hitting the ground.

The wind starts increasing, and once the sun is down there's enough light to see the clouds only during each lightning flash. Tony, Diana, and I retreat indoors, and shortly the heavy rain and hail start. Usually the most violent part of these prairie storms comes before the rain, so I assume the greatest threat of a tornado has passed. Strangely, though, I feel disappointed when the storm subsides. Nebraska weather can be dangerous enough to excite, inspire, and terrify all at once. No other natural phenomenon comes close to achieving this effect for me.

I go to sleep thinking about Mary in her tent. I hope the rough weather misses her.

June 7

The day begins sunny and clear, though by afternoon gray clouds will increase as another low pressure disturbance from the Rockies descends on us. Because there's little wind, after breakfast I decide to have Annie and Judy try IS 2, the colony on the end of the diversion dam where we netted earlier during bad weather. Kathy and I will visit CR 2.

Annie seems to be coping better with working independently, so I feel better about her and Judy netting alone today. I drop them off at the diversion dam, and this time I don't set up their net. By now they can do it themselves. No fishers are at IS 2, and I hope none will appear this morning: often fishers stand on the catwalk in the very spot where we must drop the net. People have been catching a lot of trout off the dam lately, though, and I bet that Judy and Annie will eventually attract spectators.

CR 2 is a different architectural style than most of the canal bridges. It's designed only to funnel water from the canyons to the south across the canal and into the North Platte River to the north. In a heavy rain, the runoff from the hills and bluffs along the southern edge of the river valley is concentrated in a few ravines. Without a way to redirect that runoff, the canal could flood after a summer cloudburst. The bridge here is concrete with moderately tall walls to hold the flowing water in a flood and quite narrow—only about five feet wide. It's not used for any vehicle or livestock traffic, making it a good place for netting.

Another of CR 2's nice features is that the south end of the bridge extends under the elevated canal road like a culvert to connect with the pasture to the south. We can sit inside the enclosed part, out of sight of the birds, and we have only a few feet to walk into position to drop our net. The only drawback is that it's usually damp and cold under the road, even on a sunny day like this one.

It's soon obvious that the cliff swallows here are not willing to play ball. As soon as we move into the open to drop the net, the birds flush out and *pew* at us. Each time we get only three or four laggards that are slow to flush. How do they know we're coming? The colony seems to be incubating, meaning most of the birds are under the bridge in the nests at any given time. We should be successful, but I think they hear our footsteps on the concrete floor of the bridge. Mary had good luck here last week, but for some reason the swallows are now much warier. This happens every year at CR 2 and is frustrating as hell.

Many of the CR 2 birds are old ones. I'm tempted to speculate that this colony is so difficult because the birds here have experienced netting before and *know* us. They've learned to associate our presence with getting caught. But that probably attributes more intelligence and learning capacity to a twenty-four-gram bird than is really warranted.

On the other hand, I do think cliff swallows can recognize individual humans. Mary's bike tour once made an evening stop in Ogallala. Her bicycling friends wanted to see the swallows. We went to Whitetail in their car, and I was cleaned up and not wearing my usual field clothes and cap. I walked to the top edge of the culvert, wanting the birds to put on a good show by roaring out in a massive flush. Instead they just ignored me. It took clapping and foot stamping to get even a few to flush. The next morning when I arrived in the blue truck dressed in my usual field clothes, as soon as I opened the door the entire colony flushed out and swirled above me, alarm-calling. They clearly hadn't recognized me the night before, in a different car and without my crap-stained baseball cap. Mary's convinced that they never respond to her as vigorously as to me, because they know she's "just a pawn" and that I'm the real source of their troubles! Sometimes when I'm walking down the road at Cedar Point, far from any colony, a passing cliff swallow will give an alarm call at me. They never *pew* at Mary.

We end with a measly total of fifty-nine birds by noon. Only nine were unbanded, illustrating why CR 2 holds so much attraction—and frustration.

Annie and Judy had a good morning at IS 2, getting about seventy birds. They had problems with spectators, though. Some fishers appeared with their kids, and the kids naturally preferred to watch Judy and Annie catch and band birds rather than watching their parents fish. The little girl generally kept her distance, but the little boy—about six or seven—was a major pain. He kept yakking and tried to touch some of the birds entangled in the net. Annie had to scold him, telling him to stand back and leave them alone. But Judy and Annie are more put out with the parents, who seemed oblivious to their children's interference. I'm proud of Judy and Annie for being able to continue working, without any data errors, despite the distraction.

By lunchtime the wind has increased steadily. It's out of the north and has a chill to it. I decide the wind is going to make netting impossible this afternoon everywhere except Whitetail, and even there we'll have to do the north end.

The assistants are happy that I want to do our processing in a grassy area by the roadside rather than sitting down in the cold, damp west tunnel. It will mean more walking for me to carry birds from the net to the processors, but it might be better for the help's morale given the blustery afternoon. As usual, the swallows initially freak out with us on the north end, especially since we're sitting in the open. But they're further into nesting now—many have eggs—and thus more tolerant. Soon they settle down.

The sky continues to worsen, and by midafternoon there aren't many birds around. They've gone off to feed. Several times I increase our captures by doing a flush: I walk through the dry west tunnel to the south end and jump out into the creek in front of the middle tunnel. Huge numbers of incubating birds flush out of their nests away from me and into the net on the north end. We've sometimes caught sixty or seventy birds in a single flush and often could have gotten more except that once the loose mesh of the net is full of birds, others just hit it and bounce out.

Another interesting feature of flushes—whether done on the north or south end of the culvert—is that most of the birds we catch have been banded in a previous year. We get few unbanded birds that way. For some reason, first-time captures (unbanded birds) come only from undisturbed traffic in and out of the culvert. This pattern holds again today. The different netting methods clearly yield different subsets of the swallow population. I've speculated about the reasons for this for years, and later this summer I'll finally realize what these differences mean.

We eventually catch 309 birds at Whitetail. This week is half over, and so far we've done well. We've caught approximately 1,300 birds since Mary left four days ago. I'm skeptical, however, that we can maintain our average of 300 birds a day for the rest of the week.

More bad weather is forecast.

June 8

Heavy rain fell most of last night and had barely stopped by breakfast. The day is cold, windy, and damp. I tell the assistants to find something else to do this morning. Annie is happy to go back to bed. Judy stays in the lodge to read a trashy novel, and Kathy goes over to the lab to again tackle the manuscript of *Coloniality in the Cliff Swallow*.

I negotiate the muddy roads and head into Ogallala to visit the bank and pick up Cedar Point's mail. The field station has a post office box in town, but mail reaches us only when someone goes to the post office to get it. Mail is our contact with the outside world, and receiving letters is a highlight of each day. I'm in the minority in that I'd like to go the entire summer without any mail. Whatever finds us out here usually requires attention and forces us to devote time to something besides swallows.

As I return to Cedar Point, I notice many cliff swallows foraging low around the lab building and adjacent junipers, in the same area where we studied food calls. I watch them zigzag across the open grass, darting among the junipers that dot the field just west of the laboratory. Most of the birds are only a couple of feet above the grass. They're probably feeding on the midges that rest in the grass or junipers during cold weather but occasionally fly high enough to be caught.

I wonder about netting these foragers. At times, nets set among the junipers can catch a lot of swallows in cool, cloudy weather. We don't know where these birds are breeding, but catching them helps us in estimating survival of birds from earlier years. Chances are that many of the foraging birds we'd catch would be banded ones. My guess is that most are from nearby colonies. In the past we've caught banded residents from as far away as Whitetail foraging here during bad weather, suggesting the birds often have to travel widely—three miles or more—to find food during hard times.

I hem and haw briefly over the wind, so I walk out into the field and look for openings where nets could be placed and possibly buffered by the junipers. In several places the wind doesn't seem too bad. We'll net.

I find Kathy in the lab and Judy in the lodge, but I have to go up to their cabin to get Annie. I bang on the door, and Annie awakens, disoriented and looking a bit shocked to find me standing there telling her we're going to net this morning after all. She tells me she'd been dreaming about me, and to be suddenly awakened by me in middream has flummoxed her. My merry band of helpers soon assembles at the lab, where we're greeted by Josef, who's also grounded by the weather. He offers to let us use some of his forty-two-foot nets, and I accept because my forty-two-footers are rigged for use on tall bridges. We don't want nets too high today in this wind.

We start setting the nets in the more protected spots among the junipers. With the poles somewhat masked by the trees, the nets are relatively hard to see despite the wind that billows them at times. The assistants let the first net drag on the ground while we're setting it, and it snags on a large tumbleweed. It takes five minutes to get it off. Josef notices this and keeps asking if I'd like some help. I hate to bother him, and initially I say no, thanks. After the second net drags in the tumbleweeds, I reconsider. In no time Josef and I get four more nets set up among the junipers.

We start catching swallows as soon as the first net goes up. The foragers can see these nets, because some birds actively avoid them. Many others, however, just plow right into them, distracted by the search for insects. Hundreds of cliff swallows are foraging over the field and the Cedar Point grounds, and we catch birds at a steady pace. A couple of us patrol the nets while two others process our catch inside the lab, releasing the birds out the door. Our activities draw the attention of Joan, the associate director of Cedar Point, who brings her kids down to see us. Her daughter, Alison, becomes fascinated by bird catching and sits in the lab with the processors the rest of the day. Alison is well behaved and closely supervised by Joan, a big contrast to those kids who pestered Judy and Annie at IS 2.

Netting in the Cedar Point field is relaxing and a different kind of fun from catching birds at the colonies. This is low-stress netting: we just wait for the birds to come to us. Here we don't have to worry about disturbance to a colony, keeping the birds off their nests, catching too many at once, or other problems that may develop when we take our nets where the swallows live. I feel that anything we catch in this lousy weather is a bonus.

The four of us eat lunch in shifts to keep the nets open during the noon hour. By midafternoon captures start to diminish, in part because of increasing wind. Fewer cliff swallows seem to be around. One way to remedy this is to try to increase the number of insects in the immediate vicinity. We resort to our insect flushing methods of the food-call days. Each with a stout stick, we fan out among the junipers and start hitting their boughs. Midges flush off the branches to form temporary swarms before settling back into the grass or trees. As soon as we start beating the trees, more swallows appear and our captures in the nets increase. We must look like idiots out here flagellating the poor trees. Plant abuse. It's effective, but we have to keep at it constantly; otherwise the insects decline and so do the swallows. Hitting the trees vigorously enough to be effective is hard work, and after a while the assistants lose interest. They find excuses to gravitate back toward the lab or lodge. I keep on beating the bushes until supper.

I decide to leave the nets open until dusk, and Judy tends them while the rest of us eat supper. I don't anticipate getting many more birds today, but about an hour before dusk birds suddenly increase around the nets. The wind has declined, and we start catching swallows rapidly. I told Annie at supper that we wouldn't need everybody and she could stay in the lodge; now I'm sorry that all of us aren't here. Before long it's getting dark, and our nets are still filling up. Kathy and I have to sprint from net to net, closing them as we remove the last birds.

We eventually finish in a frenetic ending to what has been a productive day despite the weather. The final count is 178 cliff swallows, a record for a single day in the Cedar Point field. Of those, over a quarter are birds banded in an earlier year, including one first banded seven years ago. I'm gratified by this high percentage of previously banded birds in a random sample of passersby, since it reflects the enormous effort we've put into banding cliff swallows in the past several years.

We also caught several rough-winged swallows and a yellow-breasted chat. Chats are garrulous, thrush-sized warblers known for their songs, a miscellaneous collection of whistles, warbles, and clucks. Mary and I have been hearing one singing at night outside our apartment, probably the one we caught today. It will hang around the junipers by the lab all summer, usually singing throughout the night.

It's after 8:00 before I get back to the apartment. Mary hasn't phoned lately, and I'm expecting her to call tonight. It's so late I figure I missed her, and sure enough there's a message from her on the answering machine. She's in Ponca, after a rough day because of the weather. Her voice is hoarse, and she sounds exhausted. I learn later that today was among the worst she's ever spent on BRAN. She awoke to temperatures close to 30° in that part of the state, then rode seventy-six miles in a strong headwind and heavy rain. Most of the riders gave up and were carried into Ponca on sags. Rumor had it that Mary was one of only seven women who finished.

I'll have to wait another day to talk to her.

June 9

When I awake this morning I realize how comparatively good yesterday's gray, cloudy weather was. The wind has increased today, and it's colder. By midmorning it's raining heavily and occasionally hailing. Even after the rain stops, I see very few birds foraging on the Cedar Point grounds. With the stronger wind, there are no protected spots by the lab to set nets. I have to convey to the assistants the sad fact that there's nothing we can do on a day like this—but by now they know it.

When the phone rings this evening I'm expecting Mary, but instead it's Bruce calling from New Haven to report the progress he's making on his dissertation. He's completed his data analysis and has written most of his dissertation. Bruce spent the past three summers at Cedar Point, collecting data, and much of his work was done at colonies along the South Platte River.

Bruce wouldn't have been doing anything with those colonies this summer. I describe the water level this year, and he realizes he dodged a bullet. Had this summer been part of his fieldwork, the lack of colonies where nests are accessible would have kept him from completing his degree on time. Even short-term graduate research projects that involve fieldwork carry a large element of risk. Extreme years like this summer may be valuable and tell us a lot in the long term about how the birds react to wide environmental fluctuations, but a season like this can really snooker a graduate student.

Bruce's most exciting news is that he's developed a statistical method to estimate the proportion of immigrant swallows moving into our colonies daily. To calculate how often swallow bugs get transported from one colony to another, we have to know how often "new" birds move into a colony. Our netting at different sites on different days provides that information in raw form. For instance, we net at Whitetail today, then return four days later to net there again. On the second visit, we catch some birds we had last time plus many we didn't catch then. Some of this latter group are probably residents we just hadn't caught yet, but others may be new birds that have immigrated into Whitetail since our last visit. By knowing the colony size (the number of active nests) and the various fractions of different classes of birds caught, one can estimate statistically the number of immigrants and where they're from. Only these birds can be carrying bugs into the colony. Other data tell us how many of the immigrants are likely to be transporting bugs.

Bruce has applied the new method to some of our mark-recapture data, and the results sound interesting. For example, the first colony he tells me about is Whitetail, and he says I'll be surprised at the high number of immigrants passing through Whitetail each day—over a thousand birds, it turns out. I am surprised. Of course many of those birds don't stay; they pass through the culvert maybe just one time (when they get caught in our net) or stop briefly and look at a nest or two before leaving. But it means there is considerable movement by birds between colonies, and this movement is going on all summer. We'd never have known this was happening without netting.

In a couple of weeks the significance of Bruce's analysis of immigration rates will hit me.

June 10

The clouds and rain moved out during the night, but not the wind. It's straight out of the north at thirty miles an hour, keeping the temperature down and stressing the swallows for the third day in a row. Netting is out of the question. I assumed this was obvious to the assistants, but at breakfast and again at lunch they complain about having nothing to do and wanting to catch birds. Déjà vu!

By late afternoon I notice the wind diminishing to a tolerable level. We can go out after supper and try to use this bad weather to our advantage at CR 2. Perhaps the birds there will be less wary and not as hard to approach after several days of marginal weather. They may have less energy to spend avoiding us. It seems a little dirty to net them after such bad weather, but it's critical that we catch as many of the banded birds at CR 2 as possible. This may be the only way.

Only two of us can really be effective at CR 2, so Annie and Judy will try CR 4. Although we used two drop nets at CR 4 last time, I think a single net can also be effective because the colony residents don't seem skittish. We leave immediately after supper, and after dropping Annie and Judy at CR 4, Kathy and I return to CR 2. The birds fly out of the nests under the bridge as we set up our drop net above them, but they return as soon as we retire inside the hidden portion of the bridge.

We start a series of drops and have much better success than three days ago. The birds are less likely to flush before we do a drop, and consequently we catch more per drop—up to fifteen or twenty on some attempts. They come back quickly after each disturbance; we don't have to waste time waiting for them to calm down. Considering how tough it was here the other day, I can hardly believe our good fortune. By dusk we've caught sixty-two birds, and only nine were unbanded. I kick myself for not having brought Judy and Annie, since more processors might have increased our haul even more.

Judy and Annie did well at CR 4, though, so their time was still well spent this evening. They ended up with twenty-seven birds, almost half of the colony residents. I'm proud of them for doing so well at a small colony and tell them this is excellent, though they still don't realize the importance of getting data from the smaller colonies or recognize how challenging these sites usually are. They seem almost bummed out by getting "only" twenty-seven birds.

I finally speak to Mary tonight. Her ride ended today in Omaha, where she was met by her brother, Dave. Dave will bring her as far as Kearney, the midpoint between Omaha and Ogallala, and I'll meet them there tomorrow. I go to bed in a good mood. We've been fairly productive during Mary's absence, going only one day this week without catching any birds.

June 11

I'm scheduled to meet Mary about noon, which gives me enough time to organize Kathy, Judy, and Annie for the day. It's time to return to Barn Owl, which should be an easy site for them to do alone. But since I won't be back until after lunch and they'll be netting at CR 4½ this afternoon, I'll need to leave one of the trucks with them. Annie is the designated driver.

Kathy is not looking good this morning. For at least a week she's had a cough, and today she woke up feeling achy. She may be coming down with summer flu. I don't realize how bad she feels until we get to Barn Owl, and I offer to take her back to Cedar Point. I'm afraid she might have a fever, and Annie volunteers that she has a rectal thermometer Kathy can use. Kathy refuses to even consider not working today, despite my admonitions that she must take care of herself.

I'm vaguely uneasy for fear her symptoms might be caused by a hantavirus. Field station personnel are very conscious of the potential for contracting these rodent-borne viruses. Mice are everywhere, and a researcher at a biological station in California died from a hantavirus infection three years ago, the same summer that an outbreak occurred in the Southwest. It starts out like the flu, then if untreated leads quickly to respiratory failure. If Kathy's worse by this afternoon, we should be on the safe side and take her to the clinic in town. I repeatedly tell her to stay in this afternoon if she's still feeling bad at lunchtime.

The route to Kearney takes me by some colonies that need to be checked. The swallows have lost interest in one of the wooden canal bridges they were on earlier, but they still seem firmly established on the other. We need to net there. I wince once again when I see that Aqueduct is deserted. No owl today, but no swallows either.

I get on the interstate at Roscoe. At the interchange there are several abandoned gas stations. These were in business when we first came here in 1982, but they've long since gone bust. I guess most tourists would rather stop at the Ogallala exit only seven miles away. But one of the abandoned gas stations has attracted cliff swallows. The birds are swarming under an awning that covers the old gas pumps, and they're also under the eaves of the building itself. We've named this colony Skelly after the kind of gas station it used to be.

This site perennially attracts swallows, yet they never successfully nest here. When the birds moved in during the first summer the gas station was closed, house sparrows attacked the colony. There were tons of sparrows around the nearby buildings, and they took over the cliff swallow nests after the swallows laid eggs. The destructiveness of the sparrows was especially evident that year, with over a hundred swallow eggs tossed out of nests and splattered on the concrete pavement below. A kid with a BB gun who lived in one of the gas stations was also a problem, shooting at the birds and their nests. Eventually the swallows abandoned the site.

By the next year the property apparently had a new owner who was opposed to cliff swallows and the "mess" their mud nests made, and he began (illegally) knocking their nests down. For several successive summers the swallows had a morbid fascination with this wretched site and futilely tried to colonize it. After finally forgetting about Skelly for several years in the early 1990s, the birds were back two years ago. Why are the birds interested in this place when scores of similar buildings throughout the area are always ignored?

Today there are several hundred birds swarming under the awning and the eaves. They're gathering mud from a mudhole in a dirt road to the east. I'm sad to see this because I know these birds are doomed to fail. It's getting so late in the summer that they may run out of time to nest elsewhere once the old guy knocks their nests down. I start to wonder, though, if we could catch some of these birds before they're forced out. Roscoe is just down the road, and the birds here could be some of the missing Roscoe birds from last year. We'll have to hope the birds can get slightly further along in their nesting without being disturbed, and then we can try to net them.

I get on the highway and head east to Kearney. Interstate 80 parallels the Platte River all the way, and I see swallow colonies on almost all the bridges and overpasses. Cliff swallows are common in western Nebraska to about Kearney but become progressively scarcer east of there. Some large colonies can be found in the eastern half of the state—there's a large one on the Platte River bridge between Lincoln and Omaha—but for unknown reasons the colonies are more widely spaced and less predictably used as one goes farther east. This trend continues into Iowa and Illinois, where the cliff swallow is relatively uncommon. You'd think the climate and food would be perfect for large numbers to live in eastern Nebraska, Iowa, and places farther east. So why don't they? No one knows.

I find Mary and Dave at the Wendy's restaurant in Kearney. We transfer Mary's gear and bicycle to the *Valdez* and start the drive back to Cedar Point. Mary is relaxed and refreshed from her week of bicycling. This time off energizes her for the rest of the summer, the hardest part, that lies ahead. She regales me with "war" stories from the week just past, especially the hard day going into Ponca in the cold wind and rain. Weather that lousy now seems only a distant memory, because today is sunny and warm, a more typical early summer day in southwestern Nebraska.

We reach CR 4½ in midafternoon. Mary drops me off and continues to Cedar Point to unload. The assistants are doing well, though when I arrive they have some spectators—several old ladies out for a drive along the canal—who are starting to become a nuisance. I act brusque, and a few minutes after I arrive the women leave. Judy, Annie, and Kathy caught ninety-four swallows at Barn Owl this morning with no problems; Annie thinks that colony may have declined in size since she was last there. The total catch at CR 4½ this afternoon is almost two hundred birds. Kathy seems to be feeling better and isn't achy anymore, so I quit worrying about hantaviruses.

The assistants, on their own, managed to catch close to our sought-after average of three hundred birds today. They're now capable netters, and with Mary back, we're at full strength again. The weather is forecast to be good for the coming week. The stretch run is starting.

7

Moving Eggs

*A husband and wife team of naturalists ... have been five
years near Ogallala, Nebraska, observing cliff swallows
... slipping eggs from their own nests into neighboring
nests. If they spread their eggs around it ensures that
some of the family will survive. Their instinct may dwarf
human wisdom.*
— Paul Harvey, *News and Comment*, KOGA
radio, January 19, 1988

June 12

I've been stewing for a week over our failure to catch birds at
Diversion Dam on that day with perfect weather. Today I plan to
try again.

Knowing what birds live there is especially critical this year, because Bluffs, Mule Deer, and Diversion Dam are the only small colonies accessible to us for netting. Small colonies are always unpredictable: some years we have many and other years very few. I've
always been fascinated by small cliff swallow colonies and by why
some birds want to live in them. Perhaps our netting will eventually
reveal what characteristics define a "small colony" cliff swallow.

Annie and I tote our gear across the dam to the river gates out in the
middle. By the time we get our buckets filled and the drop net set up,
the wind has increased, and the net keeps trying to blow over. Other
than the wind, the day is beautiful, with the bright blue water
reflecting the puffy white clouds scattered across the sunny sky.

Below the dam in the North Platte River to the east I see about
fifteen white pelicans cruising in a V-shaped flotilla. They're fishing
cooperatively; by moving along in a coordinated front, they flush fish
ahead of them, often into the waiting bill of another group member.
I'm impressed by so much apparent teamwork among individuals

that probably aren't related. Someone should study white pelicans, not just because they feed cooperatively but because they're colonial. Like cliff swallows, I bet they do many interesting things in their breeding colonies.

We catch only one swallow on the first drop across the west side of the river gates, but I'm encouraged when we catch eight on the next try. We've already tripled the catch Kathy and I got here the other day. Our luck doesn't last, however. Soon the swallows are back to their evasive tactic of flying out the narrow slit on the east side whenever we drop the net on the west side. Besides that, they're cranky and swirl overhead, alarm-calling at us.

As we sit and wait for the birds to calm down and return to their nests, Annie asks about the great storm that trapped me on the diversion dam several years ago. She's heard it mentioned often—it's legendary at Cedar Point—but hasn't heard the complete story. It's been on my mind too since we arrived this morning, as it is every time we come here. I think about it not because I'm afraid of a storm today, but because I was nearly killed at this site. All we can do is wait for the swallows to quit crabbing at us, so I tell Annie the story.

The summer of 1992 was Bruce's first year to collect field data for his study of swallow bug population genetics. His goal was to determine how often cliff swallows carried bugs between colonies, and knowing this required sampling the ectoparasites on adult birds. But unlike baby swallows, which are naked so that their parasites are easily seen, adults are covered with feathers that hide them. To overcome this problem, Bruce had to use a collecting jar to kill the parasites on the adult birds.

A collecting jar is simply a wide-mouthed jar with part of its plastic lid replaced by a piece of flexible rubber with a small hole cut in the center. The adult swallow's head is inserted through the hole in the lid, and with the bird's body suspended inside the jar, the lid is screwed on, creating an airtight seal. We put a few drops of ether on filter paper at the bottom of the jar, and the fumes kill any parasites in the birds' feathers. Since its head is outside the jar, the bird isn't affected. We leave each bird in the jar for twenty minutes, long enough for all the parasites to die and fall off. Other than glaring at us and looking like martyrs, the swallows suffer no ill effects. We did over five thousand birds without a single fatality or injury. Many fumigated birds were back in the net within an hour.

Mary and I had designed this jar method and used it on cliff swallows in earlier years, so we had some existing data. But doing this to many birds is laborious, and we had data for only about three thousand birds scattered over a five-year period. Bruce's genetics models required a thorough parasite sample from several thousand birds in a single season if he was to estimate bug immigration among colonies. The only way he could get such numbers would be to devote a full season to nothing but fumigating adult birds.

One challenge we faced was shading the birds while they were in the jars. When it was sunny, the black rubber top of the jar next to the bird's head would heat up. We first tried to stick the jars under our chairs or in the shade of the truck, but eventually Bruce constructed a wooden frame three feet square with holes cut in its bottom. He placed the jars in the holes to hold them and then, using plastic piping and a blue tarp, rigged a sunshade over the frame. "The contraption," as we called it, must have weighed forty pounds, and we had to haul it wherever we went to net.

The afternoon of June 16, we decided to net the Diversion Dam colony. Bruce needed data from cliff swallows living in small colonies, so he came with me. The rest of the crew split up to go elsewhere: Mary and Laura to Keystone and Winnie and Veronica to CR 4. Mary took the *Valdez* and dropped Winnie and Veronica off. Bruce and I took the blue truck and parked on the canal road opposite the south end of the diversion dam. The lot nearer the dam where we usually park was closed that day because of construction, meaning we had a longer walk than usual out to the river gates.

The weather had been unsettled that entire spring; only three weeks earlier we had endured the record-setting cold and snow that killed cliff swallows. Thunderstorms had been frequent. Two days before, while I was retrieving Mary from her bike ride, Bruce and the assistants had gone out to net only to see a funnel cloud forming directly above them. That close call had made Bruce a little nervous about stormy weather. The afternoon of the sixteenth began sunny and pleasant, with little wind. Thunderheads were developing around us, but the day looked like countless others during a Nebraska summer.

We toted our gear, including the god-awfully heavy contraption, out to the middle of the diversion dam and set up in the very spot where Annie and I now sit. Unlike today's birds, the residents that year were cooperative. Netting was easy. They didn't go out the slit on the east side, and we caught them by just dropping our net over the west end where everybody flushed out. We started catching birds, jarring each one we got. By midafternoon we had caught over thirty. Bruce had erected the contraption's sunshade, and it sat there like a big blue tent.

About 3:30 I noticed a thunderhead building to the southwest. I wasn't concerned, though, because years of experience out here had taught me (I thought) to accurately judge the distance and movement of these prairie storms. Bruce kept asking what I thought, but I assured him we had time for at least one more drop. I badly miscalculated for two reasons: the high bluffs rising above Cedar Point to the south and the massive Kingsley Dam two miles to the west obscured my view of the bottom part of this storm, and it was moving unusually fast.

We did another drop, catching six birds. As soon as we pulled the net up, I glanced at the southwestern sky again and noticed that in only two minutes it had turned dark and menacing. We stuck the net poles in the buckets, and I started to work feverishly at getting the birds out of the net. I knew by then I'd misjudged this mother and it was bearing down on us. I shouted to Bruce that he'd better release the four birds still in the jars. Their time wasn't up yet, but that no longer seemed important. I just kept praying that the wind would hold off and not blow the net over before I got the birds out.

As I extracted the third bird, I looked across Keystone Lake and saw the edge of the storm. For a few seconds I stood there with not a breeze blowing around us and watched huge waves suddenly form on the lake surface, several feet high and rolling straight at us. The sky to the west over Kingsley Dam was an eerie green. I could *see* the wind coming before it hit us, rather like when you stub your toe and wait for the pain to register in your brain a half-second later.

The wind smacked into us ferociously. The net went down, the lawn chairs were flung across the diversion dam and down the leeward side, jars went everywhere. But the gravity of the situation hit me when I saw the contraption lifted off the ground and thrown down the opposite side of the dam as if it were made of cardboard. Bruce shouted that we should run for it, but my concern was the three birds still in the net. The net was lying in the grass, the birds badly tangled but not hurt. I knew I had to extract them immediately, and I grabbed the Swiss army knife from my pocket. Using its scissors, I quickly cut the birds out of the net and put them with the other three birds in the holding bag tucked under my belt. For their safety I didn't want to release them in that wind.

I'd been kneeling to cut the birds out, with my back to the wind. As I turned around, my heart was in my throat at the sight of the lake. Waves were crashing against the dam in front of us, the spray drenching us. The surface was white with waves. The top of the diversion dam is only about ten feet higher than the lake in normal times, and the water was churning so violently that right then we were only a couple of feet above it. I'd never experienced wind like that, and I fully expected to see a funnel cloud bearing down on us. I grabbed the clipboard and was amazed that our data sheets hadn't been ripped off it. I stuck the clipboard in a knapsack and clutched it. Bruce and I could hardly hear each other in the roar of the wind and waves. One of us—I don't remember who—suggested we hunker down on the leeward side of the dam. We made our way down the east side to take refuge along a concrete retaining wall adjacent to the river gates' release point. So much spray was coming over the dam that we were soaked.

After a few minutes Bruce said again he wanted to make a run for it. But I could see his jars scattered all over the lee side of the dam and yelled back that he'd better retrieve them or his data would be down the drain, since we had no replacement jars. I think he was more concerned about his own survival than about the jars, but he quickly gathered them up. To my surprise the cardboard box we used to carry them was still there, and Bruce stuffed the jars into it. The wind was so bad that I was being blown over unless I crouched. I had no interest in trying to walk across the top of the dam to get to the truck, yet we didn't know how much worse it might get. Bruce finally said he was going to make a run for it and took off across the top of the dam toward the truck, carrying his box of jars.

I waited another minute and thought the wind might be slackening. I climbed back up to the top of the dam and saw the tops of the waves crashing less than a foot from me. For all I knew, the dam might have been about to wash away. One half of the diversion dam is lower than the other half by a foot or two, designed (we'd been told) so that in a flood the lake would flow over the low half and spare the other half. We were on the low half, and I started to imagine that a storm like this was what the power company had in mind. I grabbed the little army shovel we use to fill our net pole buckets, though I don't know why I wanted it. Clutching it and the knapsack with the data, and carrying the six cliff swallows still in the holding bag attached to my waist, I started across the dam after Bruce. I couldn't see him. Either he wasn't visible in the spray coming over the dam or something had happened to him.

I got only a few yards before I felt myself being lifted off the ground. I had no control of my movement, and I was absolutely terrified. I really thought I was going to die. As I felt myself being blown off the top of the dam, I crawled down the leeward side again. I remember telling myself not to hyperventilate or have a heart attack! I was stabilized as long as I crouched there, and I remember thinking I should try to dig a foxhole in the side of the earthen dam with the army shovel.

I hunkered there for what seemed like an hour but was probably only a few minutes. Finally the wind lessened, and I was able to make it to the truck. After I got back to the canal road and thought I was safe, a large branch from a cottonwood tree crashed down only a few feet behind me. The road was littered with limbs. I was relieved to see that Bruce had made it to the truck, but I had the keys, and he had just been standing there with the limbs falling all around him.

We sat in the truck watching the storm, both of us badly shaken. Our equipment was lying out on the dam, but we had saved the irreplaceable things: our data, the jars, and the six birds. The poor swallows were as soaked as we were but still energetic and wiggling in the bag. As the wind continued to diminish, we soon saw cliff swallows flying. The waves were dangerously close to the nests at IS 2, but the birds were out enjoying the storm, zooming past in the wind at speeds they never attain normally. I bet they were just having fun.

As I regained my wits, I began to worry about Mary and the assistants. I didn't have to fret for long, because soon I saw them approaching in the *Valdez*. Mary said later that Bruce and I looked as white as ghosts. I don't doubt it.

They'd been caught in the wind too. Shortly before the storm struck, a man working for the rural telephone company had seen Winnie and Veronica at CR 4 and told them the cows were bunching together, meaning we had a bad storm coming. He frightened them enough that they started shutting down, then he went to warn Mary and Laura, who were only a half mile down the road at the Keystone bridge. By then the sky was getting bad; it must have been about the time Bruce and I did our last drop. While Mary and Laura packed up, the telephone man went back to CR 4, picked up Winnie and

Veronica, and brought them to Mary. Winnie said she'd been taught never to accept rides from strangers, but that rule didn't apply with a Nebraska windstorm bearing down.

The four of them got into the *Valdez*, but the wind was so bad Mary didn't dare drive down the canal road into the storm for fear the truck would be blown into the canal. Instead they headed away from the storm to the tiny town of Keystone, just a mile away. Keystone consists of only a few buildings and house trailers, but Mary thought they could find refuge there. They parked along the east side of the bank, the only brick building in town, which partly blocked the west wind. They wanted to go into the bank, but the wind was so strong they couldn't get the truck doors open! They didn't stay there long, because the wires to an electrical transformer on a nearby pole were pitching so violently that sparks were flying, and a tree's limbs were being blown into the sparks, close to being set on fire. It looked as if the wires were about to come down—and they would have fallen across the road, blocking the only exit.

I gave Mary our soaked birds and asked her to take them back to the lab at Cedar Point, only a mile away, to get them dried off and processed. Bruce and I hoped to retrieve our gear, but the wind stayed so strong that we too headed back to the lab and didn't get the equipment until several hours later. Our net was ruined, but we found everything else intact, scattered all over the east side of the diversion dam. Mary had lost only one band and a little cloth bag used for weighing the birds.

We later learned that winds of ninety-eight miles an hour were recorded in Ogallala during this storm. We were in winds at least that strong. Cedar Point didn't escape unscathed. A gigantic cottonwood maybe a hundred years old was split by the wind, and half of it fell onto the Mouse House, where we and our assistants lived, and poked a hole in the roof. That day ended with Bruce and Doug up on the rooftop with a chain saw trying to cut the broken tree free from the house.

After telling Annie the story, I shudder once again at that close call. There's comparatively little wind right now, but our net is trying its best to blow over. The top of the diversion dam is just about the windiest place in Keith County, and with the possible exception of the top of Kingsley Dam, we couldn't have been in a worse place to experience hundred mile an hour winds. The weather is so gorgeous today that I'm sure Annie has trouble picturing how violent that storm really was. But Bruce and I will never forget it.

Our morning here is turning into another bust, so we must try a new method. It's possible to lower a net into the slit on the east side of the gates. The space is only about a foot wide, so we can't flip the net over in the usual way. Instead, we have to turn it upside down and hold the poles by the ends where the net loops are attached. Positioning the net over the slit, and stretching it as tight as possible between us to keep it from snagging on the metal catwalks that border the slit, we lower it straight down by leapfrogging our hands up the poles. When we reach the end of the poles our net is in place, and we loosen the tension to give the net some loose mesh to entangle birds. This method can work only if wind doesn't snag the net as we lower it through the narrow opening. I've never tried it on a day this windy, but except for a couple of miscues we eventually get it lowered.

Usually a net in the slit on the east side is highly effective. These birds are crafty, though, and again we come up dry. They see the net and turn and fly out the open west side. We lower the net twice and get only one swallow.

I've become obsessed with getting these little butt-heads, and I refuse to admit defeat. I want to try something else, so I leave Annie with the net and walk back across the dam to CR 1 where Mary, Judy, and Kathy are netting. The increasing wind is also causing problems there, and the CR 1 birds are not being cooperative. I ask Kathy to grab a lawn chair and come to Diversion Dam with me. The idea is for Annie and me to lower the net through the slit while Kathy simultaneously reaches over the west side and waves a chair back and forth. Perhaps this will keep the birds from coming out the west side and startle them into the net. We try this several times and still don't have much luck. We get a couple of birds, but generally they seem unimpressed with the moving chair, and most fly out that way despite Kathy's efforts.

I conclude that we need two nets here, one on each side. Again I walk back across the dam to CR 1. I ask Mary and Judy to shut down and bring their net and buckets over to Diversion Dam. Mary is reluctant to leave because they just got a good drop, and their catch is now up to seventy-four birds. But we need to know if there's any way to get the Diversion Dam birds, and two nets is the only method left to try. I'm frustrated and in a bit of a lather, so Mary tells me to calm down—they'll be there as soon as they can.

It's nearly 11:00 by the time Mary and Judy arrive with their net. We wait for the birds to settle down. I want a bunch of them in the nests when we first try the double nets. After most of the colony returns, we quickly creep out onto the structure, and Annie and I lower a net in the slit while Mary and Kathy fling the other one over the west side. We get six birds the first time, three in each net.

Two nets is definitely the method of choice here. The assistants and I start a series of double-net drops while Mary does the processing. By lunchtime we've caught a total of forty-two birds, over half of them in the last thirty minutes of using two nets. This is more than half the colony, and I'm satisfied at last. We need to come back here and use the double-net method again, perhaps some evening after supper. It needs to be done soon, though, because I saw some birds flying around carrying insects in their mouths—big moths, probably corn borers or millers. Diversion Dam must be among the first colonies to have hatched young.

After lunch, I take Annie and Kathy to CR 6. Our colony numbering scheme mostly reflects the order in which we discovered sites in years past and doesn't indicate relative positions along the canal: CR 6 is a distant site, fourteen and a half miles from Cedar Point and the next to last colony along the canal before reaching Paxton. We don't visit the site often, usually once or twice a year to look for dispersing birds. But this year it's large, the biggest it's ever been, and I'm hopeful we can catch a lot of birds there.

We drive down the canal, seeing birds still at the wooden bridge and nothing at Aqueduct. I notice there's a small colony at CR 7—a bridge that in some years contains hundreds of nests—and a big colony at a site called Pigpen. Farther down the canal we pass an enormous cattle feedlot to the south of the canal, and the stench is overpowering. When the wind's out of the south, as it is today, you can get nauseated just driving past. I point out a bridge over the canal that leads to the feedlot and tell Annie and Kathy that swallows sometimes nest on it. They can't believe I'd try to net there with this odor, but I assure them we've done it in the past and will do it this year should any birds move in. They roll their eyes and express their fervent hope that the cliff swallows stay away from it this summer. I have to admit to myself I sort of hope the same thing.

CR 6 is beyond range of the feedlot odor, and I see that the colony is still large. This is a bridge like CR 4½, installed by the power company to connect the local landowner's pastures that are divided by the canal. This section of the canal is deserted, and no fishers ever bother us here. But the unfortunate consequence is that these swallows aren't used to people and are wary. As at Prairie Dog, they're unwilling study animals.

I've never had great success at CR 6, and it's soon obvious that today will be no exception. We start a series of drops, but everybody flushes out before we can get onto the bridge. A typical drop is three or four birds. We spend a lot of time waiting for them to calm down and stop alarm-calling. Time starts to drag. The afternoon sun is hot, and we have no shade. Kathy crawls under the truck—the only shady spot—and lies there reading poems by Henry Wadsworth Longfellow.

As we're doing a drop, suddenly I hear Annie let loose with an expletive. My immediate thought is that she's dropped her pole, but I see the net still hanging normally. As she was bending over the railing of the bridge, her sunglasses fell off and dropped into the canal. We get the net back up and moved to the processing area. Distraught, Annie wants to try to wade into the canal to find the sunglasses, but I tell her it must be at least ten feet deep, with a nasty current. It turns out the sunglasses were Kathy's, which she had traded to Annie because they were the only ones Annie had ever found that fit her. I think to myself they must not have fit too well to have fallen off when she bent over.

The loss of the glasses mars Annie's afternoon, and the birds' lack of cooperation mars mine. After a while we're barely getting one or two birds per drop. I resolve to try to catch as many as we can, because it's clear we won't be coming back. By quitting time we have sixty-eight birds, pitiful considering the five hundred or so active nests here. Eight were previously banded, almost certainly from other colonies. These eight recaptures made the trip to CR 6 worthwhile, although in looking at the data sheets tonight I'll notice that Kathy erred in writing down the band number on one of the eight banded birds. There are too many digits, and it's impossible to tell what the real number is. Make that *seven* recaptures at CR 6.

We drive past Aqueduct again on the way back to Cedar Point. Initially I see nothing, but as we're about to drive away I notice a swallow fly up to a nest and go inside. I should check this out. Walking up to the bridge, I see birds come out of nine nests. I can identify the active ones because they've been repaired and refurbished with new mud. These are scattered among dozens of old, unused nests in various stages of disrepair. Perhaps we should call this the "ghost town effect," in which a few birds can hide their nests from predators (and biologists) among deserted ones that are falling apart. Surprisingly, the nine active nests are on the west end, not far from where the great horned owl sits. I wonder if the owl is still around.

We leave, knowing Aqueduct is active but a very small colony. This is unusual, given that the smallest it's ever been in our experience is 150 nests, and some years it's exceeded 600. We'll have to bring our big nets down here and try to catch these eighteen birds. It's important to learn who they are, and the decline in colony size is theoretically interesting, but I had more grandiose hopes for Aqueduct this summer.

After supper Mary and I take our evening walk along the shore of Keystone Lake. We go across the diversion dam and over to the beaver marsh on the far side. The swallows on the dam seem to have forgotten about us from this morning as they flit in and out of their nests, busily feeding their babies. A family of Canada geese—mom, dad, and six goslings—has taken up residence on the diversion dam. They stand on the top or graze on the grassy sides. Whenever a human approaches, mom and dad herd the babies down to the lake's edge. To avoid disturbing them, we sometimes turn around and go back when we see them ahead of us. Tonight, however, they see us first, and the family has already moved down to the water's edge when we spot them. They effortlessly ease into the water and nonchalantly steam away into the sunset. Their stately black silhouettes stand out against the brilliant orange reflection of the setting sun on the still waters of Keystone Lake.

As we return to Cedar Point, we smell the strong odor of a grass fire. This is reason for concern. The tops of the bluffs above Cedar Point are brushy pastureland, and a fire could come roaring down the canyons and be on us before we knew what hit us. It seems too wet for much fire danger, but the odor is unmistakable. The nearest "fire station" is a single truck on the north side of Lake McConaughy staffed by volunteer firemen, many of whom live miles away. Needless to say, should a fire start, we'd be on our own.

No one seems to be trying to locate the source of the odor, so I walk up the canyon directly behind the lodge. The student cabins are nestled along the sides of the hills. Despite the strong odor, none of the students seem concerned; the cabins look mostly empty, though I hear laughter coming from one. I see no evidence of a fire anywhere in the canyon. Meanwhile Mary has encountered Joan, whose job is partly to worry about fires at the station. Joan is concerned, but she's been walking all over the place and can't find the source of the smell either. The three of us stroll back to the apartments, where Diana, the plant ecologist, assures us it's much too wet for a grass fire. We all tend to agree, but Joan announces she's going to scout the land south of Cedar Point from the highway that leads into town. She heads off to her car.

We never do find where the odor came from. Joan drove a five-by-five-mile square around the pastures south of the field station, and the smell was even stronger to the south. The fire must have been south of Ogallala somewhere and its odor was carried to Cedar Point by the wind.

When all else fails during a swallow summer, blame the wind.

June 13

Today's schedule calls for Kathy and me to go to Spillway. We've only netted there once this summer, that inaugural day when Kathy went out for the first time. We hadn't returned, because Spillway underwent a major reduction in size soon afterward. Hundreds of active nests are still on the high crane housing, but many of the birds that had settled in the nests on the retaining wall where we net disappeared. When we arrive today, I verify that there are only a handful of active nests in two widely separated clusters along the wall.

This illustrates that capture data must be interpreted cautiously: we began netting here before most of the swallows had chosen where to nest, and many of them moved elsewhere. A single capture of a bird at a colony site may not tell us much. This is especially true early in the season while birds are still selecting colonies and later in the summer when postbreeders start visiting colony sites. We really need at least two captures of the same bird at the same site before we can have any confidence that it actually lived there. Today we will see if any of the swallows we caught at Spillway in mid-May have remained.

We can see the birds going in and out of their nests above us on the crane housing. As Kathy watches, she asks about egg transfers. She's been making progress reading the book manuscript, and recently she read the section on brood parasitism. She wonders how often we've seen the birds move an egg. Egg transfer is relatively rare, I reply, and we've seen it happen only three times in fourteen years. But that's not to say brood parasitism in general is infrequent, because it's rather common in cliff swallows.

As soon as a swallow arrives at a colony and establishes ownership of an existing nest or is almost finished building a new one, it becomes intensely interested in its neighbors and their nests. Some birds—males and females alike—seem to get hot pants and can't stay put in their own nests. They constantly try to enter their neighbors' bungalows. Usually a neighboring nest owner is home, sitting in the nest entrance, and repels the attempted trespass. A simple lunge is enough to make the intruder fly back home or to somebody else's nest. The amount of time many cliff swallows spend trying to get into their neighbors' nests is remarkable, with birds almost constantly flying from their own nest to one nearby, then back home, then over to another one.

On the occasional sortie when an intruder finds a nest unattended, these little birds do rotten things to each other. Some trespassers will steal wet mud from a nest, carrying it back to put on their own nests. Others will pilfer grass stems that a neighbor had used to line its nest. I watched one bird completely clean out his neighbor's nest one afternoon, making at least ten trips and taking every stalk of grass. Sometimes the consequences of leaving a nest unattended can be dire: some trespassers will toss out an egg. Other times a male intruder may try to copulate with a female neighbor if her mate is away. Mary likens trespassing to waiting for your next-door neighbor to come home with a load of groceries, and while her door is left open as she gets the food out of the car, you run in and steal her bedsheets or throw her infant out the window.

Brood parasitism happens when a female trespasses into a neighboring nest and finds it unguarded. A female can lay one of her eggs there in less than a minute. She then returns home, leaving her egg completely in the care of its foster parents. Even when a female enters a nearby nest and doesn't lay an egg there, she may still be assessing the nest's suitability as a foster home. One of our more interesting discoveries about brood parasitism is that parasitic females can judge which of the nests around theirs are most likely to later fledge young. By putting their parasitic eggs in those nests, they can be more certain that their foisted-off young will survive. The parasitic birds do this in part by figuring out which nearby nests have the fewest ectoparasites, since it's almost axiomatic that nests with fewer swallow bugs are more likely to be successful.

We knew brood parasitism occurred in cliff swallows as early as the first year of our study, when we started seeing two or more eggs appearing in a nest in a single day. A female bird is physiologically incapable of producing more than one egg in twenty-four hours, so multiple eggs laid in a day meant multiple females had to be involved. We later verified parasitic laying by watching female trespassers do it.

But laying an egg is not the only way cliff swallows parasitize their neighbors' nests. After the 1984 field season, we were analyzing the data we had obtained from checking the contents of nests. We noticed several instances where an egg appeared in a nest quite some time after the other eggs there had been laid. We had been considering these cases of parasitic laying where the female happened to mistime it and laid her egg after the host had laid hers. But the later eggs hatched at the same time as the hosts'. Sometimes an egg that appeared in a nest hatched with the others only five days later. Cliff swallow eggs require a sixteen-day incubation period. What was going on?

The only explanation was that these eggs had been incubated somewhere else for a while and then physically *moved* into the nest where they hatched. We concluded that the cliff swallows must be transferring eggs between nests. A few bird species—primarily woodpeckers—had been reported to move their eggs, usually when one nest was damaged and the birds had an alternative nest to put their eggs in. These reports were rare and not well documented, however, and no birds were known to move eggs often. Our data, on the other hand, suggested that in some colonies cliff swallows might be doing this regularly.

We began the next season with the objective of demonstrating convincingly that cliff swallows move eggs. At two colonies we numbered the eggs as they were laid. To do this we had to cut a small hole in the side of a nest, carefully remove the eggs, and write the nest's number on the outside of each egg with a magic marker. We replaced the eggs and plugged the hole with wet mud, using the concretelike ooze from Mule Deer. Each day we checked all the nests in the colony, looking for numbered eggs that showed up in the wrong nest.

It didn't take long to find a transfer. Two days after marking, an egg from nest 6 at Clary appeared two doors down, in nest 8. Although I was certain from our indirect data that egg transfer happened in cliff swallows, the discovery of the numbered egg in a different nest was among the most thrilling moments of any swallow summer. Later we found that a numbered egg had been moved at Mule Deer.

This was exciting stuff, and the next year I received a grant to study brood parasitism in cliff swallows. One of the peer reviews of that grant proposal was the most memorable I've ever seen. The reviewer asked how Brown knew his assistants weren't slipping out in the middle of the night and moving the eggs themselves! Why they would want to do this wasn't clear, and the reviewer didn't suggest a motive. This reviewer obviously had never been in the long tunnel at Mule Deer with its dead things or waded in the liquid cow crap at Clary, and he or she certainly didn't know how our assistants loathe these places. Mule Deer at night is no place a sane person would ever want to be.

Part of the plan in our research grant was to do an intensive dawn-to-dusk watch of nests to identify parasitic females. I hoped we'd *see* birds moving eggs. Whitetail was of course my choice as the colony to watch. The incidence of brood parasitism increases in larger colonies, and by then Whitetail had grown to a point where brood parasitism was frequent among its residents. For three weeks during the egg laying period, Mary and I spent every day closely watching sections of the colony. We had caught many of the birds and painted their white forehead patches with distinctive color combinations so we could identify individuals and determine which birds owned which nests. Each bird got a unique two- or three-color stripe down its forehead patch, a perfect way to mark birds whose head is all that's usually visible when they're sitting in their nest.

We came to know the personalities of many of the marked birds in the nests we watched. Mary was shocked at what a little criminal OPW (orange-pink-white) was. He constantly intruded into his neighbors' nests, and at least twice he threw out some of their eggs. He stole nesting material and mud and forcibly copulated with neighboring females. In contrast, YO (yellow-orange) was the quintessential victim. Totally clueless, he left his nest unattended, his eggs were thrown out, and he and his mate were parasitized by several neighboring females. We doubt they raised any of their own young, instead having a nest full of parasitic eggs. OPW and YO represented the extremes, with most birds—such as Mary's favorite BSB (blue-silver-blue)—somewhere in between. Joe Average Cliff Swallow isn't averse to doing rotten things to others but generally holds its rude behavior in check, if only to keep its own nest guarded.

We discovered, perhaps not surprisingly, that the more often a bird left its own nest to do things to others, the more often things got done to its unattended nest. The cliff swallow's Golden Rule is that you will get done unto as you do unto others, but you should still try to get away with whatever you can without getting caught. Trespassing and its outcomes represent a balance between exploiting your neighbor and keeping that neighbor from returning the favor.

What really struck us in watching these birds closely was how competitive and cutthroat cliff swallow society can be. Trespassing is the avian equivalent of crime, and it's rampant. The parallels with human society are hard to ignore. Swallow crime usually happened when the perpetrator was desperate and had few other options to achieve high reproductive success; the weak (like simpleminded YO) were often the victims; and crime was more frequent in the larger colonies (big cities) than in the smaller ones (rural communities). As scientists, we're not supposed to anthropomorphize our observations and conclusions, but the swallows are so much like us when interacting with others of their group that we're hard pressed not to ascribe human attributes to them. A bird can steal from its neighbor, then go back to its own nest and look oh so innocent.

After the first year of intensive watching, we had seen several cases of parasitic laying by our marked birds, and one female had thrown an egg out of a nest at the same time she parasitized it. This established a possible link between brood parasitism and throwing eggs out of neighboring nests. But we had still seen no egg transfers. I was not very optimistic that we'd have better luck the next summer, but as usual the birds proved me wrong. On May 16, 1987, at about 2:00 P.M., I saw WKW (white-black-white) emerge from her nest with an intact egg in her beak. Barely hesitating, she flew to an unattended nest twenty-two doors down (about four feet away), popped into it, and within a few seconds was back out sans egg. The sought-after egg transfer had at last been seen.

We later calculated the frequency of egg transfers using nest-check data from almost five thousand nests. From that we estimated that about 6 percent of nests have eggs moved into them. This is a remarkably high frequency considering that egg transfer is virtually unknown in other bird species. Moving eggs is risky: you might drop your egg or get in a fight with a neighbor that's guarding its nest. For this reason, cliff swallows probably move eggs only when they're sure a neighbor is gone.

Perhaps the major advantage of egg transfer is that it expands the window of time when you can parasitize nests. If you do it by laying an egg, it has to be while the host is laying her eggs so that the parasitic egg hatches slightly before or at the same time as the host's own eggs (not after). If your parasitic egg hatches late, the young bird will be smaller than the host's nestlings and at a disadvantage in competing for food. When laying parasitic eggs, you have about four or five days—while the host herself is laying—to do your dirty deed. But if you move an egg, you have the entire time the host is incubating (sixteen days or so) during which you can wait and watch for the split-second opportunity when a host nest is left unguarded, incubating your soon-to-be parasitic eggs yourself in the meantime. And theoretically anyway, males can also parasitize nests by moving eggs, although no case of a male's carrying an egg has been seen.

Why do cliff swallows parasitize nests? This question has been debated at length by us and other scientists, and we're still not sure. Some bird species parasitize others to avoid having to do any parental care. This is the case with interspecific parasites like European cuckoos and the brown-headed cowbirds of North America. They make no nests and lay all their eggs in the nests of other species. But parasitic cliff swallows have nests of their own. All the birds we saw parasitizing nests were residents of the colony, and they raised young themselves. They have normal-sized families in their own nests, so they're not avoiding parental care. Instead, it looks like they're simply supplementing their reproductive output. Add an egg or two to other nests in the colony, and you leave more total descendants.

But the real story probably isn't this simple. Birds pay a cost to be parasites. We found that birds that parasitize others are often parasitized themselves because they leave their own nests unattended more often as they seek to get into other nests. Get done unto as you do unto. They raise other birds' offspring in their nests, just like any other host. Consequently the parasites may not actually produce more offspring of their own than birds that are not parasites but that also aren't parasitized. The difference is that the parasites' eggs are spread among several nests.

One reason cliff swallows parasitize nests could be to put their eggs in more than one basket. Put all your eggs in one nest, and you could end up with zero reproductive success if something happens to that nest. On cliff nesting sites, overhangs often crumble and fall off, destroying nests. Bull snakes get into colonies and will eat the eggs in several nests. If these events were frequent enough in the birds' past, perhaps they evolved the habit of spreading their eggs among nests to insure themselves against total reproductive failure. Unpredictable falling of overhangs doesn't occur on the bridges and culverts the birds now often occupy, but the behavior is still present.

As I watch the birds at their nests on the crane housing, I'm reminded of how much fun it is to watch activity at nests. Doing the brood parasitism observations was more entertaining and satisfying in the short term than the netting we do now. As we were watching the birds, we generally knew what we were seeing and what it meant. In contrast, we often cannot conclude anything from our mark-recapture data until several years later after we've "followed" the same birds for additional seasons. Even better, watching swallows at their nests gave me an excuse to go to Whitetail every day! But we took the brood parasitism study about as far as it would go, and except for the DNA fingerprinting analyses of parentage, there's not much more we can do with it. Obviously, when you see an event like egg transfer only three times in hundreds of hours of watching, it can't yield numerous articles in journals or a series of research grants. Those are the criteria by which a scientist is judged nowadays, so events that occur rarely—no matter their importance—are not ones most of us can afford to study.

We do another drop and process our standard Spillway quota of two birds. I glance up at the crane housing again, and my attention is suddenly drawn to one bird. It's hovering in front of a nest with a white object in its bill. I stare at it in disbelief.

"My God, Kathy, that bird has an egg!"

"Where?"

"Along the lower horizontal tier of nests, to the left. See it?"

"Wow, is that really an egg?"

"You bet it is. It's trying to get in that nest."

We watch as the bird hovers for a few more seconds. It seems to be having trouble flying, perhaps not surprising when a bird is trying to hold an object as large as an egg in its open mouth without breaking it. Another bird is in the nest it's trying to enter. Soon it flies a few nests' distance to the right, goes into a nest with its egg, and vanishes. We keep watching for a minute or two, but it doesn't show. When another swallow enters that nest a short while later, the one inside exits normally and flies away. It carries no egg.

What did we just see? Kathy asks. Of course I can't be sure, because the birds weren't color-marked and we don't know who owns what nest. But my guess is that this bird tried an egg transfer. The transferrer had probably scoped out a nearby nest that was unguarded, only to find that the neighbor had come back in the time it took the would-be parasite to go home and grab its egg. When it got to the selected nest with its egg, it found the unwilling transferee guarding its nest. Momentarily bewildered, the transferrer hovered there briefly, then went back to its own nest with the egg. When its mate came home, it had already returned the egg to its rightful place, and it went off to feed, leaving its mate to guard their nest against neighbors that might try what it just did.

This is an exciting observation, not only because it's only the fourth time we've ever seen an egg transfer, but also because it suggests that sometimes birds try transfers and are unsuccessful. You'd expect this, yet until now we had no evidence for it. What an incredible coincidence was Kathy's asking about egg transfers and our seeing one only five minutes later! We were simply at the right place, and I glanced up at the right time. This is why fieldwork is so exhilarating.

We end the morning with a total catch of fifty-eight birds at Spillway. As I had guessed, most of the earlier settlers went elsewhere: only four of today's birds were also caught on our visit in May. I know that at least one bird from Spillway was caught at Barn Owl a week or so ago, but I'm not aware of others' turning up at other colonies so far. Perhaps the Spillway birds went over to the nearby—and for us, inaccessible—colony at Morning Glory.

It's been warming up steadily the last couple of days, and the temperature is supposed to reach the mid-nineties this afternoon. We have to be careful in heat like this, since birds exposed to direct sun can quickly overheat in a net or a holding bag. At lunchtime we decide Whitetail would be a good place to work in the heat. We can sit in the damp, shaded west tunnel, which will keep the birds in holding bags cool, and the net placed over the creek is usually cooled slightly by the water flowing under it.

I take Judy and Annie to Whitetail. The afternoon is the hottest yet this summer, but we and the birds in our holding bags stay cool inside the tunnel. I'm surprised at the huge number of birds still building nests in the culvert. The birds continue to make progress on the many new nests in the east tunnel, and others are starting nests in the middle tunnel. From end to end of the middle tunnel, nests are now stacked five and six deep in tiers. I remember seeing the big sections of bare wall where nests had fallen at the start of the season and questioning whether the colony would be a large one this year. Clearly the cliff swallows decided they wanted a big colony here and rebuilt nests in record numbers.

Although a lot of birds here are still only building nests, others have already hatched young. I watch neatly broken eggshells float by the net. When an egg hatches, it cracks in two even pieces, and the parents pick up the shells and drop them out of the nest. Here they fall into the water and are carried away by the current. I don't think many birds have young yet, because most of the adults still seem to be sitting tight in their nests. The traffic in and out of the culvert is less now than earlier when everybody was nest building and less than it will be later when most of the birds will be coming and going to feed their babies.

By midafternoon our capture rate is slowing. I decide to juice things up by doing a flush. I really should have known better, given the many birds incubating inside nests. As I stick my head around the corner of the culvert's end opposite the net, a massive rush of birds boils out. A dust cloud blows back in my face, kicked out of nests by hundreds of birds quickly exiting their adobe homes. The sound of whirring wings reverberates through the culvert. Over this racket I hear Annie exclaim, "Oh, my God!"

I run back through the west tunnel to get to the net, which is black with birds. I've never seen this many birds in a net, ever. It's a flush from hell on a day that's hot as hell. There are so many swallows caught in the net I barely can decide where to start in getting them out. Judy and Annie ask if I want them to help me extract birds, but I reply that they need to process—fast. I start taking birds out of the net as quickly as I can, filling bags and passing them on to be processed. I get the upper birds first, because the ones closer to the water will stay cooler. The assistants start working like crazy, Annie handling the birds and Judy recording and dispensing bands. By now they're fast and good, as efficient a team as I've ever had at White-tail.

Eventually we get all the birds from the flush done without any casualties. By quitting time Judy reports that we have 264 birds, and exactly 100 of them came on that one flush. This is a record I didn't intend to set on a beastly hot day like today. The same old pattern of getting mostly banded birds on the flush continued. In fact we didn't get many unbanded birds at all today. We've netted White-tail often enough to have already banded many of the residents, and new birds have stopped arriving.

Mary and Kathy netted this afternoon at CR 3, another canal bridge. Mary reports that several birds there had swallow bugs on them, which crawled off during processing. She saw several more bugs moving along the top of the bridge. That's a long way for a bug to disperse along the substrate and may mean that CR 3 is heavily infested this year. I wouldn't be surprised, because the site was active last season, and the birds appear to be occupying the same nests. The bugs surviving from last summer must be having a field day, and bug populations will certainly be large there. We should watch for a mass abandonment of CR 3, a response the birds sometimes show to a heavily infested colony.

Kathy, Annie, and Judy are excited tonight. I promised to take them to North Platte tomorrow to see their first rodeo.

June 14

Yesterday's heat is forecast to continue today. The environmental extremes of the High Plains are illustrated by my worrying only five days ago that some cliff swallows might starve to death in cold weather. Today it may be too hot to net. Taking the afternoon off to go to the rodeo is a good call in this heat. Assistants wear out quickly in hot weather. Over the years I've found that maintaining their enthusiasm is impossible when we have to work in extreme heat day after day. When it comes to outdoor work, humans seem to hold up better to being cold than hot.

The temperature is not supposed to reach the mid-nineties until the afternoon, however, so we can net this morning. Mary, Judy, and Kathy are going to CR 1 to concentrate on the sparsely populated north end of the bridge. They won't catch as many total birds, but they'll get ones we haven't had yet. Annie and I will try Pigpen for the first time this summer.

Pigpen is about thirteen miles east of Cedar Point. Like IS 1, it's a device to divert the canal down a ravine to the north should an emergency arise. It consists of a narrow bridge spanning the canal and gates in the side of the canal under the adjacent road. The opening for the gates is about as wide as a culvert entrance with no way out the back side. Drop-netting the gates under the road is like taking candy from a baby.

The first birds to arrive at Pigpen this year settled under the bridge. This is the traditional portion of the colony site that is occupied every year. Some years Pigpen is a relatively small colony, with only about a hundred nests. It's among the first settled each spring, and birds were in their usual nests under the bridge when we first drove by on May 11, over a month ago. But just recently, hundreds more birds moved into the portion under the road. This is only the second time in eleven years that the birds have used the side gates. It's a weird coincidence that the birds at Barn Owl, a similar structure eight miles to the west, also are using its side gates for only the second time.

Annie and I set up alongside the road just east of the bridge. This is an open and exposed site, much like Prairie Dog, with the canal and road we're on rising well above the adjacent river valley to the north. Just below us is a farm. With its traditional white house and weathered red barn surrounded by plowed fields, it looks like the quintessential family farm that's disappearing across much of the Midwest. When we started visiting Pigpen over a decade ago, this farm was thriving, with people always coming and going. In those days pigs were kept in a pen not far from the canal road, imparting a distinctive fragrance and giving this site its name. I think people still live in the house, but the grounds aren't kept up. I sometimes sit here between drops and daydream about life on a farm like that. It's there that the pony named Wildfire in Michael Martin Murphy's song might have lived during a cold Nebraska winter, or where John Wayne's family in *The Searchers* might have been massacred by Indians. When I'm disillusioned with academia, which happens more and more often nowadays, I wonder what living on the Pigpen farm might be like. I tell myself it would be a simple life where the major challenges are those of nature, many of them the same kinds we face during a swallow summer.

As Annie organizes our equipment, I watch the colony. There isn't much bird traffic under the bridge, meaning the residents of that section are probably incubating. In contrast, the birds in the side portion under the road are busily gathering mud. Hundreds of birds are streaming back and forth between the colony and a mudhole in the farmyard about a hundred yards to the north. I bet that most of the nests in that side section of the colony need extensive repair, being last used four years ago. The Pigpen birds are relatively tolerant of people, even though not many humans come down this stretch of the canal. They seem to accept us, at least while we're standing on the roadside, and haven't started to alarm-call.

Having two distinct waves of birds settling at a site at different times—as here at Pigpen—presents some problems in interpreting capture data. The first birds chose to live in a one-hundred-nest colony, much smaller than what eventually formed here. Now there are probably eight or nine hundred birds, and the earlier settlers are clearly part of a larger group if the issue is one of foraging or predator avoidance. Advantages in finding food and avoiding predators vary with the size of a colony, and these advantages in turn affect survivorship, which we are measuring in our mark-recapture study. In analyzing the survival of these earlier settlers to next year, therefore, is the relevant colony size the larger one they're now part of or the smaller one they initially chose? I'd probably use the larger one where they spend most of the summer, but this illustrates the ambiguities involved in interpreting field data.

It also illustrates that individuals often have no control over their colony's size. They may settle in a colony of one size only to have other birds arrive or depart, changing its size. The original settlers then are faced with the choice of leaving to find another colony that better suits their needs or staying in the "new" colony. If they're well into nesting, as these early Pigpen birds were, they probably have little choice but to stay. Fortunately, most cliff swallow colonies are settled more synchronously, and these separate waves of incoming settlers don't happen at most sites.

I decide that today we should emphasize netting the birds on the bridge over the canal because they're furthest along. There'll be other days to come back and get the birds that are still nest building in the side section. We start drop-netting over the canal and have moderate success, usually getting between four and ten birds per drop. After a while, however, the birds over the canal seem to realize they can avoid us by exiting the opposite side. It becomes the Diversion Dam all over again. We need to bring two nets to go after these suckers.

We switch to netting the side nests under the road. There are hundreds of birds in the side part of the colony, and we get at least twenty on each drop. We end with 116 birds.

I notice a striking difference in the presence of previously banded birds in the two parts of the colony. About a third of the swallows on the bridge were already banded, but virtually none of the birds under the road were. My guess is that the first birds to settle here—on the bridge—were older ones, reflected by some having been banded in previous summers. The birds that moved in later under the road are probably mostly yearlings and thus unbanded.

The heat is getting bad, and I keep telling Annie to drink water out of the jugs we bring with us. She says she's okay and doesn't drink anything, probably because she doesn't want to have to pee outside. She'll have to learn the hard way about dehydration. By the time we start back for lunch, she comments that she doesn't feel too good and sleeps for most of the drive.

We arrange to leave for the rodeo in early afternoon. It takes only an hour to get to North Platte, but I'm going to use our trip to check colonies en route. We don't net at all of them; the only data we collect on some are whether the site is used in a given summer and its size. In some years we use the rodeo trip to gather annual colony-size information, but this year the birds are so far behind their normal breeding schedule that it's too early to get any definitive data on colony size or use. I want to have a look at some sites today only as possible netting places.

Everybody convenes for our departure, and for perhaps the first time this summer all of us are wearing clean clothes. Netting is a dirty job, and it doesn't make much sense to wear nice clothes or even clean ones. The front of my shirt is frequently solid brown and stiff with swallow excrement, especially after a day at Whitetail. Some of the other biologists at Cedar Point say they can tell how our day went simply by looking at how much additional poop has appeared on my shirt! But today we're spruced up, and some of us even smell as fragrant as the students in designer outfits who populate the Cedar Point classes.

Our first stop is Skelly, the abandoned gas station. On the way we cross the bridge at Roscoe. The river is still outrageously high, but it seems to have dropped perhaps a foot, enough to spare the adjacent fields to the north. At Skelly we find the birds still busily building nests, blithely unaware that they can't be successful here because of the cranky owner. They've made a lot of progress on their nests, and we could probably net them now. We'll try it in a few days if that old guy doesn't knock the nests down before then.

Just down the road from Skelly at the interstate interchange are several single-tunnel highway culverts that sometimes contain small cliff swallow colonies. These have been used erratically over the years. Last year, with the large number of birds using the new concrete bridge at nearby Roscoe, we thought that might be the end of the birds' occupying these culverts. No one lived in the culverts last year, but I notice action in them now.

The first one we come to is called Mosquito, for reasons not hard to imagine. It lies under the earthen approach to an overpass spanning the interstate. A relatively small colony appears to be present, with a few birds going in each end. We cross the overpass, and on the other side I can see two culverts called, appropriately enough, I 80 North and I 80 South. The northerly one is a long tunnel, like Mule Deer, under the interstate. The other one is under the eastbound exit ramp, about fifty yards south of the long culvert. As at Mule Deer, these two culverts are functionally separate colonies whenever they're active. It's two hundred yards from the overpass where we're parked to these sites, and I peer at them with binoculars. I see what looks like a cliff swallow go in the south culvert, so I'll have to walk down there.

Kathy wants to come with me; Mary and the others wait in the *Valdez*. We trudge down the overpass embankment and out across a wide, grassy right-of-way between the interstate and the exit ramp. We've put on black knee boots to keep our shoes from getting covered with sticktight grass seeds, but they fit poorly, are hot, and make walking in the tall grass difficult. As we approach the culverts, a cliff swallow flies by and alarm-calls at us. Shortly, at least a hundred birds flush out of I 80 South. It's the largest it's ever been. The birds have refurbished most of the old nests and built many others from scratch. They appear to be incubating, meaning they've been here a while. We need to pay them a visit with a net. We see nothing in I 80 North, which isn't surprising since it's been used only once in the past six years.

By the time we hike back up to the truck I'm hot, thirsty, and probably no longer smell very good, but I'm thrilled about having two more culvert colonies for netting. It will be interesting to see which birds have moved into Mosquito and I 80 South, especially since these colonies are used so erratically. I suspect that some of them were part of the big colony at nearby Roscoe last year. Annie is sleeping in the back seat of the truck and wakes up when Kathy and I get in. She looks groggy and finally asks for some water.

We continue to Mule Deer. We pause there only to show it to Kathy and Judy. A mile and a half down the road past it is another of the power company's diversion dams. This dam holds water in the South Platte River and diverts it into another canal—called Korty—that ultimately empties into the same Sutherland Canal where our CR colonies are situated. With the river at flood stage, the water is flowing uninterrupted downstream through the dam's gates and the Korty Canal is at maximum capacity. The concrete gates that release water to the canal provide the same sort of nesting structure as at IS 2, and cliff swallows often use this colony site. We call it the Roscoe Diversion. I was here earlier this spring and saw no cliff swallows, just lots of barn swallows that nest on the gates over the river. No cliff swallows are here today, either.

We've stopped in a parking area along the edge of the Korty Canal. An enormous turtle, probably a western spiny softshell, is sitting on top of the sloping concrete canal bank in front of the truck. Kathy gets out to look at the turtle more closely. As she approaches slowly the turtle keeps sitting there, peacefully sunning itself. Annie, who had been sleeping again after we left I 80 South, suddenly awakens and announces loudly and urgently that she has to get out of the truck. Mary, startled by Annie's obvious distress, quickly moves over toward me and pulls the passenger seat forward so Annie can exit. Annie belly flops out the door, stands up, spins around as if dizzy, and falls down again. She gets up before anyone can assist her and staggers directly toward the turtle. As she reaches the canal bank, she falls to her knees and starts vomiting directly onto the sunning turtle. The poor turtle scurries down the bank toward the safety of the water as the vomit rains down on it.

Annie finishes and gets back in the truck, this time in front by the window in case she needs to hurl again. She's clearly dehydrated because she's refused to drink a lot. We give her some water, and I ask if we should take her back to Cedar Point. She insists she'll be fine, probably because she doesn't want to spoil the long-planned trip to the rodeo.

We continue along a dirt road that parallels the Korty Canal all the way to Paxton. After several more miles we come to a colony called Dead End Bridge, named officially for a nearby sign warning of a dead-end road. But the name could just as well refer to our decided lack of success each time we've come here to net; the birds at this site are wary and uncooperative because they seldom encounter people. This year the colony has about nine active nests. While we're looking at it, Annie realizes she's about to have diarrhea, another symptom of dehydration. She asks about toilets, and I tell her I know of none within six or seven miles. She's afraid she'll have to go outside, not something any of us are eager to experience given her earlier problems at Clary! I suggest she hunker down beside the truck.

She finally decides she can hold it for a while, and we proceed with our tour. Perhaps appropriately given the prevailing conversation, we come to a bridge colony called Stinkpot, named for a pig farm to the south. The wind isn't bad today, so we're spared. Near Stinkpot there's a spot where the canal road was cut through a large sandbank about fifteen feet high. This bank is part of the naturally rolling terrain and is perfect for bank swallows. The soft sand of the cut bank is riddled with their burrows, horizontal tunnels that may extend back a couple of feet. The birds dig these themselves, pushing the sand out with their feet. At the end of each tunnel they line a wider chamber with grass and feathers and lay their eggs there. There was a colony of fifty nests or so here last year, and many of the burrows from last summer are intact. A few bank swallows are flying around today. It looks like the site is active but not as large as last year. I hear their buzzy call notes overhead, and I think how much smaller and more delicate than cliff swallows the birds seem.

The bank swallow is the other highly colonial North American swallow. Although generally not as large as those of cliff swallows, their colonies sometimes contain several hundred nests. As I watch them flying up to the burrows in the bank, I silently express my gratitude to them for making my cliff swallow research possible. Without John Hoogland and Paul Sherman's study of bank swallows in the 1970s, I probably wouldn't have started a study of coloniality.

We bid farewell to the bank swallows and move on down the canal road. We get to the county road leading to Paxton, and I decide we'd better get Annie to a toilet. The closest one is the gas station south of the Paxton bridge, the one she waded through the swamp to visit when we were big netting at Paxton a month ago. We pull in, and Annie sprints for the restroom, darting in ahead of a gray-haired woman whose husband is buying gas. The rest of us sit and wait for what seems like twenty minutes. The woman eventually gives up and leaves. When Annie finally emerges, she's carrying a wad of toilet paper. She buys a bottle of Gatorade, and we make her drink it all.

By now we have only enough time to go straight to North Platte. Checking colonies is over for today. Thirty miles later we pull into the city and are greeted by a comforting sign of civilization: a Wal-Mart. The assistants want to stop. Annie's not too ill to do some major shopping. Before long she's loaded up several pairs of shorts, batteries, a new Neil Diamond tape, Father's Day cards for herself and her friends back at Cedar Point, and of course several pounds of Twizzlers. Judy finds a new shirt and a brush to clean her sandals. I finally have to herd Annie out the door.

We have supper at a pizza restaurant called Valentino's, a Nebraska chain famous for its unique tomato sauce. Native Nebraskan Mary has been looking forward to coming here more than going to the rodeo. The restaurant's major asset tonight is that it's not Cedar Point food, which is declining in quality with each passing day. Four of us gorge on pizza and spaghetti. Annie, however, eats large amounts of a disgusting-looking purple blueberry mousse.

The rodeo tonight is the culminating event of a weeklong celebration in North Platte. Called Nebraskaland Days, the festivities are designed to celebrate the area's Old West heritage while pumping tourist bucks into the local economy. The week begins with events like pancake breakfasts, cooking competitions, talent shows, parades, dances, carnivals, and concerts by such country music luminaries as Diamond Rio and Charley Pride. The rodeo is held at the Buffalo Bill Wild West Arena, whose stands can accommodate several thousand spectators. Buffalo Bill Cody had a ranch and home in North Platte and was based here during much of his later life. The Nebraskaland Days rodeo is a major event on the professional rodeo circuit and attracts contestants from across the nation.

We buy tickets and get settled to watch the opening ceremony. Soon about a hundred people come riding into the arena: the color guard, the announcers, the rodeo queen candidates, Miss Rodeo USA, the Velvet Spurs riding club—a group of middle-aged women carrying pink flags who seem to be the rodeo equivalent of the high-school drill team, clowns mounted on donkeys, advertisers and sponsors carrying banners for their products, and the rodeo organizing committee. The last group consists mostly of fat old guys in cowboy hats who seem to be having a tough time just staying on their horses. At the end a wagon comes in transporting a fellow in buckskin with flowing white hair and goatee who looks just like Buffalo Bill. The rodeo officially begins when he fires his pistol into the air and shouts, "Let's rodeo!"

The assistants are alternately awed and disgusted by the different kinds of competition. They've never seen a rodeo before. The violent neck snapping as calves are roped and thrown to the ground to be hog-tied is always a shock. Rodeo is more dangerous for the contestants than most sports, and midway through the evening a bucking horse throws a cowboy into a metal gate and mashes his nose into a bloody mess. Kathy sketches scenes, while Judy and Annie take photo after photo. All four female members of our group comment repeatedly on the cowboys in their Wrangler jeans. Mary cheers for the livestock, applauding whenever a lariat misses a calf or a steer outruns the cowboy trying to tackle it from above. The locals sitting around us take the rodeo seriously, though, writing down contestants' scores and keeping track of who needs what sort of finish to win prize money.

After the calf roping, bronc riding, team roping, and steer wrestling, it's intermission and time to crown the new rodeo queen. The five candidates come galloping around the arena, waving to the cheering crowd and showing off their riding, all while trying to maintain their painted-on beauty contest smiles. Now it's my turn to reflect on the attractions of tight jeans. These women have some of the biggest hair I've ever seen. Their pinned-on cowboy hats are dwarfed by their profuse and precisely styled coiffures. I bet they all have a bad case of hat hair when they take off their Stetsons. Each wears a sequined outfit of a different bright color. Judy, Annie, and Kathy, like many of our female assistants over the years, seem offended by the meat-market aspect of this exhibition. When the winner is announced she rides forward to accept her prizes—a new saddle and a "diamond" tiara that's affixed to her cowboy hat.

The rodeo ends with my favorite event, bull riding. I can't fathom what could possibly motivate a sane human being to try to ride a 1,200-pound animal with horns that wants to stomp the living hell out of its rider. We must not have any world champion bull riders here tonight, because only two out of ten manage to hang on for the required eight seconds to be judged. But no one gets killed either.

We drive back to Cedar Point in the dark, and it's 11:30 before we get everybody unloaded and say good-night. The diversion this afternoon and evening has been good for the assistants. As the summer wears on, burnout is always a potential problem. I've seen no sign of it yet with this group, but it's still early. Yet a day like this also disrupts our flow and routine. It's too late and I'm too tired to write my daily field notes tonight, so I'll have to double up and spend more time on that tomorrow. And I'd bet money that after the excitement the assistants will be more tired than normal tomorrow. They'll probably be late for breakfast, and we'll get a late start on a morning—naturally—when we're going to Garden County.

8

New Colonies

If you build it, he will come.
—W. P. Kinsella, *Shoeless Joe*

June 15

Our objective today is to visit our Garden County colonies for
perhaps the last time this summer. Besides Ash Hollow and
Clary, I've decided to net at a third colony, Bluffs. The day starts off
well, because to my delight we leave on time. Mary made lunches
without any "help" this morning, in part because I didn't tell the
assistants where we were going until after she had the food packed.

While Mary was making the lunches, Joan gave her a phone message she took last night. Duane Dunwoody, a rancher, called Cedar
Point to report swallows "nesting under the railroad tracks by where
he moves his cattle." He'd never seen anyone studying them and
wanted to make sure the field station knew about them. Joan said he
seemed excited about it, telling her she should send some Ph.D. student out there.

Duane Dunwoody is a name we know. John Janovy and his students have done some parasite studies at a pond on Duane's land,
just north of Keystone. John's invited Duane over to Cedar Point for
supper a time or two, and I met him last year. Mary's had more contact with him. He's seen her along the roadside netting on several
occasions, usually at CR 4 or the Keystone bridge over the North
Platte River. Duane invariably stops to chat, often driving his massive land barge of a car down into the ditch beside the road to get
closer. One cold and blustery morning over a decade ago, our assistants Todd and Laura were sitting by the road at Whitetail counting
foraging swallows. Duane stopped and quite seriously asked if they
were on their honeymoon. Sitting by the road at 9:00 on a cold Sunday morning in a howling gale watching swallows might sound like a

good way to spend a honeymoon to me and I guess to Duane, but probably not to most people and certainly not to Todd and Laura.

The more important question to muse on today is whether Duane really has cliff swallows. I'm not aware of any colonies around Keystone that he could be referring to. Locals often confuse cliff swallows with barn swallows: the two species look superficially alike, both build mud nests, and both breed on man-made structures. Barn swallows are more common around buildings and farmyards. You seldom see large colonies of barn swallows, however, and if someone reporting "cliff swallows" says there are only a few, they're likely to be barn swallows.

Yet the possibility that Duane might really have a colony we're unaware of gives me something else to stew about. I've been wrong before in discounting these reports. Two years ago a local guy named Jones encountered Mary netting one day and stopped to ask how he could get rid of a bunch of "those birds"—implying cliff swallows—that were trying to nest under his carport. Swallows under a carport sounded like barn swallows, so she said something to appease him and we didn't think any more about it. Several days later we were at Whitetail and Jones stopped again. He said he'd been knocking nests down and killed a bird by mistake. He handed me a band, one of ours, that he'd found on the bird! I just about fell over.

Sure enough, Jones had cliff swallows—about eight hundred. They were swarming under a carport he'd constructed to cover his boat and RV. It was a perfect design for cliff swallows, with parallel support beams under the ceiling along which the birds were building nests. The carport was open on all sides, and Jones had even inadvertently supplied the swallows with a mud source by watering his garden only a few yards away. Mud and poop were showering down, and the birds' chattering was enough to wake the dead. He'd moved his boat and RV away to keep them from getting covered with mud and crap. Cliff swallows are not subtle when they decide to nest somewhere, and a massive horde of eight hundred birds swarming all over the yard was considerably more than this guy could deal with.

I tried to act sympathetic to Jones's plight and promised to help him. I knew his opposition meant these birds were not destined to successfully nest there, but I wanted to string him along until we had a chance to net them. It was important to know which birds were starting a new colony like this. I told him we could net them, and though we couldn't kill the ones we caught, just the act of catching them often caused them to leave a site. It was mostly a fib, but he agreed to let us net. An assistant and I showed up the next day and put regular nets on two sides of the carport. That day was windy, though, and we caught only 109 birds. I planned to return and use big nets, which could completely seal off the carport, but before we could return, Jones got wise and rigged up a sprinkler to continuously spray the underside of the roof with water. The birds left. We often pass by Jones's house, and every time I think, if we could have had just one more good day there. . . .

We reach Garden County and stop first at Clary. Mary and Kathy will net here. We drop them off, and this time I leave Mary to set the net. I don't want another disaster caused by my haste to get on to the next site. I've asked Judy to work alone at Bluffs. The other assistants seem to regard her selection to be the solitary worker as a badge of honor, and it does reflect how much confidence I have in her. With only seven or so active nests, Judy won't have a busy day.

We stop on the road above the Bluffs culvert, and I point out a shallow canyon about a hundred yards to the west. Judy will have to sit there, since it's the closest place to hide from the swallows. At a small colony like this they'll be extremely wary, and they probably wouldn't tolerate even a car parked on the road above the culvert. Sure enough, as soon as we've stopped the truck and before we get out, all the birds roar out of the culvert, alarm-calling.

Annie and I set nets on each end of the culvert. We're using the low-visibility ones, which should help. Judy totes her equipment over to the canyon. I'm pleased to see a juniper growing there that provides just enough shade for one person. I instruct her to watch the nets from her hiding place and walk over at least every half hour even if she sees no birds in them. Sometimes a bird will hit the net low and be obscured by the grass. I tell Judy to be careful and that we'll pick her up at 4:45.

When we get to Ash Hollow, it doesn't take long to start catching a lot of swallows. The colony is incubating now, and the birds seem more motivated than last time to enter the culvert, by going either over the top of the net or through the west end. Annie and I empty the net, take the birds back to our processing area under the gigantic cottonwoods on the edge of the arroyo, process them, and then go get the next load. We work constantly all morning, and by 1:00, when we finally try to eat lunch between bags of birds, we have over eighty captures. Many of the birds are already banded, either in an earlier year or from the previous visit here. We seem to be getting a higher percentage of past-year birds than on the earlier visit. With the many banded birds we're catching, it's hard to keep track of which ones we've already caught today.

Captures slow down during the afternoon. We're releasing a lot of same-day repeats directly from the net. The afternoon is pleasant and relaxing. The resident kestrels are still nesting in the cotton-wood above us and still seem oblivious to the swallows. Insects are becoming more abundant with each passing day, and grasshoppers buzz in the nearby pasture and on the hill above the arroyo. This is such a beautiful, peaceful scene that I don't understand why Annie wants to diminish it by wearing headphones to listen to music. This is not the place for Neil Diamond.

At about 4:15 I go to the net for another check. Mostly we've got repeats, but as I'm removing one bird I notice its band number. The prefix begins with 2010. This is a bird banded in 1984! Annie and I are excited, and we process the bird, a female, immediately. My guess is that she was banded as a nestling during the third summer of our research. That makes her eleven years old. She's only the third eleven-year-old we've ever caught.

As I hold this bird, I think of the incredible life she's had and everything she's seen and done. This little animal that we just weighed at twenty-eight grams has made eleven round-trips between Nebraska and Argentina, each one about six thousand miles. She's nonchalant, looking at us with her big brown eyes and wiggling just like any other cliff swallow. We know she's special only because of the metal bracelet she wears; how many unbanded eleven-year-olds have we held and not known it?

I'm reluctant to let her go, preferring to just hold her and marvel both at her as an individual and at what this recapture says cliff swallows as a species are capable of doing. She also makes me proud of our study. Not many people have the opportunity to recapture an animal they first marked eleven years ago. Keeping the research going that long has required hard work and some sacrifice. I've often been frustrated by colleagues or funding agencies that don't appreciate either what it takes to sustain long-term field studies or their inherent value. This little bird I'm holding, number 2010-12901, is what makes all the years, all the hard work, all the frustration more than worth it.

Wishing her luck, I release her. We watch as she flies away to join a group of swallows foraging high over the hills to the northwest. Soon she becomes just another cliff swallow. It's an emotional moment.

Annie can't wait to tell the others about our 2010. I'd promised to reward the assistants with ice cream sundaes at the Dairy Queen if we caught a 2010 this year. Now I'll have to pay up, and Annie promptly reports that to the others when we retrieve them. Mary and Kathy had a good day at Clary, getting 147 birds from a colony of 125 nests. Judy also cleaned up, catching 13 birds at Bluffs. I had estimated that 14 live there, so there's little need to go back. Annie and I ended up with 167 at Ash Hollow. This has been one of our best days this summer.

When we return to Cedar Point, the assistants want Mary to look up the 2010 on the computer. Mary takes out our laptop containing a copy of all the data files and types in the bird's band number. As I had guessed, she was banded as a nestling in 1984, making her eleven years old. She hatched on June 13 in nest number 168 at Clary, a nonfumigated old nest about a meter and a half from the center of the colony. She came from a clutch of five eggs and a brood of four. An egg transfer had occurred in her natal nest. Thus there's one chance in five that our eleven-year-old began her life being carried to a foster nest and that the "parents" weren't her real ones. From 1985 to 1988 we didn't see her. In 1989 she nested at Bluffs, a colony of 245 nests. The next year she moved to Clary, a colony of 190 nests. After disappearing for the next two summers, in 1993 she was back at Clary, a colony of 255 nests. She disappeared again last year, and this year she's at Ash Hollow, which contains 108 nests. She seems to prefer medium-sized colonies, which a variety of analyses have suggested may be the best for cliff swallows. This bird's longevity supports that conclusion. She's often lived in Garden County, but where was she in the missing years? We'll never know.

After supper I call Duane. He insists there are lots of cliff swallows at his site. He describes it as being along the railroad tracks, but I don't understand his directions. Finally I ask if he'll just show it to us. He starts talking about when in the next couple of days we can get together. Forget that. My curiosity is so aroused that I ask if we can come over to his house *now*, this evening before dark. He says sure, so I go find Mary and we head off. She keeps telling me not to get my hopes up, that they're probably barn swallows.

We drive to the Keystone road, but when we reach it we continue straight north rather than turning west to Whitetail. We go two miles down a bumpy dirt road before reaching a crossroad that leads east to Duane's house. He told us to home in on a large red metal barn, and it's big enough to be obvious for miles in this open country. We turn into his "driveway," a pair of ruts through a pasture, and pull up to the double-wide house trailer where he lives. He, a woman I take to be his wife, and a friend are sitting on the porch drinking iced tea. The front yard is full of farm machinery, and close by is a pen full of chickens. A pack of barking dogs runs out and surrounds us. One of the dogs, a big yellow Lab, is carrying a kitten in its mouth. The kitten is plastered with dog slobber, but the Lab doesn't seem to be trying to eat it. A neighbor runs up to extricate the kitten.

I feel real out of place here.

We exchange a few pleasantries above the roar of the dogs, then Duane tells us to follow him. He and his friend get in a little foreign-made pickup, and we're surprised not to see his land barge anywhere. They strike out through a nearby pasture on an even more obscure grassy trough of a road. We go for a mile or so, eventually losing any trace of a road and driving across open pasture. We go through dense stands of enormous sunflowers. The wet spring really has them growing, though none are blooming yet. We comment that Diana should come here if she wants to study sunflowers.

Soon I can see the railroad embankment that bisects Duane's pasture. After a few more yards we spot some corrals, and I see cliff swallows overhead. Duane stops by a metal gate, and just beyond it is a concrete culvert under the railroad tracks. Lots of cliff swallows are in the culvert. Damn! Duane has birds after all.

The four of us get out and climb over the metal gate to approach the culvert. The interior is muddy, with a Clarylike smell of manure. There's a big pool of it with green slime on top at the end closest to us. We didn't bring rubber boots, but I can get close enough to see over 150 nests being built on the walls. The culvert is a single tunnel, only as long as the railroad embankment is wide. Strangely, it's of a style in which the walls join the ceiling at a forty-five-degree angle, unlike the more typical ninety-degree juncture. I had always believed cliff swallows wouldn't use a culvert like this because of the difficulty of attaching their nests. These birds have proved me wrong big time, with nests placed all over the angled interface between wall and ceiling and others farther down on the vertical part of the wall. The culvert is about seven feet tall and perfect for netting.

I ask Duane about this site's history. He says the culvert has always been here; he uses it to move his cattle between the pastures divided by the tracks. But recently the Union Pacific Railroad has been laying down a second set of tracks to accommodate parallel trains along this section of the line. Duane says over fifty trains a day pass here, hauling coal from Wyoming mines to eastern power plants. The construction widened the embankment, so the culvert was lengthened. He swears this is the first summer the birds have nested here. He ought to know. You can't miss a colony of cliff swallows in a place like this, and all the nests do look new.

I ask for permission to net the birds on his land, and he replies that he wants us to. He wants to know where these birds are from, and so do I. But there's more. He says his neighbor to the west, Dave Knight, has a similar culvert under his section of the railroad, and there's another cliff swallow colony there. Holy cow, we didn't know about that one either!

Although I can hardly wait to go look for Dave Knight's colony, Mary and I spend a little time chatting with Duane. It turns out he's a rancher by day and a Presbyterian minister nights and Sundays. He preaches in nearby Keystone, in Lemoyne on the north side of Big Mac, and in Arthur thirty miles up in the Sand Hills. I wonder to myself if Duane uses the famous Protestant-Catholic church in Keystone. Legend has it that early pioneers cooperated to build the only dual-faith church in the country. One end contains a Protestant altar and the other end a Catholic altar, and the pews in between are reversible. The church still stands, but apparently now it's just a tourist stop and regular services are no longer held there. It doesn't take long before Duane starts asking if we go to church. We try to avoid the issue. I have a vision of him requiring us to come to his church as payment for being allowed to study his swallows. We thank him, promise to let him know what we discover about his birds, and follow him back out of the pasture.

Duane told us we can get to Knight's culvert and his by driving up to the railroad tracks on the road we came in on and then turning onto a gravel road used by the construction workers that parallels the tracks. This route obviates going through the pastures. We decide to try to reach the other culvert this way and see what it has before we talk to Dave Knight. We find Duane was correct, and as soon as we turn onto Union Pacific's road along the tracks we see the culvert. We stop on top of the structure, and I climb down. The birds flush out, and this colony looks larger than Duane's. It has the same angled juncture of wall and ceiling. This culvert is dry throughout and so will be easier to work than Duane's. Judging from the hoof-prints in the dirt, it also serves as a walkway for livestock.

Since netting here entails being on Dave Knight's land, we retrace our route and find his farm—the Red Cedar Ranch—just south of the railroad intersection. His traditional farmhouse reminds me of the one at Pigpen that I often fantasize about, but when he answers the door he certainly doesn't look like a farmer. I expected someone at least in his middle fifties and wearing bib overalls, but Dave Knight is about my age, well educated, and interested in our swallow research. We later learn that he moonlights as a cowboy poet, reciting verse at local rodeos and fairs. He's seen us along the road at White-tail and tells us we're welcome to net at the culvert.

But there's more. He asks if we know about the swallows in the tube under the railroad just west of here. *Another* new colony? He says this tube is a metal cylinder that Spring Creek flows through. We can reach it by driving through his pasture that abuts the rail-road tracks near the road intersection, and he says we're welcome to go look at it. This one *does* sound like a barn swallow colony. We thank Dave and drive back out to the railroad tracks. We decide we'll go have a look, though we're sure no cliff swallows will be nesting in a metal tube.

A thunderstorm is developing to the west, blotting out the setting sun. This sucker could get nasty, so we hurry to find the entrance to the pasture. We find the tire ruts that lead west, paralleling the rail-road tracks. The "road" winds through the pasture and virtually dis-appears after a hundred yards or so. We're out in the middle of an open prairie with a thunderstorm bearing down on us that's already spitting lightning bolts, searching for birds nesting in a tube under a railroad. What a great way to spend a summer!

Soon we spot the metal cylinder, its front framed with a concrete sleeve. I slow down and don't want to get too close, because I can't tell for sure where the creek is. A couple more lightning flashes to the west help us decide this is just a barn swallow place and we'd better get out of here. I turn around and start back to find the tire ruts. Suddenly we see a cliff swallow pass overhead, heading toward the tube. Mary looks out the window behind us. She sees it go straight to the tube. I can't believe it.

Despite the lightning and the storm's approach, I slam on the brakes and turn around. We get as close as we dare, not knowing the lay of the land. I jump out and walk toward the tube. Several cliff swallows are going in and out. This is definitely an active site. There's a barbed wire fence in front of the entrance, and I'm not eager to climb it and wade the creek right now. We'll have to come back when we have more time. I run back to the truck, and Mary and I turn around once more to get out of here before the storm hits.

As we drive back to Cedar Point, I marvel at the discovery of three new colonies right in our own backyard—only about three miles from Whitetail. I'm also a bit embarrassed. We know, or thought we knew, the whereabouts of every potential colony site in our study area, yet Dave Knight said the birds have used that tube every summer! And I didn't know about it until tonight. The other two new colonies are probably first-time sites this year, but I worry that we hadn't been monitoring this part of our study area closely enough to know that the railroad construction was creating new colony sites. We'll be coming back soon to thoroughly survey this region for other possible colonies.

My self-reproof for not knowing about these sites is fleeting, however, because mostly I'm thrilled at having three new colonies. I'm very curious to know what birds have colonized the two first-time sites, and I also wonder how many old friends banded in earlier years have been escaping us by living at the tube. We'll find out soon.

June 16

Despite my desire to begin studying the new colonies along the railroad tracks, it's more important to focus first on another new colony. Skelly is new in the sense that today will be our first attempt to net there. The birds' days at that site are numbered, and we need to strike before the gas station owner knocks their nests down.

I'm a little uneasy about going to Skelly. The owner of the property doesn't like cliff swallows, and I don't think he likes us. When the birds first moved in twelve years ago, we naively assumed that since the gas station was vacant it had no owner. We started checking nest contents, and until house sparrows destroyed the colony, we used it as one of our main research sites. Mary and our assistant

Todd were at Skelly one day, and a man stopped to tell them he owned it. He didn't seem to mind our studying the birds. A few days later Todd and I were back, and a less friendly fellow pulled up. He bawled us out for not having asked his permission to come there. We thought we had the owner's blessing, but it turns out the first guy was this fellow's brother, a co-owner who didn't have much to do with the property. The belligerent Bubba didn't make us leave, but we certainly felt unwelcome, especially after he launched a tirade about his taxes going for this. I was just a graduate student at the time and had no federal dollars in my pocket, but that didn't seem to matter to him.

Two years ago when the birds last nested at Skelly, Linda, a graduate student who was studying swallow hormones, wanted to use this site. She managed to learn the owner's name and called him to ask permission to work there. I don't know if it was the same guy as a decade earlier, but he told Linda he was going to knock the nests down (which is illegal) because the birds were "messy." He did, too, about two days later. This year I figure it might be better not to say anything to him. Not calling his attention to the swallows might prolong their existence, at least until after we net them. But basically it means we have to sneak in.

Annie and I drive up to the gas station and see large numbers of birds. I estimate about 125 active nests under the awning and the front eaves of the building, most of them complete. But we have a problem: no dirt for our buckets. Asphalt surrounds the awning, and the only way to erect a net is to fill buckets with dirt and anchor the net poles in them. Nowhere do I see any dirt, and our need to be inconspicuous precludes digging up sod in the nearby lawn.

We also have another problem: a cop. As we sit in the truck and muse on how to net here, a highway patrolman parks near the interstate entrance ramp just a few yards to the south. He isn't concerned with us but is watching for interstate speeders. His presence makes me nervous, though, because he probably lives locally and might even know the gas station owner. So we casually drive back to the road, wave as we pass the patrolman, cross the interchange overpass, and stop along the side of the road on the other side. The overpass blocks us from the cop's view and there's dirt here. We get out and quickly fill the buckets. I figure it won't be long before the patrolman goes after a speeder, and sure enough he roars off after somebody before we finish filling our buckets. Now we can sneak back to Skelly.

We unload our buckets and spread out a forty-two-foot net. It's soon obvious that this net, though long, isn't tall enough to be effective. Most of the birds are flying over it. It also covers only a small portion of the available flyway. Netting birds on buildings is tough because of the openness and the many directions they can approach or exit from. I appreciate again how ideal culverts and canal bridges are for netting. Our major problem, however, is the wind. It's strong, and Skelly isn't protected at all. The net mesh is pulled so tight that most birds that hit it bounce out. After thirty minutes we've caught only seven birds, and the net keeps blowing over. Fortunately the asphalt doesn't have a lot of sticks and grass to tangle it, but we finally give up.

We pack up our gear and depart with a sigh of relief at not having encountered the cranky owner. Yet I know we need to try again. The seven birds we caught were all unbanded ones, so we really learned nothing about this colony today. We return to Cedar Point to find that Mary, Kathy, and Judy also got winded out. They tried at IS 1, where the birds were uncooperative and the net kept blowing over and snagging on the bridge railing. They finally quit after getting only fifteen birds. Wind can kill a day just like cold or rain.

After lunch, Mary spreads nets in the hallway of the lab. They've sustained some tears, usually when one snagged on part of a bridge or on brush. Mist nets used to be so cheap you'd just throw one away when it got torn up, but prices have skyrocketed. Until recently almost all mist nets were made in Japan, and many were exported to countries that didn't closely regulate who could use them. Nets were often used to catch protected or threatened species to sell as pets or as food in less developed countries. Under pressure from conservationists, the Japanese government put heavy export restrictions on whom nets could be sold to and where, driving many net manufacturers out of business almost overnight. As supply went down, prices went up. Repairing nets is now a more cost-effective option.

I ask the assistants to help Mary mend the holes. The mesh is reconstructed by sewing it back together using a needle and thread. It requires considerable patience, some eye-hand coordination, and the ability to focus on a fairly unexciting task for a while. Mary can turn on music or a book on tape and spend hours mending a net. I can't. Neither can Annie; she has trouble sitting still. She finds an excuse to leave, but Judy and Kathy stick with it all afternoon. They're slow, but with their help Mary gets all the nets repaired by supper.

Kathy works especially diligently. Some friends in Omaha invited her to go canoeing with them this weekend along the Niobrara River. Kathy immediately told Mary about the invitation, but she seemed reluctant to bring it up with me. The intimidation problem, I guess. Mary finally urged me just to tell Kathy it would be okay. We can get by without her for a couple of days, so I'm happy for her to go. She's leaving tonight, but I can tell she's feeling guilty, with Judy and Annie here working. I think that's why she worked so hard on mending the nets.

After supper Mary and I return to the railroad tracks. We want to see if there are more new or enlarged culverts east or west of the sites we discovered last night. The most efficient way to look for them is to follow the gravel road paralleling the tracks. It doesn't look like a public road, though, and I'm a little uneasy about using it despite Duane's assurances. But there are no railroad construction workers there this evening, and these tracks go through about as remote a region as one can imagine, so no one will see us anyway. We first go east from Duane's and find another culvert like his. It looks new, but it's not as tall and has no birds or nests. We travel east to the end of the construction zone and find nothing else.

Backtracking, we follow the tracks west. We find three more culverts of a size and style similar to Duane's and Dave Knight's, and they all look newly installed under the enlarged railroad embankment. Periodically a coal train blows by, a creepy experience since the road we're on is just a few feet from the tracks. No birds or nests are in the three new culverts, but I predict they'll eventually be occupied. If not this summer, perhaps next year. I'd be surprised if any more new sites are colonized this late in the breeding season, but it's been a delayed spring so we should still keep an eye on them.

We follow the tracks west to the junction with Highway 61 just north of Kingsley Dam. In a sense I'm glad we didn't find any more new colonies. We have a lot to do with our existing sites, both the three new colonies and the many others where we must continue netting. Some traditional places like Aqueduct, Pigpen, Skelly, Mosquito, I 80, and the wooden bridge have barely been touched, if we've done anything at all. My euphoria of last night has turned into a feeling of pressure and stress. It's not helped by a forecast that calls for several more days of this god-awful wind. The assistants will be here only about three more weeks. We can't lose any more time.

June 17

By breakfast the wind is already as strong as it was yesterday. Wind is particularly frustrating when the weather is otherwise so sunny and mild. I'm tempted not even to try going out, but Mary suggests we go look at the new colonies. Sometimes culverts are surprisingly well blocked from the wind by their embankments. I'm skeptical, but we load up and head out.

At the railroad tracks we turn east and immediately encounter Knight's Culvert, as we've officially named it to distinguish it from Knight's Tube. I climb down the embankment to assess the wind. It's not bad, mostly because of a dense line of cottonwoods just south of the culvert between us and Dave's house. These were probably planted long ago to shield the farm from cold northerly winds during the winter, and today they're blocking the south wind from us. We unload our gear and carry it down the embankment, crossing the tracks and several barbed wire fences. Mary and I erect a net across the south end of the culvert.

I'm always excited when we net for the first time at a new colony. As soon as the first bird goes into the net, I feel as if we've started to unlock more of these birds' secrets. Today is no exception as I watch the swallows plow into the net. The sense of discovery grips me, especially when I notice that the first bird into the net is banded.

The residents of Knight's Culvert are extremely cooperative for a new colony that probably hasn't had much contact with humans. All four of us stay busy, Judy and Annie processing and Mary and I tending the net. Mary takes photos of me at the net as coal trains roar past only six or seven feet above me. Whenever a train isn't passing, the railroad workers are moving heavy machinery along the tracks. I can't tell exactly what they're doing, but they make a lot of noise. The disturbance here is extreme, yet the birds ignore the noise and seem little concerned about us. That the birds are thriving in an environment this artificial attests to their adaptability and bodes well for the cliff swallow as a species.

I'm flabbergasted that we can net here in this wind. The nearby cottonwoods are flailing away, but our net isn't even billowing. Knight's Culvert has to be the only site in the state where we could net today, and I consider this a major victory over the elements. By noon we've caught 180 cliff swallows and one barn swallow. A single pair of barn swallows is nesting in the culvert, and I'm surprised cliff swallows haven't usurped their nest by now. Perhaps the reason is that those barn swallows have built their mud nest on top of a curled metal rod that protrudes from the roof of the culvert. The rod serves as a bottom anchor for the open-cup nest, which is perched precariously between it and the ceiling. I've never seen a barn swallow nest built like this, and I guess it's too weird for any cliff swallow to want it. I walk through the culvert and count 225 active cliff swallow nests, all new this summer.

Judy reports that fifty-two of our captures had been previously banded. Among those, fifteen are birds banded this summer at other colonies. The swallows have been moving around this season, illustrating again that it's necessary to catch a bird repeatedly at a site before we can feel certain it lived there. Almost half of the banded birds are ones first caught last year. That almost 30 percent of the residents at a new colony are already banded reflects how thoroughly we've been marking the swallows in the local population. That should give me satisfaction, but all I'm thinking about now is catching more birds.

We return to Cedar Point for lunch, and by then the wind is ridiculous. We can hear it howling even when we're inside the lodge, and periodically the screen doors blow open and napkins and lettuce salad are flung across the dining room. The only possibility for the afternoon would be to go back to Knight's Culvert. But we were getting a lot of repeats by the end of the morning, and the wind is so bad now that I doubt even that site would be shielded enough to net. The assistants get the afternoon off.

Mary checks the computer for the banded birds we got at Knight's Culvert. Our new data won't be entered in the computer until this fall, but we're curious where these birds are from. We discover that most of the birds banded last year were first caught as juveniles, primarily from Whitetail but a few from Aqueduct. They're yearlings now. This result is consistent with the pattern at other sites: new colonies often contain many young birds. Why this should be isn't clear, however. These youngsters aren't being forced out of existing colonies by older birds, because there's plenty of nesting space at all the sites and some yearlings do nest at the traditional colony sites. Many of the other previously banded birds date from the summer of 1993, meaning they're two years old. Again, relatively young birds in a new colony.

Yet there are always some exceptions. We caught one bird this morning that was banded as an adult in 1988, making it at least eight years old. We had another that was at least six years old and two five-year-olds. Still, that's a smaller percentage of older swallows than we'd see at a perennially used site like CR 2 or Whitetail. Knight's Culvert is clearly being settled by local birds, since most of those caught in an earlier year were at Whitetail or one of the close canal colonies.

We notice that several of the past-year birds have multiple gaps in their capture histories, showing we missed them in those years. I wonder if the birds settling in these new colonies might be ones that had been avoiding us lately, perhaps by settling somewhere else we weren't aware of. We'll have a better idea of this after we've also netted at Duane's place and the tube. It's exciting to encounter these birds we'd been missing, and our capturing them will improve our estimates of annual survival.

I continue to be troubled by the discovery of the new colonies because it means others might be out there, especially in the open country north of Whitetail. Given the terrain, I'd assumed there were no suitable colony sites up there, but only twice have Mary and I gone more than a mile or so north of the Keystone road. I want to scout that area tonight. I'm satisfied we checked the railroad tracks thoroughly enough yesterday, but there might be something farther north, perhaps a colony on a farmhouse or barn.

After supper we drive north from the railroad tracks along a dirt road. This road looks like a shady country lane, lined in places with large cottonwoods. We pass a few farmhouses, most old and weathered with dead cars in the yard but still inhabited. We see no cliff swallows. Before long we're driving through the Sand Hills proper. A sea of grass extends to each horizon, dotted only by patches of blooming yuccas and herds of cattle. We're getting far enough from the North Platte River that I can know with some certainty that there'll be no colonies in this area. We turn around.

I'm satisfied there are no more undiscovered colonies in this part of our kingdom.

June 18

I don't even want to get out of bed this morning. It's still windy.

At breakfast Mary and I debate what to do and finally decide to try Whitetail. It's less critical to net it today than many of our other colonies, but one reason Whitetail is so special is that we can catch birds there when conditions don't allow it anywhere else. This is the third day of a howling gale, and tomorrow's forecast doesn't sound much better. I'm almost grateful that the National Weather Service doesn't give long-range wind forecasts, because I'd probably get completely despondent.

When we get to Whitetail, I decide we'll set the net but tell everyone to be prepared to admit defeat and quit if the wind is too bad. We'll obviously be on the south end, where all the birds are going out. The wind howls and roars, sounding like a wintertime blizzard, which seems odd as warm as it is today. Mary and I tell each other several times as we set the net that it's folly to be out in a gale like this.

To my astonishment, we start catching cliff swallows. A lot of them. Before long I'm constantly standing in the creek extracting birds. The net is flapping in the wind and is obvious as hell. I'm sure every cliff swallow can easily see it. But the wind is so strong that the birds have some trouble flying, and many just can't avoid the net. They *have* to exit the south end into the wind to have any control of flight, and the net's there waiting for them. It occurs to me that we might be catching some of the smarter individuals that avoid the net on less windy days by cleverly going over or around it. I know there are such birds. The wind keeps howling, the net keeps flapping, and we keep catching swallows. Quintessential Whitetail.

The wind gets worse as the morning progresses. The net is blowing so badly that I keep thinking we'll have to quit, yet each time I glance up after removing a bird there are more in the net. It's far more stressful for me than on a "normal" day, because the birds are more tangled up in the net. I worry that some will get yanked by the blowing net and be injured or choked, and with the mesh pulled tauter than usual by the wind there's often less slack around a bird as I try to work the net off it. We're pushing the envelope by being here.

In midmorning I hear a car stop on the road above. I can't see it, but it must be somebody who saw Mary and the assistants sitting by the creek bank. The last thing we need now is a spectator. I hear Mary talking and realize "it" is Duane. He wants to know if we've netted his birds. Mary says we plan to as soon as the wind abates. Duane's on his way to preach at Lemoyne on this Sunday morning at "the same church [football coach] Tom Osborne goes to," as he proudly told us the other day. He tells Mary he'll pray for us. In this wind, we'll need it.

By noon, when we finally stop, we've caught almost 375 birds, most of them banded. As we look over the tally, we notice that one bird, a male, was from 1985. When we get back to the lab, Mary looks him up and finds that he was first caught and banded as an adult, meaning he was born in 1984 or earlier. Thus he's at least eleven years old like the bird at Ash Hollow and possibly older. I regret we didn't have a chance to look at him more closely, but netting was so stressful this morning that I don't think I'd have been in the mood to be too philosophical or emotional about this oldie.

We were lucky to do so well this morning and to have no injuries or accidents in the wind. I decide not to push our good fortune by going back after lunch.

June 19

This morning I refuse to concede defeat. I'm tired of watching Diana, Tony, and Josef—who aren't doing wind-sensitive research—go out and have great days while all we can do is gripe about the wind. We may not catch anything, but we're going to go try. Although the forecast is for "breezy" later today—the National Weather Service euphemism for a prairie gale—it's not too bad yet.

We've been needing to get back to Prairie Dog for a second and probably final session. That colony was among the earlier ones, and it will soon be too far along to net. But I should have known it would be a bad call to go to Prairie Dog, one of our windiest sites, on a day like this. As soon as Kathy and I stop at the bridge, we see the lush grass in the nearby pastures rolling in gigantic ripples like waves on a sea. It's a beautiful sight—if you're not trying to net cliff swallows.

Except at Whitetail, the birds everywhere are more skittish when it's windy. Perhaps that's because they have less control of their flight in wind and must be more careful if a predator (which we presumably represent) is around. The birds at Prairie Dog are uncooperative at the best of times, and in wind—well, forget it. The wind wraps much of the net's loose mesh around the pole Kathy carries, so by the time we drop there's no slack left in the body of the net. After catching thirteen birds and constantly fighting to keep the net poles from blowing over, we admit we're licked.

I leave with a serious sense of frustration because I know there are many banded birds at Prairie Dog that we'll miss this summer. Over half of our thirteen today were banded. We're not likely to have any more opportunities to come back here, and the birds themselves are clearly not going to cooperate anyway. Prairie Dog is so large that I'm certain that's where most of last year's Aqueduct birds went, but I won't be able to prove it.

Instead of quitting completely, Kathy and I stop at Barn Owl. The section of the canal containing this colony is sheltered slightly by some bluffs to the south, and we find that it's possible to net here. Barn Owl, like Pigpen, consists of a narrow bridge over the canal and side gates under the canal road. During our first summer we found a barn owl roosting in the side part, although it hasn't been seen since. As at Pigpen, cliff swallows last used the side part in 1991, but unlike Pigpen, both portions of Barn Owl were colonized at about the same time this year. We don't have problems here with earlier birds choosing one colony size and later ones choosing another.

We spend the rest of the morning netting both parts of the colony and have surprising success. By lunchtime we have ninety-nine birds. I notice the same pattern as at Pigpen: the side structure contains mostly unbanded birds or swallows first banded earlier this summer, whereas the bridge has most of the older birds. Arrival times didn't differ here, however, so that can't explain the age differences in where the birds settled. For some reason, yearlings seem more likely to move into newer sites *within* the existing colonies. Their preference for being pioneers is not confined to new culverts like Knight's or Duane's.

As we pull into the Cedar Point entrance late for lunch, I suddenly realize we left our stepladders at Prairie Dog. We keep them out on the bridge there between drops, and when we packed up we forgot them. They were there all morning while we were at Barn Owl, and I imagine some fisher has carried them off by now. Even if we can retrieve them, Prairie Dog is ten miles from Cedar Point, and we'll waste time going back for them. I sheepishly ask Mary—who's already finished lunch by the time we arrive—if she'll go get them. She agrees to go while Kathy and I eat what's left of the oriental stir fry and noodle dish that passes for lunch. Being so lamebrained with the ladders has made me cranky and irritable, even though we had a good morning: over 280 birds counting the 169 that Mary, Annie, and Judy got at CR 4½.

They noticed a lot of new, unbanded birds at CR 4½ today. The birds of this influx were doing considerable nest building. It's unusual for new waves to settle at a colony this long after the site was first colonized. Sometimes these late arrivals will hang around a colony for a while and even start to build nests but then leave after a few days. Possibly these birds don't really intend to breed this year, not being in the appropriate condition or hormonal state. Or they may assess the ectoparasite load in an existing colony and determine that swallow bugs are so abundant by now that any late nests would be overwhelmed. Later this summer we'll make a major discovery about birds like these, but today I don't think much about them.

By the time I've organized the gear for the afternoon, Mary returns with the ladders. I'm surprised they were still there. I guess it proves just how deserted the Prairie Dog section of the canal is. Mary's retrieving the ladders puts me in a better mood, which is a good thing because this afternoon we're headed to another site that may be very frustrating.

Although windy, today is not as bad as the past few days, so I think we can have a productive afternoon if we pick our sites wisely and stick to wind-tolerant places. We decide that Mary will take Annie and Judy to CR 3. Partly blocked by hills to the south, CR 3 is often doable in a south wind. Kathy and I will go to McDougals for the first time this season.

McDougals is on the north side of Lake McConaughy not far from the Garden County line. Passing by there a couple of times earlier this year, I had noticed that a few birds seemed interested in the site. Perhaps just one or two pairs might be resident. If so, we have only a small chance of catching them. Singletons or duos are extremely wary and rarely approach their nest when a net's up. We find solitary pairs each summer, but to date we have few data on them. Besides being hard to catch, solitaries by definition don't represent many total birds. For example, it's hard to statistically estimate annual survival for small cohorts, so we usually have to combine solitaries with birds from the very small colonies (ten nests or fewer) for analysis. Solitaries and the residents of these tiny colonies fascinate me, however. What makes a bird willing to settle where it has none of the benefits of group life? I hope that if we catch the McDougals birds they'll already be banded, which would reveal something about the individuals that select small colonies.

We park at a wide spot on the shoulder above the culvert. Rolling pastures surround us, and a clear blue Big Mac lies within sight off to the south. The terrain here is hilly, and the cryptic culvert is under the highway at the bottom of a steep ravine. Getting down there from the road requires descending the high road embankment and then crawling down the sloping wall of the culvert entrance. We use one of our Prairie Dog ladders to climb down from the top of the wall. It's a physical workout to go back and forth from the culvert to the truck, and we'll have to do this all afternoon. The truck is the only place to sit out of the birds' sight.

A couple of birds fly out of nests as we enter the culvert, and I see two more flying nearby. I can already tell that several pairs live here. The south wind is very strong; there's nothing between us and the lake to block it. The inside of the culvert itself feels like a wind tunnel. I realize this could be good, since everybody will be exiting the south side, and if we can keep our nets from blowing over, we might have a chance to catch these birds. While we're still working on anchoring the poles and buckets by digging pits in the sand, we catch three birds that come flying through the culvert! I'm elated and rush to remove each one, sending Kathy back to the truck to get a holding bag. The only disappointment is that all three are unbanded.

We begin our routine of sitting in the truck and going down at intervals to check the net. Kathy offers to take turns going down, but I do it because I'm trying to get a sense of how many birds live here. Each time, I enter the culvert through the north end, flushing birds out of the nests away from me and toward the net. Everybody except one bird, that is. This swallow lives in a nest near the north end and refuses to fly out to the south. Each time I start to come through the culvert, it pokes its head out of its nest and looks at me for a few seconds before flushing. I wave my arms to try to redirect its flight toward the net, but it still flies over my head to escape. This bird starts getting bolder as the afternoon wears on, often just looking at me and not flushing until I get directly under it.

Within the first hour of netting, we've caught six birds. The residents come back to the colony surprisingly soon after each of my visits to the net. The wind is actually a big help by forcing them all to come in at the netless north end. In calmer weather, some would try to go in the south end with the net. They'd see the net and swirl around, getting everybody worked up. Today none of them even think about entering the south end.

Netting here is so effective that we start getting repeat captures, catching some birds as many as three times. From the number of birds flushing out of nests and flying nearby, I'd judge the colony at four active nests. Eight birds live here. After another hour, we catch our seventh. The third hour brings no new birds, and it's finally time to quit. Seven out of eight birds is as high a percentage of the colony as you can expect anywhere, and I know who the eighth is. I doubt that a return trip for just one bird would be time well spent.

Unfortunately, all seven birds we caught were unbanded. If we had 100 percent unbanded birds in a larger colony, I'd be certain the colony was mostly yearlings, but seven is too small a number to conclude anything about. That none were already banded is the only blot on a highly successful afternoon. It's some compensation that those birds will now be marked so that if we encounter them next year we'll know they're "small colony birds." Kathy seems amused that I'm so excited about getting only seven birds, given our emphasis on big numbers this summer. For once the wind clearly helped us, and I'm thrilled at turning it to our advantage for a change.

We quit with a total of 471 birds for the day. Who says you can't catch birds when it's windy?

June 20

We plan to visit another of the new colonies today, but a return trip to The Deer is on the schedule first. We were last at Mule Deer three weeks ago. If we're going to have a second capture session before the eggs hatch, we need to do it now. Mary also urges that we return to CR 4½ today to catch more of the new birds that have recently arrived. By this time in a swallow summer, we can start to see the end of the drop-netting season. As more and more eggs hatch, the adults spend most of their time foraging for their broods and are at the nests less and less. Our chances of catching them in a drop net dwindle. If we've got places where drop netting is still effective, we'd better take advantage of them while we can.

Mary suggests she take all three assistants to CR 4½. If she'd four people yesterday, she thinks she could have caught over two hundred birds. That means I'll have to do Mule Deer alone. The number of birds there is small enough that one person can handle it, and a morning without riding herd on assistants sounds refreshing. Our assistants are great kids, but the intense, constant nature of our as-

sociation is mentally fatiguing for all. I was getting frayed around
the edges yesterday. Little things were annoying me. I have to calm
down and tell myself this season isn't over yet. The time when people
are tired, hot, bored, thinking about going home, and just burned out
still lies ahead.

I arrive at Mule Deer and set the nets at each end of the long
tunnel. Getting a net up without a second person to help is slower,
underscoring the value of assistants despite the occasional irrita-
tion. The water level in the culvert has declined slightly since we
were last here, but it's still mucky, dank, and dark, with dead things
down in there. Today's dead things are crayfish.

I sit in the truck and watch as the swallows swirl around the nets,
trying to decide whether to go in over them. I plead with them to
adjust quickly today, because I didn't bring a lunch. We're doing only
a half day here because of our pressing need to go to other sites. I've
had productive half days at Mule Deer in the past. I've also sat here
for most of a morning without catching a thing while the birds freaked
out over the net. What'll it be today?

Fortunately, this morning the birds cooperate and start going into
the culvert in a relatively short time. I do my net checks about every
twenty-five minutes, processing in the truck and daydreaming in the
interim. I catch twenty-two cliff swallows by quitting time—half of
them previously banded—but the birds in general don't seem as catch-
able at Mule Deer today. The smaller haul is most likely a consequence of a smaller colony. I walk through the culvert before I leave
and look in the nests, just to count how many have eggs or young.
Thirty-two nests do, most with small babies recently hatched. That's
down ten from the last time we checked. Soon the entire colony will
be heavily into feeding nestlings.

At lunch I discover that Mary didn't have the big day she'd hoped for
at CR 4½. Fewer of those unbanded "new" birds were around this
morning; only a handful were collecting mud. Many of these
latecomers apparently have no intention of staying even at the sites
where they do some nest building. It seems wasteful to work on a
nest for a few days only to abandon it. So who exactly are these birds,
where have they been, and where do they go?

Mary is also ranting about Annie. She repeatedly banged her net
pole against the bridge railing, making enough noise to spoil several
drops. She complained constantly about her dry skin and about be-

ing tired, perhaps not surprising since the other assistants report that she stays out every night until 2:00 or 3:00 A.M. She sat listening to tapes with her earphones on, not obeying Mary's instructions. All this is more proof that Annie's better off with me, because I haven't had these problems with her.

Let's just try to get through the next three weeks without killing each other.

Lunch is highlighted by a speech from Joan. Last night some students broke into the Cedar Point food supply and stole, among other things, a five-gallon carton of ice cream, enough to feed the whole camp. Ice cream is one of the masses' most treasured desserts, although it's a luxury the field station can't really afford. Joan is incensed that someone would have such a blatant disregard for the rules and be so inconsiderate, and she threatens retribution if she discovers the culprits. I wince. Annie's active night life immediately makes her a suspect, simply because she's among the subset of field station residents who would have been awake at the time the theft occurred. I convey my suspicion only to Mary, though, who's been thinking the same thing.

This afternoon we're to do Knight's Tube for the first time. Netting at the tube may be an adventure, since that site looked more challenging than a standard culvert. I'm not even sure what we'll need—for example, what size net or how we'll anchor the poles—because I've been there only for a few minutes. We load a variety of equipment into the truck and hope we've anticipated everything. I usually scout a colony better before we go there to net.

When we get to Dave Knight's pasture by the railroad tracks, I'm pleased to see the gate still open. We drive down the ruts, going overland through the tall grass that dances in the wind. Annie and Judy are excited by the setting—a pasture out in the middle of nowhere—and awed that we could have found a colony out here. We park along the bank of Spring Creek that meanders through the pasture. A barbed wire fence crosses the north end of the tube, and we find a low spot to step over it. Wearing knee boots, Judy, Annie, and I wade through the foot-deep stream flowing through the tube.

This is the most remarkable colony I've ever seen. The walls and ceiling of the tube are made of corrugated metal. The birds' nests are plastered on and between the parallel ridges. There's no horizontal overhang under which the nests are placed, because the ceiling is just an arch continuous with the walls. Some nests are attached at the highest point above our heads, with their entrance holes pointing directly downward. Others are along the sides. Though the tube is long and the middle relatively dark, the flowing water cleans it out, so it's not stagnant or filthy like Mule Deer.

Obviously the tube has been lengthened during construction. The north end is the original portion, and it must have been here forever. The concrete sleeve on the north entrance along the earthen embankment has a big 1938 etched into it. The south end is where the expansion occurred, and inside we can see the seam where additional corrugated metal was spliced onto the original. The south end has a similar concrete sleeve with 1994 inscribed. There are new nests, clearly built this summer, clustered toward the south end, but in the middle and the north end the nests look very old. Dave Knight was right: the birds have been using this colony for years, maybe decades, unknown to us all that time. Damn.

There's a strong south wind by now, so we set our net on the south side. This end of the tube is more open than the north, with no fences nearby. I can tell that setting a net on the north end will be a challenge, but we won't have to worry about that today. Many of the colony residents are exiting the south end in this wind, and we start catching birds before we have the net completely set.

There's no decent place close by to process. I'm sure the birds are so unused to people at this remote site that we'll have to hide or sit far away. We decide to go back to the truck, and Judy and Annie open the tailgate and sit in the back, blocked from view by the camper shell. A tailgate party out in the middle of a pasture. I do net duty, walking back and forth through the tube to gather birds. This is a nice arrangement because I always enter the tube from the north, flushing the birds away from me through the long dark tube toward the net at the other end.

We catch birds constantly and stay busy all afternoon. It's fun netting here. The open fields that surround us on three sides make me think this must be like the isolated Sand Hills prairie where Tony does his grasshopper research. We spend most of our summer in, on, and around culverts and bridges, and it's refreshing to be away from roads. But the birds we study are never far away from human habitats, and we can remind ourselves of that just by looking to the south where the railroad embankment towers thirty feet above us. Periodically a Union Pacific coal train blows by, and the peaceful solitude is broken by the engine's roar and an engineer's greeting us by blowing his whistle.

I'm surprised by how many previously banded birds we're catching. We're getting more here than at Knight's Culvert, and I notice that in general they're "older" bands. By the time we quit we've caught 146 birds, 95 of them previously banded. We got 65 percent banded birds at a site we'd never netted before! Fewer of these banded birds were last year's, meaning there are fewer yearlings here than at Knight's Culvert. A quick count shows at least 16 birds that date from the 1989–91 seasons, meaning these birds are at least five to seven years old. But this isn't surprising, because the tube is an older colony. One wouldn't expect it to consist of mostly yearlings. More important, many of these older residents have probably been living here for several years and thus are ones we'd been missing in our netting until now. Mary will later determine from the computer that many of the tube's birds were first banded at Whitetail. The tube also seems to have relatively few within-season immigrants from other colonies, since we caught only two birds first banded at other colonies earlier this summer.

When we reconvene with Mary, we find that her afternoon was more frustrating than ours. The wind along the canal played havoc with her and Kathy's drop net at CR 3. They got only thirty-one birds. Mary is mad at the birds and the wind, taking it as a personal affront that she caught so few swallows. She wants to go back to even the score.

Two new colonies netted so far, one to go. Duane's culvert is next.

June 21

So many colonies still need our attention that I feel pulled in twenty directions. It's been almost a week since we discovered the active colony in the culvert under Interstate 80 on the way to the rodeo. With the wind since then and the need to net the new sites, we've had no chance to visit I 80. I decide to make time today, because if we wait too long and most of the eggs hatch, we won't be able to catch anything.

I take Annie to I 80. She's the model assistant this morning, cheerful and focused on the tasks at hand. I guess she's right when she says she gets along better with men than with women, though from observing her I can't figure out exactly why. Mary says that's just because I'm male and don't understand the social dynamics of female groups.

We set our net on the north side of the I 80 culvert, because the wind was supposed to be northeasterly today. But we find it's straight out of the east, and the birds don't seem to know which end of the culvert to go in or come out of. Many of them are trying to get in on the north end with the net, but this culvert is so low (the ceiling only about five feet off the ground) that they have trouble flying over the top of the net to get in. And our net is too long to fit very well across this narrow, single-tunnel culvert. We have to set it farther out than I'd like, and many exiting birds miss it.

It's quickly apparent that the karma is not right at I 80 today.

The birds spend a lot of time swirling around, agitated at the net and at us parked on the side of the exit ramp above the culvert. We wait at least an hour before birds start going in the south end. I finally decide to try to flush them into the net, so I get out of the truck and run down the shallow highway embankment to the south end. But I make so much noise thrashing through the tall grass that the birds are alerted, and many flush out the open south end before I can get there. When I reach the south entrance, most of the residents remaining in nests fly straight out at me anyway, almost hitting me as I stand there and wave my arms. An entire colony of birds like that one we missed at McDougals! This is going to be a tough place.

We get a few birds in the net on the north end, but by midmorning the wind is predominantly southeasterly. We move our net to the south side after considerable fumbling around trying to find ground soft enough to drive in the net poles. This doesn't do much good, though, because the swallows are seriously disrupted by the displaced net, and it takes them another hour to calm down and start entering the now open north end. By then it's almost noon and time for us to leave. We should have planned to do a full day here.

The haul for the morning is only 29 birds. I'm even more discouraged by our effort when I walk through the culvert and count eighty-five active nests. There are 170 birds here, and we got hardly any of them today. I can foresee that numerous trips to I 80 may be necessary.

I'm depressed as we drive back to Cedar Point. I feel we've wasted the morning, and we have too many colonies needing attention to be able to blow half days like this. I feel better when I learn that Mary had a good morning at Pigpen. She, Kathy, and Judy caught 108 birds.

As often seems to happen when we have a lousy morning, the schedule calls for Whitetail in the afternoon. We also need to net at Duane's culvert, now officially called Dunwoody. Mary and I debate for a while who should do what, and we finally decide she and Kathy will try Dunwoody. Annie and Judy are a very capable Whitetail team, so I'll take them there. I'm a bit envious of Mary getting to see a net go up at Dunwoody for the first time, but if it's a choice between Whitetail and any other site, it's no contest for me.

At Whitetail we start to set the net on the south end. Judy holds one end of the net while I wade across the creek with the other end, but as I reach the east tunnel I encounter a big hole. More and more water has been flowing through the east tunnel lately, and the creek bank funnels that water through a narrow channel on the south end. An abyss has formed there. I can't get across it in hip waders. Damn! This is a major problem. One of Whitetail's ideal features was the shallow creek on the south end. For several years we'd had a similar abyss on the north end, but it was seldom a problem because we rarely netted there. The creek changes with time, though, and now the water flow pattern has filled in the north hole and created one here on the south.

We temporarily put away the net. My only recourse is to use chest waders to wade through the abyss, but the only pair is back at Cedar Point. I tell the assistants to wait here and be inconspicuous; I'll drive back for the chest waders. As I walk across the road to the truck, I notice that Annie has moved her chair outside the tunnel to be in the sun. She's also in full view of the colony, only a few feet from the nests on the south end. I have to holler down that she needs to stay inside the tunnel to remain hidden. Frustrated by the abyss, I'm probably not as diplomatic as I should be in telling her to shift it.

It seems to take forever to find the boxed-up chest waders among stacks of our supplies in the lab. Finally I return to Whitetail and crawl into the waders. They're hot, bulky, and make walking difficult—especially in water, for which they're supposedly designed. I wade into the abyss and sink to my waist. We get the net set, but it's already clear that I'm going to have trouble reaching birds that get into the net above the abyss. By pulling the slack in the net downward and stretching, I eventually extract all the birds, but this is no fun today. When I move out of the abyss the water is only a foot or so deep, and I'm standing there wrapped in rubber like the Michelin Man.

We do a couple of flushes and get mostly banded birds as usual. We don't get any hundred-bird flushes today, for which I'm thankful; I move around with all the grace and agility of Herman Munster. I notice, though, that we seem to be getting a higher fraction of unbanded birds. Many of these birds are in fresh plumage, their colors extraordinarily bright for this time of year. The blue of their crowns and backs is more vivid, and the chestnut of their throats and the orange of their rumps are deeper and richer, than we see on the banded birds. My bet is that these sleek-looking unbanded birds aren't residents here and are some of the thousand or so immigrants a day that Bruce estimated come through Whitetail. Most of them won't stay here. The timing of their appearance at Whitetail this year is of major significance, but it doesn't dawn on me today—I'm in too much of a stew over the new abyss.

With our late start, I feel fortunate to catch about 250 birds. While Judy and Annie process the last ones, I put on my gloves and mask to fumigate, making myself an even stranger sight. I've been fumigating once a week to remove the many swallow bugs introduced from other colonies. Early in the year I was thoroughly fumigating the colony because there was so much bare wall and the existing nests could be misted with insecticide on all sides. Now, however, there's no more bare wall in the middle tunnel: the birds have built nests in solid tiers five and six deep across the entire length of the culvert. It's again hard to get fumigant into all the cracks and crevices in the labyrinth of mud nests. Perhaps as a result, I'm seeing more swallow bugs on the nests now.

I can hear babies in many of the nests, and I'd judge that at least half of the nests have young. As they get older, I'll have to stop fumigating. When the nestlings are close to fledging—leaving the nest—they're very sensitive to disturbance and will often fledge prematurely if a predator or a person gets near their nest. They end up flopping into the creek and are doomed unless I can retrieve them.

I'm eager to get Mary's report on Dunwoody. She and Kathy are late getting back for supper, and both look frazzled. They caught 136 birds, most of them in the last two hours. When they arrived no birds were at the colony, and Mary was afraid it might have been abandoned. They went ahead and set a net on one end and sat down to wait beside the truck, shielded behind a gate and some corrals to the south. Mary occasionally saw a group of cliff swallows pass overhead as if feeding. They'd caught just one bird (that had flushed out of a nest while they were setting the net) until almost 3:00, when the entire colony descended.

Immediately scores of swallows were swarming in the culvert, flying through it and plowing into the net while Mary and Kathy were standing there extracting birds. The swallows no longer seemed concerned by the presence of people. All avian hell broke loose. Eventually Mary sent Kathy back to the truck to process alone, but she couldn't keep up with Mary's extractions, and Mary couldn't get the net clear enough to go back and help her. They were overwhelmed and stayed that way until quitting time.

I ask about banded birds. They got fifty-nine, an even higher percentage than at Knight's Culvert. Like that colony, Dunwoody seems to have many birds that moved in from other colonies this year: twenty of the fifty-nine bands had been put out elsewhere this summer. And also as at Knight's Culvert, many of the birds were yearlings. Twenty-one of the banded birds were first caught last year, and most of those were banded as juveniles soon after fledging. Mary remembers getting only one relatively old bird—from 1989, she thinks.

The two newly established colonies thus are almost identical in composition: a lot of yearlings plus birds that first spent some time earlier this summer at nearby colonies. It's rewarding to see this congruence in our mark-recapture data between two similar sites, validating our methods and the conclusions that can be drawn from such data. It's also satisfying to see that our banding data suggest a different colony composition at the older Knight's Tube: fewer yearlings, fewer within-year immigrants, and more older birds.

I ask Mary how many nests are active at Dunwoody. She counted 205, which happens to be exactly what I estimated at Knight's Tube and only 20 fewer than at Knight's Culvert. One of the striking features of the cliff swallow population in southwestern Nebraska is the extreme diversity in colony size we see among sites that may be only a few miles apart. Yet here are three colonies all within a 1.1-mile span along the railroad tracks that are essentially identical in size. Why? One is an older site and two are new ones, so I don't think colony age can explain it. I don't know. I do know that if you were studying only these three colonies, you'd be tempted to conclude that 200 nests is the optimal cliff swallow colony size—because "all" colonies are that size. Colonies of this size might be ones where the birds are most successful, as other data suggest. But you couldn't know this by looking at the overall distribution of colony sizes in our population: the "optimal" one at 200 nests is relatively rare compared with the other sizes, which range from one to 3,700 nests.

This illustrates the value of studying lots of colonies on a relatively large spatial scale. So often I read about studies on other colonial birds that are confined to one or two sites. I shudder to think how biased and wrong anything we might conclude about cliff swallows would be if we studied just these three colonies along the railroad tracks. I have to wonder the same thing about published studies done on small areas and in short periods of time. You have to know what's going on in the population as a whole and over a span of years before you can correctly interpret what you see at a single site.

I can relax slightly tonight, knowing we now have one sampling session at each of the new colonies. We'll return, because we've caught only some of the birds that live there, but we already have substantial information on the composition and characteristics of the swallows occupying these sites. Taken with similar data from other new colonies in past years, we can say with certainty what "kinds" of cliff swallows found new colonies. And we've located, especially at Knight's Tube, a set of birds that had for years been escaping detection and inclusion in our statistical estimates of survival.

The summer is already a major success.

9

Boat Rides and Black Flies

*Evidence of this age-long occupation of the cliffs is fur-
nished not only by the muddy cicatrices left by fallen
nests, but, wherever the wall juts out or overhangs, so as
to shield a place below from the action of the elements, by
beds of guano and coprolitic stalagmites.*
　　　　—William L. Dawson, *The Birds of California*

June 22

The time has come to survey the swallow colonies on the cliffs
along the south shore of Lake McConaughy. We want to know
what colony sites are active this year and their sizes. For this annual
event we need to use the Cedar Point boat. Since Mary and I are no
sailors, we've arranged for Ron—the field station's maintenance
chief—to take us on a cruise.

Usually I go on the boat ride, even though I dislike water and can't
swim, because I want to see the natural sites. But today the schedule
also calls for going back to Oshkosh, and Mary refuses to deal with
the unfriendly game warden there. We decide that she'll go with Ron
and take Judy. Kathy and Annie seem a little surly about not getting
to go along, though I explain that the boat can't carry us all. Having
to spend the day at Oshkosh doesn't help their mood. They remember the earlier trip and how hot it was sitting by the roadside.

Before we leave for Oshkosh, I walk down to the boat garage to
tell Ron that Mary and Judy will be his passengers. He's backed one
of the station's Boston Whalers out of the garage and is checking it
for emergency supplies, life vests, and gas. Although Keystone Lake
and Lake McConaughy are close by, researchers and classes at Cedar Point seldom use boats, so another purpose of today's trip will be
to run gas through the engine. The boat chosen is the newest of Cedar Point's fleet, and Ron isn't sure its engine works properly. It might
conk out once they're on the water. I ask if there are oars on board.

If the motor quits, at least Ron will be there to fix it. He can build or repair anything. A native Ogallalan, Ron has almost single-handedly kept the field station's aging buildings in top condition. He personally constructed three buildings at Cedar Point, including the four-unit apartment complex Mary and I live in, and is now working on a fourth. When not building some major structure, Ron has roofed the lodge, built decks on some of the faculty cabins, torn down three dilapidated house trailers, constructed library cabinets in the lodge, installed air conditioners in the kitchen and new picture windows in the dining room, and dug up and replaced sewer lines and septic tanks. Besides this he constantly helps researchers like us fix equipment and vehicles. And he's an excellent boatman.

Around Ron I feel like an unskilled nitwit.

The presence of cliff swallow colonies on natural sites was one of the many features that first attracted me to southwestern Nebraska. In his letter to me in 1981, John Janovy mentioned that some swallows nested on rocky outcroppings not far from the biological station. During my graduate school days, before I started collecting data, my fellow students and some of the Princeton faculty were discussing whether it was really desirable to study cliff swallows nesting on bridges and in highway culverts. Does the birds' behavior on these artificial structures differ in any important ways from that seen on the ancestral cliff nesting sites where the birds evolved? If so, it could be dangerous to make inferences about how or why colonial nesting might have developed based on what we see on bridges. We might be misled by the birds' "unnatural" responses to these artificial habitats. This problem potentially applies to all field studies of animals occupying human-influenced environments and is increasingly an issue as people continue to alter natural habitats. Theoretically, small environmental changes could affect aspects of an organism's life history in ways we can't detect, much less measure, since unaltered habitats often aren't available for comparison.

One solution, of course, is to study only organisms in completely undisturbed areas. The problem is that the few such places left are in remote parts of the world. And aside from greatly restricting the kinds of things you can study and the sorts of questions you can ask, travel to unspoiled jungles, deserts, or mountaintops is a luxury most of us can't afford. So the other option is to stay closer to home and try to determine what effect, if any, human-caused environmental disruption may have had on an organism. This can be done by comparing habitats that have been altered to various degrees and observing whether changes in an organism's behavior correlate with the extent of environmental change. This was what we needed to do with the swallows: compare natural and man-made colony sites. The issue of how legitimate it is to study birds on bridges wouldn't go away until we did. During my first uncertain year as a graduate student, I was comforted many times by John's comment that cliff swallows nested on natural sites near Cedar Point.

"Having natural sites" had been so emphasized by people at Princeton that finding some was my first priority during the inaugural swallow summer. The southeastern corner of Lake McConaughy's shoreline consists almost exclusively of rocky outcroppings that are part of the North Platte River valley escarpment. These formations are similar to the cliffs where George Suckley and Henry Carleton saw cliff swallows nesting in the mid-nineteenth century. The outcroppings along the lake are irregular in shape and height, some having horizontal overhangs that provide protection for swallow nests built under them. At intervals the overhangs break off, destroying a particular cliff's suitability as a colony site, but others erode to replace them. At any one time there appear to be numerous overhangs that could support swallow colonies, though not all are occupied.

Our access to these crumbling sandstone cliffs depends on the level of Lake McConaughy. When the lake is low, a beach extends up to a hundred feet out from the base of the cliffs. At these times we can walk under the nests and use ladders to reach them. But when the lake is high, the water extends to the base of the cliffs and rules out reaching or even seeing these colonies except from the water. That first summer the lake was low enough so we could walk along the beach. Mary and I spent our first couple of days in the field checking the cliffs for evidence of past colonies. We were hampered by the lack of public access to the beach where the cliffs were most suitable as nesting sites: we finally resorted to parking in front of a seasonal cabin whose owners hadn't come for the summer and sneaking down the stairway to the beach.

We initially didn't find much that first summer. At the time we didn't know that swallows using the cliffs arrive slightly later than those at places like Morning Glory or Whitetail. When I reported to John Hoogland that we'd found only one abandoned colony site on the cliffs, he advised me to call various swallow biologists to ask if they knew of other locations in the country where cliff swallows used natural sites. For a short time I was devastated by the prospect of not having found my ideal research site at Cedar Point. Two fruitless days on the phone produced no alternative sites. No one could name another natural setting accessible for research. In retrospect I see that John and I overreacted, but at least my phone search emphasized again that Cedar Point was *the* place for cliff swallow research. We'd just have to use what was available on the cliffs along Lake McConaughy.

Eventually we discovered six colonies on the cliffs that year, and we regularly checked nests at two of them. Four were in places where we probably would have drowned in the deep water had we tried to get to them with ladders. One colony happened to be on a cliff almost directly under the cabin where we trespassed to get to the beach, and we didn't have to carry the ladder very far. Still, going there to check nests every second day was a monumental pain. By the time we wrestled a ten-foot ladder down the stairway and across boulders partly submerged in the water beneath the colony, looked in all the nests, and hauled the ladder back up to the car, half a day would have elapsed. It's little wonder that nest checking was all we did that first year.

But our efforts paid off. We learned that virtually everything that we suspected—and later verified—was going on in the artificial colonies was also happening on the cliffs. Swallows in both kinds of colonies laid eggs in each others' nests; swallows in both used their neighbors to find food; swallows in both faced the risk of having older, unrelated fledglings intrude into nests and steal food brought by the parents of younger babies. Snakes attacked both kinds of colonies. Swallow bugs infested both. In short, our work that summer and in later years showed that cliff swallow social behavior is the same no matter what colony structure the birds use. Thus we've been able to defuse the criticism that our study was "unnatural" because it relied on data taken from bridges and culverts.

Yet I'm the first to admit that natural colonies differ in a few respects. One is structural stability. The overhangs are unstable, and many last only three or four years. Once they fall the birds have to relocate, usually to an overhang nearby. Bridges and culverts don't have this problem. Some cliff sites are also less protected from the elements. In severe thunderstorms, rain and hail can blow underneath overhangs, soaking and destroying many nests. Waves are another problem for the cliff-nesting birds. When the lake is high, storms can whip up waves far enough to wash away nests. In one single storm eight years ago, over 1,400 cliff swallow nests on natural cliffs along the shoreline of Big Mac were destroyed in less than an hour. Bridges and culverts are generally more sheltered, and weather-related nest losses there are infrequent. One could argue, though, that nest loss from storms in the lakefront colonies is unnatural, since the lake is man-made. "Natural" colonies away from the lake, such as those near Ash Hollow, don't have this problem. The better-protected bridges and culverts might actually be more representative of what the birds historically experienced.

This just illustrates the problem of defining exactly what part of the environment has been altered by humans and whether the change is relevant.

One of the first questions that must be answered for any colonial animal is whether colonies form simply because nesting sites are in short supply. If a species requires specialized structures to nest on, or if it's pelagic and there are only a few isolated islands and coastlines where breeding can occur, individuals may congregate in a location strictly by necessity. This is believed to be why seabirds often breed in huge colonies on remote islands. In these cases the animals may have to pay many of the costs of living in groups, but they don't receive any cooperative benefits. Their only compensation is that breeding in a colony allows them to reproduce, period. If they refuse to join a colony, there's nowhere to go because nesting sites are so scarce. When I first expressed an interest in studying why cliff swallows live in groups, some people told me that they're colonial simply because their nesting sites are limited. The implication was that the problem was solved and consequently not very interesting.

Even by then I had observed cliff swallows enough to know this explanation seemed bogus. The birds clustered their nests in high density on some bridges, yet identical ones just down the road had no birds. The birds obviously grouped their nests more closely than they needed to, given the extensive space where nests could be built. In Nebraska and everywhere that cliff swallows are found, there is now an abundance of artificial nesting sites—bridges, buildings, culverts—and many are never used. Their nesting sites certainly aren't limited today, yet they still nest close together, often in large colonies. I knew from this that there had to be other reasons why these swallows formed colonies.

But what about birds nesting in natural colonies? Appropriate cliffs with the right kind of vertical wall and horizontal overhang could be limited, forcing the birds—at least historically—into colonies at the few sites that do exist. It took us a bit longer to determine that natural nesting sites also were not limiting for cliff swallows, in line with what we see for the bridges and culverts. Some of our evidence came from colony-site surveys like the one we're doing today.

In the early years of our research, we had no access to a boat and knew little about how many total colonies were on the south side of Lake McConaughy. Our boat surveys began eight years ago. That summer a group of limnologists was studying algal communities of the lake. Kyle, the faculty member directing the project, was looking for "boat people." The limnologists' work required scuba diving from a boat along the face of Kingsley Dam. For safety reasons they needed someone to wait in the boat to hand them equipment, take readings from instruments, and wave off speedboats that might come too close. Kyle was having trouble finding boat people that summer, so I proposed a trade. Some of our assistants would carry out the duty if he'd take us on a survey of the lakeshore cliffs by boat.

Kyle agreed. Our assistant Lori fulfilled our end of the deal, and in mid-June Kyle and Mary took the first census of the cliff colonies. They slowly cruised the southern shore, checking all the outcroppings and recording colony sizes. The boat survey revealed that the cliffs petered out about halfway down the lake, at which point the shore becomes relatively flat. But more important, Mary discovered many active cliff colonies in inaccessible sections of shoreline. She also saw many apparently identical cliffs that had no colonies. When viewed on a larger geographic scale, there appeared to be plenty of suitable nesting sites along the cliff faces. Cliff nesting was much more widespread than we would have guessed by studying the one small section of lakeshore that we could reach on foot.

Kyle had so much fun doing the survey that in later years he took us out for an annual census even when he didn't need boat people. We expanded the tour to include a cruise below the Morning Glory to count the nests built under its eaves and catwalks. We usually do each summer's survey in mid- to late June, late enough in the season that all birds intending to settle have done so but before young start fledging and colonies are abandoned. Collecting data on annual use and size of the cliff colonies shows patterns in the swallows' use of these sites. It's already given us some information on the average structural stability of many of the overhangs.

Three years ago Kyle's research changed, and he began doing less fieldwork at Cedar Point. We had to arrange another way to survey the cliff colonies. One option we rejected early was to rent a boat from the gas station and bait shop at the south end of Kingsley Dam. A few years ago, a cinematographer who was filming cliff swallows for the BBC's *Trials of Life* television show needed to reach some of the cliff colonies along the lakeshore, and he rented a boat from the bait shop. He got halfway out, the motor quit, and he ended up drifting out into the middle of Big Mac, with no oars on board. Hours later another boater spotted him and towed him in. When Ron heard about our plight he offered to be our captain, and now a boat tour with him is an annual ritual.

When we get to Oshkosh, I decide I'm not in the mood to deal with the cranky game warden. We'll chance it that my earlier contact will keep him at bay today. The wind is strong by the time we arrive at the bridge, which doesn't bode well. Already the birds seem flighty and are alarm-calling at us. The wind could also be a problem for the boaters. The vast expanse of Big Mac is no place to be in a strong wind.

Annie and Kathy continue their surliness, and I can tell this is going to be a long day. They're just standing around instead of setting up the net and chairs, and I have to start giving orders. Annie slept during the drive over from Cedar Point, and she looks exhausted. Her nightlife is really beginning to tell, which doesn't help her mood or mine. I'm annoyed that she's letting these activities interfere with her readiness for swallow research, and I resolve to continue to keep her as busy as possible. It's not the fieldwork that's tiring her, so I'm stingy with sympathy.

As we set up the net, hordes of black flies descend on us. These insects bite, painfully, and they buzz around us in clouds. We smear ourselves with insect repellent, but the chemical only keeps them from actually biting. They still hover around eyes, ears, nose, and mouth and are incredibly annoying. The black flies are all Kathy and Annie can think about, and they constantly swat at them to no avail.

As soon as we start dropping the net, it's obvious that the Oshkosh birds are too far along in nesting for drop netting to be effective. They flush out as soon as we start across the bridge. Someone always seems to be overhead and gives an alarm call. Many of the nests probably have small babies by now. The birds' change from being so easily caught in drop nets early in the season to being almost impossible now is based on their biology and occurs everywhere, but it's always immensely frustrating. It's especially so for me because I know it heralds the end of the field season.

Kathy and Annie are obsessed with the black flies and can barely function. Fortunately we're not getting many birds to process, so intense concentration isn't required. I maintain my composure and try to be stoic in hopes of showing them it's futile to get in a dither. I'm reminded of our assistant Laurie. I assigned her the task of observing swallows at a mudhole at Clary one summer, since we wanted to know which color-marked males engaged in extrapair copulation attempts with females that gathered mud there. To get close enough to see the birds without alarming them, Laurie had to sit motionless in a pile of brush at one end of the culvert. The brush partly hid her from the birds but attracted huge swarms of black flies. Laurie endured the black flies without a word of complaint, and in the process we got some of our best data on the identities of the males that perpetrate extrapair copulations (they mostly did not live in the colony). Laurie was one of those spectacular assistants who comes along only a few times in a researcher's career. There must be something about Garden County and black flies: only here and at Clary have they ever been a problem.

We keep trying drops, but we're usually getting only one or two birds. Sometimes we walk out on the bridge and get nothing. The wind is part of the problem; we can net only the east side of the bridge, because on the west side the wind blows the net shut. We have no coverage of the flyway, and the birds go around our bunched-up net. Kathy and Annie obey, but they step up their complaints about the black flies and the rising temperature beside the asphalt road. Annie's discomfort is magnified by her weariness from lack of sleep.

After four successive drops that yield nothing but a lot of pissed-off cliff swallows, I decide it's pointless to stay here. I'm satisfied that it's our inability to catch birds rather than the assistants' complaints that warrant our leaving, and we've probably stayed longer than I would have had they been more pleasant. There's a dramatic improvement in mood when I announce we're quitting. I'm frustrated on multiple counts—only sixty-one birds caught, the wind, the approaching end of being able to drop-net, the assistants' behavior—

but I'm relieved that the game warden never appeared. I guess no public-spirited passerby called in to report us today. I don't foresee any more trips to Oshkosh this summer, so we've survived a season without a confrontation with him.

It's almost lunchtime, and there's not enough time to drive the forty-three miles back to Cedar Point to eat. Instead we escape the black flies by going into Oshkosh and looking for a city park. Oshkosh consists of two streets running north and south and five or six running east and west. It takes about two minutes to cruise the town and determine that the only parklike place is a Little League ball field with one baseball diamond. It has a public restroom—which Annie appreciates—but no picnic tables, so we spread our lunch out on the truck's tailgate and eat our soggy sandwiches in the parking lot. The ball field is deserted, as is most of Oshkosh. I always have trouble believing that this town of just a thousand people, the county seat, is the largest city—almost the only city—in Garden County. There are six Nebraska counties that cover larger land areas, but Garden County is still over four hundred square miles larger than the state of Rhode Island.

While we eat, Annie brings up her nightlife and how tired she's getting. She's been helping one of the students in the behavioral ecology class with his term project. I can't tell if she's romantically involved with him or the other male student she hangs out with or maybe both. One of them is doing a census of birds by counting pre-dawn songs. Many species start singing at 2:00 or 3:00 A.M., well before first light, and some, like the yellow-breasted chat that lives near Mary and me, sing all night long. Annie's role in the project is unclear, but I use the opportunity to admonish her about letting that interfere with her daytime swallow work.

Annie also confesses that she did eat some of the stolen ice cream the other day. She says she saw it sitting out after it had been taken and thought it was okay to have some. My suspicion is confirmed, though she swears she wasn't involved in the theft. She tells me it was stolen by a student who until recently had been Josef's assistant. Josef had to dismiss him because he was incompetent at fieldwork and so interested in partying at night that he was exhausted during working hours. I point this out to Annie. Now this fellow is still hanging around, pulling stunts like stealing ice cream. I tell Annie to avoid him. Being a visitor to the station, I don't want any public relations problems caused by my assistants' behavior. But

Annie's open acknowledgment that she's been burning the candle at both ends, her promise to get more sleep, and her assurance that at the moment she values her swallow work above all else make me feel better. Perhaps I've been too hard on her and Kathy today.

By now the wind is too strong for any further netting. Instead we use the time to check some natural colony sites here in Garden County. These are in the Ash Hollow area and may be close to those observed by the nineteenth-century naturalists. We discovered these colonies six years ago, almost by accident, as we were trying to find an old bridge over the North Platte River south of Lewellen that had cliff swallows. We were driving down a dirt road that ran along the base of a line of tall cliffs just south of the river. I had never thought to search these cliffs for colonies; I assumed for some reason that the birds used only the bluffs along the lake well to the east. Also, these cliffs were rather overgrown with vegetation that would make them unattractive to cliff swallows. Or so I thought. Along the roadside I suddenly noticed a single cliff swallow gathering mud at a puddle. I knew of no colonies in the area except at the old bridge, which was too far away. We screeched to a halt and watched the bird. It flew straight toward a colony on one of the massive cliffs almost directly above where we were parked! The birds didn't care that portions of this bluff were overgrown with juniper trees. Obviously many cliffs in the study area that I had judged inappropriate were suitable for occupancy after all.

By thoroughly searching the cliffs along this road we found seven more colonies. Those, and other newly settled sites in this area, have been used sporadically in subsequent seasons. Each summer seems to be boom or bust for these sites: birds occupy either most of them or none. Unfortunately these sites are inaccessible, since they're on the sides of bluffs at least fifty feet high. Our "use" of them as research sites is confined to scoring their occupancy and size each year.

This summer appears to be an off year for the Garden County cliff colonies. Kathy, Annie, and I drive the road until it dead-ends in a pasture belonging to the Grace Land and Cattle Company. We find no active colonies. The birds' absence doesn't reflect a lack of overhangs, however. Most of the overhangs we discovered in 1989 are extant today. Old nests last for many years at these sites. The stable Garden County cliffs, with no water around them, make me wonder if perhaps the crumbly cliffs on Lake McConaughy are the "unnatural" ones.

I get the boat ride report from Mary when we return to Cedar Point. Although the lake was rough, Ron followed a course close to the south shore that was well protected. He was the complete captain, also serving as tour guide by pointing out landmarks and relating local history. They had no motor problems, although Ron really opened it up at times to give the engine a good test. Mary was most impressed with the high lake level. With the extensive flooding downstream along the Platte, the power company has been holding water in Lake McConaughy, trying not to compound problems by flooding the North Platte River. The lake is up to maximum capacity. There's no beach, and water is under all the cliff colonies. Most of them are perilously close to the water already, and some nests will flood if the lake rises or if a strong wind stirs up high waves. Mary found five active colonies on the lakeshore cliffs. The numbers are low this year, possibly because of the high water. They cruised below the Morning Glory and counted about 1,500 nests under the catwalks and eaves. That's the smallest Morning Glory's been in years. I wonder if the bad weather this spring has caused some swallows not to breed.

There are a lot of signs that some cliff swallows may not be nesting this summer.

10

Predators

Sometimes, when subjected to unusual conditions. . . ,
grackles resort to wholesale killing.
> —Alfred O. Gross, Bent's *Life Histories of North*
> *American Blackbirds, Orioles, Tanagers, and*
> *Allies*

June 23

Yesterday Mary went by Skelly and found the colony intact. I'm surprised it's lasted this long. Maybe the gas station really is abandoned. As much as I don't want to, we'll have to try Skelly once more. It means sneaking in again.

We erect our net near the nests under the gas pumps' awning. The net is more conspicuous than I like, both to the birds and to passersby—more precisely, the owners of the property—who might be driving down the road. We wait in the truck, and I emphasize to Annie that we need to minimize our visibility. She assumes this is because of the birds; I don't tell her I'm mostly concerned about attracting the notice of the law or the owner. Our truck blends in well with some junk cars and tractors parked on the premises.

We begin catching a few birds, but we have the same old problem of their having a lot of flyway. The swallows tend to go around the net. This is the best we can do at Skelly, though. The expanse of asphalt rules out anchoring the poles of the big nets. With big nets, it would also be harder to shut down and slink away if an uncooperative owner should suddenly show up. Each time a vehicle passes on the road or exits the interstate nearby, I watch nervously until it disappears. I feel like an animal worried about predators.

I finally decide that our best chance of catching anything might be to flush the birds toward the net. In a flush they might momentarily forget to go around. The only way to do it will be to quietly get out of the truck and go around the back of the gas station. Then we can suddenly appear under the nests. The only problem is that flushing will increase our own conspicuousness, especially when it may look like we're prowling around the back of an abandoned building.

We try it anyway. I do the first flush, taking the birds by surprise, and we catch seven. Annie tries the next one, and we get nothing. We let the birds calm down, and it's my turn. We get three. When Annie next tries it, we catch nothing. She comes back to the truck asking how is it that the birds get in the net when I flush them but not when she does. But within half an hour, even my flushes are yielding only one or two birds. The cliff swallows are learning to go around the net even when I come running out, waving my arms like an idiot.

As the morning wears on, we start waiting longer between flushes, hoping the birds will "forget" about us in the interim. During a wait, I see a car turn into the driveway. It's a beat-up brown sedan, 1970s vintage, the big gas-guzzling type that Mary calls a land barge. The thing's roaring as though it has no muffler. The car pulls up beside us and comes perilously close to the net. I'm sure the driver never saw it, despite the buckets and poles sitting there in plain sight. Uh-oh, I say to myself, when he rolls down his window.

The guy's in his twenties, unclean-looking (though who am I to talk, with bird shit all over me) with long, scraggly hair. I quickly deduce he's not the owner.

"Does so-and-so still own this place?" he asks.

"I don't know. We haven't been able to figure out who owns it."

"So-and-so used to own it. He has a farm south of Ogallala. I saw you here and thought maybe he sold it."

"No, at least not to us. We're banding the swallows here."

"Oh?" The guy turns to look toward the net. "I'd seen them nests there and thought maybe they was bats."

"No, they're birds."

"So they get in that net. That's something. Well, have a good one." The guy fires up the land barge and takes off, again narrowly missing the net. I have visions of him driving right through the net and roaring off down the road trailing mesh and net poles as though he was just married.

Our scraggly-haired friend's information that the owner lives south of Ogallala is useful. That means he probably doesn't get over here by Roscoe very often. At least I won't have to worry that he lives in one of the house trailers visible a half-mile away. But it really doesn't matter because the Skelly birds aren't interested in being caught. We catch our last bird at 11:13, and after getting nothing in the next half-hour we take the net down. We end with a paltry thirty-three birds. Most were unbanded, suggesting that the poor misguided souls that have settled here may be mostly yearlings. Of the seven banded birds, five were ones from last year, also consistent with the idea that this colony is made up of younger birds.

The time has finally come to net at Aqueduct. I know there were a handful of active nests—nine or so—a week ago. I want to know which birds have chosen to live in such a small colony. But recently we've been seeing more birds there. Maybe some of these aren't residents; I don't know what's going on. I speculate that one assistant and I can probably handle Aqueduct, especially if there are only eight or nine nests. I'd like Mary to take two assistants to Pigpen for perhaps a final time.

My initial plan is to take Annie, but Mary tells me I should work with Judy occasionally. The assistants are keenly aware of how the personnel are divided up, and Mary tells me they analyze the working assignments. She's afraid that the ones who seldom work with me may think they aren't good enough or suspect I may be displeased with them. On the contrary, I spend the least time with the best assistants because they don't need my supervision. I'll tell Judy this later. But I agree with Mary and decide to take Judy to Aqueduct.

As soon as we stop along the road north of the flume, I wonder how wise it was to bring just one assistant to Aqueduct. There are hundreds of birds swarming under the structure. We walk beneath the nests and see that many of the old partial nests have bits of fresh mud on them. Obviously a lot of birds have moved in here recently and have begun nest construction. It'll now be impossible to know which birds among this horde are the original eighteen. Here's another example of birds' settling in a colony of a given size only to have more swallows move in and change the colony's size. I'm disappointed at not being able to identify those first small-colony settlers. We should have come sooner.

We erect a big net along the side of the flume. Many birds sit in nests above us while we work, seeming very interested in what we're doing. The birds here typically react to us nonchalantly because at big-net sites like Aqueduct we're always well *below* them and extend our net upward. Terrestrial predators represent little threat to these birds, and they're not too concerned by people eighteen feet below. Most predators of cliff swallows attack from above, and their vigilance against aerial attack is one reason drop netting can be so tough.

Judy has never done big nets before. She learns quickly, however, and we get the first net up in only fifteen minutes. I decide to try a second one on the opposite side of the flume and offset to the east. The wind has diminished this afternoon, and the day is ideal for big nets. By the time we get the second net up the first one is full of birds, and birds immediately start getting into the second net. The swallows hardly care that the nets are here, coming and going all around us, fighting with each other and creating general bedlam. I can tell it's going to be a busy day.

While we're extracting birds from the first net, I see two Cedar Point vans stop. It's Ted and Josef with the behavioral ecology class. Ted yells out the window, asking if he can bring the class over to watch us for a few minutes. We've got at least thirty birds in the nets by now, and the last thing we need is spectators, but I can hardly say no. Ted, Josef, and about twenty undergraduates pile out, troop over to the nets, and gather around us. It's a chaotic scene: Judy and I trying to get birds out, Ted explaining what we're doing, more birds getting in the other net by the minute, the swallows swarming at their nests above us—probably enjoying the commotion—and poop raining down on the students.

Josef is standing nearby, eyes wide, looking at all the birds in our net. He's having trouble restraining himself from helping. He's trying to be Mr. Teaching Assistant, watching the students and telling them not to get too close or wander off. Suddenly he can't stand it anymore. He sprints to the net and starts taking birds out. He can extract them as fast as I can, and at one point I look up and see him hand Judy four birds at once. How did he hold the first two while he was taking the last two out? Josef is almost giddy, doing what he loves best, and his efforts help us get the first net emptied of birds.

We pull the first net back up on its pulleys, and that seems to be the signal for the class to depart. Ted has finished his spiel about banding and cliff swallow biology and announces that everyone should return to the van. The students, most of them looking decidedly bored, are glad to get out from under the bridge and the falling poop. Josef glances at the second net full of birds and apologizes because he can't stay and help us. "I must go to drive the van," he sighs wistfully. I wish he could stay too.

Judy and I begin a routine of clearing the two nets, walking to a shady spot under some cottonwoods about a hundred yards to the north, processing the birds, and returning to the net as soon as we finish each load. By then both nets are full again. It's so relaxing to work with Judy. She's competent with the data recording and bands, and I don't have to constantly glance at the band numbers to make sure they're correct. She's pleasant and efficient and doesn't talk about anything except the task at hand. Although I've worked with her several times at Whitetail, today I realize just what a good worker she really is.

I glance up and see a kestrel fly under the bridge. The cliff swallows flush out, alarm-calling at it. The kestrel doesn't pause, continuing past the bridge and disappearing in the canyon to the south. I bet it was checking out the chances of getting a bird here. Kestrels sometimes buzz the colony at Aqueduct, going under the bridge close to the nests. Only once have I seen one chase a swallow here, however, and it was unsuccessful. Kestrels are usually detected before they can get close enough to strike successfully, and this was what we just saw. Most of the swallows had flushed out before it reached the bridge.

The swallows are upset and swirl overhead for several minutes. They consider kestrels bad news and respond more vigorously and indignantly to them than to other predators. But kestrels represent only a minor threat to cliff swallows. I've seen them get swallows only a couple of times in all the years we've been in Nebraska, and in those cases they caught newly fledged juveniles that weren't flying strongly. My guess is that the swallows' response to the kestrel is designed to tell it that it's been seen and is unlikely to be successful. Presumably, if a predator knows it has lost the element of surprise it will leave. This kestrel has vanished, but whenever one circles overhead the swallows will fly up to its level and mill around it, alarm-calling. While they're below it and vulnerable to its dive, they fly in a tightly bunched flock. Once above the kestrel, the swallows are no longer in danger and spread out in a loose flock, sometimes quite close to it. They'll follow it as it moves, constantly yelling at it. At that altitude and distance, you can barely hear the alarm calls from the colony site. The calls thus don't seem to be for the benefit of other swallows at the colony—young birds in the nest, for instance—but instead are apparently directed at the kestrel. Move on, you bastard: we know you're here and you won't catch any of us.

The swallows spotted the incoming kestrel so quickly because there are so many birds here. With lots of eyes, chances are someone will see a predator coming. I wonder if the outcome might have been different if those first nine pairs had been the only ones here. Odds are no one would have seen it, and the kestrel might have been able to surprise a bird. The greater probability of detecting an approaching predator at a distance is a benefit of living in a large colony.

I can't think about predators for long, though, because the nets are full again and we need to get the birds out. As we start back toward the nets, I'm alarmed by some building thunderheads. I tell Judy to go on to the nets, and I walk up the road a short way to get a better view of the horizon. Aqueduct is at the bottom of a canyon, so storms can surprise us if we're not vigilant. When I'm level with the canal, I can see that the western sky looks threatening, with numerous white puffy thunderheads starting to turn bluish gray. Although I don't think there's any immediate danger, we'd better watch it. With only two people here and two big nets full of birds, a fast approaching storm could spell disaster.

We keep netting for another half hour before I decide the clouds are too ominous. After we clear the nets, we close them and hurry back to process the birds. I'm enormously relieved when Mary, Kathy, and Annie drive up. They saw the clouds at Pigpen, and Mary decided to come back to Aqueduct in case we needed help with the big nets. Mary and the others start disassembling the nets while Judy and I finish processing the birds.

We end up with 125 birds. Although over 40 were previously banded, I'm surprised that we didn't have more from earlier years. We've thoroughly netted Aqueduct the past three years—on a scale rivaling Whitetail—and I expected more of the residents to be ones from past years. It seems these late-arriving birds are not predominantly ones that lived here in the past. The large number of unbanded individuals probably means many of them are yearlings, as is often the case with late-starting colonies. The traditional Aqueduct birds went somewhere else this year—probably Prairie Dog.

Although there was no sign of the owls today, after we took the nets down I searched for owl pellets. Owls regurgitate the undigestible hair, bones, and feathers of their prey, spitting this stuff up in a solid mass. Usually one can find pellets littering the ground under their roosting areas, but I couldn't find any here. Perhaps the owls left, explaining the influx of new swallows. Still, I resent those owls. Even if they're gone, I'm sure they affected the cliff swallows' use of Aqueduct this summer, and I'm certain they destroyed the great blue heron colony in the nearby cottonwoods.

This evening we take the assistants into Ogallala to celebrate the eleven-year-old bird with ice cream sundaes and attend the "Crystal Palace Revue" at Front Street, another traditional swallow summer event. Ogallala has a re-created western town, complete with saloon, general store, sheriff's office, and livery stable. Front Street is mostly a photo op for tourists and doubles as restaurant and bar. Each night during the summer the restaurant puts on a dance hall show starring local high school kids or students home from college. It consists of singing, dancing, and corny jokes by girls in colorful dance hall dresses and guys in cowboy hats and boots. Mary and I have seen it so many times we know all the jokes and most of the song lyrics: "Way out in Ogallala, where you can whoop and holler. . . ."

I've always been surprised that a town the size of Ogallala (population 5,600) could support a live variety show every night of the summer. Seeing it about once a decade is all most normal people would want. The nightly attendance bespeaks the tourist industry here, and they have a full house tonight—forty or fifty people—as they do every time we come. When the emcee goes around the room asking where folks are from, we learn that eleven states from Utah to Tennessee and from Minnesota to Oklahoma are represented on just this one evening.

But why would anyone come to Ogallala unless they were studying cliff swallows?

June 24

The morning finds Kathy and me back at I 80. We're trying out a custom-made short net that Mary constructed the other day. She cut the loops off one side of a torn regular-sized net, removed the damaged mesh, and reattached the loops to make a net whose length matches the width of single-tunnel culverts like I 80. We've been able to place the short net on the north end much closer to the culvert entrance than ever before.

I'm somewhat preoccupied this morning. En route to I 80 we stopped at the post office in Ogallala and picked up the day's mail. In it was a package notifying me that my grant proposal to the National Science Foundation requesting funds for the DNA fingerprinting study of cliff swallow parentage had been rejected. Without that money there's no way we can analyze blood samples to determine how many of the young in a nest are the result of parasitic egg laying or extrapair copulation. The immediate consequence is that it's now pointless to collect blood from the families at Bluffs. I don't want to waste the time and subject the birds to the disturbance blood collection would involve if there's no short-term prospect for analyzing the samples. This is a major disappointment, though frequent nowadays. So little money is available for ecological research that scientists compete like hyenas over a carcass for the pittance the NSF distributes each year.

I read over the reviews of my proposal as we wait for birds to get caught. Usually I get so mad at these that I stay upset for a day or two. Even if what's said in the reviews is wrong or debatable, the author of a proposal has no recourse, no chance to respond or to refute the criticism, until a year later when proposals can be resubmitted. It's up to panels of scientists appointed by the NSF to sift through the comments made by anonymous reviewers and determine which criticisms have merit. These panels then decide on the proposals that should be funded, usually about 10 percent of those submitted. With these odds of success, scientists have to spend most of their time writing and rewriting grant proposals. Many people spend more time trying to raise money than actually doing science.

Yet I'm a bit surprised by these reviews: some of them are constructive. We want to know how often young are produced that aren't related to one or both of a nest's owners. If this happens, a pair's average reproductive success will be lower than it seems, because a parent won't be related to all the young fledging from its nest. Do brood parasitism and extrapair copulation increase in larger colonies? We suspect they do, and if so, they will change the average reproductive success estimated from our nest check data on how many young survived.

But two reviewers point out that we have to assign parentage for *all* nestlings in a colony and identify the parents of everybody either as members of the colony or as nonresidents. If all the brood parasitism and extrapair copulation is occurring among colony residents, the *average* reproductive success in the colony won't change. Frank might have some offspring in Joe's nest, Joe might have some in Bob's nest, and Bob might have some in Frank's nest, but this won't change the average number of young raised per bird in the colony. Only if some nonresident comes in, lays an egg in a nest or successfully fertilizes a resident female, and then leaves will the average reproductive success in the colony decline owing to unrelatedness between parent and young. We had planned to take data from a sample of nests in each colony, but I can now see that we have to assign parentage for *everybody* in the colony, including the larger colonies. That's going to be a major challenge.

As we sit, I watch a cliff swallow colony visible a couple of hundred yards to the south of the exit ramp. This site, called Stuckeys, is another abandoned gas station. Two years ago the birds moved in there, nesting under the awning over the pumps. I don't think the owner at Stuckeys is as hostile to them, and the birds nested successfully. Kathy asks if we're going to net there, but I don't think so: a wire cable is blocking the driveway, and Keep Out signs are posted prominently. Given the difficulty of catching birds on wide-open buildings, it's probably not worth the trouble of identifying the owner and asking his permission.

I watch for kestrels. One day while we were sitting here two years ago, I glanced up and saw a kestrel go up under the awning at Stuckeys and then fly away. I thought that seemed odd, since at that time I didn't even know a cliff swallow colony was there. Using binoculars I saw a handful of swallow nests under the awning. Shortly the kestrel returned, and I watched as it flew up to the entrance of a swallow nest, hung there briefly, and tried unsuccessfully to extract a nest owner or baby with its talons. That was the first time I'd seen a kestrel cling to a nest and try to prey on birds inside. Usually they just chase swallows in flight. Kestrels had been reported to attack nests in California, but I hadn't seen it happen in Nebraska and had begun to wonder about the veracity of those reports. I no longer doubt them.

No kestrels appear this morning. The colony at Stuckeys is larger than two years ago, so kestrels may be less likely to attack it now. They'd be detected sooner and would lose the advantage of surprise. But a larger colony doesn't always deter predators, and in some cases its conspicuousness may attract them. That's probably what happened with the heron colony at Aqueduct; it got bigger this summer and caught the attention of the owls. The attraction of predators to big cliff swallow colonies will be well illustrated to us this afternoon.

On the drive back for lunch, we pass by Skelly. Something doesn't look right: I don't see any bird activity. We turn in the driveway, and I stop under the awning. As expected, the colony has met its demise. Over 90 percent of the nests have been knocked down. Pieces of nests and broken eggs litter the pavement, and only a few swallows are flying overhead. I bet the owner did it, as he does every time the birds try to nest here. That jerk. I knew this would happen, but it still upsets me. I hope these birds will go somewhere else and try to renest this summer, though it's probably too late in the season to start over. I wonder too about the timing of the destruction: less than twenty-four hours after we netted here. Perhaps it's only a coincidence that the owner happened to show up now, but could that scraggly-haired guy who stopped yesterday have told the owner we were here?

This afternoon we decide to take advantage of the north wind and do the north side of Whitetail. We've had only a couple of good sessions on the north end this year. Despite the birds' being less lovable on the north side, I'm relieved to be netting where there's no abyss. I won't have to wear those abominably hot chest waders today.

I take Annie and Judy, the standard Whitetail team. As we park along the road above the culvert, I notice that the birds are flying at the north end of the culvert in successive waves but aren't going in. Each wave approaches the entrance but peels off and goes above the culvert. Rolling down the window, I hear a scattering of alarm calls coming from the birds approaching the north end. This behavior indicates a predator is in the colony, and I suspect it's a bull snake.

Before we can get out of the truck, a common grackle flies out the north end, carrying a baby swallow in its beak. This causes more agitation among the colony residents, with birds swirling above it as it disappears into the thicket of leadplants along the creek bank. A grackle has discovered the colony. It's hunting by lighting on nests and pulling babies out the entrances. Whitetail has a long and bloody history with grackles, and I immediately wonder if that history is going to repeat itself this summer.

Grackles are long-tailed blackbirds about the size of a blue jay. The common grackle is widespread throughout the eastern two-thirds of the United States. Males are iridescent green, purple, and bronze but look jet black. They have a long, wedge-shaped tail that's used in displaying to females. The dull brownish females are smaller with less obvious tails. Both sexes have fiendish yellow eyes and strong, massive, spearlike bills. Grackles are semicolonial, with groups of up to twenty or more nesting in the same stand of trees. They are omnivorous, eating seeds, insects, fruit, refuse, and carrion. They also hunt small birds like cliff swallows and raid nests, devouring eggs and young of other species. In southwestern Nebraska grackles usually live in trees along the river floodplains and around ranches and farms. They are a successful species that thrives in edge habitats, and they have increased with the relatively recent cutting and fragmenting of the eastern deciduous forest.

Whitetail's association with grackles began eight years ago. One day we drove up and noticed a grackle impaled on the barbed wire fence just south of the culvert. The bird apparently had flown into the fence, or been blown into it, and one of the sharp barbs had pierced its neck. It was a gruesome sight. The grackle hung there all summer, twisting in the wind. Perhaps our failure to dispose of the corpse annoyed whatever higher power watches over grackles and led to the carnage two years later.

Whitetail had been steadily increasing in size, and in 1989 it reached 2,200 nests, an increase of 800 from the previous year. The birds nested in all three tunnels, including the west tunnel that's over dry land. One afternoon our assistant Barbara and I visited to check nest contents. As we entered the west tunnel, we saw the ground littered with dead cliff swallows. Something had been eating most of them, though some were intact except for the skull, which had been bashed in and only the brains eaten. We were aghast as we counted twenty-four adult swallows lying under the nests. I had no earthly idea what was killing these birds.

Barbara and I returned the next morning. We had collected all the corpses the day before, and we were astounded to see twenty-six new ones! These had only the brains eaten. But this time we saw a big male grackle fly out of the west tunnel as we approached, suggesting that grackles were responsible for this mess: at least fifty cliff swallows killed in two days. I knew grackles occasionally hunted cliff swallows. Once Mary and I watched a grackle slowly stroll toward a group of cliff swallows gathering mud in the riverbed at Roscoe, jump on one of the birds, and kill it with a couple of jabs to the back of the head with its beak. The grackle then ate almost all of the swallow. A natural predation event. But this . . . Could a grackle really be killing dozens of birds a day?

That evening Mary and I faced a dilemma, one that we discussed with our assistants and other Cedar Point biologists. Grackles are natural predators—not introduced pests like house sparrows—and for this reason one could argue we shouldn't intervene. We should just watch what happened. Yet we had created a potentially unnatural situation at Whitetail. Through our fumigation, we had perhaps caused a larger than normal swallow colony to form there. Maybe the colony would not have been so large and thus so attractive to grackles had we not removed parasites from the nests. I told myself we had provided an atypical concentration of prey for grackles.

We already knew what grackles were capable of, and I was certain they would keep on killing. I finally resolved to discourage the depredations, but not until I knew more about how this was happening. Was only one grackle doing this, or a whole flock? How were they getting the swallows? The next day was cloudy, cool, and unsuitable for netting, giving me a perfect excuse to go to Whitetail to watch grackles.

I stopped along the roadside above the culvert and began waiting. The swallows' activity seemed normal, and some were collecting mud along the creek bank despite the cloudy, raw weather. With the window down, though, I could occasionally hear a muted alarm call. The birds didn't really act like anything was wrong, but I decided to go have a look anyway. I got out of the truck and crept down the highway embankment toward the south end of the west tunnel. I crouched behind a leadplant where I could see into the tunnel. Although some swallows were alarming at me, most were carrying on at their nests as if I weren't there. Then I saw it. A grackle was standing on the dry ground in the west tunnel. He was peering up at the birds at their nests only three feet above him. They acted as if he weren't there either.

I watched spellbound as a bird from a nest on the wall dropped down to the wet earth under the nests to collect mud. I knew the swallows were getting some of their mud from inside the tunnel, but while a grackle was there? As soon as the bird lit, the grackle pounced on it, grabbing the fluttering swallow with its feet and killing it with a couple of pecks. So that was how he got them; they're so dumb they were flying right to him!

I watched from the truck the rest of the morning. The grackle came in periodically, but by midmorning all mud gathering had stopped because of the weather. He killed only a few birds that day: unless they were on the ground, he wouldn't bother trying to get them. It appeared that only one grackle was involved, because the only one I saw near the colony had a missing wing feather. His missing that feather was fortuitous, because it showed we had only one mass murderer. Without that telltale sign, we couldn't have known how many different grackles were hunting at Whitetail.

The next day I was back, and having satisfied myself that I had learned all I needed to from this episode, I was armed with a pellet gun. I was not eager to have one grackle wipe out all three hundred or so birds living in the west tunnel, occupying nests we planned to use in observations of foraging behavior later that summer. I discovered, however, that trying to gun down a grackle is as futile as shooting at house sparrows. He seemed to sense the situation and refused to come close when I was there. This grackle had learned—how, I don't know—that I was an enemy.

Later that morning he began using a new hunting technique. Many of the swallows were lighting in the grassy pasture to the north to collect grass stems for their nests. The murderous grackle began flying patrols out over the field, and on spying a swallow on the ground, would drop straight down onto it. I watched as he killed several birds and didn't eat any of them, not even their brains. This was getting out of hand.

At intervals the grackle would fly off toward the ranch to the southeast, the same ranch that's the source of Whitetail's sparrow problems. I saw there was a colony of grackles in a grove of trees around the buildings. Driving slowly past the ranch, I looked for the murderer but saw only innocent grackles. Most of the males were busy courting females, following them around and guarding them from other males. They were tame and ignored me, even when I got close. None of them had a wing feather missing. I finally concluded that the murderer was some sort of outcast, a bird that had no mate and had probably decided to spend the summer just raising hell. He was doing a good job of it at Whitetail.

I gave up trying to shoot the grackle, and instead we spent the next couple of days netting at Whitetail. I hoped that our presence would discourage him. He stayed away while we were there, but when we'd leave for lunch and return an hour later, we'd find four or five birds he'd killed while we were gone. Eventually he left when the swallows finished their nest building—no more easy meals. We confirmed at least seventy kills by this grackle, and I'm sure he got more than that. Of the twenty-four banded birds he killed, twenty-one were yearlings. First-year cliff swallows must not know how to avoid grackles.

Later in the summer other grackles arrived. These were birds from the colony by the ranch looking for food for their babies. They mostly scavenged nestling swallows that fell from nests. A female grackle would perch along the lower strand of a barbed wire fence that spanned the creek downstream of the colony, snatching grasshoppers out of the water. But she particularly liked the doomed baby swallows that came floating by. She'd carry her prey back to her nest at the ranch. These grackles were engaging in normal behavior, and we didn't interfere.

In later years other grackles have preyed on isolated birds at Whitetail, but none have been anything like the mass murderer. One year a grackle would occasionally fly toward flocks of cliff swallows assembled on the wires above Whitetail, trying to collide with a bird but rarely succeeding. Another enterprising grackle would sit on the fence and try to chase down juveniles that had just fledged. Despite their large size and clumsy tails, grackles are surprisingly agile and can catch juvenile swallows in flight. One impetus to my present practice of not fumigating once the young swallows approach fledging age came one day while I was spraying the nests and a fledgling flew out in response. A grackle was sitting on the fence watching, and he easily caught the juvenile as it flew past.

Seeing the grackle predation today extends to seven consecutive years Whitetail's streak of having at least one grackle attack per summer. Before 1989 we never saw grackles here. They were in the area but didn't come around the colony. Once Whitetail exceeded 1,500 nests, however, as it has every year since 1989, grackles began to show interest. I'm certain this reflects the greater conspicuousness of a large colony. Visually hunting predators like grackles notice the bird traffic around a big colony and are attracted there for easy meals.

We once did an analysis tabulating how many predator attacks we'd seen in colonies of different sizes over the years. As we expected, the number of attacks per colony went up as colony size increased. But one benefit of living in a group is that it may dilute each individual's personal risk of being a predator's victim. If there are enough colony residents, odds are somebody else will be the prey. This is a popular explanation for why some animals form groups or colonies. But we found that predators attack the larger cliff swallow colonies so often that an individual's personal risk is actually *greater* in a large colony than in a small one. The attraction of predators to colonies is another cost of social life.

To my surprise the swallows hardly mind a net on the north end today. They resume coming and going in minutes, and we settle into a busy routine. After about an hour, I hear a *chuck* call behind me. A grackle! I turn around, and looking through the culvert I see it sitting on the fence at the other end. It's a big male. I can see his crazed-looking yellow eyes as he walks along the fence, sizing me up. I keep watching him as I remove birds from the net. The swallows don't seem overly concerned by him, and the alarm calls I hear could be directed at me as much as at the grackle. After a few minutes the bird makes his move. He flies into the culvert about a third of the way toward me, lights on a nest, and while perching there tries to reach into an adjacent nest with his beak. By now the swallows are upset, and they've started swirling at the south end. The grackle can't seem to get anything, though, and he soon flies out the south end. I wonder what I'd have done had he come this way and gotten into the net.

He comes back a half hour later and tries again but has no luck. His coming into the culvert, however, illustrates another cost of colonial nesting for cliff swallows. By clustering their nests together, the birds provide convenient toeholds for predators like grackles. A grackle clings to one nest to reach into another. Nesting close together may give a predator access to your nest. Bull snakes also attack nests by hanging onto neighboring ones. Isolated nests without close neighbors are harder for snakes to reach, and grackles don't like to hover in front of a single nest. There must be some powerful reasons to cluster nests together, given these costs.

In addition to watching for grackles, I've been keeping an eye on the southern sky. Thunderstorms were forecast this afternoon, and there's a nasty-looking one to the south. It's generating heavy rain, which we can see coming down in sheets. I think the storm to the south will miss us, but I'm a little uneasy because we're catching so many birds it would be impossible to shut down quickly. As quitting time approaches, however, I'm feeling good that we went the full afternoon despite the looks of the sky.

Suddenly I notice some evil clouds to the northwest. I was so worried about the storm to the south that I overlooked the development of a much closer one. I can see occasional lightning, and it looks like it has a lot of rain. I quickly close the net and tell Judy and Annie to speed up their processing. They look at me as if I'm crazy, because they've been going at their maximum rate all afternoon, not leaving their lawn chairs once since we arrived and processing over 360 birds.

They finish the last bird as the wind gusts pick up. I can see the storm coming directly at us across the pastures to the northwest. This sucker is moving southeast, an atypical storm track but one that's been frequent this summer. The rain starts as we throw our equipment into the truck. By the time we get back to Cedar Point it's a downpour, with hail. I'm relieved to see that Mary and Kathy had quit at CR 3 in time; they're gone by the time we pass. That was a close call—too close. I must be more vigilant. Still, the narrow escape was exciting, even fun. Events like this help make the summer so exhilarating. You know they'll happen but you don't know when.

This evening Mary and I drive into Ogallala to see the Great American Cattle Drive. A herd of Texas longhorn cattle arrived in town yesterday, a reenactment of an event that was common here in the 1880s, when Ogallala was one of the major cow towns along the railroad where herds from Texas were driven. A promoter is staging a realistic cattle drive from Fort Worth, Texas, to Miles City, Montana, retracing the route taken in Larry McMurtry's novel *Lonesome Dove*. The herd and entourage make twenty miles or so a day, and when they get to the larger towns like Ogallala they stay for a couple of days. The cowboys tending the herd look rugged and authentic, with handlebar mustaches, beat-up hats, long coats, and chaps. Tonight the town's having a rodeo and dance to celebrate the herd's arrival. We've had our yearly dose of rodeo, so Mary and I pass on Tony and Diana's invitation to attend. We just want to see the cows.

The longhorns are the most impressive, dignified cattle I've ever seen—huge curved horns that extend outward several feet, hides variegated from brown to red to gray to white to black. These are tough-looking animals, unlike the fat, dumb Herefords and Angus we see on the range every day. I bet they'll make it to Montana.

June 25

The time has come to start surveying colony sizes at places where we don't net. This gives us information on annual patterns of site use.

Among other things, it tells us how many apparently suitable colony sites in the study area are occupied by cliff swallows each summer—typically about two-thirds. There are about 150 colony sites between Oshkosh and Maxwell. Since we net at only about 30 of them, we have to begin censusing nests at the other locations. This morning I'm going to start by visiting some of the colonies near Sutherland.

I leave Mary with all three assistants. The four of them are going to try the double-net method at the wooden bridge over the canal. We figure that colony has only about fifty active nests. With a colony so small, the only hope of catching the birds is to do simultaneous net drops. I feel a little guilty leaving Mary to organize and direct everybody this morning, but I have to leave immediately after breakfast if I'm going to make it to Sutherland and back by noon. Spending a morning alone will also be relaxing, and this too makes me feel guilty for leaving Mary to go to the wooden bridge.

Among my first stops is the Roscoe diversion dam on the South Platte River. I don't see the turtle that Annie vomited on, and the site also looks devoid of cliff swallows this year. I watch some barn swallows sunning on top of a metal shed. There are about nine, all in the weird positions these birds assume when they sun. They tilt to expose their flanks to the sun, roll their heads over so one eye points straight up, open their beaks, spread their tails, and partly extend their wings. A sunning swallow looks like it's in some sort of catatonic state. Sunning exposes the bare skin under the feathers to sunlight, which may help control ectoparasites.

The barn swallows are sunning peacefully until two cliff swallows land in their midst. The barn swallows shift uncomfortably, as if a couple of undesirables have arrived, but continue their nude sunbathing. One of the cliffers waddles toward the top of the roof, jams its head up against the roof's vertical lip where it adjoins the next building, and goes into a sunning pose. The other cliffer looks around nervously as if it doesn't know what to do. Well, if all else fails, whale at somebody. It attacks the nearest barn swallow and drives it away. It then attacks a second one. By now the rest of the barn swallows are alert, looking at the troublemaker. But I guess the cliffer has gotten tired of beating up wimpy barn swallows, and within a few seconds it takes off, soon followed by its sunning friend. The remaining barn swallows yawn and go back to their sunning.

I think how well this interaction illustrates the two species' personalities. Barn swallows are peaceful, unaggressive souls that get along with each other. Cliff swallows are delinquents that seem to thrive on conflict. They're little butt-heads, and I guess that's why they're so endearing.

I continue east. The bank swallows are still in their roadcut by Stinkpot. At Paxton I stop at the bridge and am surprised to see hundreds of birds swarming on the west side. These cliff swallows appear to have arrived recently. This is awfully late in the summer for so many birds to still be trying to settle. Could these be birds that won't stay, like those we saw at CR 4½? Regardless of their plans, I can't estimate a colony size at Paxton yet. We'll have to come back later. The birds on the east side, the original part of the colony where we first netted this summer, are feeding large babies. The river is still deep, wide, and flowing swiftly, so netting remains out of the question.

I follow the canal road to its terminus at the Nebraska Public Power District's coal-fired power plant. I pass all the higher-number CR colonies: CR 10, CR 11, and so on up to CR 17. We've occasionally netted at some of these sites, to look for dispersing birds from our main colonies, but these cliff swallows are wild and wary and netting them is usually Frustration City. At the power plant I turn north toward Sutherland, passing the colony called Cemetery where Bruce installed some of his plaster nests. The site's active, but I don't have time to wade into the culvert to check the fake nests.

It's soon time to start back to Cedar Point, the morning almost gone. I drive back on Highway 30, which used to be the major route across Nebraska before the interstate was built. Now it serves only local traffic, and it's a more pleasant road to take unless you're in a hurry. Today I want to check some culvert sites along it. Although there are many culverts under Highway 30, most are used only by barn swallows. Cliff swallows have shown interest in just four culverts along a four-mile stretch of the highway a few miles from Roscoe.

The first one I come to is called Alkali Lake Station, named after a nearby historical marker commemorating a Pony Express station. No birds fly out, but I see some cliff swallows flying overhead. Hmm, this place might be active. Only a half-mile down the road I arrive at another site, this one called the Roscoe Gun Club after a nearby skeet-shooting range consisting mostly of outhouses. This colony is active for the first time since 1992. I walk down to one end of the culvert, and I see that birds have started building new nests. In some cases small blobs of wet mud are all that's been put up. These birds, if they persist with nesting, will be here well into August. I wonder if some of these swallows are ones that lost their nests at Skelly two days ago. Skelly is less than three miles away as the swallow flies. We'll find out when we net here.

The next two sites, Rattlesnake and Goats, have no birds, but the recent colonization of the Gun Club illustrates the lateness of the season. My tour this morning revealed that the birds in general are well behind schedule, a consequence of the May weather. In past years the first babies had fledged by now. This summer there are no young out of the nest yet, many birds are still incubating, and some are still trying to find colonies and build nests. I marvel again at how different each summer is from those that have come before.

Mary is on cloud nine when I meet her at lunch. She cleaned up at the wooden bridge using the double-net method. They got ninety of the one hundred birds living there. Though the total number for the morning is small, that's probably a record for percentage of a colony caught with drop nets. I'm ecstatic too; we won't have to go back there. Mary says proudly that this morning was her finest hour of the season so far, and I don't disagree.

The afternoon finds us back at Knight's Tube trying to get the birds not netted on the first visit. This means we have to figure out a way to install a net on the north end. Last time we found it easy to do the south end, but the north side of the tube is overgrown with vegetation. A barbed wire fence is in the exact spot where a net would best be placed. We flounder around for a while trying to anchor the net poles. Even after we get the net positioned, though, I'm not satisfied. There's too much room for the birds to go around it. We set up to process in the truck as we did last time, but with a net on the north end I can't flush birds toward it when I approach the tube from the truck. The swallows flush away from me and go out the unobstructed south end. There's no place to sit on the south side to drive them the other way into the net.

It's no surprise that captures are much slower this afternoon than on the last visit. By midafternoon we have only nineteen birds.

Judy and Kathy suggest we put the net back on the south side. I explain that I want to sample birds from all parts of the colony, and if we return to the south end, we'll have no chance to catch the residents of the older nests on this end. In general, swallows nesting on the edges of culverts are harder to catch. This can bias our sample, with center nesters overrepresented among the captures. The only recourse is to net enough at each end so that the edge birds will eventually get caught. Here at the tube, at least a third of the colony consists of nests just a few feet from the north end, so netting on that side is critical.

Captures finally increase as the north-end birds gradually get used to the net. We end up with eighty-two for the afternoon, substantially fewer than the last time, but most of our haul consists of birds we didn't catch then. That was our goal, so I'm pleased.

After her brilliant morning at the wooden bridge, Mary didn't have a particularly good afternoon. She and Annie went first to Diversion Dam. The birds there are all feeding young, and few of them are in the nests at any one time. They caught six before giving up and going to IS 1. At IS 1 they found the same scene: birds feeding young and hard to catch. They ended up getting only thirty birds, a sure sign that the drop-netting season is over at IS 1. That will be the story for more and more colonies in the days to come.

Mary also had an intimate encounter with a turkey at IS 1. She'd gone over to an area of tall grass to pee, and as she was assuming the proper pose, a wild turkey came walking out from under her. If it hadn't moved, it would have been directly in the line of fire. This was only mildly less shocking than a similar encounter she had at Barn Owl several years ago: in that case a nesting turkey suddenly flew up directly at her rear end as she was squatting. Turkeys on nests are hard to see, but what could be the odds of twice pulling your pants down only to have a turkey in that exact spot? How disconcerting it must be to have a large fowl come roaring up so close it brushes your naked butt with its wings! At Barn Owl it just about caused Mary to fall down the side of a steep ravine. But then imagine the poor turkey's feelings.

June 26

The forecast today calls for light wind. Time for a big-net day at Aqueduct. All five of us will go, and we can use three big nets: maximum effort.

As soon as we stop on the road north of the colony, we see two great horned owls fly out from under the flume. They'd been sitting on the westernmost support piling, the place we've seen them each time. The swallows were swarming all over the structure even while the owls were there, acting normally. They alarm-call when the owls fly off into the canyon, but they quickly go back to their business. These birds now don't seem to care that the owls are roosting here. Maybe I've given the owls a bad rap. I wonder if their presence really has had any effect on the cliff swallows' use of Aqueduct this summer. Perhaps it was this site's large size last year and the many ectoparasites left over that caused the birds to avoid the nests here earlier this summer. Might it be that only after enough parasites had died during the past six weeks could the site be inhabited by these latecomers?

I start to convince myself of this as I remember the reported cases of cliff swallows nesting close to raptors. Colonies have been built underneath nests of golden eagles and ferruginous hawks on the sides of tall cliffs in mountainous regions. Small birds sometimes nest close to big birds because the big ones may deter or eat the predators of the little ones. Of course this scheme works only if the little birds are so small or so agile that the big birds don't try to eat them too. That could be the case for great horned owls and cliff swallows. I doubt an owl that large could hang from a nest and grab the occupants inside, and they usually don't catch birds in flight. There might be no reason for the swallows to fear these great horned owls.

We set up three big nets in a crisscross arrangement. All birds have one clear approach to their nests but have a net blocking the other. As when Judy and I were here alone, they quickly adapt to us and our nets, swarming at the nests, flying around and into the nets, and mostly acting as if we're not here. With three nets it doesn't take long to become busy. Mary and two assistants sit in the shade of the cottonwoods and process, while the third assistant and I constantly extract birds.

Aqueduct is wonderful for watching the birds while we work. They carry on at their nests above us in full view. How leisurely these guys are about nest building! Most of them have nests only about half intact. Portions of almost all existing nests fell over the winter, so everybody has some nest construction to do. Yet the birds go get some mud, put it on the nest, then sit and watch us or their neighbors. In many of the half nests, two birds sit together for long periods, not interested in working. Other birds are fighting with each other, usually during an attempted trespass by a neighbor. It's almost July, and these birds seem to feel no urgency to get done. Reminds me of some graduate students I've known. It also makes me wonder if many of these birds—which our netting the other day suggested are mostly yearlings—really have any intention of breeding this year. Maybe they're just playing house.

In midmorning Mary brings an empty holding bag and starts taking birds out of a net. Soon I hear her ask the bird she's working on, "What are you?" She tells me she has "something odd." We frequently catch other species here; Judy and I got a chimney swift the other day. I walk over to see what Mary has. At first glance the bird looks like a juvenile cliff swallow, but the throat is pure white with none of the characteristic speckling of fledgling cliff swallows. Damn, that bird's a cave swallow!

Cave swallows are the closest relatives of cliff swallows among the North American swallows. They have a patchy distribution in parts of northwestern South America, the West Indies, and Central America. A somewhat isolated population occurs in central Texas and south-central New Mexico. As their name implies, they often occupy caves, and they are the swallows that live with the famous bats at Carlsbad Caverns. Cave swallows closely resemble cliff swallows, but they don't have the cliffer's white forehead patch and dark chestnut throat. Another major difference is that cave swallows usually live in smaller colonies. They frequently breed in groups of fewer than fifty nests, and colonies of a thousand or more nests are virtually unknown.

The cave swallow has recently shifted to using human structures for nesting, showing the typical swallow adaptability to artificial environments. Many cave swallows in central Texas now nest in highway culverts and under bridges. In Mexico these birds nest on Mayan ruins. With the conversion to culvert nesting, cave swallows are now moving east and north in Texas into areas where they never occurred before. As they do they're encountering barn swallows, and the meeker barnies are suffering. The cave swallows take over their nests, forcibly copulate with female barn swallows and produce hybrid offspring, and generally treat them a lot worse than the cliff swallows do.

So far cave swallows haven't interacted much with cliff swallows, maybe because there are just fewer cliff swallows in that part of Texas. But if the cave swallows keep moving north, eventually they're going to run into a lot of them. I'd like to be there when the confrontation starts.

Perhaps our little friend today is a scout. It's clearly a juvenile raised earlier this year. My guess is that it was hatched in early May in central Texas, and after fledging it headed north, maybe as part of a migrating cliff swallow flock. Cave swallows breed early in Texas, and there'd be enough time for this to have happened. It's probably confused. I'm sure it doesn't live at Aqueduct but was merely attracted by the swallow activity.

We take it back to the processing area to band and weigh it. I want some photographs, because this is only the second cave swallow recorded anywhere in Nebraska. The first one was also a juvenile that we caught at Clary four summers ago. Vagrant cave swallows have been reported from locations all across North America, usually in areas where cliff swallows aren't common. Cave swallows are hard to detect because of their similarity to cliffers, so the more cliff swallows live in an area, the less likely bird-watchers are to look for cave swallows.

I shoot an entire roll of film while Mary holds the little guy by his feet. He looks martyred, but he doesn't struggle much. The assistants are amused by my excitement and especially by my excessive photography. They tell us they expect to get a Christmas card from us with a snapshot of him in one of those holders people use for pictures of their kids. After a fifteen-minute photo shoot, we release him. He disappears over the flume, and like the cave swallow four years ago, we don't expect to see him again. We won't.

I wonder if cave swallows will ever move this far north in any numbers. Why do they live only in a restricted part of the American Southwest and in the tropics, whereas the similar cliff swallow is all over the rest of North America? Maybe the two species have fought it out in the evolutionary past, and this is how they've divided up the universe: live in different regions to minimize competition. If so, we'd expect the cave swallow's range expansion to stop when it reaches true cliff swallow country. Someone needs to go down to Texas and study this. Maybe it'll be me. I can't imagine walking away from here, but if I did study another species, there's no doubt it would be the cave swallow.

As I go back to the net, I see something else in it. We've caught a red-headed woodpecker. This is the third time we've had one in a net here, and I wince at the thought of removing it. I motion for Mary to come help me. The previous redheads screamed so loud when we touched them that they hurt my ears. This one is no exception. Before we even get to it, it starts yelling with a raucous, wheezy sound like hysterical laughter. It also bites with its rather formidable bill as soon as I start to work on it. Mary holds it and tries to control its bill while I loosen its grip on the net mesh. It screams loudly and constantly the entire time. What a handsome bird, though. Brilliant red head and throat with big patches of jet black and snow white on its back and wings. The assistants gather around and get out their cameras.

What would a red-headed woodpecker be doing here? It might have just been flying by and hit the net. The canyon Aqueduct spans is a natural bird flyway. It might also have been trying to prey on cliff swallows. There are reports that the red-headed woodpecker and its western relative the acorn woodpecker attack swallow colonies by perching on the outsides of nests and using their beaks to drill through the mud walls to get to eggs or nestlings inside. Woodpeckers usually aren't thought of as predators, yet they're willing to eat other birds' eggs or young. We've never seen them do this in Nebraska, but we catch red-headed woodpeckers at Aqueduct frequently enough to make me wonder. Like grackles, woodpeckers could be attracted to large cliff swallow colonies.

At lunchtime Mary goes back to Cedar Point to get food. We didn't bring sack lunches because we're so close to the station. Since I don't want to take down three big nets just to go eat, Mary will bring us a serving of whatever Dennis has fixed today. Annie goes with her because she needs to use a toilet and still hasn't mastered the art of peeing outside. That's just as well, because I'd worry about Annie's psyche if she worked up the nerve to pee outdoors and then had a close encounter with a turkey. Kathy also wants to go back to do some food preparation for a specialty dish she promised to make for the station's evening meal tonight. Suddenly it's just me and Judy and three big nets.

She and I are busy for half an hour, and then captures begin to slow down. Many colony residents seem to have gone off to find their own lunches. These birds are acting as if it's May, when everybody quits during the afternoon and heads off to forage. Mud gathering has stopped.

In an hour Mary and the others return. Judy and I get the usual soggy sandwiches: at the station was disgusting frozen pizza, which is being served about every third day now and wouldn't travel well. But Kathy promises cabbage pie tonight. Judy and I take a breather to eat and turn net duty over to our relief team.

With the Aqueduct birds less active this afternoon, I suggest that Mary take someone and go down the canal to another colony. Three of us can handle it here. She's not enthusiastic about this plan but finally agrees. I suggest she try Prairie Dog, since it's closest, though I figure the party's probably over there. Also not far away is CR 7, a small colony of about forty nests. We divide up the bands, data sheets, and other gear, and she and Kathy leave.

By midafternoon we're into a slow-paced routine. Captures have declined to the point that the nets need to be checked only every twenty minutes or so, and in the interim we sit in the shade of the cottonwoods. I drink in this beautiful, serene summer scene. The gentle breeze rustles the leaves of the cottonwoods, grasshoppers buzz in the grass nearby, puffy white clouds drift lazily across the blue sky, and an orchard oriole sings from the branches behind us. Moments like this are the compensation for the hard work and stress of field research.

Right in front of us is a large cottonwood limb downed long ago by a windstorm or lightning. In a portion of it that sticks up there's a hole, possibly made by a downy woodpecker. A pair of house wrens are nesting there, and they're feeding young. One of them, probably the male, sings from atop the broken snag containing his nest, quivering his wings as he calls. He frequently flies down to the grass to grab a caterpillar or other insect to take to his young. He feeds them, then jumps back up to sing for a few minutes. He alternates between singing and feeding his young the entire day and is virtually never out of our sight. There's also a house wren that lives in the cliff swallow colony. It occupies a crack in the concrete of one of the support pilings, the one the owls sit on. We often hear it singing, and it got into the net earlier today but escaped. House wrens sometimes take over cliff swallow nests and use them as their own. Wrens can be pugnacious and may destroy swallow eggs when taking over a nest— pint-sized egg predators. But the one here is content to live in its crack and hasn't harmed the cliff swallows.

As quitting time approaches, Mary and Kathy return.

"How'd you do?"

"We got eleven."

"At Prairie Dog?"

"No, at CR 7. We got one at Prairie Dog."

"Well, I thought you might have better luck. . . ."

"It's over at Prairie Dog. Kaput. Finished. Done with. I'm not going back. Deal with it."

I guess I have to agree with Mary on that. Yet she says CR 7 might still be feasible if we had two teams to use the double-net method. It's a small colony and the birds are wary, but the magic of the wooden bridge session might be re-created there if we want to budget four people to that site for a half day. I'll think about it.

We finish with 240 or so birds at Aqueduct. If all the nest fragments that have owners are active, there are about 275 nests here. Though we had a good day, we still got fewer than half the residents. And I bet some of the birds we caught, especially those banded elsewhere this summer, are drifters that don't really live here. The total haul of actual colony residents was probably lower than our numbers suggest.

On the drive back we see hundreds of birds swarming under the CR 5 bridge. These birds have only been there a few days. Apparently another late colony. What's going on this year?

June 27

Yuck. Another morning sitting on the exit ramp, trying to catch birds at I 80.

The novelty of coming here has worn off. We're using a short net on the south side, and we've got the net in a good position. Except the birds refuse to go into the culvert. Come on, birds.

After a while, fifty or sixty swallows start congregating on a barbed wire fence south of the culvert. It looks like they've decided to wait us out and are going to sit down while they do. Before long everyone is preening nervously, with birds constantly coming and going and squabbling with each other over where to sit. It's already hot this morning, and soon the perching crowd moves farther down the fence to sit in the shade of a small tree. They clearly prefer the shadier area, and before long they're fighting for places. There's plenty of shade, but they all want to be in one little spot. Incoming birds try to knock others off, and there's so much conflict that no one can preen. Finally the whole flock gives up and flies off.

Eventually a few birds start going into the culvert. But each time I go down to check the net, the colony freaks out, and it takes them another thirty minutes to start coming back. The I 80 birds seem to be getting less tolerant the more we're here. At most sites it's the opposite.

Again it's almost quitting time before the birds finally start to cope with us. We end up with twenty-eight captures, and two-thirds of those came in the last hour. It's painfully obvious that a half day just won't cut it here. We'll have to do a whole day. Oh, boy.

On the way back we stop to see what's happening at Mosquito. More birds are there than the last time we visited. Another colony with a recent influx of late nesters. It's also another hellish place that's going to be a lot like I 80 to net.

At lunch Mary reports a mediocre morning at CR 4½. They got only fifty birds, primarily because the colony is now feeding young. Few adults are in the nests at any one time, and the parents are more wary now that they have youngsters to look out for. All the birds that had moved in at CR 4½ last week and started nest construction are gone. It makes me wonder if the late birds we're seeing at the other sites will also vanish. Mary also had a problem with two horses that spent the morning standing on the bridge. They just stood there in the way. With the hot weather, they were probably trying to escape flies and to keep cool over the cold canal water. Mary and the assistants had to drop-net around them.

Mary's catch of only fifty birds at CR 4½, our bread-and-butter drop-netting site this year, means the drop-netting season is practically over. The workload will start to dwindle, and it'll be a challenge to keep all three assistants busy for the rest of the time they're here. Not surprisingly, Annie and Judy were getting bored this morning. Fifty birds is barely enough to keep two people busy, and a third person is mostly standing around. I'll need to come up with creative ways of using all three assistants, but I'm getting tired of organizing people. Six weeks of it without a break is starting to wear on Mary and me.

I've decided the small colony at CR 7 is too good to pass up. This afternoon we should go back with two nets. Mary agrees to take the three assistants, and they'll try to duplicate the double-net success they had at the wooden bridge. I'll stay in and go through the accumulating data sheets on my desk. I always skim the data sheets, looking for problems such as illegible band numbers. Some problems can't be fixed after the fact, but this check keeps me aware of how the data recording is going. I try to do this whenever we have time off, and lately there hasn't been any. I've got a stack of data sheets an inch thick, dating back at least a week. I want to go to CR 7, but since we need only four people there, someone would be a fifth wheel. There'll be enough unavoidable situations like that later.

Sitting inside looking at columns of band numbers is not a fun way to spend an afternoon. I feel guilty for not being out. As the clock ticks closer to suppertime, I start to feel like a ground crewman waiting for a World War II bomber mission to return. I listen for vehicles coming up the gravel driveway to the lab. Each time I hear a truck I get up to look out the window. The first one is Tony coming back from a day at the prairie; the next one is Michelle, a student who's doing research on acanthocephalan parasites. Finally the *Valdez* rolls in.

The assistants look hot, sweaty, tired, and grumpy, and they head off up the hill to clean up before supper. Mary reports the haul was thirty-eight birds. They weren't as successful as at the wooden bridge, mostly because the birds weren't as cooperative. Mary thinks thirty-eight is as good as it gets there, and she's not sure a return trip would be warranted. Counting the handful they got yesterday, we've caught about half the colony. The heat was getting the help down this afternoon, and Mary said they kept asking to quit early. Mary refused, in part on principle but mostly because she knew that if they could get a few more birds, we wouldn't have to go back to CR 7.

At supper Joan gets a phone call from a local woman who had a shrike attacking her barn swallows. The shrike killed at least two swallows that were nesting in her barn and impaled the dead birds on a barbed wire fence. She didn't know what the predator was, and from the description Joan identified it as a loggerhead shrike.

The size of a mockingbird and resembling one in color, shrikes are chunky little killers. They have a strong, hooked beak and attack and eat snakes, lizards, insects, and small birds. Shrikes have the gruesome habit of impaling their prey on barbed wire fences or thorns; their reasons are still debated. They don't hesitate to attack birds as large as swallows. A decade ago I saw one fly directly into a group of cliff swallows at CR 2, collide with a swallow, drive it to the ground, kill it with a couple of pecks, and then pick it up and carry it to a thorn tree. It could barely fly with something as large as a cliff swallow.

Although that's the only time I've seen a shrike get a cliff swallow, I'm sure they could be important predators if they were more common. During the mid- and late 1980s shrikes virtually disappeared from this part of Nebraska, and their numbers nationwide are still alarmingly low for unknown reasons. But they've been making a come-back here recently, and we're seeing more of them. Last year one tried to get a cliff swallow that was caught in a net at Grand Canyon, over in Garden County, and it would have killed the entangled bird if I hadn't seen it and chased it off.

The woman on the phone took more drastic measures with her shrike. She told Joan she killed it. Joan responded by talking about the virtues of shrikes and urging her not to kill any more, and the woman admitted she'd started to feel bad about it. It's hard to stir up much sympathy, though, for a creature that wastes someone's back-yard songbirds and ghoulishly impales them on a fence barb.

June 28

I threatened yesterday to do a whole day at I 80, and now's the time. The morning is cloudy, with temperatures only in the sixties, and it's supposed to stay cool all day—a good forecast if we're destined to spend hours sitting in the truck on the exit ramp.

We have a strong north wind, so the only choice is to put a net on the culvert's north end. As usual, a lot of birds *pew* at us, and we wait and wait for the swallows to start going in the south end. Even when they do, however, most of them also exit the south end. These guys are wise to nets. I try to flush them toward the net, but by now they're used to coming back toward me. We catch a few birds but it's slow.

Annie's happy, though, because she has a fresh pound bag of Twizzlers to occupy her for the morning—or maybe half the morning at the rate she eats them. This is my fourth trip to I 80 this year, and I'm getting mighty tired of this place. When I 80 was last active, in 1993, I think we came here only twice.

In midmorning I look up to see the *Valdez* suddenly pull up behind us. What in the world are Mary, Kathy, and Judy doing here, forty miles from Clary, their morning's target? Mary tells me they got to Clary and found the Great American Cattle Drive camped in the pasture by the culvert. The longhorns had already been driven out onto the highway for today's march, but with camping vehicles and temporary corrals not far from where we process, Mary decided netting at Clary was not in the cards. She decided instead to go get the colony size at Blue Creek, just west of Lewellen. On the way they passed the herd not far from the Blue Creek bridge. As the herd was bearing down on her, Mary ran out on the bridge, clapped her hands and shouted to verify that no birds live at Blue Creek, and jumped back into the truck just before the longhorns thundered past. Such heroism.

We decide they'll go back to Cedar Point and after lunch they'll net at Dunwoody. They leave, and Annie and I resume sitting.

About noon we break out the sandwiches, although Annie doesn't have much appetite after her morning of gorging on Twizzlers. By now I'm getting frustrated because even our extended presence doesn't seem to be helping much. By 1:00 we have only thirty-three birds.

It suddenly occurs to me that a drop net might work here. Whenever I get out of the truck to flush them, they hear me and fly out before I can get to the entrance. If we could throw a drop net over the south end before they flush, either we'd get a lot of them in it or they'd go out the north end and hit the net there.

We decide to try. I've never drop-netted a little culvert like this, but the short net made to culvert dimensions will fit perfectly. We set up the drop net, with poles in buckets on the roadside directly above the south entrance. The wind is increasing, and the net billows. The birds are agitated and seem to know something's up. We wait another half hour before they start going in again. I tell Annie our plan will be to get out of the truck as quietly as we can, run to the net, grab the poles, and quickly fling the net down across the entrance.

It works great. We surprise the birds, and many flush out the south end as usual—into the waiting drop net. Others turn around and go out the north side, hitting that net. We catch eighteen birds in the two nets on the first drop. I worry a little about our conspicuousness; our standing on the side of the exit ramp with a mist net full of birds must not be a frequent sight along Interstate 80. No one stops, though. Thank God all the gas stations at the Roscoe exit went bust, and there's no reason for tourists to pull off here. We haven't even had any cops stop to ask if we've broken down. I guess by now the local state patrolmen have come to recognize our blue pickup and know it's apt to be parked in odd places.

After one drop in midafternoon, Annie decides she's held it as long as she can. This is not a good place to be when the urge to urinate hits, especially for a woman, because it's totally exposed. The only place to be out of sight is in the culvert itself, and there's a foot of stagnant, standing water there. Annie heads down into the culvert. She emerges a few minutes later with a frown.

"What's wrong?"

"Oh, I took off one of my boots to get my pants off, and then it fell over and filled up with muddy water and pee."

I try hard to keep from laughing as Annie takes off the wet boot and puts it on the hood of the truck to try to dry it out. I don't ask, but why would you need to take your pants off? Can't you just pull them down? Was she standing there with one leg in the air? There's something here I don't understand, but what I do know is that Annie has not yet mastered the art of peeing outdoors.

By 4:00 the cliff swallows seem to have gotten wise to us again and refuse to return to the culvert. I've started to worry about the disturbance to this colony today. It's been unusually cool for late June; the temperature is staying in the sixties, and it's cloudy and blustery. Although swallow eggs can tolerate a lot of chilling, the birds are making me feel bad. Thirty or forty are sitting on the same barbed wire fence where yesterday they were quarreling and fighting over shade. Today they look pitiful. They sit with drooped wings, feathers puffed up because they're cold. Nobody is squabbling; they're too miserable to argue with each other. Well, if they're just going to sit there and pout, there's no point in our staying here to net empty air.

Time to go home. But we're going with data for ninety birds. By drop netting and being here the whole day, we achieved our goal of finally doing well at I 80. We've now caught well over half the colony. I can finally quit thinking about this place.

Annie's boot still isn't dry.

June 29

A mist is falling at breakfast, and we decide to defer netting until the rain stops. The assistants have been working hard lately, and this is one morning off they enjoy. The clouds are forecast to break by noon. I'm looking forward to getting to Whitetail this afternoon to make sure everything's okay. An incident there yesterday upset me.

After supper last night Mary and I drove over to Whitetail to see if any juveniles were flying. In most years, scores of babies are fledging daily at Whitetail by now, and we want to be sure we net there when the big push of juveniles starts. The fledglings have distinctive calls that are easy to distinguish from the adults', and they call constantly. We parked on the roadside near the culvert, rolled the windows down, and listened for juveniles among all the birds coming and going. Any that were flying should have been coming back to the colony to sleep. We didn't hear any.

We were sitting there enjoying the sunset when two men drove up, parked on the roadside opposite us, and got out their fishing poles. They were young guys in pastel outfits and looked more like fraternity boys than the grimy local fishers. They marched down to the creek and stood there fishing only a few feet from the culvert entrance. All hell broke loose with the cliff swallows. The birds came boiling out of the culvert, alarm-calling like crazy and swarming above the guys' heads. The fishers were completely oblivious. What bothered me was that it was dusk, and a disruption like this might prevent the birds from getting into their nests for the night. Deb and the toads at Clary all over again.

Why would anyone try to fish at Whitetail? The water averages only two feet deep, is sandy and dirty, and contains only carp, the pinnacle of trash-fish evolution. There are lakes, rivers, and canals nearby full of trout and walleyes, and these guys were at Whitetail. Pretty soon they crossed the road and tried their luck on the other side, me glaring at them the entire time. If Mary and I looked suspicious enough to them, maybe they'd leave. How relaxing could it be to stand there and fish with four thousand screaming birds overhead and poop falling like rain?

As the sun sank lower, finally I decided I'd go down and ask them to leave. Before I could get out of the truck, though, they decided they'd had enough, and they came back up to their car and drove off. The colony settled down, and everyone got to bed. I breathed a sigh of relief, but it still upset me. Whitetail is so vulnerable to that kind of thing. I'm sure fishers stop there when we're not around. I'm glad I usually don't know about it.

When we arrive at Whitetail this afternoon there aren't any fishers, but we do see Will, a Swainson's hawk who's a fixture at Whitetail. He sits on a telephone pole along the roadside almost directly above the culvert. This species was named after naturalist William Swainson—hence the name we gave to what we bet is the same bird who hangs out here year after year. He's present for hours on end almost every day. Will is a *Buteo* hawk, the type that has broad wings and hunts by soaring at high altitudes in open areas. These hawks eat mostly rabbits, rodents, and snakes that they spot from high up and swoop down to catch. They seldom prey on birds. Perhaps recognizing this, the cliff swallows ignore Will. They'll occasionally alarm-call when he flies in or leaves, but once he's sitting he's just part of the telephone pole for all they care.

Will, or at least a Will, first appeared at Whitetail three years ago, and we were perplexed by his constant presence. He must have been hunting, but he wasn't going after the swallows. We joked that he was a couch potato who liked to sit and watch the cliff swallows: bird television. Then one evening while I was there an RV blew by, hitting a flying swallow and hurling it into the ditch along the roadside. Will was onto that dead bird in seconds. He grabbed it and flew to the top of a fence post. Holding it with his feet, he tore off the feathers with his beak and gulped down the body in two minutes flat. When I went over to the fence post later to see if he might have left an uneaten banded leg, I found nothing. Will doesn't waste food.

So he hangs out here looking to scavenge deadheads. Since birds are always getting hit by cars on the road at Whitetail, the colony represents a ready source of food. If you're a Will, you can just sit there like a bump on a post and wait for lunch to be served. His attraction to the colony coincides with its becoming larger and again illustrates how colonies like Whitetail are beacons to predators. At least Will's a benign predator. He might even indirectly benefit the swallows by preying on bull snakes that come along to attack the colony.

Once again we have a north wind. I can happily avoid the abyss on the south side. After years of wishing for a south wind each time we net Whitetail, I now dread doing the south end with the chest waders. Even the birds don't seem to mind our being on the north side anymore.

I'm expecting the grackle to be back this afternoon, and I'm not disappointed. Within half an hour of our arrival, I see him sitting on the barbed wire fence at the south end of the colony. He gives a few *chucks* but leaves without going into the culvert. I bet he's coming here regularly. He usually flies off toward the ranch, and I guess he's nesting in the woods over there. But he doesn't reappear this afternoon: either our presence intimidated him or he has an alternative source of food.

In midafternoon I start hearing alarm calls at the south end of the culvert. I turn around and see waves of birds flying toward the entrance but not going in. This is the typical response to a predator at the nests, and I figure the grackle is back. I don't see him in the middle or east tunnel, though. I keep watching and still no grackle. This means only one thing. There must be a snake in a nest.

I ask Annie to watch the net in case any birds hit it low and sag into the water. I wade through the culvert, scanning the rows and rows of nests. It can be hard to find a snake in the labyrinth of nests at Whitetail, especially if it's curled up inside one. Bull snakes sometimes get completely out of sight. Several years ago our assistant Kristen got a severe fright here when she stuck a mirror and penlight into a nest to count eggs and saw the maw of a bull snake. Snakes capture adult swallows by waiting in a nest and grabbing the unsuspecting nest owners when they return.

I figure the snake is toward the south end, and soon I see it. It's a big thick one, probably between four and five feet long. It has grasped one nest and has the upper third of its body inside an adjacent nest, feeding on the babies. Usually snakes attack the extreme edge nests of a colony, because those are the first ones they encounter. They move progressively inward but are usually satiated before they get very far. This snake is at least twenty nests in, maybe two yards along the wall. I wonder if it has cleaned out a swath of nests extending back to the south end.

Bull snakes are probably the most significant cliff swallow predator in Nebraska and certainly the most important one that attacks nests. Nonvenomous constrictors that kill their prey (mostly rodents) by squeezing it to death, they are abundant in the Platte Valley and adjacent Sand Hills. We see them everywhere: at Cedar Point, crossing the roads, on our evening walks across the diversion dam, around colony sites. They are beautiful snakes, with a regular series of reddish brown splotches along their backs on a background of yellow. Their bellies are yellowish with black splotches along the sides. Even though they prey on cliff swallows, they are my favorite snakes. Unlike many snakes that go slithering off through the brush when you approach, bull snakes are bold, tame, and not easily intimidated. If you happen upon one, it will hold its ground and just look at you. When we see one crossing a road, we stop and try to herd it to the side so it won't be run over by cars. Often you have to kick dirt or pebbles on it before it will leave, and sometimes then it gets stubborn and goes into its rattlesnake imitation. A bull snake will flatten its head into a viperlike triangle, coil up, and vibrate its tail. It can be a scary mimic, especially at first glance.

We see snake predations every year. Bull snakes are skilled climbers and can reach nests on metal and concrete bridges, cliffs, and culverts. At culverts like Whitetail they have trouble scaling the vertical concrete walls from below, so instead they come over the top. They hang onto the concrete facing of the culvert and the ground above, curl down, and reach the uppermost edge nest along the ceiling. Once they grab onto that nest, they have enough purchase to swing the rest of their bodies down. Any culvert colony with nests built near the edge is vulnerable to bull snake attack.

Bull snakes can really clean out nests once they get into a colony. One year we watched a snake stay in the colony at CR 4 for three days. It would eat, then curl up inside a nest and doze until it was hungry again. This snake preyed on the contents of about fifty nests, eating at least 150 eggs. Like grackles, bull snakes seem to be attracted to big colonies like Whitetail. How they're attracted is unclear because they don't rely on eyesight. Maybe they smell the big colonies. Virtually all cliff swallow colonies larger than a thousand nests can count on being attacked by bull snakes. About half of their attempts to reach the nests in a colony fail because they don't take the right approach and can't effectively climb the wall or cliff face at the chosen point. But a snake will keep trying and eventually find a way, often coming down from above as they do here.

When Mary and I began studying cliff swallows, many biologists believed—as many still do—that animals formed colonies mostly to improve their defense against predators. Group living could make it easier to detect incoming predators. Once the colony detected a predator, the residents could mount a defense: physically assault it, "mob" it by swirling around near it—perhaps to show it had been seen—or sound the alarm so their babies could escape. We decided to test whether large cliff swallow colonies detected predators better than small colonies. But since actual predators infrequently attack colonies, we devised an experiment. We presented a fake predator to colonies of different sizes and watched to see how quickly it was seen.

Our "predator" was an inflatable rubber snake sold by seed companies to keep birds out of gardens. It bore an uncanny resemblance to a real bull snake. Besides faking out the swallows, it also fooled passersby who saw us with it along roadsides. During one experiment while we were hidden out of sight, some guy passing in a truck saw it, stopped, and was about to blast our rubber snake to bits with a shotgun before we stopped him! Another fellow saw Mary walking along the roadside carrying the inflated snake and stopped to comment, "I'm glad you're not my wife."

We would erect a small blind at the edge of a colony, where the observer waited. The rubber snake went into another wooden box a hundred meters away. With monofilament fishing line attached to its head, we'd tow the predator from its box to the blind. With the observer hidden, any alarm response was to the snake. The birds didn't like it, and as soon as they saw it, they circled over it and alarm-called. At that point we stopped the tow and measured how far from the colony it had been seen.

We spent three summers doing these experiments at colonies of different sizes. They involved a lot of set-up time, hauling the blind in and erecting it and waiting for the birds to settle down after each "attack." Eventually the data showed that cliff swallows in large colonies detect snake predators more quickly than birds in small colonies. At the small colonies the rubber snake always made its run all the way to the observer's blind without being seen by the birds living there. In the big colonies they saw it almost as soon as it emerged from its box.

But did early detection of predators really benefit cliff swallows? Even if a bull snake is seen, it still moves in, unfazed by the birds' *pew* calls. Cliff swallows are small and not equipped to assault predators. Perhaps the alarm calls tell predators that hunt by surprise— the kestrel at Aqueduct, for example—that they've been seen and thus the attack is likely to fail. If so, there could be an advantage of coloniality in helping the birds avoid certain kinds of avian predators (but obviously not grackles). Yet early detection of snakes makes little difference; most attack anyway.

It's hard to see that cliff swallows avoid predators all that effectively by living in colonies. With high nest density enhancing predator access and large colonies attracting more predators, birds in small colonies or those nesting solitarily might be safest from predators. I wonder what John Hoogland thinks about that conclusion. He is a major proponent of the idea that coloniality's major function is to help animals avoid predators. He suggested I study cliff swallows in the first place to help his case in the debate over why bank swallows formed colonies—to avoid predators, he thought.

I yell for the assistants to come see the snake. Judy doesn't care to get wet, but Annie rips off her shoes and wades in. I'm going to remove the snake. If we leave it, the birds will be so disturbed that netting will be over for today. I don't care if snakes attack Whitetail when we're not here, but the limited time we have for netting has to justify our interfering with the predation attempt. Annie wants to touch the snake, so I tell her to pull it out. She grabs it by its lower body and yanks. It has gripped the nest so tightly that both snake and nest fall into the creek with a huge splash. Part of the nest it was preying on comes down too, but there are no babies left. The snake swims away, carried out of the culvert by the current. I see it climb up on the creek bank near the abyss. It'll be back.

I check and find only a couple of nests that the snake raided. How did it get this far into the culvert without eating anything on the way? It had to have come over the top and in via the edgemost nest. They're supposed to attack the first nests they come to. Chalk up something else new for this summer.

"Be careful with that band number."

Cliff swallow nests attached to corrugated metal inside Knight's Tube.

Setting a net on the south side of Knight's Tube.

A swallow colony on a natural cliff at Lake McConaughy.

A big net at Aqueduct can catch a lot of cliff swallows.

A bull snake attacking a cliff swallow nest at Whitetail (from Charles R. Brown and Mary Bomberger Brown, *Coloniality in the Cliff Swallow* [Chicago: University of Chicago Press, 1996], © 1996 by The University of Chicago; reprinted with permission).

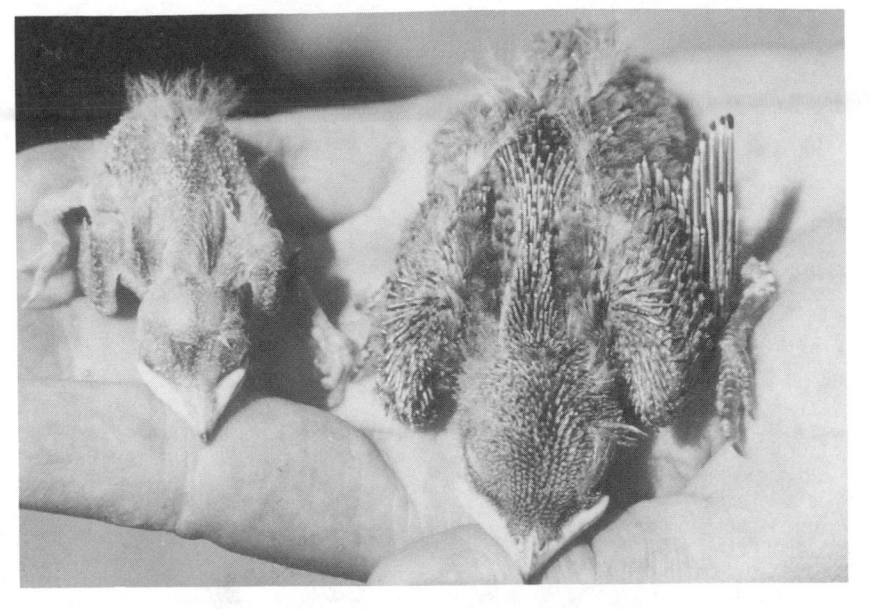

The cost of being parasitized: ten-day-old cliff swallow nestlings, one from a fumigated nest that had no swallow bugs (right) and one from a nonfumigated nest that was naturally infested (from Charles R. Brown and Mary Bomberger Brown, "Ectoparasitism as a cost of coloniality in cliff swallows [*Hirundo pyrrhonota*]," *Ecology* 67 [1986]: 1206–18; reprinted with permission).

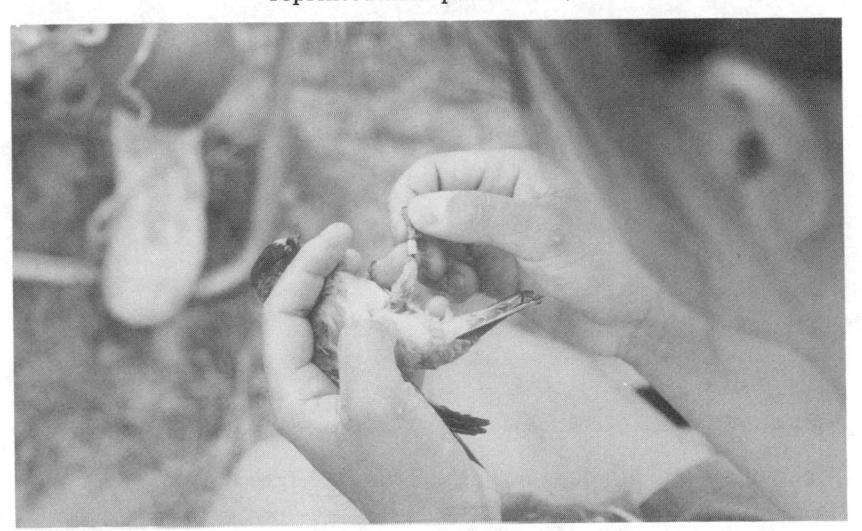

Banding another nonbreeder.

Cliff swallows flocking together in crèches soon after fledging.

A parent feeding its young in a crèche (from Charles R. Brown and Mary Bomberger Brown, *Coloniality in the Cliff Swallow* [Chicago: University of Chicago Press, 1996], © 1996 by The University of Chicago; reprinted with permission).

Swallow bugs clustered at the entrance of an unoccupied nest; if a bird lands, some bugs will crawl onto its feet to be carried to a new site (photo courtesy of Art Gingert, Wildlands Photography).

The wonder of Whitetail: birds always in the net.

11

Information Centers

*The wind ... drives with unusial force over the naked
Plains and against this hill; the insects ... are thus
involuntaryly driven to the Mound by the force of wind...;
the small Birds whoes food they are, Consequently resort
in great numbers to this place in Surch of them.*
—Captain William Clark, August 25, 1804

June 30

With our need for five people dwindling, I told the assistants I'd start giving them each half days off. This morning it's Annie's turn. Perhaps it's good that Kathy and Judy are separated from Annie for a while today. Mary tells me the strain between them is growing. Annie's nightlife is one point of contention; she usually doesn't come in until after the others have been asleep for several hours. Or her alarm clock goes off in the middle of the night when she's not there. The others seem most disturbed by uneaten Twizzlers left in the cabin that are attracting ants and mice. I just hope the lid stays on for another week.

Judy and I spend the morning at Mosquito, another small culvert, where the birds are every bit as tough as those at I 80. We sit in the truck on the elevated earthen overpass approach, a vantage point that provides a splendid view of the surrounding fields and highway stretching to the eastern and western horizons. It was at this location that, in the second summer of our research, we started to understand why cliff swallows live in colonies.

I began studying cliff swallows with the intention of determining whether advantages of either avoiding predators or finding food applied to these birds. The previous studies on bank swallows had suggested that both benefits might result from colonial living. It would take years of rubber snake experiments and collecting other data before we could address predator avoidance. But it took only one morning of watching cliff swallows for me to know that food-related benefits are important for these birds.

I first observed cliff swallows foraging at a colony at Lake Texoma, on the Texas-Oklahoma border, in the spring of 1982. Since it was March and early April, the birds weren't doing much then except foraging. It was immediately obvious that they always fed in groups. The colony residents came and went as a group, traveling from the nests out to the fields and along the shoreline, where they always stayed together as a cohesive band while feeding.

That the birds fed in groups meant they would be a good species to study, apart from issues of coloniality, because at that time many ecologists were interested in animals that fed together. People had realized that a group of foragers could convey information about food to others. Individuals could watch where other group members were finding food and learn where to go to be successful. As a foraging group got larger, the additional searchers meant food sources could be located faster—someone was always bound to be finding some food somewhere—so food intake rates could increase for everyone. And if members of a group were to give a call that signaled their discovery of food, as we would later discover that cliff swallows do, information could be transferred among the group more effectively and the advantages of social feeding could increase.

Ten years before our study started, ecologist Amotz Zahavi proposed that birds nested in groups because a colony serves as an "information center"—it was at the colony itself that individuals could get information on where food might be. A bird unsuccessful at finding food could return to the colony, observe other members, identify which ones had just found food, and then follow those knowledgeable individuals when they went back for more. Zahavi's idea was controversial, and other studies had failed to find any evidence that bird colonies met the requirements for being information centers. But if cliff swallow colonies were information centers as Zahavi had proposed, colonial life could improve the birds' ability to find food simply by reducing the time wasted in searching for it. This could be one reason the swallows formed colonies in the first place. To nail this down would require years of work, but I knew at the outset that food would be a key to understanding much of the cliff swallow's social behavior.

During the second summer, when we spent every day watching the birds at Whitetail, we noticed that a swallow would arrive at its nest, wait a few seconds, and then follow another bird that was leaving the colony. It certainly looked as if returning foragers were monitoring their neighbors' success and picking out which ones to follow. We also noticed that as the colony at Whitetail began to dwindle as babies left the nests, the remaining birds waited longer to find others to follow. With fewer birds, less information was available and it took the swallows longer to find food. The implication was clear: small colonies would not be as effective information centers as large colonies, and therefore feeding efficiency could be less in the smaller colonies.

That summer we weren't studying multiple colonies, so we couldn't test our ideas about foraging differences among colonies of different sizes. However, a late colony of only thirteen nests became active at Mosquito that season. With our work at Whitetail nearly over, we had the unexpected opportunity to watch how the foraging behavior of birds at a very small colony compared with that of birds at a larger one. Our principal discovery at Mosquito that year was that birds virtually never waited at their nests to look for other residents to follow. There were so few birds in the colony that it probably didn't pay to wait for a knowledgeable neighbor to come home.

But that didn't mean the Mosquito birds didn't look for other swallows that might lead them to food. At times foraging birds would fly out of the culvert and circle high above the colony as if looking for someone to follow. They would continue to circle in "holding patterns" until another bird departed in direct flight. Then the circling bird would make a beeline after the other bird and follow it until both reached a swarm of insects in one of the adjacent fields. In contrast, whenever a group of two or three birds happened to leave their nests together, they went straight toward a feeding site with no circling. Cliff swallows at Mosquito clearly spent more time circling overhead than did birds in larger colonies such as Whitetail, where we never saw birds circle. This meant more time was wasted in the smaller colonies.

Those early observations at Mosquito hinted that cliff swallows had different ways of finding food in different colonies and foreshadowed much of the work we were to do for the next decade. Sitting here today, I gaze out over the nearby pastures and the interstate right-of-way. The area looks much the same as in 1983, and periodically I see small squadrons of three or four cliff swallows leave the colony together and travel out varying distances. Using binoculars, I follow them and see that they soon begin foraging, shown by their erratic twisting and turning movements as they chase insects. Each little group sticks together while feeding, as if keeping track of each other's whereabouts. They may be little butts to each other at the nests or on perching sites, but they're all best friends when it's time to feed.

As our own lunch hour approaches, it's obvious that more trips here will be necessary. We've caught only seventeen birds, and the colony has at least twenty nests—forty birds. I walk through the culvert before we leave and count about forty total nests that have been built this summer. Only half of them have eggs, however. We caught a couple of house sparrows this morning, and they may have raided some of the nests. These two sparrows won't be destroying any more cliff swallow eggs, but the damage is already done.

On walking down the tall embankment to reach the culvert, I noticed that often we could get directly above the culvert entrance before any birds heard or saw us and flushed. This means we could probably drop-net Mosquito as we did I 80. We've never done it here, but it should work. That will be the next order of business. A few good drops could save several days of waiting for the birds to get into stationary nets.

This afternoon Mary and Kathy are going to CR 10, one of the farther canal colonies near Paxton. They tried to net there yesterday, but when they arrived fishers were all over the bridge and Mary didn't even set up the net. Instead they went to Mule Deer—despite Mary's vow to never go there again—and tried to catch the single pair of birds that, I thought, lived in the north culvert. They netted for two hours and never saw any birds. The solitary nest must have failed, a common fate of single nesters. Perhaps solitaries can't find food efficiently enough without the information provided by other colony residents. I had to bribe Mary heavily (she likes animal-shaped earrings and hair clips) to do Mule Deer as her secondary target in case CR 10 didn't work out yesterday. Now I'm glad I did, because we found out there's no further need to net there this summer. The assistants will welcome that news.

I'm taking Judy and Annie to Knight's Tube, because I'm still not satisfied that we've caught enough of the edge nesters. This may be a problem with all three of the new colonies along the railroad tracks. We've caught many of the birds nesting in the middle of the culverts, but the edge birds are escaping us each time. Yet I suppose it's a measure of how thoroughly we've been able to do our colonies this summer for us to have time to worry about getting edge nesters at three relatively small sites. So I feel good today.

I drop Judy and Annie at the tube, help them set a net at one end, and leave them to handle it. I need to fumigate Whitetail again. It's been almost two weeks since I doused the nests, and when we were dealing with the snake yesterday I saw bugs on them. As I drive out of Dave Knight's pasture and reach the road, I see that I need to get to Whitetail and return quickly. A large thunderhead is developing to the west, and the tube would be a bad place for Annie and Judy to get caught in a storm. They'd be out on the open prairie with no protection.

As soon as I get out of the truck at Whitetail, I hear juveniles calling overhead. Babies must have finally started fledging. This means that fumigating will be tricky, with relatively old babies in the nests ready to jump out when I spray. As I enter the culvert, however, I'm glad to be here with the fumigant. Dozens of swallow bugs are crawling on the outsides of nests. I'm taken aback by the numbers. We began the summer fumigating Whitetail more thoroughly than usual because so many nests had fallen, and I expected to see fewer parasites this year than ever before. Instead there are tons of them, attesting to the rate at which birds bring them in from other colonies.

I start spraying the nests and watch the bugs drop off, falling into the creek and being washed away by the current. Whitetail was one of the first colonies we fumigated and where we saw the terrible effect the bugs could have on the birds. Early in our research it was clear that cliff swallows had an inordinate number of ectoparasites, probably because of their long-lasting nests. A mud nest that remains at least partly intact from year to year provides a good refuge for nest parasites such as fleas and bedbugs that are adapted to withstanding long periods without a host. They can wait in the nests until the birds happen to return or, if they have a chance to get on a bird, disperse to another nest or colony.

The only way to know what effect the parasites had on the birds' nesting success was to do a fumigation experiment. Mary and I devised a plan to remove the ectoparasites from some nests and see how the birds did in the absence of parasites compared with those in nests exposed to natural levels. One of our major goals during the summer of 1984 was to do these parasite removals at as many colonies of different sizes as possible. We divided each colony in two, with half of the nests to be fumigated and half left untouched. To keep parasites from moving between the two halves, we applied a vile, smelly, olive green sticky substance called Tanglefoot in a line—the iron curtain—along the concrete wall. Tanglefoot is designed as an insect barrier, and it effectively kept swallow bugs from crawling along the concrete from one part of the colony to another.

The fumigation experiment was an immediate success. It was plain after one season that swallow bugs represent a major cost to cliff swallows. In the larger colonies, the fledging success of birds in nests exposed to natural numbers of parasites was only half that of birds in fumigated nests. Baby swallows died like flies, drained of their blood by the bugs, especially in the nests active later in the summer after the parasite population had increased. Even the babies that survived to fledge from the parasitized nests were sickly and of low weight, and many apparently didn't live to come back the next season.

As expected, the effects of the bugs were worst in the larger colonies. Parasites are more numerous there because they can move among the more closely packed nests and find hosts more easily than in small colonies. Ectoparasites also are more likely to be introduced into large colonies because of the many birds settling there. Odds are at least one bird colonizing a large colony will be loaded with parasites, whereas small colonies may not have any such birds settle. It's like the principle that the more people you're exposed to in the flu season, the greater your odds of encountering an infected person and getting sick yourself. In small colonies with few bugs, we didn't see a difference in reproductive success or condition of the babies among the birds using fumigated versus nonfumigated nests.

One of the first things John Hoogland asked me eleven years ago when I showed him heavily infested Clary was how an information center could compensate these birds for the costs of parasites. There have to be advantages of larger colonies; otherwise the negative effects of the bugs would cause the birds to try to escape them by distributing themselves in smaller groups or as singletons. By improving their ability to find food in a large colony, presumably birds can provide more food to their babies. This extra food could enable them to withstand the effects of the parasites. But John raised a good point, and I had to admit I also doubted that food-finding advantages alone could balance the harmful effects of swallow bugs, especially among the highly infested later nests in the largest colonies. It would take almost another decade of fieldwork before we could address John's question.

When our original fumigation experiments ended, I decided to continue fumigating one site to see how parasites—or more directly, their absence—might influence the birds' use of a nesting site. Could the presence of parasites limit the size of a cliff swallow colony? Perhaps if a colony gets too large there will be so many swallow bugs and fleas that the birds would have zero reproductive success. If so, colonies should stop growing when they approach that maximum size. If parasites restrict colony growth, when they're removed one might see the colony increase until it's limited by something else, such as local food supplies or places to build nests. We chose Whitetail as the site for continued fumigation and began spraying the entire site in 1985.

The birds' initial response to the fumigation was dramatic. Whitetail went from 125 nests in the year half of it was fumigated to 456 nests the next year with complete fumigation and grew steadily in successive years: 750 to 1,100 to 1,400 to 2,200. It peaked at 2,350 nests in 1990, dropped the next year to 1,700, and has been 1,500, 1,450, and 1,600 the past three years. It's tempting to speculate that the site has reached the local carrying capacity, somewhere in the range of 1,500 to 1,600 nests. If so, it's not nesting substrate that's limiting. There's still plenty of bare wall below the existing tiers of nests where birds could build more, and they used these spots when the colony was at its largest. And only this year have the swallows expanded into the east tunnel in large numbers; many more nests could be accommodated there. If the colony has hit a ceiling, it must be food based. Perhaps only so many pairs of cliff swallows and their young can be supported in a given area. We know that young swallows sometimes starve in larger colonies, especially when a pair has a large family of five or six nestlings. An information center can only help the birds find the existing food more quickly. Foraging advantages of a large colony can't create new food.

After I finish fumigating, I wade back through the culvert and count all the nests. I use a hand counter, pointing to each nest as I click the counter. I go through the stacked tiers of nests as systematically as I can, trying not to miss or double count any in the packed adobe maze. The total is 1,698 nests among both active tunnels. Allowing for a few nests I probably missed, an estimated colony size of 1,700 nests seems reasonable for Whitetail this summer. Today will also be the last time I fumigate here for a while. Many nests contain large, well-feathered babies, and at least ten fledglings jumped out of the nests while I was spraying. A couple were old enough to fly and escaped. The rest of them flopped into the water below the nests, but I was able to grab them as they floated in the creek and got them back into their nests. I'll wait to let the bulk of the babies fledge before I fumigate again.

I rush back to the tube, relieved to see that the threatening thunderhead has slid off to the north and doesn't pose any threat. I rejoin Annie and Judy, and the three of us continue the quest for the edge birds. As we sit and wait, I'm struck by an opportunity provided by these three new railroad track colonies. Knight's Tube, Knight's Culvert, and Dunwoody each have about two hundred nests. It might be instructive to begin another fumigation treatment at one of these, replicating what we've done at Whitetail. We could entirely fumigate one of these sites and leave the other two as controls. Would the fumigated colony increase in size the way Whitetail did? If so, would it reach a ceiling? Having a nearby colony that was not fumigated but was situated in identical habitat would give us the sort of direct comparison with a naturally infested site that we don't have for Whitetail. Probably Dunwoody and Knight's Culvert would be the better pair of colonies to use, because they were both first occupied this year, they're identical culvert structures, and they're only three-quarters of a mile apart. I wonder if the one we fumigate would reach the same maximum size as Whitetail.

Our haul for the afternoon is a disappointing thirty-four birds. I hope they're largely the edge birds we hadn't caught earlier, but we can't tell until the data are computerized. We'd have done better if we'd come for an entire day.

Mary kicked butt at CR 10 this afternoon: 92 birds from a colony of about 140 residents. CR 10 is a drop-net site, and to catch that a high a fraction of the colony with a drop net on this late date is remarkable.

What's even more remarkable is that we've reached the end of June and haven't yet caught any juvenile cliff swallows. This summer is starting to seem endless.

July 1

Everyone's back to wearing coats. It's only 53° at 7:00 and forecast to get not more than ten degrees warmer by afternoon. A signature day for this cold swallow summer. Insects will be harder to find in weather like this, and the information-center function of colonies will be important today, especially for the thousands of cliff swallows that have babies to feed.

For over a week we've been seeing swallows swarming at CR 5, another canal bridge. I don't know how many of the birds are for real, because many late settlers will leave without laying eggs. But we can use this weather to our advantage: any birds we catch at CR 5 on a lousy day like this are bound to be serious. The dilettantes will be out foraging, and we should get a fairly accurate sense of how many birds are actually nesting there. Mary and Judy are elected to go to CR 5. I'll take the other two assistants to Knight's Culvert, where we need to focus on—what else?—edge birds.

It's clear that babies have hatched at Knight's Culvert. Broken eggshells litter the ground under the nests. I notice that the parents go all the way into the nests to feed their newly hatched young. It's probably harder for a colony to be effective as an information center when the babies are this small. An unsuccessful bird returning to the colony needs some way to identify who's been successful and who hasn't. We discovered early in our research that the birds apparently use the same cues human observers do: they look to see who comes back with its mouth and throat stuffed full of insects. A successful forager is obvious with its bulging throat and insect appendages sticking out the sides of its beak. When the babies get older, they sit in the entrance of the nest and a parent clings to the outside—in full view of its neighbors—to feed them. It's easy then to see who comes back with food. But while the young are small parents go into the nest without pausing, making it harder for neighbors to monitor their catch. Also, when babies are small the parents bring back less food per trip, and the smaller amount is not so obvious to onlookers.

Does that mean colonies serve as information centers only when the babies are large and sit in the nest entrances? If so, that would restrict the time during the season when birds could learn from each other and diminish the importance of information centers. But cliff swallows use additional cues to identify successful birds. A common one is when a colony member suddenly leaves and makes a beeline toward the foraging grounds. When a bird heads out unhesitatingly, it's a good bet it's returning to where it just found food. If you know where there's an insect swarm, you want to get back as fast as you can before others find it and eat everything or the swarm moves. Following a departing bird that seems to know where it's going doesn't require that you actually see a bird feed its young and will work even before eggs hatch. In this way a swallow colony serves as an information center throughout the summer.

In the largest colonies like Whitetail, the thousands of foragers ensure that some birds will be leaving the colony almost constantly— virtually every second of the daylight hours. These streams of birds travel between the colony and various foraging sites in adjacent pastures or marshes. The locations of food are continuously tracked, even as they change, by the constant departure and arrival of foraging birds. It reminds me of the spokes on a moving wheel, with the colony at the center and the streams of birds leading to different locations on the perimeter. When there are enough birds to form continuous streams, a forager doesn't need to wait at its nest for a neighbor to return with food. It can join a stream and always find food rapidly. This is the single greatest advantage of living in a large colony.

At a colony like Knight's Culvert, only 225 nests, there aren't enough birds to form continuous streams. So here they have to watch for a successful forager to arrive, and birds usually follow their closest neighbors, since they can see them most easily. The advantage of having neighbors that provide information on the whereabouts of insects is obvious as babies hatch and the birds devote all their time to collecting food. It's these benefits that presumably compensate the birds for all the rotten things their neighbors may have done to them earlier in the season.

We seem to be getting a few of the edge nesters on one side of Knight's Culvert but virtually nothing on the other. With so little to do, Kathy spends most of the morning sketching sunflowers. I have to admit I'm glad when quitting time comes. The morning has been cold, gray, and depressing. We end with 102 birds, but I have a feeling we've caught many of them earlier this year.

At lunch Mary reports there were hundreds of birds at CR 5 despite the weather. Many were collecting mud and fighting over nests, as if it were May. If they're building nests in cool weather like this, they're serious and probably will stay to breed. Mary and Judy caught 113 birds before the wind got so bad they had to quit. The catch was a potpourri of birds: some unbanded, some banded in past years, some banded elsewhere earlier this year. There seems to be a lot of bird movement between colonies this summer. Mary says CR 5 is probably the second largest colony we have now after Whitetail.

I give the assistants the afternoon off because of the wind, but I'm too restless to sit and do boring paperwork. I've been obsessed with the idea of drop-netting Mosquito since Judy and I were there yesterday. I cajole Mary into coming with me to Mosquito to see if it might be possible this afternoon. She thinks it's far too windy but agrees to go. On the way we stop at Aqueduct. Swallows that are incubating flush out of a hundred or so complete nests, and these are probably the serious nesters. Many of the incomplete nests that birds were working on five days ago have barely progressed, and none of those swallows are around this afternoon. Those guys won't be breeding this year.

When we get to Mosquito, netting is out of the question. The truck shakes as we sit on the elevated overpass, and when we step out the wind almost knocks us over. There's no point in trying to put up a net—we'd get blown to Oz. But I've satisfied myself that nothing's possible this afternoon. It's back to the boring paperwork. I told you so, smiles Mary.

After supper Mary and I do our usual walk down to the diversion dam. The wind is still strong. Huge numbers of cliff swallows are foraging on the north side of the massive sandstone outcroppings that rise at least fifty feet above the road. The bluffs provide a splendid windbreak for a south wind, and insects have concentrated along their base. There are swarms of midges, hundreds of huge dragonflies that feed on the midges, and seemingly millions of flies that land in big nasty clusters on our legs. Where there are insects, there are cliff swallows. With the wind blocked, the birds find it much easier to pursue and catch prey here. Although I hear a few food calls, for the most part the birds are silent. The weather today has been yucky enough that you'd expect more food calls. Perhaps the birds aren't calling much because the wind disrupts the insect swarms (except along the base of these cliffs) and makes the calls harder to hear.

As we walk along the road, cliff swallows are darting all around, always busy. Some are so preoccupied with looking for food that they nearly collide with us. You can get dizzy watching the birds swarm-

ing everywhere, almost as far as you can see. We hear a high-pitched
zwreep call and notice four rough-winged swallows sitting on a wire
above us. The nondescript little birds are brownish on their upper-
parts and whitish below. They are similar ecologically to bank swallows, nesting in burrows in the side of banks or crevices in rock ledges.
Roughwings are widespread in the Cedar Point area, nesting in the
canyons behind the station and in banks along the canal. Unlike bank
swallows, though, they're almost always solitary. I've never seen more
than two pairs in any one location here. The four birds on the wire
are sitting quietly, gazing around and only occasionally preening their
backs. They're not interacting with each other; they don't even seem
to know the others are there. Model citizens.

Soon a cliff swallow lands in their midst. It starts shaking its feathers vigorously, preening hurriedly, looking anxious and hyperactive.
The roughwings eye it suspiciously but don't move. Unlike the smaller
barn and bank swallows, roughwings don't have a size disadvantage.
The cliff swallow takes a few steps sideways along the wire toward
two of the roughwings, the precursor to an unprovoked attack. The
roughers hold their ground, staring at it. The nervous cliff swallow
shakes its feathers more, preens another time or two, and takes another step sideways. The roughers still don't move. Finally the cliff
swallow seems to decide that these roughwings won't be bullied, and
it flies off. The roughwings continue sitting.

I conclude that rough-winged swallows don't put up with any crap,
nor do they dish it out. I wonder if this sort of personal dignity might
be a common characteristic of solitary, self-sufficient organisms.
Maybe only deviants, bullies, and wimps live in groups.

July 2

Drop netting at Mosquito is something we should have been doing
for years.

This morning Annie and I find we can easily get down to the top of
the culvert without the birds' detecting us, and the short net fits across
the entrance perfectly. We catch everyone that flushes out. The only
downside is that by the time we climb up the highway embankment
to put the net poles in the buckets, some of the birds have blown out
of the net. The wind is strong again and seems to be increasing, especially up on the embankment. It takes a while for everyone to come
back after each drop, but with no nets set up near the culvert en-

trances, the birds are fairly cooperative. Eventually we're just catching the same birds over and over.

By lunchtime we've caught twenty-eight different individuals, which appears to be about all we're going to get today. With our earlier haul, we're close to being done here for the year. The realization that we can drop-net culverts like Mosquito and I 80 is a major methodological advance of the summer. I don't know why I never thought to do it before. I guess it's the same time-honored reason that dictates the way many things are done in academia: "Because that's how we've always done it."

Back at CR 5 this morning, Mary initially found as many swallows as yesterday, but when the clouds broke in midmorning and the sun came out, many of them left. That's weird; usually it's the opposite pattern. Maybe some of these birds are drifters after all and were just hanging around the bridge while the weather was crappy. Once the sun came out and it got warmer, they headed out to feed. Mary and the assistants caught 105 birds.

Seeing juveniles at Whitetail lately makes me eager to begin catching them. Banding as many juveniles as possible is a priority this summer. A bird banded as a fledgling is of known age, so when it's recaught in later years, we can use it to estimate age-related survivorship and how colony choice may change with age. Banding a juvenile is in many ways more useful to us than banding an adult, because we have no way to know an adult's age or anything about its past. In the early years of our research we concentrated on banding nestling cliff swallows when they were ten days old—well before they fledged. But banding babies is laborious and highly disruptive to a colony, requiring us to spend long periods at the nests and keeping the parents away. Netting juveniles gives us much the same information, disturbs the colonies less, and also yields recapture data for adults. In recent years we've been banding about 1,500 juveniles each summer.

Doing Whitetail today will be no picnic. The wind is southerly, meaning we have to net the end with the abyss. Back to the Michelin Man chest waders. As we set the net I find that the abyss has deepened recently, and I sink so deep there's a part of the net I can't reach. I'll have to hope nobody gets caught there. The wet summer has promoted growth of some poison ivy near the west tunnel entrance, and it's developed into a dense stand. It's no threat to me in my rubber armor, but I warn the assistants to keep their bare legs away from it.

Less than twenty minutes into our netting, we catch the first juvenile of the summer.

We've netted at Whitetail so much this year that the birds hardly notice us as long as the assistants are in the west tunnel and I stand still at the net. These creatures' tolerance of us is perhaps the most remarkable of their many fascinating traits. Birds of virtually any other species would have long ago deserted their nests because of the disturbance. I watch a swallow repeatedly come into one of the edge nests, cling to the entrance to feed its large babies, then sit on top of a lower nest and look at me. Invariably it directs four or five muted *pew* calls at me and then flies away—always back out the north end away from the net. It's as if this bird has resigned itself to my being here but still protests each time it visits its nest. It wears a band, so we've met in the past.

The activity in the culvert is extreme, with birds traveling in big streams to and from the feeding areas in the surrounding pastures. The young in the nests are noisy, all of them calling almost constantly. The racket inside the culvert ebbs and flows with the bird traffic. If everyone flushes out, alarming either at us or at the neighborhood kestrel that passes over several times this afternoon, the babies quit cheeping and the colony is eerily silent. As soon as some parents start coming back in, the bedlam resumes.

I can tell by the noise in the culvert that the birds at Whitetail are having high reproductive success this summer. Virtually every nest seems to have young, and the babies are healthy and vigorous enough to have a lot of energy for calling. The young raised at a fumigated colony like Whitetail are in much better shape than those in nonfumigated colonies. The babies here weigh more, and their feathers grow faster. Plenty of food and no bugs to suck their blood. Only in a fumigated colony have we ever seen a single pair of cliff swallows rear six or seven young. Usually broods are three or four, and the birds often have trouble raising even five babies without one's becoming a runt from lack of food. Take away parasites, and the benefits of an information center allow the birds to raise additional young.

Among swallows with normal levels of parasites, we found that the condition of the babies doesn't change much among small, medium, and large colonies. Initially we were puzzled by this because we were certain that birds in larger colonies were finding more food, and therefore their babies should be fatter and in better condition. But it dawned on us that the babies in larger colonies are also more heavily parasitized by swallow bugs. The heavier parasite infestations siphon off any gain from better foraging. The result was that everybody did about the same, regardless of what size colony they lived in. An egalitarian society.

As I stand here and watch the birds busily feeding young, I'm convinced that food-finding advantages have to be the main reason these birds are so social. I've believed this ever since I started to study cliff swallows, but it's been tough to show in a scientifically rigorous way. Mary and I devoted seventy-eight pages in *Coloniality in the Cliff Swallow* to social foraging, information centers, and food-related benefits of group life, yet I doubt we've convinced everyone. Information centers have been controversial for a quarter of a century, and some scientists refuse to accept that they occur in some birds. I wish I could bring those people to Whitetail and have them watch the foraging birds stream in and out of the culvert.

The only negative effect on reproductive success here appears to be crumbling nests. The sandy soil that the nests are built from is disintegrating. Some nests have big holes in their bottoms or sides. In some cases the babies are still there, literally hanging on for dear life. In other cases too much of the nest has broken, and the nest contents are gone. In a couple of spots along the wall, it looks like several upper nests crumbled and lower nests attached to them also fell. This is another cost of nest clustering, especially when the mud is as poor as it is here. You can save time and effort by sharing nest walls with someone else, but if the neighbor's nest breaks and falls, you're screwed.

Today we catch the first bird of the year carrying a swallow bug. The bugs disperse from one colony to another by riding on the birds' feet and legs. This bird has one bug clinging to its toe. It's lucky to be so lightly infested; some swallows have their toes covered by these insects. The bird with the bug is one we banded earlier this year. My bet is that it's an immigrant that picked up the bug at a nearby colony and was passing through Whitetail when caught in the net.

We also catch a distinctively colored cliff swallow, one with part of its forehead patch a cinnamon brown. Almost all birds in Nebraska have white or cream-colored forehead patches, and this anomalous individual stands out. Annie and Judy swear we had the same bird at Knight's Culvert yesterday. I later find that they were right. Its appearance at Whitetail, and the banded bird with the bug on its toe, mean some swallows are starting their late-season wanderings.

12

Nonbreeders

For many years I have belonged to a little circle whose
members have decided that the celibate life is best.
—P. G. Wodehouse, *Bachelors Anonymous*

July 3

On the way to Whitetail this morning, Judy, Annie, and I pass
CR 2. We pause to have a look: hundreds of birds are swarming
under the bridge. They hover in front of nests, going in briefly, then
everyone zooms away only to return en masse in a few seconds. I've
been seeing birds doing this at CR 2 for the past several days, always
in the early morning. By noon they've left and don't return until the
next morning.

These birds are showing the classical postbreeding swarming that
begins in late June every year. Swallows that have completed breeding spend a lot of time late in the summer going from colony to colony,
apparently checking out nests. We believe this is a way they assess
the different sites—for example, to learn how many ectoparasites
are at a bridge. Information they collect this summer may help them
next spring when they have to choose where to nest.

Watching the birds at CR 2, it suddenly hits me. These swarmers
can't be postbreeders—no one has finished nesting yet. The first babies started flying only two days ago, and these "postbreeding" swarmers started showing up at various sites at least a week ago. Probably
99 percent of the breeding cliff swallows in the area are still incubating eggs or feeding babies, and there won't be many local birds relieved of nesting duties for at least another week. In the past the
swarmers' appearance coincided with many of the known breeders'
fledging their young, so we assumed the swarmers *were* these breeders, which then had free time to play around. The cold spring delayed all the local birds' nesting, yet the swarmers showed up right
on schedule. They have to be a different subset of the population.

What a blessing the bad weather was after all! Had it not delayed the nesting cycle, we'd have continued to confuse the true postbreeders with this late-summer influx of swarmers.

But if these swarmers aren't birds that have just completed nesting in the local colonies, who are they? The inescapable conclusion is that they're nonbreeders, birds that haven't bred and won't breed this summer. They may hang out and goof off at colonies for another two or three weeks, but swarmers don't build nests or lay eggs, and they'll eventually leave when all the cliff swallows migrate south. The bad weather this year tells us they can't have already bred: there hasn't been enough time, and the weather in May was too bad for them to be birds that got an early start. Could they be birds that immigrated from farther south, where cliff swallows breed earlier? Possible but unlikely. The cold spring extended as far south as Oklahoma, delaying birds there too. Breeders from Oklahoma wouldn't have had time to nest and then move this far north, right on schedule.

And I realize another piece of the puzzle fits too. Each summer in late June, we get an influx of unbanded swallows at Whitetail. We net there so much that almost all of the colony residents are eventually caught and banded. This is reflected in our capture totals in mid-June, by which time we're getting few unbanded birds in the net. However, virtually overnight we start catching scores of unbanded birds. By early July, over half of all the adults we're catching at Whitetail each day are unbanded. But these birds don't hang around. We recatch almost none of them at Whitetail. They move on, and about the only time we ever recatch one the same summer is when we net at a different colony. Sometimes we put out four hundred bands a day at Whitetail.

I hadn't known what to make of all these unbanded birds. I doubted they could be of local origin, because we band birds at so many nearby colonies that there couldn't be that many unbanded Cedar Point–area cliff swallows available to come circulating through Whitetail. We've noticed something else about these unbanded birds. Almost all of them are in fresh, bright plumage, like birds that arrive in April and May. They stand out like a sore thumb next to the known breeders. The nesting birds at Whitetail look ratty by now: their feathers are worn and broken off, the bright sheen on their bluish crowns and backs has been replaced by a dull, powdery appearance, the chestnut of their throats and the orange of their rumps are faded, and some have bald spots on their heads. The breeders look as if they need a good molt to get pretty again. The fresh, sleek plumage of the unbanded birds at this time of year is more evidence that they haven't bred anywhere else this summer.

The implications of this revelation are staggering. There must be a huge pool of nonbreeding cliff swallows in any given summer. Why don't they breed? One possibility is that these are birds that can't get into breeding condition until late in the season—that can't get fat enough or gather enough energy to endure the rigors of nesting or making eggs. Perhaps these are birds that for some reason take longer to migrate north. When they finally get here, by then in sleek breeding dress, there's time only for them to visit different colonies. The summer's about over, so breeding is impossible.

It's assumed that most populations of animals contain nonbreeders, but it's often hard to detect or census these individuals. Not having nests or places where they regularly live, they represent an underworld of nomadic drifters. How many are there? Are the same individuals the nonbreeders each year? Do some alternate seasons as breeders and nonbreeders? And what are mortality rates of nonbreeders? It's often assumed that raising young is costly for parents as they invest resources in offspring that could be used to promote their own survival and future chances for reproduction. A nonbreeder doesn't have to pay those costs and should theoretically have a greater chance of surviving to breed in the future. If a bird is in lousy condition to start with, it might be better to defer reproduction this year and put its effort into ensuring that it survives to breed next summer.

But there's not much information on the survival rates of nonbreeders in most species, simply because of the problems in identifying them and following their fates. As we set up the net at Whitetail this morning, I realize we have a great chance to identify hundreds—if not thousands—of nonbreeding cliff swallows. We can use our netting results to estimate their survival.

I'm also thinking about an analysis Mary did last winter. We hadn't appreciated who these birds were, but the question arose whether we ever recaught any of these late-summer sleek birds in a later year. If we never saw them again, there wouldn't be any point in continuing to band them. Mary did a quick percentage calculation of how many "late" birds were caught in a subsequent summer and compared it with that for birds from earlier in the season. I was surprised to hear that the percentage of late birds encountered again was *higher* than for the earlier ones. This means the birds that are part of the late influx don't just vanish. We get them again later. And their higher rate of recapture is consistent with nonbreeders' having higher annual survival.

I'm energized by the realization of who these birds are and the possibilities for studying them. It seems to make wearing the chest waders and fighting the abyss more bearable this morning. Sure enough, before long we start getting unbanded adults. Many of them come hurtling through the culvert like a bat out of hell, crashing into the net at full speed. This alone tells me they're newcomers that don't know anything about this site or about nets. The residents here are wise to the net by now, and they often expertly avoid it by going around it, over it, under it, or out the other end. And these unbanded birds are sleek-looking today: bright plumage, vivid colors, no powdery bird dandruff.

I wonder how many of the *banded* birds we get are also nonbreeders. Being unbanded is not a prerequisite for being sleek. We get some birds banded in earlier years that are in fresh, bright plumage. We've had several today. These birds too just pass through and won't be caught again at Whitetail this summer. Finding so many unbanded birds among the late captures suggests that many nonbreeders are first-year birds, but the bands from earlier years on sleek swallows indicate that older birds also sometimes don't breed. What determines whether an older bird breeds? Where it lived last year? Last year's colony size? How tough it was to pull off successful nesting? It'll take years to answer these questions.

I've learned something new about cliff swallows today. Parts of the story had been known for years, but until this morning I hadn't put it all together. And it took a fortuitous event such as the bad weather to reveal that the nonbreeders aren't local postbreeders. This is precisely why I come to Nebraska every year: each summer tells us something new.

The assistants had asked me some time ago if they could have an afternoon off. They want to go up to the Sand Hills prairie site, Arapahoe Prairie, where Tony and his assistants study grasshopper community ecology. Except for mowing of certain areas and fire suppression by the adjoining ranchers who don't want their grazing range burned up by wildfires, Arapahoe is undisturbed. It's owned by the Nature Conservancy and managed by Cedar Point. The prairie is thirty miles due north of the field station, a heck of a long commute every day for Tony and his crew. They eat a lot of sack lunches. Since Arapahoe has no cliff swallows, I've been up there only once. Our assistants have become friends with Tony's helpers, and his people invited Annie, Kathy, and Judy to come up to the prairie to see their experiments and have an evening cookout.

Mary and I are going to spend the afternoon surveying more colony sizes at sites near North Platte. We have freedom this afternoon: no assistants to organize. It's a relief knowing someone else is in charge of them for the rest of the day.

Our route takes us down the canal road all the way to Paxton. Along the canal, we notice birds swarming at CR 7. This colony was small, one where Mary and the assistants did the double-net technique. Mary says there are more birds at CR 7 today than when they netted. It's hard to judge whether these new birds are nonbreeders or latecomers that plan to nest. The only way to know is to keep watching and see if they stay to build nests and lay eggs. Late nesters that move into colonies in June may be birds that are in barely good enough shape to nest, whereas the nonbreeding swarmers are ones that just can't attain breeding condition in time.

Not far from CR 7 we come to Feedlot. Perhaps our most important discovery of the afternoon is here, where we find that the colony site is active. Feedlot must have started late. At least two hundred swallows fly out from under the bridge when I pound on the metal railing with a rock. Their behavior indicates that most of them are incubating. Feedlot is a netting site for us, and we'll still have a chance to catch these birds if we move quickly. The stench here is sickening. The southerly wind blowing toward us from the pens has a sweetish odor, perhaps from the sorghum the cattle are fed. I can imagine the reactions of the assistants when I tell them Feedlot is active!

We go on to Paxton and through the town to the bridge over the river. I figure we can now estimate how large the colony really is; when I last visited, the many new arrivals made its size unclear. As we stop along the approach to the bridge, I see that the colony is huge! This is one of the longer river bridges in the study area (725 feet), and cliff swallows are nesting from end to end along the west side, nests stacked a couple of tiers deep in most places. All the nests on the west side are recently started ones, and it looks as if new birds have also filled in around the original early colony on the east side. This is the largest Paxton has ever been. With binoculars I count active nests in several sections of the bridge and then multiply by the total number of sections: 1,900 total nests is the estimate.

This colony seems enormous because it's so spread out, but it's only two hundred nests bigger than Whitetail. I think how remarkable it is that in the Whitetail culvert almost as many birds are crammed into only 6 percent of the space. The huge size of Paxton makes me think wistfully of what might have been if the river hadn't flooded this summer. If it were its normal trickle, we could spend the rest of the summer big-netting at this one place. We could've caught *a lot* of birds here. But the river is still high, water stretching from bank to bank, and easily over our heads throughout. Mary and I wonder if the high water might have made the bridge somehow more attractive to the birds this summer. It's hard to say, though. Roscoe had high water, and it seemed *less* attractive this year.

Eventually we end up near Maxwell, the eastern edge of our study area and about sixty miles from Cedar Point. With our research sites spanning about a hundred miles along the North and South Platte valleys, we have a larger geographical scale to our study than many field projects. I'm proud of our work for that reason, but more important, I know that a large study area is necessary because it's more informative. Focusing on a smaller set of colonies would lead us to conclude things that are untrue when applied to the wider cliff swallow population. That's why we're out here standing on a bridge at Maxwell sixty miles from home with an evil-looking thunderstorm bearing down on us.

We drive back to North Platte, skirting the edge of the storm. We'll miss that one, though the town of Maxwell will probably get clobbered. KXNP out of North Platte is broadcasting thunderstorm warnings for the counties just south of us and also talking about another storm between North Platte and Ogallala. We'll probably get into it going back. But first we have one more stop to make, at a city park in North Platte.

Four years ago Peter, my graduate student at the time, was studying dispersal of swallow bugs among cliff swallow nests. He was in North Platte one day and drove by the city park, which consists mostly of baseball fields. Baseball and softball—played by all ages—constitute a major form of entertainment in southwestern Nebraska during the summer, and it seems that every business in every town sponsors a team. Peter discovered an unusual cliff swallow colony in the park. Along the edge of a pond is a rectangular cinder block building completely open on the side facing the water. The roof is supported by parallel concrete beams deep enough for the birds to attach their nests. Somehow cliff swallows found this site, and over three hundred nests were started on the beams.

When Peter showed me the colony, I was puzzled about why the birds decided to use this particular structure amid the thousands of other buildings in town they could also nest on, and pleased at how easy it would be to catch them. There was only one way out—the open side of the rectangle—and a regular-size net would just about cover the flyway. The ideal design of this colony for research and the proximity of the baseball fields suggested just one name for the site: Field of Dreams.

It was indeed the Field of Dreams for netting, and we caught half the residents in one day. But it was the Field of Hell in terms of spectators. Catching birds in the sparsely populated Ogallala area is one thing; doing something as odd as netting birds in a city park in the middle of downtown North Platte (population 22,000) is something else. It was a constant battle to concentrate on processing birds while having to yak with a steady stream of interested onlookers. Of course someone called the law on us, and a friendly game warden came out to watch the show. We got no recaptures of Cedar Point–area birds, however, which would have been useful in trying to estimate swallow dispersal. Unfortunately, the easy access to this colony—the nests were barely seven feet off the ground—and the concentration of people in the park meant the birds and their nests were vulnerable to disturbance and vandalism. It was really no surprise when Peter later found that kids had knocked down most of the nests.

The same fate befell the birds when they tried to nest at Field of Dreams two years later and again last summer. Although we are able to catch birds here, I now hope the birds will stay away. It's another Skelly. We wind our way through town and finally come to the park. No birds at Field of Dreams. I get out and walk over to the structure. There's no sign that any nests were started this summer. Good. I reflect again on what a weird little building this is. We were told it's a shelter used in the winter by kids who skate on the adjacent pond; dilapidated wooden benches line the three walls.

Driving back to Ogallala, we get into a major rainstorm. For several miles the rain is so intense it's hard to see the highway, and wind gusts pummel the truck. I'm a little uneasy, especially when semis blow by as though it's not even raining. We wonder if the assistants are having storms like this up on the prairie. They're forty or fifty miles northwest of us, though, and these storms are so isolated that it's impossible to predict what their weather might be.

My impression before today was that colonies in general seemed smaller this summer, based mostly on the numbers of swallows in the ones we've been netting. That made sense, especially in light of the discovery of the nonbreeders. In a cold, late, stressful breeding season, fewer birds might be in good enough condition to nest. Consequently the nonbreeding pool would be larger, and colony sizes would be smaller on average. But I didn't get the sense that colony sizes were smaller among the sites we toured today. Look at Paxton— bigger than ever. Airport was in line with its past sizes, and one of the Maxwell colonies was larger than it's ever been. Maybe the birds are just distributed differently among the colony sites this year. Another benefit of having a large study area is that we can identify local fluctuations that are insignificant at the population level.

13

Crèchers and Kleppers

*There are plenty of neighborhoods where the kids think of
swiping things as the daring and manly thing to do. It's
not proper, but it's not vicious and it's not a sign of malad-
justment. . . . [The child is] only obeying a normal instinct
to make his place in the group.*
—Benjamin Spock, *Baby and Child Care*

July 4

Today is Independence Day both for our country and usually for a
lot of young cliff swallows. In most summers the Fourth of July
marks the peak time of crèching—the flocking together of young
swallows that have just fledged from their nests. But this year most
young birds are still being fed in their nests. Independence Day for
many of them is still a week or more away.

The morning is sunny and pleasant except for a strong north wind.
I decide to net at the Roscoe Gun Club, hardly the best place to work.
It's along a stretch of Highway 30 that has virtually no shoulder. We
park on the grass barely off the pavement, and the verge slopes down
abruptly. The single-tunnel culvert is at the base of a ravine, and the
road embankment we walk down is high and steep. We have to climb
over a barbed wire fence each time we check the net and technically
trespass in someone's pasture. There's a deep pit just beyond the
south end of the culvert, probably made when the culvert was built.
Full of tumbleweeds and dry brush, it prevents us from setting a net
on the south end. Even on the north side, the barbed wire fence in-
terferes with positioning the net, and we have to set it farther out
than I'd like.

The colony is not as large as when I stopped a few days ago. Some
birds had started nests, but in the interim they've abandoned them.
These probably were birds that weren't in good enough condition to

sustain nesting. It looks like only thirty-five or forty nests are occupied. Data from this small colony will be valuable.

As Annie and I wait in the truck up above the culvert, it doesn't take long to see that it's too windy to net. The net is flapping, and the exiting birds see it so easily that they're mostly going over it.

This sure ain't Whitetail.

As we wait, I gaze at the dense stands of yucca that cover the pasture to the north. The yuccas have continued their incredible flowering for several weeks now. Nearly every plant has a tall spike covered with chiffon-yellow flowers, turning the hillsides golden. I hadn't appreciated how abundant yuccas are; when not flowering, they blend inconspicuously into the short-grass Sand Hills prairie.

By midmorning we've caught only twelve cliff swallows. The wind's getting worse, and it's clear that we're done here. Fortunately we'll have other chances to come back this year, and I'm afraid we'll probably have to do so repeatedly. We pack up and drive just three-tenths of a mile down the road to Alkali Lake Station. I walk down to look in the culvert. I'm surprised to see at least 150 active nests, some still with wet mud but nearly all completed. This colony has no deep pit and will be a snap to net. Alkali Lake's occupancy and growth this summer coincided with the demise of Skelly, only three miles away, and I bet some of these birds are Skelly refugees. Netting here will be a priority once this wind—now in its fourth day—subsides.

I had hoped to do Whitetail this afternoon to get more juveniles, but the thirty mile an hour wind rules that out. Kathy went to Clary with Mary, and Judy had the morning off in anticipation of our doing Whitetail after lunch. There's nothing else that she, Annie, and I can do. I hate to be idle, especially now. With the end of this summer in sight, we must maximize what little field time is left. Before long the birds will be gone and opportunities to collect 1995 data will be lost forever. The finality of the season's end is beginning to hit me.

Clouds start to build after lunch, and a midafternoon thundershower dumps a brief rain on us just as Mary and Kathy return from Clary. Wind was a problem there all day, and they quit early. They still managed to catch about ninety birds, a good haul that will close the books on Clary for this summer.

Thunderstorms continue to develop for the rest of the afternoon. It seems that rain threatens the Fourth of July celebration in Ogallala every summer. The town's volunteer fire department sponsors a fireworks show that attracts hundreds of viewers, including us. Their extravaganza is rather good—commercial-grade fireworks that light up the night sky impressively. Fortunately the nearby storms subside as dusk approaches, though there's still one off to the northwest. It makes its own show, brilliant flashes of sheet lightning low on the horizon.

We invite the assistants to join us, but only Annie accepts. Judy and Kathy are going with Tony's assistants to do their own celebrating, probably on one of the Lake McConaughy beaches. I wonder if there's a story behind Annie's not going with them, but I don't butt into their business. We drive into Ogallala, passing what seems like a dozen state patrol cruisers. Lake McConaughy is a major Independence Day tourist mecca, with over sixty thousand people visiting the lake on a typical Fourth of July weekend. In past years the partying got so rowdy that the local authorities couldn't keep order. The Ogallala jail filled up, and there was nowhere to put more prisoners. It must have been like that when cattle drives came to town in the 1880s. The Fourth came to be dreaded by us "locals," except of course the merchants who sell beer, bait, and gas. Several years ago the state patrol was called in, and their presence has kept things under control.

The fireworks are set off on an elevated road next to a baseball field on the edge of town. The night air has cooled off, and in the crisp, cool evening the vast sky is studded with thousands of stars. A ribbon of stars—the Milky Way—crosses the sky above us. Oohs and aahs rise from the crowd as each barrage of fireworks goes off. Seeing them always transports me back to my boyhood, when I eagerly looked forward to the Fourth and the chance to shoot off as many firecrackers as I could afford to buy. Watching the fireworks display, I reflect that I've spent every Independence Day of my life in the only two homes I've ever had. One was where I grew up in Texas. The other is here with the cliff swallows.

July 5

Day five of wind. It's the worst today, over thirty-five miles an hour by noon. Just being outside is unpleasant. On days like this I always ask myself why the hell I'm doing a research project that requires catching birds in nets. Surely there must be other things to study about cliff swallows, things that don't require nets and light wind.

My response, of course, is that the most interesting questions about these animals can be answered only by following the same birds over multiple seasons. We have to net.

But we won't be netting anything today. This may be the windiest day of the summer. It's one of those north winds that come barreling down across the open Sand Hills with nothing to block them. My frustration grows because this makes two days in a row we've been unable to go to Whitetail to catch juveniles. I'm sure babies are fledging in large numbers now, and we need to be over there banding them. Each day missed reduces this summer's eventual capture total for known-age birds. So far that total is so pathetic I don't even want to think about it.

The assistants vanish after I announce we're grounded. They don't mind the time off now, particularly Kathy and Judy. They're scheduled to leave in just a few days, and there are lots of things they've been planning all summer that they haven't done. Kathy wanted to collect some sunflower seeds and sketch some of the flowers in the canyon by the cabins. Judy wanted to hike up onto the bluffs to take photographs. Both of them wanted to tour the hydroelectric power plant at Spillway. The novelty of netting has clearly worn off.

I usually tell our assistants to plan on leaving about July 8, because in most years the netting has declined to the point that Mary and I can handle it alone by then. Kathy and Judy made their plans accordingly. This summer, though, with the birds delayed by the bad weather, we need an assistant for longer. Three people are still essential for netting at Whitetail and will be for at least another week or ten days. Fortunately Annie's plans are flexible, and she asked me if she should stay longer. She's told me the past eight weeks have been the best time of her life, and she doesn't want the fun to end. Me neither.

After lunch, Mary goes for a six-mile walk around Keystone Lake and adjacent Lake Ogallala. When she returns she reports a large crèche of juvenile cliff swallows assembled on the far side of Keystone Lake. This is the first crèche we've seen this year. It had several hundred birds, so fledging of young has finally started in earnest. Damn this wind! That enough birds have fledged to form this crèche means we're probably missing a lot of juveniles that are flying at Whitetail at this very moment.

The crèche was assembled on a barbed wire fence that runs along the edge of a beaver marsh. The marsh and fence are below the level of the road and the artificially raised shoreline of Keystone Lake, so the birds probably are more protected from the howling gale. Crèching is yet another fascinating behavior cliff swallows engage in and one that is almost unique to them among small land birds.

As soon as a young cliff swallow is old enough to fly and leaves its nest, it seeks out other young birds to associate with. A flock of young—a crèche—forms when juveniles band together in one place. Often it seems that parents try to lead the babies directly to these nursery groups—to "park them," as Mary says. The babies assemble on relatively visible perches such as fences, wires, dead trees, the irregular sides of cliffs, or as a last resort, leafy tree branches. A single crèche sometimes has up to a thousand young swallows, all gathered in one small area. The juveniles are still dependent on their parents to provide food while they're in a crèche, and the dependency may last up to five days after they fledge. Parents don't abandon their young once the babies leave the nest. They have to keep track of their offspring's whereabouts to be able to feed them until the young birds can forage for themselves.

Crèches seem to develop in fairly random places. One year they'll be on a certain stretch of wires, and the next summer no birds will come near those same wires. Often a crèche forms a considerable distance from the nearest colony. We discovered, for example, that some juveniles travel three miles or more from the colony where they were raised to join a crèche. Each juvenile stays in a crèche until it learns to catch insects itself. Once independent, a young bird starts drifting around for the rest of the summer and isn't confined to any one place. A crèche is maintained by newly fledged birds that replace the older birds as they leave. Sometimes babies from several colonies mix together in the same crèche. The crèche Mary saw probably has birds from Whitetail, Diversion Dam, Spillway, and other colonies.

How can parent cliff swallows find their own young in these large crèches? Just coming back to the same spot in the crèche where you left your fledgling won't work. The birds in a crèche frequently flush from their perches, usually in response to a potential predator that passes nearby. The young birds swirl around for a while and then resettle on the perches, but almost never in exactly the same spots. These frequent reshufflings mean that a parent returning with food faces the problem of locating its young each time.

Parents do it by voice. By the time the babies are ten days old they've started developing a call, and they vocalize almost constantly while they're in the nest. The parents learn their own young's distinctive calls, which constitute a vocal "signature." The parents can discriminate subtle differences among birds and tell which young ones are theirs once they fledge. In a crèche, the young birds call loudly and constantly whenever an adult flies in with food. The parent travels through the horde, listens to the voices, and picks out its own juveniles to feed. This remarkable feat testifies to these birds' extraordinary sense of hearing. To the human ear all the babies sound the same, although we can *see* obvious differences when the calls are analyzed by a spectrograph or oscilloscope to produce voiceprints.

Another way parents might locate their young is by looking at their distinctive faces. Baby cliff swallows have a mottled throat and forehead, speckled with combinations of gray, brown, cinnamon, and white. The variability among juveniles is extreme: no two look exactly alike, even to the human eye. I'm not aware of any other species with such extreme plumage variability among the young. It must be related to the cliff swallow's colonial lifestyle and habit of crèching, though no one has studied the facial patterns of the young birds and learned whether parents really do use them to identify their broods.

Yet even if you can recognize your own young, it still may take time to find them, especially when a crèche is large. Wading through a thousand young birds all perched in the same twenty yards of fence begging to be fed can be a chore. The more time it takes a parent to find its own young, the less time is left for finding food. Early in our research, we estimated how efficient parents were at finding their own fledglings in crèches of different sizes. Mary watched incoming parents that were bringing food, and she counted how many juveniles a parent hovered near before feeding one. Often the adult bird paused at a fledgling, the baby called loudly and quivered its wings, but the parent went on without feeding it, moving to another. Not my kid. How 'bout you? They do this repeatedly until they find one, presumably their own, that they feed.

Mary found that the bigger the crèche, the longer it took an incoming parent to find its own offspring. More time was wasted in large crèches. Then why do cliff swallows crèche? If a parent parked its young on an isolated fence or tree branch, it could easily keep track of them and locate them whenever it wished. That's what most other kinds of swallows do: they keep their broods separate from the broods of other parents. But that would be antithetical to the very essence of the cliff swallow. You join with others, man, as soon as you can.

It's hard to come up with a convincing reason why cliff swallows form crèches of a thousand birds. The costs of crèches this large seem substantial: it's harder for parents to locate their own babies, and they're conspicuous enough to attract predators. Presumably, by congregating in a crèche the fledglings are improving their vigilance and ability to spot predators that might attack them. There are always adult birds hanging around the crèche, and if a human approaches, all it takes is one *pew* from one bird to flush everybody into the air. The resulting bedlam might be enough to confuse any poor predator. But only once in fourteen years have I seen a predator attack a crèche.

Maybe the best conclusion is that crèching is just a reflection of the uncontrollable social desires of cliff swallows, which start early. At any rate it is certainly common, and most young birds begin their life that way. We can look forward to crèches' increasing steadily over the next two weeks. Unfortunately, as juveniles move to the crèches and away from the colonies, they're also moving away from our nets and reducing the likelihood of their getting banded this summer.

For the summer to be a complete success, I figure we need to band at least a thousand juveniles. We don't have even a hundred yet.

July 6

The wind blew itself out during the night. There's only a gentle northerly breeze, perfect conditions for a big day at Whitetail. It should also be a good day for doing Feedlot: the wind is blowing toward the smelly pens and away from the bridge. Even so, I have to admit I'm glad it's Mary and Kathy going to Feedlot and not me. It's not the odor I mind—you habituate to it and after a while you barely notice it—but the birds there. They don't get much fisher traffic and are butt-heads as a result. I've only netted at Feedlot once, several years ago, and I caught three birds out of a colony of a couple hundred. Mary's had better luck there in the past, I tell myself, but I'm not too hopeful. At least we'll make an effort.

The first two juveniles we catch at Whitetail are already banded. I can tell from the band series used that they were done when we were here three days ago. Why would babies that were flying then be hanging around the culvert today? Shouldn't they be at a crèche somewhere? They should, unless they're kleptoparasites—juveniles that steal food from smaller babies still in the nest. These "kleppers," as we call them, illustrate yet another way cliff swallows exploit one another. Do unto others before they're big enough to do anything about it.

In the first summer we studied cliff swallows, we spent much of our time checking nests when the babies in each were ten days old. We weighed and banded the babies and checked them for ectoparasites. Nestlings at ten days old are still not very well developed: their feathers have just started to break out of the caselike sheaths, they're still sluggish and always seem sleepy, and some have barely opened their eyes. We were surprised by a lot that first year, and one of the bigger surprises was to find fledged juveniles in some of the nests with these ten-day-old babies. These juveniles would fly away as soon as we began to extract the babies. At first we dismissed this as isolated weirdness, but in the bigger colonies we often saw fledglings in nests with small babies. Something was going on, so we began to watch the nests.

We discovered that the juveniles would fly into a colony, go to a nest, and especially if the nest had small babies, enter it. A klepper would then sit in the entrance blocking the parents' access to their young. When the parents returned with food, invariably they fed the klepper instead of their own babies—a sort of brood parasitism. A closer look revealed that the kleppers were not simply trying to get back to their own nests and missing. We began trying to capture any klepper we found in a nest. Babies banded as ten-day-olds would later be caught as kleppers in the same colony, but often far from their own nests. The early nests in a colony produced many of the juveniles that turned into kleppers and came back to steal food in the later nests of that colony.

Why do the parents of smaller babies tolerate the kleppers? They could evict them, just as they oust trespassing adults. Probably the major reason is that the parents of the small nestlings haven't yet learned their own young's calls. It apparently takes an adult a couple of weeks to "imprint" on the calls of its brood, and if someone else gets in there before then, it's treated like one of the parent's own. Since the fledglings are bigger and stronger, they can dominate the smaller babies and take all the food. It's a neat trick by the kleppers.

Juveniles we catch in the net at Whitetail either are those that have just fledged and are on their way to a crèche or they're kleppers. Those caught repeatedly at the colony, especially as long as three days after fledging, are almost certainly kleppers. I suspect that many fledglings have the choice of going to a crèche and being fed by their own parents or hanging around the colony and stealing food from others. We don't know what causes a young bird to do one or the other. One possibility is that kleppers are juveniles that have somehow become separated from their parents. Perhaps their parents took the rest of the brood to a crèche and the stragglers don't know the way, so they survive by being kleppers. But this isn't the whole story, because some kleppers are clearly birds that are independent and old enough to find their own food. They come back and steal food from smaller babies because that's easier than hunting for it themselves. Cliff swallows never pass up an opportunity to exploit each other.

We've often wondered if kleppers get into nests with older babies, ones about to fledge. We haven't collected any data on nests with large young, but there are a couple of reasons to think that kleppers don't parasitize older young. They don't have as much size or strength advantage over larger nestlings, and it might be harder to dominate them. And parents have presumably learned their own babies' calls as fledging time nears and by then should be able to recognize the intruding klepper and evict it. Philip Stoddard has seen parents evict foreign young—probably kleppers—from nests in the Pacific Northwest. Apparently they recognized that the intruder's call was wrong.

But we've never seen adults evict young from nests in Nebraska. Given the frequency of kleppers and the enormous size of colonies like Whitetail, you'd think we'd see at least occasional evictions. One reason we haven't may be that the huge Nebraska colonies, relative to the smaller ones Philip studied, create so much noise that parents have trouble hearing the fine differences among calls. There are only so many variations in the way a call can sound, and in a big colony inevitably you may have some babies from different nests sounding much the same. Parents may sometimes make mistakes and feed babies that sound like theirs. This could happen in a crèche too, probably the larger ones. In small colonies and small crèches, it seems likely it would be easier to recognize your own young, not make mistakes, and keep kleppers away after you've learned your babies' calls.

I keep asking, Why put your baby in a big crèche?

Perhaps the parents' better ability to recognize kleppers in small colonies is why we've not seen kleptoparasitism there. Kleppers rarely come to colonies smaller than one hundred nests. But this could also be because in small colonies there aren't many nests to parasitize. At big colonies you have better odds of finding the right nest, one with small young and hardworking parents that will bring you lots of food. For precisely this reason, it may be that juveniles raised in small colonies that want to steal food travel to the larger colonies. We once found a juvenile raised at Clary that was caught three days after fledging as a klepper at Whitetail, over thirty miles away!

By noon we've caught only thirty-three juveniles, although our total captures are almost three hundred birds. We hope the afternoon will be better for getting juveniles. Back at Cedar Point, Mary reports that she and Kathy caught seventy-two birds at Feedlot. Kathy says the odor wasn't bad, but she's also glad that her departure in two days guarantees she won't have to go back. Mary thinks seventy-two is about as good as it will get at Feedlot and is skeptical that going back would yield much. Like most colonies this year, Feedlot includes some immigrants: four of their birds were banded elsewhere earlier this summer.

Mary saw another crèche near Prairie Dog. Birds are fledging all over the study area.

After lunch we resume at Whitetail, but our haul of juveniles is no greater than this morning. In a sense I'm relieved, because that means we didn't get burned too badly by the several days of wind. Many of the babies still haven't fledged.

In midafternoon we have some excitement when a large bull snake, perhaps the one we removed from the nests a week ago, swims through the middle tunnel. It repeatedly tries to scale the culvert's concrete wall from below but has no success, barely getting a foot of its body out of the water before it falls back in. The strong current keeps trying to wash it downstream. The swallows give a few alarm calls but don't seem too disturbed by it. Twenty minutes later the birds start swirling at the south end in their characteristic "snake in a nest" display. I walk through the middle tunnel and see nothing in the nests. But when I get to the end I see a bull snake—undoubtedly the same one—that has come over the top of the culvert and is clinging to an edge nest in the east tunnel. It's directly above the abyss. I don't have the chest waders with me today. How am I going to remove it? While I stand there trying to decide what to do, it suddenly drops off the nest and falls into the abyss with a splash. I guess it couldn't get a good enough purchase on the nest. The snake swims off, to try again another time.

That snake clearly knew about the nests as it swam through and tried to climb the walls. I still wonder how snakes find Whitetail. I bet they're attracted by the smell of guano emanating from the culvert. Baby cliff swallows back up to a nest's entrance and poop out the door, beginning when they're about seven or eight days old. Before then the parents pick up the fecal material and drop it out the entrance. The birds are very clean in their nests, and much of the crap here falls into the creek and is washed away. But some poop that falls out of the upper nests lands on the tops and sides of the lower nests, creating stalagmites that grow upward. On rare occasions the crap builds up so high that it blocks the entrance of the nest it came from. When that happens the babies inside can't be reached to be fed, and they die. A cruel fate, to be imprisoned and starved to death by your own dookey. There's enough accumulated on the 1,700 or so nests in the colony that the odor is strong and distinctive. I bet hunting snakes detect it with their tongues, which is how they smell.

Certain nests are now having problems with entrances partially blocked by crap. I watch as these parents, to get in to feed their young, work their way around the piles of shit that are reaching dangerously high levels. Their having to wade through it to reach their goal usually reminds me of university faculty meetings.

Tonight the five of us go to the Dairy Queen in Ogallala, ostensibly to pay off with the promised sundaes for the second eleven-year-old bird we caught a few weeks ago. But it's really a chance for us to bid a collective farewell to our summer research group. This is the last time the five of us will be together. Tomorrow Annie is going on a weekend trip to the Black Hills with her boyfriend. The diversion should be good for her, especially since she's staying here longer than planned, and we can spare her for a couple of days. By the time she returns late Sunday, Kathy and Judy will be gone. Everyone's so tired tonight, though, that it's hard to get too emotional. Nothing tires you out like heat.

And the forecast is calling for a major heat wave to start tomorrow. We don't have enough energy left to deal with hot weather. The swallows probably don't either.

July 7

The plan today is to find out which birds stayed at Aqueduct. Many of those that were building nests earlier left, and I'm not sure how many birds are still nesting in the colony. Aqueduct should also be a decent place to work in today's heat. We can sit in the shade of the cottonwoods, and the nets are partly in the shadow cast by the giant flume.

We take both trucks. Mary, Judy, and Kathy will stay the entire day, and they've brought lunch with them. I'll stay for the morning and go back to Cedar Point at noon to meet a visitor. With four of us, we should be able to get birds out of the nets and processed quickly, minimizing any heat-related stress for them.

Getting overwhelmed with birds in the heat turns out not to be an issue. There are some swarmers here when we arrive, but many of them leave by midmorning. The swarmers are nonbreeders: they're sleek and bright like those at Whitetail and mostly unbanded. These birds hover in front of active nests, getting repelled by the nest owners if they try to enter. Others sit in partly built nests that were deserted earlier. But we should be able to identify the actual residents of Aqueduct by the pattern of multiple captures: any caught last time and again today are certainly birds that nest here.

By noon we've caught exactly 150 birds. Seven are juveniles. These fledglings aren't from here, because none of the nests at Aqueduct have babies big enough to fledge yet. This is an example of how juveniles wander among colonies in late summer. The ones caught this morning didn't look old enough to be on their own yet. I bet they still need to be fed by adults and came to Aqueduct to kleptoparasitize. Kleppers won't find many opportunities here, though. Only the original nine nests have young at the moment; everybody else still seems to be incubating eggs.

I go back to have lunch at a deserted field station. The second set of classes ended yesterday, and the third set—parasitology, vertebrate zoology, and aquatic microbiology—doesn't start until Monday. It's another of those lost weekends with no meals being served. I can't recall seeing Cedar Point so deserted on an intersession weekend. Diana and I scrounge around in the kitchen and find some leftover Belgian waffles and cold blueberry sauce to top them. On weekends when everyone's gone, I think of the John Wayne movie *Big Jake*, in which a gang of outlaws rides into a ranch deserted during a cattle drive and kills most of the women and children who were left behind. Cedar Point's locked gates presumably will prevent anything like that here.

The visitor I'm expecting is Christie, a biology editor who handled *Coloniality in the Cliff Swallow*. Christie is on her way to a conference being held in Lincoln next week. She uses scientific meetings as a chance to meet prospective authors, discuss ideas for books, and publicize those just published. I invited her out to see the cliff swallows, since she was going to be "only" 285 miles away. It's always fun to show our birds to people who can appreciate them, and Christie should qualify after dealing with the 566-page book.

The heat is getting bad after lunch, and I hope Christie gets here in time for me to take her to Aqueduct to see the netting before Mary has to shut down. I sit on the veranda of the apartment, waiting and sweating. About an hour later I see a strange car drive in, either Christie or outlaws. I meet Christie halfway up the hill leading to the apartments. I'm glad to see she's not a makeup and big-hair type, which is good because in this heat makeup would run and big hair would quickly become small with sweat. Christie is outdoorsy and looks ready for fieldwork, but you can tell she's an immigrant from the outside world. Her clothes are cleaner than any I've had on in two months, and there's not a drop of bird shit on her.

Driving down the canal, I provide a running commentary on the colonies we pass, including CR 5, which still has a lot of birds swarming. Many of the birds there are building nests this afternoon. If they're working in 90° heat, at least some of the CR 5 birds are dead serious about breeding this summer. When we arrive at Aqueduct, I'm relieved to see the nets are still up. We get out, and I give Christie some black (and very hot) knee boots to wear—not those Annie peed in—to keep her new tennis shoes from getting covered with hundreds of sticktight grass seeds. We walk under the nests, and as when Ted and Josef brought their class to Aqueduct, the birds put on a good show. Even though we've been netting and disturbing them all day, most of the colony residents are still tame and sit in their nests looking down at us.

I take a banded bird out of the net to show Christie. I recognize the band series as one dating from 1988, and after memorizing the number in case it gets away, I let her hold this eight-year-old bird. For me there's nothing in the world that can compare with the thrill of holding a wild swallow, even though I've done it thousands of times. I'm not sure Christie is as turned on by it as I am.

We walk back over to the processing area. Mary says captures have declined this afternoon as it got hot and the wind increased. We have about 190 birds for the day, and Mary and I agree they should shut down after Christie and I leave. The assistants are eager to quit, because Mary promised to take them to one of the swimming beaches at Lake McConaughy this afternoon to cool off. Mary said the promise of a beach trip kept the help functional today.

No visit would be complete without viewing Whitetail, so that's our next stop. I want Christie to see the inside of the culvert. We put on hip waders, and I warn her about the abyss on the south end. Christie is clearly awed by the spectacle of row after row of mud nests stacked together in a complex labyrinth from one end of the culvert to the other. We stand in the middle tunnel, and birds start coming into the culvert, flying through only a few feet from us. They're putting on a good show here too. I notice a juvenile head poking out of a nest that also contains several smaller, not completely feathered young. A klepper. I point it out to Christie, and we watch it as it looks at us. A stare-off. It's restless and can't seem to decide whether to stay in the nest. It's probably got a good deal there with those little babies that present no obstacle to its taking the food their parents bring. Soon it flies off. It flies well, and I bet that sucker is independent. I'm not sorry we disturbed a deadbeat like that and caused it to leave.

We return to Cedar Point, and I show Christie around the station. I'm a bit embarrassed that it's so deserted, and I apologize because no meals are being served. But at least I won't have to worry about her being fed frozen pizza. Instead, she and Mary and I go into Ogallala to eat Chinese food. Kathy and Judy are having supper with Tony's assistants. It's after dark before we get back to Cedar Point, and we say our good-byes tonight, since Christie is leaving before dawn in the morning.

Kathy also leaves tomorrow.

14

The Parade of Homes

*And they learn to be idle, wandering about from house to
house; and not only idle, but tattlers also and busybodies,
speaking things which they ought not.*
—1 Timothy 5:13

July 8

Hot weather is clearly going to be the next challenge facing us
this summer.

Western Nebraska is high enough in elevation that nighttime temperatures usually cool off into at least the fifties, even in the middle of the summer. When we wake up this morning, though, it's already warm. Last night's low didn't fall below 60°, and the morning air feels heavy and stifling. Once temperatures exceed 95°, it becomes almost impossible to net in the afternoons because the birds will overheat.

Kathy has the morning off to pack. Her flight leaves from North Platte this afternoon, which gives the rest of us the morning to net. We've decided to do Whitetail on alternate days, and today's an "on" day. We head back to resume our quest for juveniles.

The usual crowd of unbanded nonbreeders appears this morning. The number out there must be enormous. One unbanded bird after another keeps passing through the colony in what seems like a constant procession from dawn to dusk. Where are they coming from? It's as if the culvert spontaneously generates them.

In midmorning I pull a banded bird out of the net. I notice its shiny new band and check the number. My first thought is that it's a bird we banded a few minutes ago, but I recognize the band number as one used yesterday at Aqueduct, six miles away. The bird is a sleek nonbreeder. It's making the rounds, probably visiting all the local colonies. These drifters go from site to site, and our guess is that they're gathering information for next year, when they presumably intend to breed. Now's a good time to see how many parasites a colony typically supports, how easily food can be found nearby, how well the nests hold together over the summer. This information may be easier to obtain now than early next spring, when parasites are dormant, insects haven't hatched, and nests haven't yet been built. Late summer is the best time to do the parade of homes.

Catching these nonbreeders today has me thinking about an idea proposed a couple of years ago by Etienne Danchin, an ecologist who studies seabirds. Etienne believes bird colonies form in patches of habitat that are particularly suitable as places to reproduce. Each colony is maintained in a certain spot because nonbreeding birds visit existing colonies and observe the nesting success of residents at each. The nonbreeders can thus determine where reproduction is likely to be highest, and they return to those sites the next year. This way a colony is perpetuated in favorable areas, and lousy parts of the habitat never have colonies. Naive individuals gain information about nesting prospects on the parade of homes.

Etienne thinks this process applies to most colonial birds, and he and I had long discussions about his idea at a conference in Vienna last August. Etienne has extensively studied kittiwake gulls that breed on remote cliffs along the French coast. In kittiwakes, a substantial fraction of the population appear to be nonbreeders in a given year, and these birds continually visit active colonies. They're pests, since they hang around the breeders for days or weeks, getting in the way as they try to get close to active nests. Those that "prospect" at a site, as Etienne calls their visiting, are more likely to come back and nest there the next summer.

Etienne asked me if cliff swallows do this. Yes, I replied, but I wasn't sure the swarmers that visit colonies gain the same kind of information his kittiwakes do. Until this summer, the swarmers— which I didn't realize were nonbreeders—always appeared *after* most of the young in the colonies had fledged. That's not the best time to get information, since once the babies fledge, you can't tell whether the empty nests were successful. I told Etienne we didn't have evidence for a lot of nonbreeders. At least on that point, I'll have to correct myself the next time he and I meet.

But this year Etienne's hypothesis could apply. The nonbreeders that are circulating among colonies right now can easily observe how well the residents are doing. I'm certain the nonbreeders visit colonies to gain information of some kind. And with the lateness of this season, visitors now have a greater opportunity than usual to glean information about site quality. But whether this is a general phenomenon among all colonial birds and whether it "explains" colonial nesting, as Etienne argues, I'm not so sure.

We glide through the morning effortlessly processing our captures. We're doing the north side, which is always shaded, and the west tunnel where we sit is cool and comfortable. The birds aren't stressed by the netting this morning, and we could easily handle more than we're getting. Mary and Judy are an all-star processing team. I'm going to miss Judy's efficiency and beautifully neat data sheets.

The four of us drive straight to North Platte, not saying much. The departure of our assistants seems so abrupt each summer. Because of the nature of fieldwork we all live and work close together in intense relationships, yet the day always comes when suddenly the assistants are gone. Poof! Many of them we never see again. Some stay in touch for a while, but most fade away. I wish I knew what happened to them, because I become very fond of each one. It's hard not to when you spend as much time with them as Mary and I do and watch most work their butts off for us. Many show incredible growth in their understanding of the scientific process during their weeks in Nebraska.

Once we arrive at the airport, there's a long delay getting Kathy checked in. Some obnoxious middle-aged fat guys keep clogging up the works by cracking stupid, sexist jokes to the young woman at the ticket counter. We all feel sorry for Kathy, getting on a small plane with these jerks. Back to the real world, I guess. During the summer we live in a wonderful little enclave of people with similar values, goals, and priorities. I resent the annual breakup of our Cedar Point community and our being thrust back into society at large. The pigs at the ticket counter illustrate why. While we wait, I escape by going to watch a barn swallow that's built its mud nest on a light fixture above the airport's entry door.

Kathy finally gets her ticket stamped and her bags checked. Well, this is it. A round of awkward hugs and good-byes: "Have a good life." Farewells are usually not maudlin, though. The assistants are looking forward to going home, and Mary and I are looking forward to not being responsible for them. The most emotional moments are between assistants. They're often close friends by the end of the season, and they, too, seldom see each other again. I thank Kathy for her help this summer, and she assures me the experience was every-thing she'd hoped for and more.

With a sense of relief, I walk out the door with Mary and Judy. The sadness I'm starting to feel is not for Kathy's departure but for what the assistants' leaving represents. The end of the summer is in sight.

The three of us drive back to Ogallala with a couple of stops on the way to get more colony sizes. One stop is at a partly wooden, partly concrete bridge over the Korty Canal near Paxton. The colony is called Phoebe, named after a Say's phoebe that was living there the season we discovered it. Say's phoebes are flycatchers that, like cliff swallows, build mud nests under rock ledges on the sides of cliffs. Also like cliff swallows, they've adapted well to human structures and commonly nest on awnings over porches or under the eaves of buildings. Cliff swallow colonies seem to hold a morbid fascination for them. The phoebes often take over a swallow nest, usually a broken one that doesn't have a ceiling or narrow entry hole. They typically start breeding before the cliff swallows arrive at a site, which can be their downfall.

Several years ago a pair of Say's phoebes lived at Whitetail. Each year two birds (probably the same ones) used one of the deserted nests in the west tunnel. They had success each summer, largely because no cliff swallows cared to nest in that tunnel. One year the phoebes returned well before the swallows and took over a partial nest in the popular middle tunnel. Big mistake. Their eggs had hatched and their babies were four or five days old when hordes of cliff swallows suddenly arrived at Whitetail that spring.

A cliff swallow decided it wanted the phoebe's nest. The poor clueless phoebes seemed bewildered by the hundreds of swallows that had suddenly descended on their quiet, peaceful culvert. The parent phoebes just sat on the barbed wire fence, giving a plaintive whistlelike call, and seemed too scared to go to their nest in the cul-vert with the many cliff swallows there. The crazed swallow began to murder the baby phoebes one by one. It would perch on a baby's back, grab its head with its beak, and begin shaking it with the same side-to-side motion a cliff swallow uses to apply mud to a nest. Eventually it worked the baby phoebes, their heads pecked and bloody almost beyond recognition, up to the nest's edge and shoved them out. Once it had rid the nest of the phoebes, the swallow just sat there, looking cute and innocent and proud of itself. Soon it built up the sides of the nest and domed over the roof, and you would never have known any phoebes had lived there. At the time we were shocked by the vicious-ness of our study species, but since then we've realized that the mur-der of the phoebe family is typical inner-city violence in the bigger colonies, where rape, plunder, and exploitation of others are ram-pant.

The site named Phoebe has no phoebes this year, and most of the cliff swallows that were present before have also left. My estimate is that the colony contains only three active nests. There must have been a bunch of nonbreeders here earlier, and most of them couldn't get it in gear for nesting. A crèche of at least a hundred young birds is assembled in two trees in a farmyard just north of Phoebe. None of the colonies along the Korty Canal are far enough along to have pro-duced juveniles by now. The closest place they could have come from is Paxton, about four miles to the northeast. These are probably off-spring of the early birds at Paxton, the ones we big-netted in May before the river rose.

Cedar Point is still deserted when we return. It will decline by one more when Judy leaves early tomorrow. I feel sorry for Judy spend-ing her last night here alone, all her friends—Kathy, Annie, Tony's assistants—gone. Usually good-bye parties are held the night before for people who are departing. Mary and I revel in the solitude and quiet, though. Tomorrow another onslaught of students and faculty will arrive, the most this summer. The station will be crowded be-yond capacity for the rest of the season.

And hot.

July 9

We're up at dawn to get Judy to Ogallala for her 6:30 bus. On the drive to town, I tell Judy why I worked with her the least of the assistants this summer. She's pleased to know that I considered her so trustworthy, and this prompts her to ask me for a letter of recommendation. A constant in my life is writing reference letters for former assistants. I don't mind doing it, in part because I can provide an informed and detailed letter for most of them. I know all too well how helpful (and rare) such letters are when I'm sitting on the other side trying to evaluate potential graduate students or prospective assistants.

To our surprise the Greyhound is right on time. Judy is the only person getting on or off in Ogallala. The driver tells her she should board but that then the bus is going across the street to McDonald's for a half-hour breakfast stop. Well, no one ever said interstate bus travel was efficient. Good-byes and good lucks are said, and Mary and I watch the bus pull away, Judy waving through the window. I'll miss her, but strangely it always feels good to say farewell to our better assistants. I suppose it's knowing that they enjoyed the experience and benefited so much from it. The euphoria of graduation. I got far more satisfaction from teaching Judy in the field this summer than I've ever felt lecturing in a sterile classroom back on campus.

For the rest of the day it's just Mary and me. Annie won't be back until tonight. By the time we head to CR 5 directly from town, it's hot again. We're expecting 100° by afternoon.

This is my first visit to CR 5 to net this year. The colony is indeed huge, although Mary thinks some of the birds from last week have left. No one is getting mud today. It looks as if many of the residents are incubating, but some of the birds are clearly nonresident swarmers. This place must be a popular stop on the parade of homes.

I'm quickly impressed by the array of banded birds we get. Many are from past years, but virtually all band series used earlier this summer at other sites are also represented. We're catching birds that span the season, some banded early, others just recently. This illustrates the complexity of a colony's composition, especially a late-starting one where it's hard to separate true breeders from nonbreeders and later from postbreeders that do their own parade of homes.

By midafternoon students and faculty have begun to arrive for the final set of classes. Most have a fresh enthusiasm and are looking forward to the next five weeks with a mixture of excitement and fear of the unknown. We felt that way in May, but by now we're just exhausted, smelly veterans. At supper the dining hall is full again, everyone assembled for John's orientation speech. Our usual seats at one of the back tables have been occupied by some newcomers. Eventually people will recognize the back table as the "swallow table," though we don't have enough swallow people left to fill it anymore. Tonight we sit with some students who've just arrived and make small talk, something I despise even when I'm not worn out.

July 10

We don't know whether to expect Annie at breakfast. Although she's due back, she hadn't appeared as of 9:00 last night. But when we walk in this morning she's in the kitchen talking to Dennis. The trip seems to have refreshed her, and she's excited, talking even more than usual. Her romance seems to have intensified over the weekend, and now she's planning to visit her boyfriend in Lincoln when she finishes here. While they were camping in South Dakota the night before last, a wicked storm blew up. It got so bad that they took refuge in the dark under the end of a bridge over a little stream called Sage Creek. They spent the night there, only to be greeted at dawn by *pew* calls from a colony of pissed-off cliff swallows nesting on the bridge. The birds didn't appreciate having a couple of greenhorns cowering under their bridge.

I'm glad to see Annie back, because that means we can do White-tail. I'm doubly glad we have a third person when we arrive at the culvert. Vast numbers of cliff swallows are there. Hundreds of birds are assembled on the wires overhead, and perhaps as many as a thousand more are swarming in the culvert. And this doesn't count the two to three thousand regular colony residents still feeding young. The spectacle of several thousand swallows all clustered at this one little road culvert is incredible. The wires look black with birds. Rolling down the window, I listen to the equally impressive chatter of *chur* calls by the adults and the begging calls of the juveniles still in the culvert and flying overhead.

These enormous flocks are typical at Whitetail, especially early in the mornings as the season winds down. Many of the nonbreeders congregate at this time of the day; later in the morning and afternoon they'll pass through the culvert in more staggered fashion. With some babies now fledged and independent, I bet some of the birds in this vast horde are true postbreeders, some of them from other colonies. Others might be liberated adults that spend time sitting in their old nests and defending them from swarmers. They act like they're going to breed again, but cliff swallows seldom raise a second family. After a week or so the nest owners gradually tire of playing house and start spending more time foraging in anticipation of migration.

I know that many of the birds swarming here will leave once we get out and set the net. Nonbreeders and postbreeders become less and less interested in hanging around a colony with a net as the summer wears on. Eventually they'll stay away entirely from a place like Whitetail once a net goes up, and when that happens the summer's over for us. It's the mirror image of early in the season, when the birds become more interested in the colonies and more tolerant of our net with each passing day. They'll tell us in their own way when it's time to quit, but I'm sure that won't be happening for a while yet.

I wade into the abyss while we set the net. At least the hole seems to have stabilized and isn't getting deeper. Thousands of birds swirl overhead, alarm-calling at us. Gradually the massive flock rises higher and higher, and the *pew* calls subside. Suddenly the colony is deserted; even the babies calling in the nests sense danger and are quiet. You don't get these mass departures during the main part of the breeding season. The swallows will be back soon, but I can tell their behavior is changing, inexorably reverting to what it was in early May. With each passing day, these sudden disappearances will increase in frequency and duration, until finally everyone's gone for good. But today the birds are back quickly, within a minute or two. There are still too many active nests here for parents to be gone long.

Annie's role is now that of recorder, something she hasn't done much of this summer, especially at Whitetail. She's not as comfortable recording data as handling birds, but determining the birds' sex is more difficult now as their gonads recede, and I want Mary doing the sexing. Annie concentrates, though, and this morning there are no problems with the data sheets or bands.

The parade of homes is the peak time for the swallows to carry bugs around on their feet, and the third bird caught today has six swallow bugs wrapped around its toes. The bugs are large and look as though they'd interfere with a bird's ability to perch. You'd think the swallows would pick them off. Perhaps they do, and if so, dispersal for bugs could be risky. There must be strong benefits to getting out of certain colonies for the bugs to undertake this kind of dispersal.

Three summers ago we got some insight into the activity patterns of the birds that move bugs around. That summer we were following radio-tagged cliff swallows to see how many colonies they visited and how far they ranged. Radio tracking requires attaching a tiny electronic transmitter to a bird's back. We glue the transmitters to their skin with nontoxic colostomy cement, and they usually fall off after about ten days. Just like a miniature radio station, the battery-powered transmitter gives out a constant signal on a particular frequency, which is different for each bird. Using a receiver and directional antenna mounted on top of the truck, we can follow the bird's movement by monitoring its radio signals. We can determine what colony it's at, whether it's foraging, which way it's moving, and where it sleeps for the night.

Radio tracking revealed a lot about these birds. We found that one nonresident male went to Whitetail and hung out where females were gathering grass, repeatedly attempting extrapair copulation with them. He later settled at Whitetail and bred there. We discovered that females spend more time visiting colonies early in the season than males do, and they don't choose a nesting site as quickly. Females are more likely to sleep in trees early in the season, and some birds roost in particular trees each evening. I was surprised at how easy cliff swallows are to radio-track. Although the transmitters are small, the birds are often high above the ground, and the height makes the signals easy to receive—sometimes from five miles away. The flat terrain of Nebraska also offers an advantage, since there are few hills or other obstacles to deflect the signals and confuse the readings.

We had hoped that following the participants in that year's parade of homes would give us some insight into why the birds spent so much time visiting colonies late in the summer. We selected three birds at Aqueduct one morning in July and radio-tagged them: Raquel, a female, had been banded earlier that summer at CR 3 and was presumably a postbreeder visiting Aqueduct; Rolf, a male, was also a postbreeder originally banded that summer at Whitetail; and Rudy, a male, was an unbanded, sleek bird (a nonbreeder, we now realize) caught at Aqueduct with six bugs on his feet. We released our $150 birds (the price of each transmitter), and I spent the next week constantly driving up and down the canal road, monitoring their movements.

We knew that late in the season we ran the risk of tagging a bird only to have it suddenly migrate. That happened with Raquel. She disappeared the next day, not to be seen again that summer. But Rudy and Rolf hung around for a week and revealed a lot about the parade of homes. Rudy seemed to prefer CR 8, a canal bridge just east of Aqueduct. He was frequently in its vicinity, feeding over adjacent pastures or sitting in loafing flocks along the barbed wire fences. Yet he moved all along the canal, traveling over at least a ten-mile stretch, and briefly visited most of the colony sites in that area. He went into a nest at Prairie Dog, an inactive site that year that was heavily infested with bugs from the previous summer. Going into nests like that is undoubtedly how he picked up six bugs. Rolf showed the same pattern, seeming to prefer CR 1 as his home base, though he had nested at Whitetail. Rolf moved over an even larger area looking at colonies, and one day I tracked him to one of the cliff colonies on the shore of Lake McConaughy. Both males slept in trees at that time of year, which is smart considering how heavily infested with ectoparasites most of the nests are by now.

So it may be that the birds that circulate among colonies late in the summer are making provisional choices of their next year's nesting colony. The site they seem to hang around the most during the parade of homes may be the one chosen. If so, we'd have predicted that Rudy would have nested the next year at CR 8 and Rolf at CR 1. We netted CR 1 extensively the next year, but no Rolf. He didn't show up anywhere else either. Maybe he was there and we just missed him; maybe he died; or maybe he went somewhere else. We couldn't tell if Rudy came back to CR 8 the next summer. The layout of CR 8 is such that it's one of the few colonies we can't net. It figures that the little butt-head would have to select CR 8, of all sites, as his favorite! We didn't catch him anywhere else.

By noon we've caught 312 birds. No way could Mary and I have handled that many birds alone, and I'm grateful Annie arranged to stay longer. The number of juveniles caught today was up to 50; more are fledging each day. That gives me a good feeling, despite the oppressive heat. It's so hot that I don't want to chance it this afternoon, even here.

July 11

Alkali Lake Station and the Roscoe Gun Club are the targets today. To beat the heat, we're up at dawn. Those sites require sitting in the truck on the side of the highway, something I'm not eager to do when it's 100°.

Although the colonies we're bound for are only three-tenths of a mile apart, we take both trucks. We have nowhere else to sit at either site. I'm going to do the smaller Gun Club alone, while Mary and Annie net at Alkali Lake. We set up first at Alkali Lake. While

Mary waits for birds, I take Annie down to the Gun Club to help me set a net there, drive her back to rejoin Mary, then return to the Gun Club. After all these machinations and U-turns, it's 7:30 before the birds have calmed down enough to catch any. The heat has quickly gotten bad, and it's already terrible inside the trucks.

The morning drags on interminably. The colony at the Gun Club is small enough that I don't expect to catch many birds, although I'm doing better than the last time we were here, in a gale. The blooming yuccas in the adjacent fields that were so brilliant last week have started to wither. This is a boring site with nothing except yuccas to look at or think about. The shoulder of the highway is such that I have to park facing away from the colony, and I can't even watch the swallows coming to and from the culvert.

With no other stimulation, my mind easily gets obsessed with how hot it is inside the truck. Climbing up and down the steep highway embankment makes me even hotter with each net check. The morning's only diversion is a visit by the local landowner. He drives up, parks his pickup by a gate in the barbed wire fence fifty yards east of the culvert, and unloads a four-wheel ATV. He opens the gate, loads some fence posts and wire on his ATV, and roars off, disappearing behind a ridge to the north. Digging postholes and stringing barbed wire would be even less pleasant in this heat than sitting in a truck netting cliff swallows, I convince myself. I hope he doesn't reappear when I'm down checking the net, because it's set a foot or two on his side of the property line. He'll never notice it unless I'm down there, and I'm too hot to want to deal with him.

The net here is in the sun, and the birds begin panting as soon as they get in it. Birds don't have sweat glands to cool them off, so they thermoregulate by opening their mouths. As the heat worsens, I have to start checking the net more often. More frequent net checks mean more disturbance to the colony and fewer birds caught.

As quitting time nears, I've got twenty-nine birds. Most were unbanded, but I caught one banded earlier this year at Skelly. So the refugees did come here, as I suspected. The Skelly bird had a bug on its foot—more evidence that the immigrant birds are the ones that move bugs around. I check the nests in the culvert and find thirty with eggs. None of the other nests are active. Some were never completed, and ten or so others apparently had eggs but lost them. I see them splattered on the concrete floor. The culprits are probably a pair of house sparrows that now live in one of the nests.

I drive down to Alkali Lake, and Mary and Annie are shutting down. Annie's surly because of the heat, and no one's in a very good mood. They caught fifty-nine birds, our second haul of that exact number here. They got three birds banded earlier at Skelly. I go through and check nests, finding 103 with eggs. As at the Gun Club, many nests were never completed. A large number of birds invested considerable time and energy in building nests from bare wall to half or more finished, only to abandon them. Young ones, perhaps? Maybe they assessed the lateness of the summer and concluded that to stay here into August to breed would too seriously reduce their prospects of surviving the coming migration and winter.

The afternoon high in Ogallala reaches 105°, and in eastern Nebraska—where it's far more humid—it's up to 108°. Cattle are dying in feedlots because of the heat, several hundred in one near Omaha. I spend the afternoon doing paperwork, Mary reads a book, and Annie does the six-mile loop walk around Keystone Lake. Why she chose this afternoon for such a hike is known only to her, and she took no water with her. But at supper she seems to have recovered and shows no ill effects. I think Annie is having a little trouble adjusting to Cedar Point's new social environment. Kathy and Judy are gone, she has new roommates in her cabin, and all her other friends, including her boyfriend, have left. Diana's assistant, Nanci, is the only long-termer left for her to pal around with. Annie says she and Nanci are too much the veterans of the field station to have anything in common with the new students, who reportedly are mainly interested in taking showers to keep clean in the heat.

July 12

Two days ago I had the feeling that Whitetail might finally be close to a massive fledging of juveniles. We'll find out this morning, which is supposed to feature a moderately strong south wind. Our biggest hauls have always been with south winds.

Despite the wind forecast, when we arrive the birds are acting as though the wind's out of the north. "Weather to plan your day by" is the radio station's slogan. Fat chance of that. We set up on the culvert's north end, the easier side to do. We barely have the net up, though, before the National Weather Service says I told you so. The wind suddenly shifts to the south. Move the net. Go change into the chest waders. Tote the chairs to the other end. Watch out for the poison ivy.

It's a frequent routine here. Lately we seem to be having trouble picking the correct side of the culvert for netting, which frustrates me as we flail around moving and waste time.

Sure enough, the south end is the place to be today. We start catching more birds than we've had in a long time. The activity in the net reminds me of our seven-hundred-bird day early in the year. The increasing wind is directing all the avian traffic out the south end, but part of it today is that there are just a hell of a lot of birds going in and out of the culvert. I was right: babies are fledging like crazy, and unbanded nonbreeders continue to fly through the colony and hit the net by the score. Cliff swallows are the insects of the bird world, with what seems like an unlimited population.

Negotiating the abyss in the bulky chest waders continues to be a major pain, but this morning I don't mind because we're catching so many birds. Throughout the morning we're getting much higher numbers of unbanded birds—juveniles and nonbreeding adults—than on past days. Each time an unbanded juvenile hits the net, that's another known-age bird in our growing data set. Many of these juveniles will return next year, if not here then to other local colonies, and when they do they'll provide valuable information. They'll tell us, for instance, what colonies are typically used by yearlings. They'll reveal whether younger birds arrive later in the summer than older birds and whether yearlings are the nonbreeders. Banding juveniles last year told us that the new colonies at Knight's Culvert and Dunwoody are composed mostly of yearling swallows.

There are long-term advantages of getting bands on juveniles, too. We can determine how their use of colony sites may change as they get older. Do old birds really prefer small colonies, as we think, and do yearlings concentrate in big colonies? Someday one of the juveniles we band this morning might exceed the eleven-year longevity record for this species. (Will Mary and I still be here catching birds in eleven years? Scary thought, because we probably will.) As birds hit the net, I rush to grab each juvenile before it gets out or at least pull the mesh onto it to entangle it better. Banded adults, birds we already know something about, are my next priority. Unbanded adults get my attention last. Net triage.

Now's *the* time to get juveniles at Whitetail. The peak of fledging has finally arrived, at least ten days later than in a "normal" summer. By noon we have an incredible haul of 344 birds, caught during a little over three hours of actual netting time, and 122 of them were juveniles. I hate to think how overwhelmed Mary and I would have been today without Annie.

We head back to Cedar Point for lunch, well satisfied with our morning, though I wish we could return this afternoon. We need to get more of these juveniles, but the heat is already terrible, and the temperature is supposed to reach 105° again. Going around in chest waders would be insane, and the birds would fry in the net on the sunny south side no matter how quickly I got them out.

After lunch I'm surprised to see Annie out with Nanci in one of Diana's experimental sunflower plots. They're bending over plants, apparently counting things, and recording data directly on a portable laptop computer. Damn, it must be hot doing that. Why are they out there now? The smart move would be to wait until earlier or later in the day when the sun isn't so intense. Annie doesn't even have a hat on.

They stay bent over the sunflowers all afternoon, four hours of sitting out in 105° heat. At one point I'm tempted to go out to warn Annie not to get sunstroke, but I don't want to be a nag. At suppertime she comes in sweaty and exhausted. She had agreed to help Nanci measure leaves on the experimental plants, punching in the data as Nanci called them out. Despite the heat, Annie seems okay physically. But she rants for a while about how boring it is to measure leaves on plants. It requires no skill, college education, or intelligence, she announces. Is catching swallows any different? I ask. She replies that netting is far more stimulating and takes more skill. Perhaps, but some of what we've done over the years is no more thrilling than measuring leaves. Annie has grasped a fundamental reality of fieldwork: most of it is boring, repetitive grunt work. Many aspects of field biology require only that someone be there to count stuff or record numbers. No excitement, no technical ability required. People like me should thank their lucky stars that people like Annie and Nanci are willing to come out here and do ridiculous things like measuring leaves on plants in 105° heat.

I've been wanting to try Feedlot one more time. Getting over seventy birds there on the last visit suggests a return trip could be productive. I ask Mary to take Annie and try it after supper. Mary doesn't want to go to Feedlot. She doesn't think they'll catch much, and it's a long drive—nearly to Paxton—for the limited time after supper. But I argue that we need the mornings for Whitetail, and I don't want to waste more than an evening on Feedlot. What are *you* going to do? Mary asks. My plan is to check some barns north of Ogallala that cliff swallows have used in past years. I've been putting this off, and it's getting so late in the year that I must get these colony sizes soon. I cajole some more, and finally Mary agrees to go to Feedlot, under protest.

There are scores of farmhouses and barns throughout this part of southwestern Nebraska. Cliff swallows are usually not inclined to use buildings, and most barns don't have any nests. Yet for some reason cliffers have a fondness for a small cluster of farmyards about a mile and a half north of Ogallala. These adjacent farms, separated by cropland, are all within a quarter of a square mile, close together as the swallow flies. The area is accessible only by dirt roads. Given the flat prairie terrain there, it's not a part of Keith County that we frequent. No bridges, culverts, or cliffs.

We first became aware of these sites six years ago when some students from Cedar Point doing bird censuses in the area discovered cliff swallows using a barn in a farmyard full of pigs. We went to have a look, and found over five hundred active nests under the eaves of a weathered old barn. That site has been used off and on in the years since, although it has never again been that big.

I don't look forward to checking these colonies because it requires dealing with the property owners. Two of these farmyards aren't visible from the road. For those I have to drive up the private driveway and park at the farmhouse, then bang on the door and ask to count their swallow nests. The property owners usually look at me like I'm crazy but have always allowed me access.

The first farm I come to this evening is the one that had the five hundred nests. When I pull into the driveway between the house and the barn, there's nothing. The place is deserted by both birds and people. I think humans still live here, but no one seems to be home. Not far to the west I come to the next site. This barn, a tall white one with a steep roof, is perfect for swallows. An overhang extends out beyond the gable of each end, providing a nice horizontal shelter for the nests. I can easily see this structure from the road, and it's clear that no birds are living there. Doesn't look to be a good year for swallows on barns.

Just down the road is the third site, another one visible from the road. This is an old, dilapidated barn used for horses. One side of it is permanently open, giving the birds access to the interior, where nests are built along the rafters in parallel rows as they would be under a canal bridge. Two years ago I explored this site; no one lived here then and the property was up for sale. A neighbor told me the owners had gone bankrupt, and we named it accordingly: Bankrupt Barn. I can see that cliff swallows are using the barn today. I'm not sure I want to get out of the truck, though. A ferocious dog—it looks like a Doberman—has come running up the driveway toward me. It stands only a few feet away, snarling and barking loudly. I can't tell for sure how many nests are here unless I get out and go into the barn. With the Doberman not enthusiastic about my being here, I decide I'll just score this site as used, size unknown. Interference from vicious dogs is an example of why I don't like to do research on private land.

The final stop is at a farm north of Bankrupt Barn. As I follow the driveway through a pasture to reach the farmyard, I can see cliff swallows all around. The site must be active. I park next to the house, where half a dozen chickens are strolling around loose. I better take care not to run over one, or I'd probably not be welcome to study swallows here. I go up to the back door, where I'm met by the gray-haired woman who lives here. You're fairly conspicuous when you come driving into these isolated farmyards, and you seldom need to ring the doorbell. She barely cracks the screen door while I give her my spiel about who I am and what I want. She relaxes a little when she realizes it's just the swallow guy. She says they have swallows again this summer, and I'm welcome to look around. She also says they were thinking about knocking the birds' nests down because they're so messy. Strange comment coming from someone whose back-yard is full of chicken shit and molted poultry feathers. But a neigh-bor told them the swallows eat mosquitoes, so they've left them up.

This is a common attitude about wild animals among many rural folks. What good are they? It's frustrating to those of us who appre-ciate organisms for other reasons, ones we think are nobler. But you're never going to convince these people that they should encourage cliff swallows to live on their barns because the birds' social behavior is so fascinating. They need to see a payoff from having them, the same kind of return they get from having those soon-to-be-fried chickens running around. I assure them that cliff swallows eat mosquitoes and many other nuisance insects. Corn-boring moths and grasshop-pers are a scourge of Nebraska farmers, and I always win points for the birds by telling locals, correctly, that cliff swallows eat a lot of them. Cliff swallows do take mosquitoes occasionally, but they seldom eat large numbers.

I count fifty-five nests on the main barn and inside an adjacent shed. As at Bankrupt Barn, the nests are built on parallel rafters, and a rather narrow open door to the shed lets the birds get in. We could net these birds. Netting could tell us who some of these farmyard nesters are. I wish, though, that the colony were larger. Even if we caught most of the residents, we wouldn't get many birds. Odds are that few would be banded, and we'd need several banded ones to be able to infer much.

Mary and Annie return at dusk. I don't see Annie, since she quickly vanishes toward the cabins and a shower. Mary comes storming into the apartment, mad as hell. She had a real bad time of it at Feedlot. They caught only twenty-three birds, but Mary's mostly upset with herself that she agreed to go in the first place. Why was it so bad? I shouldn't have asked.

First of all, Annie yakked the entire time. She refused to hush up even when they were trying a drop, and her chatter invariably flushed everybody out before they could get the net over. Whenever her talking didn't flush them, the birds were warned by the scraping sounds her shoes made as she stepped on big kernels of dried corn that had spilled onto the bridge surface from feed trucks headed for the feedlot. That's largely why they got such a paltry haul. Mary says she couldn't get her to shut up and to quit stomping on the corn. Well, that's my fault. I've known all summer that I'm best able to control Annie. I should have gone to Feedlot.

The next problem was insects: huge, biting, bloodthirsty, homicidal flies that were swarming around their faces and legs. Mary's exposed skin is now covered with dozens of huge red welts. Annie left one of her Twizzlers on the seat of the truck, and as it heated up and became even more vile, it attracted hundreds of flies, seething with them as if it were alive. At one point Mary needed to pee, and the only spot was a dense stand of sunflowers six feet tall. While Mary waded through them and battled to get her sweaty pants down and to keep the swarming flies from biting her naked butt, Annie kept yakking away, yelling that a girl sure has penis envy at a time like this!

But the worst was the smell and the dust. The wind had abated only slightly by the time they got to Feedlot, and it was still blowing directly toward them from the pens. Drop netting was hard to start with, since the net was hanging up on the bridge. The odor from the feedlot was even more sickening than usual, probably because the wind was so strong. Periodically a wind gust raised clouds of dust from the pens and carried them straight toward Mary and Annie. And this was no ordinary dust. The dirt of feedlots is almost 100 percent manure. Great aerosol clouds of cow shit kept coating them from head to toe. Mary's sweat was mixing with the dust on her skin to create poopy mud that streaked her face and pooled up along the waistband of her shorts and underwear and inside her bra. At intervals a large dump truck passed by, loaded to the brim with huge piles of reeking manure. The crap was being hauled from the pens to be dumped for fertilizer in some fields to the north. The manure-mobile went by several times, contributing to the clouds of shit-laden dust as the heaped-up manure blew out the open top in the strong wind.

Another farm truck drove past, one with tall sides. Sticking out of the top at grotesque angles were legs and hooves of dead cows, piled on top of one another. The sign on the door read Tri-County Byproducts. Mary hated to think what was going to be done with those dead cows. No hot dogs for me for a while, thank you. The heat must have killed cows at this feedlot too.

It sounded like hell there.

To Mary's credit, she stuck it out and kept trying to catch birds until sunset. But once they quit, she didn't think they were going to get home. The cab of the truck was filled with the Twizzler-seeking flies, which they had to swat at all the way back, and the vinyl seat was so hot that she and Annie had to sit on knapsacks. The windshield was covered with dusty cow crap so Mary could barely see the road. Twice they almost drove into the canal. I better put in some more washer fluid.

After Mary gets the powdery and muddy poop washed off her, she finally calms down a bit. Eventually I work up the nerve to ask if there's any point in going back to Feedlot on a less windy evening. . . .

I guess not.

July 13

I didn't think it would be possible to have a better morning at Whitetail than yesterday, but I'm wrong. We catch 375 birds on the south end by noon. Over 150 are juveniles. I'm starting to feel that we're going to accomplish all our objectives for the summer.

One of those goals was to exceed a cumulative total of 80,000 birds banded. We celebrate that this morning: number 80,000 (as near as we can calculate) is the first bird banded, a squealing juvenile that seems not to appreciate his celebrity. I think back to the first summer when we banded only 945 birds, just as a way to keep track of which babies in a nest we had weighed and which ones we hadn't. The prevailing wisdom was that among small birds like cliff swallows, the young seldom returned to their birthplace. We didn't imagine then that we could gain any sort of information about the subsequent activities of babies or juveniles through banding. None would return in later years, we assumed. Yet as we kept banding babies and expanded our efforts to include adults, gradually we began getting more and more recaptures of earlier birds. By 1987 we were getting so many that we realized a major emphasis on netting and banding could yield substantial numbers of recaptures. Keep doing anything long enough, and you'll do it 80,000 times.

Our 80,000th bird this morning is a milestone, because only a handful of studies have marked that many individuals of a single species. Mary and Annie share my excitement, and I begin calculating how many more birds we need to band this summer in order to have a legitimate shot at 100,000 by the end of summer after next. If we can assume 9,000 newly banded swallows a year, we'll need 2,000 more this season to position ourselves for a run at 100,000 in two years' time. At the rate babies are fledging at Whitetail, 2,000 more this year should be possible. Although we can be proud of having banded some ungodly number of birds, I know it's not the numbers themselves that are so important. It's the amount of information we gain on recaptured birds by banding all those swallows that's the primary value of this work.

Analyzing the data on the thousands of recaptured and first-time birds we get each summer is a different kind of challenge. Some of the statistical methods for that still haven't been developed. But standing here in the creek this morning I'm comforted to know I don't have to worry about that right now. Data analysis is something to think about back on campus this winter during the cold darkness of the off-season.

All three of us are exhausted by noon. In this heat, constantly extracting birds from the net and processing them is thoroughly fatiguing. I'm thrilled with our haul and happy not to be going back out this afternoon. I feel dehydrated from wearing the sweaty chest waders all morning. Today, however, is supposed to be the last day of the hot weather for a while, and the forecast for tomorrow of a high only in the eighties rejuvenates Mary and me, at least mentally. Maybe wearing the chest waders won't be such a steamy ordeal after today. Annie's less turned on by the forecast, though, because her departure is scheduled in only two days. Sadness about leaving is starting to set in with her. I'm also wondering if Mary and I can handle it without her. We certainly couldn't have at Whitetail today.

After supper Mary and I walk down to the diversion dam. We see hundreds, if not thousands, of juvenile cliff swallows flying above the bluffs east of Cedar Point and along the river below the dam. It looks like most of the colonies are fledging their young almost simultaneously. Within a week, many of the colony sites will probably be deserted and the parade of homes confined to Whitetail and the late colonies.

Many of the juveniles this evening are being fed by their parents in flight. Toward the end of a young swallow's dependency period, as it becomes a more accomplished flier, its parents will transfer food to it in the air. We watch as a juvenile flies to meet an adult, the two birds coming together beak to beak in a near collision. The insect passes from parent to offspring. Other times the insect is dropped during the exchange. The baby tries to catch it, usually successfully. If it misses, the parent dives down to grab it before it hits the ground. It looks as if the parents drop the food intentionally. Perhaps it's easier for the juveniles to start out by catching dead or stunned insects in free fall. From that they learn to pursue live insects.

Other birds are leading their young back to sleep in the nests at Diversion Dam, IS 2, and CR 1 this evening. A parent identifies its own fledgling amid the hundreds flying nearby and, using a special call, tells it to follow. The babies follow close behind, making every twist and turn their parents make. When the parent reaches the nest and pops in, the baby is right behind it. The juveniles almost always make it to the right nest. These aren't kleppers. That the parents are leading these fledglings back to the colony to sleep means the nests at these sites must not be too heavily infested with ectoparasites, since a swallow family will avoid their nest if it's overrun with bugs. This bodes well for these sites' being used again next year.

It's a measure of how soon the sun will be setting on this summer if I've started thinking about which sites the birds will use next year.

July 14

Blessed relief from the heat today. A cold front dropped overnight temperatures to about 60°. We'll be able to work this afternoon for the first time in a week. This gives us the opportunity to try for another big day at Whitetail. Given yesterday's half-day haul, I figure we can exceed seven hundred birds by going all day.

A north wind this morning allows us to do the easier north end, but numbers are down from yesterday. I notice a marked reduction in bird traffic in the culvert, not surprising given the many birds fledging lately. Many nests are empty by now. We don't get as many juveniles today, but the nearly continuous capture of unbanded nonbreeders goes on.

We have 327 birds by lunch, but we catch only 133 more during the afternoon. Even fewer are around by midafternoon. The procession of unbanded birds virtually stops, and eventually we're getting only banded residents, many for the fifth and sixth times this summer. The disappearance of the swarmers means the start of migration is imminent. That the daily parade of homes has ceased at all the nearby canal colonies except CR 1 also signals that the birds' behavior is about to change drastically. I'm disappointed by day's end: today was probably our last chance this summer for a six- or seven-hundred-bird day. No way can we come close to processing that many once Annie leaves.

July 15

I wake up this morning with an ear infection. My hearing is impaired, and one ear feels completely clogged. Nothing's worse than being sick in the field. Mary and I have had good fortune over the years in staying healthy each summer, and today is about the most miserable I've ever felt at Cedar Point. We debate the best course of action, trying to decide if I should go to town this morning for medicine. But today is Annie's last day in the field, and we want to take advantage of having the three of us at Whitetail one more time. I decide to defer the trip to town until after lunch.

One could hardly imagine at breakfast that temperatures were over 100° two days ago. The day has begun cool and cloudy, and we're back to wearing jackets. I'm not optimistic about catching much at Whitetail, because the swarmers and nonbreeders won't be at the colony sites in poor weather like this. But we should still be able to get juveniles, the more important goal.

As we're setting up the net, I spot a young swallow sitting in the grass beside the creek. An "Easter egg" we call it, because we sometimes have to hunt around in the tall grass for a long time before we can find these semimobile babies that can run from us but can't fly. The bottom of its nest must have crumbled and dumped it into the creek, and it swam to shore. It's probably about seventeen days old and a week away from fledging. We find babies like this one rather often, and I always return them to another nest. In a sense this is an "unnatural" intervention, but I figure that rescuing these doomed babies makes up for the occasional bird (three so far this year) that dies from our netting. We repay our debt to the species this way. Mary once had a juvenile that had fledged prematurely fly up and land on her shoulder as she was processing birds. She says it needed help—to be put back in a nest—and knew where to come. Some of the rescued nestlings survive to fledge, because we've recaught them as adults in later years.

While Mary bands the little bird, I search for a nest to add it to. I'd like to find one with nestlings of similar age and a brood of only one or two. Today, though, there's not much choice: many nests are empty. Everybody's fledged. I hadn't realized until now what a large percentage of nests had been vacated. No wonder captures have tailed off. Eventually I find a nest, and the foster child quickly jumps into it when I put it in the entrance. It's still young enough that its new parents will have time to learn its signature call before it fledges.

Action is steady for most of the morning, but as expected the parade of homes is not happening in this weather. I'm glad we're doing the north end, because the abyss on the south side looks deeper than usual this morning. Heavy rain from intense thunderstorms fell in the Sand Hills north of Whitetail last night, and the creek is at least half a foot deeper than usual. There's been a lot of runoff from the prairie's sandy soil. Moving around in the deeper water to tend the net requires noticeably more effort this morning.

The clouds finally begin to break by 11:00, but the parade of homes doesn't begin even then. The swallows are becoming less interested in the colonies with each passing day, and sunny skies don't automatically cause them to resume visiting sites. We end up with 243 birds by noon, and only 83 are juveniles. At this rate Mary and I can handle it here after Annie leaves.

I tell Annie to say good-bye to Whitetail, because this is her last visit. She wants to celebrate by wading into the abyss. She has no waders and decides to just pull off her shoes and do it in her clothes, telling me to photograph her once she's in the water. She wades in and is soon up to her neck. Damn, it *is* deep this morning. She splashes around for a while and then emerges, announcing that she needed to pee and that seemed like a good place to do it.

"Did you take your pants off?" I ask, remembering the episode at I 80.

"No, I just went. The creek washed it away."

"You sit in the back of the truck, on the spare tire. I don't want you sitting on the seat in the cab."

Annie's excretory adventures in the field have thus spanned the entire summer. Never have I known anyone who made such a drama out of peeing.

We decide at lunch that Mary and Annie will go to Dunwoody this afternoon, and I'll go to town to deal with my ear. When I return I'll join them and start the new fumigation experiment there. We've chosen Dunwoody to be the new fumigated site, mostly because the nests are about a foot lower there and thus easier to reach for spraying, and we'll leave Knight's Culvert as the unmanipulated control colony.

There are three drugstores in town, and the second one I visit has medicine that seems appropriate for my malady. My stopped-up ear is about to drive me crazy, especially since I have to turn my head to hear clearly. I return to Cedar Point, apply some medicine, which has no immediate effect, and mix up some fumigant to take to Dunwoody. When I arrive Mary and Annie have set up their chairs and processing area on the railroad embankment above the culvert. It looks like a very exposed place to sit, but the swallows are coming into the culvert anyway. Netting goes well all afternoon.

At 5:00 we quit netting so I can fumigate the nests. It's exciting to start any experiment, but especially one intended to continue for five to ten years. I wonder how our knowledge of cliff swallows will progress during that time and how long it will take before we can tell whether the birds here respond to parasite removal the way they did at Whitetail. I go through the culvert spraying all the nests at least twice. Far more swallow bugs than I had expected are crawling on the outsides of the nests. This is a new colony, so *all* these adult bugs had to have been carried in by the birds. Where did these bugs come from? This illustrates that we basically don't know squat about the movement of bugs between cliff swallow colonies. And this is a big problem in trying to understand how ectoparasitism affects the birds' social behavior.

At supper Mary and I eat with a group of limnologists who've made a quick trip out to Cedar Point this weekend to collect data at Lake McConaughy. The three of them—Heather, a graduate student, and Ben and Ray, two postdoctoral scientists—are working under the direction of our friend Kyle, who used to take us on the boat ride to check the cliff colonies. Heather, Ben, and Ray are here to collect readings of ultraviolet light at different water depths in Big Mac. The amount of UV reaching different portions of the water column affects algal growth and community composition, which are their main interests. To take measurements, they've brought a $15,000 piece of equipment—a UV spectrophotometer—that they anchor in the water along the side of Kingsley Dam.

The limnologists are in a bit of a tizzy because they couldn't get all the data they needed. They want a complete daily record of how UV penetrates the water, but they need sunny skies to take measurements. Today began cloudy, and though they got good data for this afternoon, they aren't satisfied with the morning's results. Heather has to be back in Lincoln sometime tomorrow, giving them barely enough time to go back out in the morning to repeat their sampling—if it's sunny. If tomorrow is cloudy, they're exploring the possibility of leaving their equipment so someone else can operate it in the days to come and send them the data. They ask us if we know the name of a certain undergraduate student here who supposedly likes to dive and who could handle their apparatus. We don't know him, and I marvel at Heather's willingness to trust a $15,000 piece of equipment to some guy whose name they don't even know. Heather had asked Kyle if they could leave the spectrophotometer unattended in the lake all night so it would be positioned and ready to collect readings at first light. Kyle said no, you must take it out in the boat in the morning if you want a complete diurnal record.

Tomorrow Heather will regret that she didn't listen to Kyle.

Annie has arranged to ride back tomorrow with the limnologists, since Lincoln is her first stop on the way home. She's sad about leaving and tells us again that her stay at Cedar Point has been the most rewarding time of her life. I can understand that, because it's the same for me. In a couple of weeks I'll be overwhelmed with the same sadness when Mary and I leave.

After supper Mary works on my ear, repeatedly flushing it with warm water. The crud in it finally breaks free, and suddenly it's no longer clogged or painful. I can hear again. I feel like a new man, ready to start the final phase of the swallow summer.

Tomorrow it will be just Mary and me.

July 16

The chat is singing outside our apartment window at dawn. We hadn't heard him at all during the heat. He's showing a resurgence of song here at the end of the breeding season, which is typical of many small songbirds. As their gonads begin to shrink for the winter, surges of hormones are released, and some birds exhibit a temporary flare-up of nesting behavior. It's always aborted in a short time, though, and individuals soon slip into the migratory and nonbreeding activity patterns that will last until next spring. We see this in the cliff swallows. While on the parade of homes many birds will go through the motions of defending nests, courting mates, and collecting mud to put on a nest. But it never lasts long, and soon everyone migrates.

For the first time in sixty-two days, Mary and I will not have to plan the activities of assistants this morning. Annie will be leaving with the limnologists after breakfast. It's a major relief knowing we made it through another summer with no mishaps or problems with our assistants. Perhaps the greatest relief, however, comes from knowing that the departure of the last assistant means the summer is almost over. We've battled the elements for ten weeks and fought through a variety of obstacles. Our research success this summer has been determined by now; anything Mary and I do from now on won't materially alter how we judge this season.

At breakfast the limnologists are still in a dither over the weather. The morning has begun cloudy again, and they needed sun. They're trying to predict whether the overcast skies will break up in the next hour and to decide whether to wait to collect additional data. They should have known you can never count on the unpredictable Nebraska weather to fit with a constrained time slot. Don't come out here unless you have time to wait for the weather to cooperate. I remember the whole week in May when we sat around waiting for the bad weather to clear, and they're worried about waiting a few hours. Annie just wants to know when they're leaving so she doesn't miss her ride.

By the time Mary and I are ready to leave for Whitetail, they decide not to wait for clearing skies. They'll go out in the boat to retrieve the spectrophotometer and then depart, easily before noon. We say our good-byes to Annie. She tells me she's learned a lot this summer. One thing she's realized is that biological fieldwork is not something that she wants to do as a career. She's enjoyed what she's done here and loves watching and working with birds, but the intensity and single-minded focus necessary to do this are not something she thinks she has or could develop. Annie is not unique in this regard; only a handful of our assistants have continued in field biology. I sometimes worry that I'm so obsessed with cliff swallows that I give twenty-year-olds the wrong impression of what it takes to do fieldwork. But in the overcrowded, competitive academic environment, survival dictates that you must have a consuming intensity about your research. If a student doesn't hope to develop that, now is the time to explore alternatives.

I'll miss Annie. She's been an excellent assistant, and working with her was never boring. She tells us she'll see us again sometime. I wonder whether she's right, and I think once more about the strangeness of working so closely with people for weeks only to have them suddenly walk out of your life for good.

With some anxiety, Mary and I leave for Whitetail. Although recently it's been slow enough for two people to handle, we always have some trepidation about going there when it's just the two of us. There have been many occasions in the past when we've been overwhelmed by birds in the net. It's especially stressful for Mary, who has to process and record by herself. As good as she is, there's an irreducible time required to open a band, close it around a bird's leg, blow on the bird's belly to check its sex, weigh the bird, release it, and write down the information. If there are too many captures, she can't keep up. No one can. We can get backed up in a hurry, and if it's hot. . . .

At least it's not hot today.

The first day or two after the last assistant leaves is usually marred by our squabbling with each other. Each of us is used to being the boss while we're out with the assistants. When it's just the two of us, for a while we're both still in a supervisory mode: Fill that bucket full enough. Did you tape that loop? Don't let that data sheet blow away. Trying to boss each other doesn't work and isn't necessary, but it takes a little while to realize that again. A kind of empty nest syndrome, applicable specifically to swallow biologists.

Our fears about getting overwhelmed are unfounded. The morning is slow by Whitetail standards, and we get only 199 birds by noon. It's a good pace for two people. A serene feeling of contentment fills me all morning, though standing a few feet from a culvert containing several hundred screaming baby birds is not something most people would consider relaxing.

At lunch we're surprised to see Annie and the limnologists in the dining room. It's immediately clear that something's wrong. Heather is upset, and Ray and Ben are trying to console her. Annie tells us that when they went out this morning to retrieve the UV spectrophotometer, it was gone. Someone came by in a boat during the night and took it—a $15,000 piece of equipment. The speculation is that a fisher happened to see it and thought it was a fancy fish finder. The thing looks like a bomb and would be of use to only about twenty people in the entire country. No wonder Heather's upset. Kyle told her not to leave it out overnight, and he was livid when she called him this morning to report the loss. Heather's own graduate research requires this instrument, and without it her science is over. She says there's only one other spectrophotometer like it in North America.

The plan is to report the loss to the sheriff's office in case someone should turn it in. The limnologists will also inform several of the local dive shops in case someone thinks it's an air tank and returns it. Joan is going to offer a reward for it in the Ogallala and North Platte newspapers. But that sucker's gone. The thief had to make a big effort to detach it from its mooring; it wasn't as though the thing was just floating there like a piece of driftwood.

I don't envy Annie riding back with the poor limnologists. She says she's just trying to commiserate and not pester them about when they're going to leave. We say good-bye again after lunch, though Heather's in such a state that I'm not sure they'll go back to Lincoln today. Her earlier need to return pales in comparison with the loss of the spectrophotometer. And going back means facing Kyle's wrath. Annie may still be here at supper. Ironically, and to Heather's chagrin, the clouds broke in late morning, and it became sunny enough to take UV readings.

Captures at Whitetail after lunch remain at a comfortable enough pace for the two of us. We eventually get 223 birds this afternoon, for a daily total of 422. As we load everything back into the truck at quitting time, I notice the birds doing their characteristic snake alarm at the south end of the culvert. I walk down to the bank near the abyss and don't see anything, but the birds are having a fit. I return to the truck to get back into the waders and slowly make my way through the middle tunnel. I see the snake near the south end. It has gone partway inside a nest, but enough of it is sticking out that I can grab it. The brute's a big one, and it takes a good yank on its tail to pull it out.

Surprisingly, most of the mud nest it was in didn't break. I look inside. There are three juveniles, all dead. The snake killed them but hadn't had time to eat them. These babies were able to fly. Why didn't they leave the nest when the older birds started alarming and the snake approached? We know they could have flown because one is banded. We had it in the net exactly an hour ago. Its parents must have led it back to the nest before the snake attacked.

One reason we think the banded juvenile lived in that nest and wasn't a klepper is the striking similarity in the faces of all three birds. With the juveniles' variable speckling patterns on their throats and foreheads, each one we catch in the net looks different. But these three are identical. I've never seen such similarity in faces. Mary and I wonder if all the babies in a given nest—presumed siblings—look alike. Perhaps they do, if the facial plumage is genetically controlled. If so, parents would have to learn only one pattern and could use it to supplement their voice-based baby recognition system. And if siblings look alike, parents theoretically should be able to identify babies in their nest that result from the parasitic eggs other females have laid there. But there's no evidence that parent swallows discriminate against any of the nestlings in their nests, so either they don't use facial patterns for this purpose or there's no consistent similarity among siblings. The sameness of these three might be coincidental, though they're so alike I doubt it.

Someone should study the similarity in faces among juveniles. It's much easier said than done, however, because it's hard to work with them. By the time they're old enough to show their facial variability, they're old enough to fledge, or at least jump out of the nest, whenever you handle them. One would have to devise some way to restrain the juveniles to prevent premature fledging. You'd also have to come up with a quantitative measure of plumage similarity. Although I haven't thought much about it, I don't see an immediately obvious way to score the faces. And finally, such a study would have to be done in conjunction with a DNA fingerprinting analysis of parentage. Some of the babies in a nest arise from brood parasitism and extrapair copulation, meaning some nestlings are not siblings or may be only half-siblings. You'd have to know the exact relatedness between the babies in a nest before you could make sense of the facial patterns. This would be a great study, even with these challenges. Perhaps we'll do it someday.

At supper we find that Annie is gone. The limnologists left in midafternoon, after making the rounds of the dive shops and lakefront stores asking them to watch for the spectrophotometer. Its loss is all the residents of Cedar Point can talk about. The story eventually had a happy ending, since three weeks later someone anonymously turned the instrument in at the North Platte police station. The thief was apparently spooked by Joan's newspaper ad that referred to the device as "federal equipment," implying that the FBI might get involved!

This evening we walk across the diversion dam and along the north side of Keystone Lake. Juvenile cliff swallows are everywhere: crèching on a barbed wire fence, foraging over the beaver marsh, flocking in trees along the river below the dam, feeding overhead. Many seem old enough to be independent. Periodically little squads of five to ten birds pass over. I think many of the independent juveniles form small gangs that travel around at this time of year, and these little groups probably stay together until migration. I wonder how long after that they remain together. Do the same groups go all the way to Argentina and then come back in the spring to the same colony? Perhaps right now the young birds are forming associations that will last for much of their lives.

We watch several birds bathing in Keystone Lake. Cliff swallows bathe by flying down to the water and hitting the surface briefly before flying on. The collision is fairly violent, and the splash throws water all over them. It's done completely on the wing. They drink in a similar way, skimming the water surface with their bills. The birds bathing this evening appear to be mostly independent juveniles that are already accomplished enough fliers to do this tricky maneuver. As we watch two or three birds repeatedly hit the water, they're soon joined by more. Before long at least twenty-five cliff swallows are taking a communal bath in a part of the lake not larger than thirty by thirty feet. After a few minutes the bathing stops just as suddenly, and the birds disperse. Another illustration of the strong social attraction these creatures have for one another.

We walk back in the fading light, the western sky ablaze with shades of pink reflecting off thin, wispy clouds as the sun sinks below the horizon. Swallows dart all around us in the waning daylight, doing some last-minute foraging on the many nocturnal insects that have begun to emerge. There must be thousands of birds around Keystone Lake. It's comforting to see all these cliff swallows. Reproductive success has been high this summer. There'll be new birds coming back next year for us to study.

July 17

Simultaneously netting Alkali Lake Station and the Roscoe Gun Club is a three-person job. It'll be a challenge to do it today with only two of us.

On the way we drive along the canal, noticing that several of the canal colonies are completely deserted, even at 8:00 A.M., prime time for the parade of homes. At Aqueduct the residents are feeding young, but there are no swarmers, probably because the owl is still there. When we stop it flies out from its perch under the flume. The residents alarm-call as it flies away, but apparently they don't mind it when it's sitting still. I bet its presence dissuades swarmers, though. In most years Aqueduct would be overrun with nonbreeders and postbreeders at this time of the summer.

Instead, everybody seems to be at CR 8. Huge numbers of cliff swallows are swarming all over the bridge. Many independent juveniles are sitting on the outer flared lips of the parallel metal I-beams along the base of the bridge. These birds seem to be hanging out, not really looking at nests, but secure in being so close to others of their kind. The thousands of birds here mean migration is nearing.

Netting at both Alkali Lake and the Gun Club requires driving back and forth between them. Since Alkali Lake is larger and we catch more birds there, we spend most of our time there and check the Gun Club at intervals. Our method is for Mary to go to the net at Alkali Lake to get birds, and while she's doing that, I drive the three-tenths of a mile to the Gun Club. I bring any birds caught back to Alkali Lake, where we process and release them. The short distance between the two colonies is easily within the birds' foraging range, so releasing the Gun Club birds at Alkali Lake creates no problem for them. Several of them are back in the net at the Gun Club within half an hour. I get a lot of practice making U-turns.

By lunchtime we've caught 102 birds at Alkali Lake, and it's showing no sign of slowing down. We're getting more unbanded birds than I had expected; we'd already banded about half the residents here on earlier visits. Judging from the sleek plumage of some of them, there are nonbreeders passing through here too. Nonbreeding visitors must circulate among all the sites, even small ones like this. My suspicion that there are nonbreeders here is confirmed when we catch a bird I recognize as one banded three days ago at Whitetail. These nonbreeders get around. Whitetail is over eight miles from Alkali Lake as the swallow flies.

The nonbreeders seem mostly interested in Alkali Lake; we're not getting any at the Gun Club. Captures continue at a fast pace at Alkali Lake until 2:00. Suddenly the wind changes to the north and increases, and bird activity at the colony declines. The morning began clear, but clouds have been gathering, and a thundershower has developed off to the south. Before long we start getting sprinkles, and by 2:30 we're catching almost nothing. We wait another hour during which we catch only two birds at Alkali Lake and nothing at the Gun Club and decide to shut down.

I'm astounded that we caught 179 birds at Alkali Lake in six hours of netting. Almost half were unbanded, and some of those were nonbreeding drifters. Eleven were independent juveniles that had come here to visit and possibly assess the colony site for next year. Among the banded ones, we got bands used at a variety of places this summer, so some of our haul consisted of postbreeders on the parade of homes.

Today's results are important because they illustrate that the nonbreeding and postbreeding swarmers also visit *small* colonies late in the season. Until this year, all our late-season netting had been confined to large colonies like Whitetail and Aqueduct. This summer the delayed breeding by many birds meant that small colonies like

Dunwoody and Alkali Lake Station have been active late enough in the year to overlap with the arrival of the nonbreeders. Another insight made possible by that frustrating May weather.

After supper a visiting parasitologist gives a lecture on his research. It's classical parasitology: collect a bunch of animals, cut them open, and describe what sort of internal parasites they have. A destructive approach, and while listening I keep thinking how glad I am that Mary and I study parasites that live on the outside of their hosts and in their nests. You can't learn much from a dead animal. The presentation is rather dry, but it's livened up by the speaker's young son. He keeps wandering around the room in front of the audience while his father is talking, and soon he starts making hand shapes in front of the slide projector. His father seems oblivious, but the shadowy dinosaur and monster heads on the screen make it hard to read the tables of data. The entire audience's attention is fixed on this brat, and no one can concentrate on the material being presented. Eventually his father reprimands him, but the hand shapes continue until the seminar ends. I keep waiting for the kid to flash the audience the finger.

Walking back to the apartment, I encounter Tony. He asks how our day went, and I tell him about the nonbreeders we discovered at Alkali Lake. We start musing about whether this year has had an unusually high number of nonbreeders, given the bad weather early. I suspect there have been more this summer but have no way to prove it. Tony suggests we try to find a way to systematically sample the nonbreeders each year and use our netting data to estimate what fraction of the population skips breeding. We could correlate the extent of nonbreeding with climatic conditions or the availability of resources necessary for breeding. It might be possible to estimate the number of nonbreeders for past years too, using the number of unbanded birds caught at Whitetail after the threshold date when swarming started.

The biggest problem with our discovery of the nonbreeders is *proving* they're nonbreeders. A skeptic could argue that they're immigrants that bred somewhere else earlier in the season. Although the timing of their appearance this year and the geographic scope of the bad spring weather refute that argument, it's indirect evidence. A better indication of their status might be their fresh, bright breeding plumage. Since the known breeders have worn, drab feathers by now, we could quantify a bird's degree of brightness and assign each a breeding or nonbreeding status based on its plumage. That way we could identify birds' status at colonies where we haven't netted extensively and where not all residents are banded.

Next year we'll have to score plumage brightness for all birds.

July 18

Mary and I spend the morning and afternoon at Whitetail and catch 472 birds. I've never been more exhausted from a day in the field.

The morning began slowly, with our getting mostly banded residents and juveniles. By late morning and for the entire afternoon, however, we were deluged with unbanded nonbreeders. *Where the hell do they keep coming from?* They were just pouring through the culvert. Poor Mary, trying to process birds alone, got so backed up that I had to close the net and help her. We could easily have exceeded six hundred birds today had Annie been here to help. Although there are many empty nests in the culvert now, lots of juveniles are still flying through the colony, some having been independent of their parents for several days. Our total contains 189 juveniles.

In midmorning a kestrel flew over the colony several times, creating considerable consternation among the swallows. Each time they all roared out in a tight flock, got up to its level, then began following it and alarm-calling at it. Once it was carrying something, probably a mouse, although it might have been a juvenile cliff swallow. Kestrels haven't hunted at Whitetail much this summer. In past seasons we've been treated to great shows in the open pasture south of the colony, watching kestrels dive from heights of a hundred feet or more toward juveniles flying below. A chase usually ensued, but the kestrels were rarely successful even when going after juvenile cliff swallows. Kestrels seem to enjoy toying with the swallows and getting them stirred up, occasionally chasing one just for the fun of it. Mice or grasshoppers are probably more profitable prey items for them.

By suppertime we're feeling like zombies. Doing 472 birds in a day with just two people is hard work. I'm doubly tired because we did the south end, and I slogged around in the chest waders all day, fighting the abyss. We've got to do something about that hole if it's still there next year. Our mood isn't helped when we get back to Cedar Point and find most of the food's gone by the time we get through the serving line. The kitchen staff has routinely been running out of food this summer, and I don't understand why. It's always frozen pizza for the unfortunate souls who come to supper after the main wave. That's usually us and Tony's group, and tonight we get pizza for what seems like the fifty-fifth time this summer. This food is really getting me down, especially on a day like this when we come in tired and hungry and want a good meal.

After supper Mary and I go for a walk along the North Platte River. It's a relaxing and peaceful antidote to the hellish day at Whitetail. We watch the resident beaver as it emerges from the river and goes after a cottonwood sapling on the bank. This massive rodent makes short work of the tree, quickly cutting it down and stripping its leaves and branches. It munches away ravenously. There are thousands of cliff swallows feeding over the river below the diversion dam and the adjacent floodplain. Many of the birds are independent juveniles, fattening up for the coming migration. Stands of cottonwood trees on both sides of the river provide great roosting and perching spots, and there are swarms of insects everywhere you look. This is a perfect place to while away your summer days if you're a cliff swallow waiting to migrate: undisturbed, plenty of food, places to hang out. No wonder so many birds are here tonight.

No wonder nobody has migrated yet.

July 19

We need a break from Whitetail.

Looking over our records, I noticed that we haven't netted the south end of Dunwoody. The wind has been such that we've always done the north end. Not netting on the south side means we miss some of the colony residents, and since we're setting up the fumigation experiment at Dunwoody, I want to know as much as possible about the residents there. Even if most of the ones we've missed are unbanded, I still want to get bands on them so we'll know who they are and where they go in future summers. The problem is that at this time of year nonbreeding and postbreeding swarmers are hanging around some colonies, and we may confuse them with the actual colony residents. I hope the cloudy weather this morning will deter the swarmers and that we'll be able to catch only residents.

We drive through Duane's pasture and park beside the corrals. The stands of sunflowers are so lush and tall we can barely see the tire ruts leading to the culvert. Many of the sunflowers are as tall as I am, a rich green all over, but not flowering yet.

Watching the colony, I realize we're in luck. The only birds going into the culvert appear to be feeding babies in nests. No swarmers are around. We set the net on the south side, wading through the slimy, muddy poop with its green algal sheen. I don't know where the water comes from to make this "mud." There's no flowing stream here, but water has washed in from somewhere. It's probably from that downpour a few days ago that temporarily raised Whitetail Creek.

The Dunwoody birds are not in a cooperative mood this morning. Dozens of birds swirl over us, alarm-calling. They refuse to go into the culvert. We'd hoped to be able to sit in our lawn chairs, but soon it's obvious we'll have to sit inside the truck. Even after we move, the colony residents won't calm down. I know cliff swallows become more wary once they have babies, but this is ridiculous.

After an hour we've caught only six birds. At least a third of all the nests in the colony are clustered near the south end, and their owners are completely unwilling to enter the culvert on the open north side to reach their nests. The net blocks their access from the south, and they have no interest in going in over the top of it. We've waited too long to do this side; the birds have large young and are not at a stage to be tolerant. I don't blame them. By this time of the summer I don't have much patience either.

We give up and move the net to the north end. Maybe we can flush some of the south-side residents toward it. The colony calms down once the net is moved, and traffic into the culvert resumes. It's weird how they'll cope with the net being where it was on earlier visits but won't tolerate it in a new location today. I bet the pattern would be reversed if we'd netted the south end earlier.

We start catching birds at a slow pace. Many of them are this year's bands, though, so we're not getting the new birds we wanted. We recognize one band number as that of a bird banded at Whitetail a couple of days ago. There are a few nomadic swarmers around after all.

We've been watching an evil-looking thunderstorm build on the northwestern horizon all morning. It's odd to have one developing this early in the day. A storm to the northwest should track away from us, but by 11:00 this one seems to be getting closer. Before long we hear thunder, and within a few minutes it starts looking really bad. The clouds have a threatening greenish tint.

I want to fumigate today and have brought some insecticide, so Mary takes down the net while I quickly spray the nests. She has the net down in a couple of minutes, hastened by the fumigant blowing toward her. I look for bugs on the nests and don't see any. The previous dousing must have eliminated many of them. It's getting dark inside the culvert, with the grayish green clouds rolling in, and soon it's hard to see.

By the time I finish and get back to the truck, the wind is strong. It's whipping up clouds of straw and hay from the adjacent corrals, hurling them past us in ominous whirls of dust. This is not a good place to be in a storm. The open pasture is exposed for miles, and the truck is the highest point around. That's not good, since we're seeing lightning. The culvert would be the only refuge should this storm contain a tornado. The swallows have gone home to their nests, and we start the truck to get out of here. We hope we can remember how to get back to the road, because the tire ruts are doubly hard to see with the grass and sunflowers blowing so violently. No time now to take a wrong turn.

Fortunately the rain holds off until we make it to the pasture gate and turn onto the road. It's pouring by the time we get back to Cedar Point. We got only fifty-three birds, and most of them weren't ones I really wanted. It's clear that the party's over at Dunwoody this summer: no more netting there. But the slow morning was welcome after the chaos of yesterday at Whitetail.

The thunderstorm is short-lived and is over by the time we finish our lunch of tacos. No frozen pizza today for a change. The storm has given us a north wind for the afternoon, and I want to take advantage of it by doing the north side at Whitetail. I won't have to wear the chest waders, a major cause for celebration. Mary groans, remembering yesterday, but I assure her the cloudy weather this afternoon means Whitetail will be slower.

I'm right. Markedly fewer birds are around. At times the net is empty, and Mary has none awaiting processing. We're able to sit in our lawn chairs and relax in the west tunnel under the road, staring out into the pasture beyond, watching the peacefully flowing creek. We see the resident muskrat—we've named him Mortimer—come swimming down the creek carrying a freshly cut branch of a leadplant. Mortimer has a lodge along the creek not far from the culvert, and he often passes by. Whenever he swims through the culvert, the swallows alarm at him. Why, I don't know, because he's the most harmless creature you could imagine. He eats leaves.

The slower afternoon also reflects fewer active nests inside the culvert. Although business picks up slightly in midafternoon when the sun comes out, we still get only 196 birds. Once I do a flush that could have yielded a hundred birds a month ago when everyone was incubating. Today we catch two.

The slow morning at Dunwoody and the relatively slow afternoon here have been good for us. I'm not sure we could have physically done another 472-bird day. We're not nearly as exhausted by suppertime, and I feel like today has recharged our batteries. We've got our second wind.

I just hope we have enough energy to get us through what's left of the summer. Fieldwork takes stamina, and I'm about out of it.

15

Migration

This is my last view of them for a while. If you see them
before I do, say hello from me and give them my love. For
now I'll remember them as they are. . . , sitting with each
other and listening to a summer rain.
—Garrison Keillor, *Leaving Home*

July 20

As we drive down the canal road toward Aqueduct, I notice there are fewer swallows around today. We pass bridge after bridge, all deserted. It's weird—and sad—to see nothing at CR 4½, one of our largest colonies earlier this summer. The birds have declined in abundance just since yesterday morning; I correlate their sudden reduction with the passing of the storm and cold front about noon yesterday. Could the front and the switch to a north wind have been a stimulus for some birds to start fall migration?

There's not much happening at Aqueduct either. Today I count 180 nests that are complete and seem to be active, with their owners now feeding young. That's down from 670 active nests last summer. I still think that owl is partly responsible, though we don't see it today.

Our goal is to do one final big-net session here, but as soon as we start to erect the first net, the wind picks up. It's southerly, so it will only get worse as the day wears on. The nets billow rather badly, and I worry that a strong gust may topple them. We've used the big nets so infrequently this summer that we haven't had many opportunities for wind-related disasters, but I remember our trouble here last year. One big net was blown against the side of the flume on a windy day like this. It caught on an irregularity in the concrete about sixteen feet above the ground, and in getting it down we ripped a huge hole in the mesh. Mary spent an entire day repairing and reconstructing the torn net.

The small colony size and flapping nets contribute to a very slow morning. We sit in the grove of cottonwoods and relax, needing to visit the net only every twenty minutes or so. But the good news is that most of the birds we're catching are probably residents; our captures aren't being polluted by the presence of swarmers. Even the unbanded birds we catch are in worn, drab plumage and likely are breeders we missed earlier.

I wonder what fate awaits these late breeders at Aqueduct. They'll complete their nesting, but it will be early August before they're finished and their young are independent. What are the consequences of breeding at different times of the summer? What are the consequences of being raised at different times of the summer? Watching many of the swallows feeding below the diversion dam in the evenings suggests that they spend a lot of time fattening up at this time of the year. Presumably the longer you have to do this before migrating, the better your odds of making it to South America. A three-thousand-mile migration must be a dangerous, arduous journey for a twenty-four-gram animal. I suspect that late nesting is costly because it doesn't allow either the breeding adults or their young much time to get prepared.

We already know that late-hatched young pay a penalty. When we banded babies in nests before they fledged, we knew the date each one hatched. We could then estimate the probability that a baby would live to return the next year, using recaptures of marked birds. The odds that a swallow would survive its first winter and return the next breeding season declined the later in the summer it hatched. Juveniles that fledge in August—as the ones here at Aqueduct will do—face poor prospects. They don't have time to hang out along the river and hone their flying and foraging skills.

The same applies to the adult breeders. Breeding is hard work, and by the time their young fledge, many adults have lost weight and don't have much fat reserve. All their effort has gone into nesting. Without time to recoup their losses, their probability of making it to next summer isn't high.

We don't have the data—yet—to show that late nesting adults suffer a survival cost, but this summer will be wonderful for investigating this question. We've had several late colonies where we've been able to catch and band many of the residents. We'll have a large sample of late nesters that we can track through the coming years to see if they really do pay a long-term penalty—reduced life span—for nesting late.

Thinking about this as I sit in the pleasant shade of the cottonwoods gets me very excited. These sorts of questions can't be answered for many animal populations, and I wonder whether cliff swallows will conform to our theoretical predictions. But it will be a while before we can draw any conclusions, because it takes several seasons to "follow" a given cohort of birds. Just because we don't catch a bird one year doesn't necessarily mean it died. It could have been at a local colony but evaded capture. The next season we'll have another chance to catch any bird we missed the previous year. Some birds evade capture for a second season. Our next chance to catch them is the following summer, and so on. It takes three years before we can be relatively sure whether a bird survived.

The three-year rule means that the data from this summer will enable us to estimate survival for birds from 1992 and earlier, but we still haven't followed the 1993 or 1994 birds long enough to say anything about them. It will be 1998 before we'll know the survival consequences for the late nesters here at Aqueduct. I suppose some people would say to hell with it and wouldn't want to spend three years waiting to see their results. I really can't blame them, yet for me the satisfaction of getting the sort of information few people have is immense. Because each summer is different—climatically or in how the birds are distributed among colonies—each one has something new to tell us.

I often smile to myself when well-meaning people naively ask what we discovered about cliff swallows today. The correct reply is, I'll let you know in three years.

The birds at Aqueduct have one thing going for them, though. A colony of about 180 nests is close to what we think the "optimal" colony size might be for cliff swallows. Throughout the fourteen years we've studied these birds, my overriding interest has been how the sizes of the colonies a bird is raised in and later breeds in affect its reproductive success over its lifetime. Knowing this will help tell us why the birds form colonies of particular sizes, maybe even why they live in groups to begin with. Do birds living in big colonies consistently raise more young during their lives? If so, the formation of large colonies is advantageous and easily explained. What about small colonies? Do birds living there also do well, thus accounting for the diversity in colony sizes within the population? What about where a bird is born? Does that colony's size affect its lifetime prospects? It's beginning to look as though getting the full answers to these questions will represent my life's work. There's much we don't understand, but some early indications are that medium-sized colonies might be best.

An organism's lifetime output of offspring is based on two things: how many young it can produce per breeding attempt and how many breeding attempts it can make. Its number of breeding attempts is determined by how long it lives. A long-lived animal will probably breed more often than one of the same species with a shorter life span. Thus our data on survival enable us to calculate how long swallows live and how many young they can potentially raise. Preliminary data reveal that birds in the largest colonies seem to live longer—their probability of survival is greater—than those nesting in smaller colonies. A large colony with its many foragers means birds have more information on the whereabouts of food and may find more food faster. A breeder from a big colony is in better shape at the end of the breeding season and therefore more likely to make it to South America and return to nest again.

Then why do we think medium-sized colonies are best? If breeders in big colonies live longest, shouldn't they have the greatest success, and shouldn't their descendants eventually come to predominate in the population? But also important is how many of your young survive. It doesn't matter how often you breed or how many young you fledge if none of your offspring live to become breeders themselves. "Recruitment" into the population is the term for survival of young to breeding age. And that isn't highest for cliff swallows in big colonies. The survival of young to become breeders is greatest for birds raised in colonies of 100 to 299 nests: Aqueduct size.

It seems, therefore, that parents have the most surviving young if they use an intermediate-sized colony each year. This isn't too surprising. A colony like Aqueduct, 180 nests, is large enough to offer its residents the food-finding advantages. It's also big enough to spot incoming predators and provide early warning, as we saw when the attacking kestrel was quickly detected here.

But a 180-nest colony is small enough that many of the costs of group life are reduced. Ectoparasitism isn't as bad as in a big colony. Chances for confusing the identity of fledglings in a crèche are less. There's less competition for food. This translates into the babies' being in better shape when they fledge and become independent. Their survival, and their parents' reproductive success, is greater than in colonies that are either larger or smaller. The million-dollar question, of course, is why colonies so much larger and smaller than the "optimal" size exist. If medium-sized colonies are really best, all cliff swallows should settle in that kind. Huge colonies like Airport or tiny ones like McDougals should never occur. It may take another lifetime to solve this riddle.

At least our calculations and estimates suggest that medium-sized colonies confer the greatest benefits. Maybe they're wrong; they're still preliminary. With this summer's data in the bag, though, we'll be closer to making more definitive conclusions.

The netting seems to be over at Aqueduct. The wind has worsened, and I'm still anxious about having the nets up. It would be a shame to tear them up on what's probably the last day this year that we'll use them. I'm also uneasy because there are cows around. I saw fresh cow patties under the nests. A local rancher keeps a herd of cattle in the canyon to the south. They often come as far north as the cottonwoods we're sitting under, grazing in the lush wooded thicket along the North Platte River behind us. They were here most of last summer, and on some days they'd suddenly emerge from the woods around us. With no fence between us and them, or between them and the nets, it makes for a tense situation, especially since there was a bull with the herd last year. The feeling of vulnerability I get every time we use the big nets is particularly bad today. I feel we're courting disaster by having the nets up in such a strong wind when the lurking cows could come thundering out of the woods at any moment. Storm clouds have also started to build around us.

Not what you'd call a relaxing day.

At 2:00 we take the nets down, with great relief. We've avoided the cows. Our total is a measly eighty-four birds. There's little point in returning to Aqueduct: another colony off our list. Whitetail is the only one left.

By late afternoon a thunderstorm has developed. It's a short one but contains heavy rain and a lot of wind. It passes, and when we do our after-dinner walk to the diversion dam the fresh, clear air is invigorating. It has that wonderful smell that comes after a rain. The evening is gorgeous, with heavy dark blue storm clouds to the east, their massive tops snowy white. The storms are building but moving away from us; according to the radio, North Platte is getting creamed by a bad one. To the west the sky is alternately yellowish and pinkish, like alpenglow. Wispy clouds turn flaming red as the sun sets, contrasting sharply with the bluish black cloud mass to the east. The beauty surrounding us on each horizon is overpowering. God's country. I never want to leave here.

A couple hundred juvenile swallows have assembled in a huge fallen cottonwood tree along the edge of the beaver marsh. Some seem to still be dependent on their parents, so this is probably a true crèche, possibly of Whitetail birds. Last summer the birds were using this same dead tree, and they crèched here for days. It's a wonderfully scenic sight, dozens of young birds lined up along the bare branches with a beautiful green field as a background. I tried last year to set up a blind near the downed tree to photograph the juveniles and their parents. Crèches don't allow humans to come close, and hiding in a blind is essential to getting decent pictures. However, the birds refused to sit in the tree when my tentlike blind was up. I tried repeatedly, but as soon as I erected the blind, the entire crèche would take off and stay away. As soon as I left, they'd all return. I came back mad and frustrated each evening, and Mary finally had her fill of my obsession with this crèche.

"They don't have to sit there," she kept telling me. "They can go sit anywhere." She meant that they're not motivated to approach a strange item like a blind if all they need is a place to perch. It would be a different story at a colony, where they have much more incentive—their nests—to tolerate something like a blind, net, or exposed observer.

"Don't even think about it," Mary warns me before I say anything tonight about the crèche. She knows I want to photograph the birds in the dead tree.

July 21

This morning we'll find out if migration has really started. If activity at Whitetail has diminished, then we'll know that birds have begun leaving. In a normal summer, most of the cliff swallows in the study area would be gone by now. But the May weather has delayed everything this year, including migration.

Large numbers of swallows are at Whitetail when we arrive. I suspect many are nonbreeding and postbreeding swarmers and independent juveniles that are hanging out in the nests. There's considerable coming and going around the culvert, at least until we get out of the truck. Our presence makes all the birds leave, and while I slog through the abyss in chest waders getting the net up, the colony is eerily quiet. The birds' mass departures are becoming more frequent, and they're staying away longer. Their behavior this morning clearly shows they're becoming less tolerant of people. We sit for at least twenty minutes at a deserted culvert before the swallows begin to return. Even then it's only a trickle. Most of the swarmers that were here have dispersed and no longer are interested in the colony.

With the net on the south end, a gentle southwesterly breeze, and sunny skies, this morning will be a good test. Is Whitetail still attracting enough birds to warrant netting? The answer seems to be sort of. We catch birds at a slow pace all morning, interspersed with periods of nothing when everybody leaves. At such times I can hear the flock high overhead. They stay together; their social attraction to each other is as strong as ever. It won't wane even as their interest in breeding does. We catch mostly banded adults and juveniles. Very few nests with young remain in the culvert. By noon we've caught only 135 birds.

With Whitetail the only colony left to net, the season's over when we're done here. And this morning's small haul means the end is in sight. In a sense that's a relief, because we can finally begin to look ahead to our own departure. I figure we can wrap everything up in four or five days. As we sit in the culvert this morning, Mary and I list the other things we need to do before we leave. We need to have both trucks serviced; we want to visit Cabela's, the massive outdoor supply store in nearby Sidney, to shop for clothes and field gear for next summer; we must complete arrangements for storing the blue truck over the winter; we need to pack the equipment in the laboratory; and I need to fumigate Whitetail and Dunwoody another time or two. Suddenly these tasks seem as important as catching swallows.

As we drive back to Cedar Point for lunch, the canal bridges are all deserted. Even CR 1, which has been attracting swarmers each day, has no birds. We're confident that, yes, the season is almost over. The birds are telling us so.

We spend the afternoon packing up gear that we won't need in the remaining few days. I'm always amazed at how long it takes to disassemble the laboratory and pack everything away in boxes for the winter. It usually requires two full days to get all this junk unpacked and organized for use when we arrive, and another two days at quitting time to box it back up. That's four days a year just packing and unpacking boxes of research gear, plus more time doing that for our household items. I bet we spend at least a week just packing and unpacking for each swallow summer. Over the life of this project, that's fourteen weeks—easily the equivalent of an entire semester—just putting stuff in and out of boxes. And that doesn't count the time we spend on the road between Cedar Point and our off-season home. No wonder many people do their fieldwork close to home.

Our walk this evening verifies our suspicion that migration has begun. There are noticeably fewer birds foraging along the river to-night, and the photogenic crèche in the fallen tree is smaller. Birds must be leaving rapidly. I remember the summer of 1990, which still holds the record for the most abrupt migration. Over just two days in early July, an estimated three-quarters of the total cliff swallow population in the study area vanished, gone south. We don't know why the birds left so suddenly that year.

Scientists have debated the evolutionary origins of migration for decades. Are migratory birds ones that evolved in the tropics and took advantage of the retreat of the glaciers to seasonally colonize more temperate regions? Does migration allow them to escape the competition with other birds that would be inevitable if they remained to breed in the crowded tropics? Why pay the tremendous cost of traveling thousands of miles between breeding and wintering areas? A sedentary life in the warmer tropics seems less risky. And if an insectivorous bird like a swallow has to migrate to escape the harsh winter and lack of food in a place like Nebraska, why do cliff swal-lows migrate while it's still midsummer? There are enough insects here to support them until at least early September.

Deep down I'm glad they migrate. How could I ever leave here or concentrate on anything else during the academic year if the cliff swallows stayed in Nebraska year round? It must be a terrible im-pediment to a normal life when your study animal is always present, constantly beckoning you to come learn more about it.

July 22

Our expectation this morning is to get more of the dregs at Whitetail. We're in for a surprise, though. There's a resurgence of interest by swarmers, and we catch 188 birds by noon. Not so fast on this summer's being over!

"Migrate," Mary keeps telling each bird she processes.

There are even fewer active nests remaining in the colony than yesterday, but the handful here are attracting swarmers and independent juveniles. There can't be enough left to make kleptoparasitism a viable option, so the juveniles we're getting now must be fully independent ones that are looking at the colony to gain information for next year.

I'm sure the juveniles we've been catching here over the past couple of weeks were raised at many of the canal colonies, at Spillway, Morning Glory, Knight's Tube, and probably more distant places. We know that juveniles from the Garden County colonies sometimes turn up at Whitetail in their late-season wanderings. We also know that, despite their explorations, many of these juveniles will choose to settle next year in a colony similar in size to the one they were raised in. In an analysis for *Coloniality in the Cliff Swallow*, we looked at the colonies chosen for breeding by 2,090 birds first marked as nestlings and recaught the next year in a breeding colony. These first-year birds were more likely to choose a breeding colony near the size of their natal one than if their colony selection had been purely random. Birds raised in big colonies preferred to nest in big colonies their first year, while those from small and medium-sized sites also preferred the kind they'd been born in. This pattern held even if the young birds switched to a different colony location.

Does this mean that individuals are "specialized" for certain colony sizes and their young share those characteristics? Are large-colony cliff swallows ones well suited to the bedlam of big groups? Are they somehow adapted to cope with the different costs and benefits they can expect in a large colony? Are birds that use other colony sizes equipped to deal with the different environments there? We don't know, but if the answers to these questions are yes, that may explain why cliff swallow colony sizes vary so much. Perhaps the population consists of a collection of individuals that are adapted in different ways to deal with the divergent requirements and expectations of rural, suburban, and urban living.

We've also wondered whether older birds show preferences for the same-sized colony from year to year. Southwestern Nebraska is a wonderful place to study colony choice, because there are many colonies of different sizes in the area each summer. A returning cliff swallow has plenty of places to choose from. Our netting has generated a treasure trove of information on the birds' choice of nesting sites. Each swallow caught, unless it's one of the nonbreeders, has a known breeding colony, and many individuals have been caught year after year. We've started to look for patterns in the data, and our first analysis used over eight thousand cases in which we knew a bird's breeding colony size in two consecutive summers. We found that over half of the birds aged two years or older prefer to occupy colonies of similar size each year. This is the same pattern seen in first-year birds. On the other hand, some cliff swallows definitely move to smaller colonies as they get older. Why some birds show a consistent change in their colony size preferences over their lives and others don't is another question we have no answer for.

Perhaps we don't understand the complexities of the birds' colony choices because we don't yet have many instances where we've followed a bird's history over an extended portion of its life—say, five or six years. Getting its colony choices for just two years here and two years there isn't as useful because such snapshots may obscure patterns. The more we net, and the closer we come to catching everybody in the colonies, the more birds we'll get long-term histories for. This is one reason our goal all summer has been to get big numbers of birds each day. I almost salivate thinking about the additional data on colony choice—another year of it for many of our birds—we'll have at the end of this summer. Soon we'll have scores of birds we've known something about for six and seven consecutive years. Those patterns should tell us a lot about the birds' choice of where to live.

At lunch we have mixed feelings about the morning. Yesterday we believed the summer was over and that we could plan accordingly. We felt relieved because we thought the swallows had signaled us that they were done. Suddenly that's not so clear. Getting 188 birds in a morning warrants continued fieldwork. The endless summer goes on. We'll just have to suck it up and keep on going. Back to Whitetail this afternoon.

We're almost glad when afternoon captures are back to the slow rate of yesterday, perhaps even slower. The swarmers vanish after lunch, and the colony is deserted for long periods. At times only a trickle of birds enter the culvert to feed their young. By midafternoon we've caught only forty-seven more. Diminishing returns.

On our way back to Cedar Point, we detour past the three new colonies along the railroad track. We need to measure the mileage from each of them to the main road so we can locate them on our topographic maps. This will let Mary use the maps to determine the linear distances between the new colonies and all other sites in the study area, which we need to know in analyzing how far dispersing birds move from year to year. Mary has a huge matrix sixty-nine cells square written on a big roll of paper, listing all the colonies where we've netted and showing the pairwise distances between each of them. We can thus look up the actual distance between any combination of colonies. Almost all combinations have been used by at least a few birds over the years. Mary's "big paper" is where we go to find how far birds travel when they move between, say, Pigpen and Spillway (13.25 miles) or any other obscure pair of sites.

Mary's not thrilled about having to expand her matrix by three colonies during the coming off-season. She'll have to make her big paper even bigger. But we get the mileages, which is easy to do by simply driving the road beside the railroad tracks.

As we're clocking the distance, we notice swarmers at Knight's Culvert and Dunwoody. I'm not surprised to see them at these two places, because each has a fair number of late nests. Lots of birds are still feeding babies there, serving as a magnet for swarmers with nothing better to do. If action is drying up at Whitetail, maybe we ought to resume netting at these sites to get more swarmers. My rational mind tells me we should try it, but another part of me says no way. I don't have enough energy left to net at more places. By this time of the season Whitetail is about all I can summon the strength for, and I'm about out of gas even for it.

July 23

We decide to go see what's happening at Whitetail this morning and then decide whether to keep netting. Our last bird yesterday finished a string of bands, and if we start another string today we want to be able to finish it too, since it simplifies record keeping. Each string is a hundred bands. Can we catch another hundred unbanded birds before Whitetail quits?

From the number of swarmers at the culvert when we arrive this morning, the answer seems to be yes. The sunny skies and calm wind make this a beautiful morning, and I guess the swallows think so too. Looks like a lot of swarmers have come out of the woodwork, and there are more at the colony than we've seen in several days.

Mary and I look at each other: we net.

By 11:00 we've used almost an entire string of bands. Most of our catch has been unbanded adults and juveniles. The phenomenal pool of unbanded nonbreeders hasn't dried up. We've banded 3,508 adults since we first saw obvious swarming by nonbreeders on June 21, and the vast majority of these birds have been sleek nonbreeders. We can't do many more today, though, because we brought only one string of bands this morning. There isn't time to go back to Cedar Point to get more, especially since I also need to fumigate. We finish our string and shut down, having caught 144 birds.

We figure the afternoon is apt to be slow and decide to use it to visit the Cabela's store in Sidney, about seventy miles to the west. The only swallows we see en route to Sidney are a few stragglers flying near the South Platte bridge in Ogallala. This site, home to a large colony earlier, is virtually deserted. The river is still much higher than normal, but the tops of some sandbars have started to appear. The protruding sand provides a glimmer of hope that the river will be back to its normal trickle next year, allowing us access to the South Platte bridges.

We do our shopping and make an effort to get back to the field station in time for supper. It's frozen pizza again.

July 24

We have to begin the day by taking the *Valdez* into town to be serviced. It needs an oil change and a new air filter, and its engine is making a squeaking noise, probably a slipping fan belt. After lunch we'll go get it and leave off the blue truck.

Whitetail again. We did too well yesterday to quit, so we head straight from town to the culvert. Maybe all the birds have left during the night and we can close the book on this summer. Fat chance of that, though. The usual crowd of swarmers is present when we drive up. Mary warns me that if we start another string of bands this morning we'll have to finish it, even if it means staying extra days to catch the dregs. I accept the challenge, but I can't believe we can continue to catch birds the way we've been doing lately.

I'm wrong. Today is even busier than the past two days. The unbanded swarmers and independent juveniles are still attracted by the few active nests in the culvert, and their near-constant procession through the culvert and into the net lasts until noon. We're working at top speed all morning, and we still get backed up. I simply can't believe the culvert is attracting so many birds this late in the summer. Hardly anyone lives here anymore! Eventually we kill one string of bands and start a second. Whitetail magic.

With the late start, we have only two and a half hours of netting time until lunch, yet we catch 196 birds. Incredible. We could easily have caught 250 if we'd had an assistant to help process, and 300 might have been possible. The birds are still doing their periodic vanishing act, but they come back in droves. Everyone flies through the culvert at once and gets in the net at the same time.

But except for the birds at Whitetail and a fair number still at the inaccessible Morning Glory, you'd think all the cliff swallows had migrated. There's nothing at the colonies along the stretch of canal that we drive regularly. Spillway's deserted. During the past couple of days there's been a drastic reduction in cliff swallows near Cedar Point. The symmetry of early and late in the season is striking: the first colonies occupied each year are Morning Glory and Whitetail, and those two will be the last to have birds. What is it about these colonies? It can't be Whitetail's fumigation, because the birds show the same pattern every year at Morning Glory, which has never been fumigated.

We spend the afternoon packing. We'll be storing the blue truck at Cedar Point over the winter, so we'll stow all our summer equipment in the back. I take it into Ogallala for servicing after lunch and return with the *Valdez*, its fan belt repaired. We'll go back to Tulsa in it, and I spend part of the afternoon hosing out all the dried mud and Clary and Dunwoody cow crap that has accumulated in its bed. It'll be nice not to caravan in two trucks on the trip back.

In late afternoon I make my third trip of the day into Ogallala, this time to retrieve the blue truck. I hitch a ride with Ron, on his way home for the day. Ron has nearly completed Cedar Point's new two-unit apartment building, which will provide extra living space for researchers and let more scientists take advantage of this wonderful area. I've always been surprised that more researchers don't come to Cedar Point. Almost every research project undertaken out here has been successful. But with funding for fieldwork so uncertain in the present economic climate, it's hard to count on sustaining a project for any length of time. Fewer people are doing research at biological stations nowadays. Even fewer young scientists are interested in doing long-term fieldwork on a single species, a real tragedy since many of our key insights in ecology have come from such studies.

On the way to town Ron and I see a massive thunderhead building to the west. It's a beauty, and by suppertime it's been transformed into a violent thunderstorm. While we eat, torrential rain develops with wind, hail, and lightning. Midway through our meal, a lightning bolt strikes just outside the lodge. The deafening thunderclap that instantly follows almost knocks us all out of our chairs. The electricity cuts off, and one person says the lightning struck a utility pole with a transformer near the lodge's loading dock. If so, we may not be having any electricity for a long while, considering the remoteness of Cedar Point and the time it takes utility crews to find us. That means the station won't have any water, since its well's pump is powered by electricity. No showers or toilets.

The rain lets up after while, and as Mary, Diana, and I walk back to the apartments we encounter three students from the aquatic microbiology class. They were walking from the laboratory to the lodge when lightning struck about twenty feet in front of them. Fortunately they weren't harmed, but they're white as ghosts, looking the way Bruce and I probably did after the great diversion dam storm. Thankfully I've not had any encounters with lightning like theirs. We make a special effort not to take chances with electrical storms when we're at colony sites, but the students' experience illustrates that we're not safe even at Cedar Point.

A few minutes after the lightning strike, a squadron of twenty or so cliff swallows flew by, out in the rain and the lightning. These creatures thrive on excitement.

July 25

We make the final decision in midmorning. The field season is over. Time to go home.

The morning at Whitetail was slow. Almost overnight the remaining swarmers lost more of their interest in coming around the culvert when we were there with a net. Several hundred were there when we arrived, but as soon as we set the net they vanished. The colony was abandoned for long periods.

We caught 110 birds this morning, the lowest haul this summer. We could probably catch a few more if we spent another couple of mornings netting, but I'm not sure this would be time well spent. We also have a problem with band supply.

The numbered bands we use are issued by the Bird Banding Laboratory, formerly part of the U.S. Fish and Wildlife Service and now part of the U.S. Geological Survey. The lab coordinates all the band numbers used, and based on information that banders send them, they record data about each banded bird in their computers. When members of the public find such birds, a message on the bands asks them to report it to the Bird Banding Laboratory. The lab then notifies the bander that one of his or her birds was recovered and sends information about the bird to the conscientious citizen who reported it. Banding is regulated by permits, and you must go through the banding lab to do any marking of migratory birds in North America.

Each bander is also dependent on the lab to provide the bands. Until a couple of years ago, the band supply was never a problem, but recently there have been chronic shortages. Government budget cutbacks are part of the cause. The band manufacturers haven't been keeping up with the demand, and I've had bands for cliff swallows on back order for over a year. We don't have enough bands right now to get us through next summer. Each band we use now may mean one less we have for the 1996 season. I hate for something as trivial as band supply to influence our research plans, but it does. Without bands we have no research. Mary and I conclude that our limited supply of bands would best be used by conserving them for next year.

We finish the last string of bands budgeted for this summer at 10:18 A.M. when band number 2151-19600 goes on an unbanded female swarmer. Although it's nice to have made the final decision to terminate fieldwork, and now we can plan our departure, I'm overcome with sadness as I close the net for the last time. I'll greatly miss the cliff swallows. My only consolation is knowing that soon none of them will be left here anyway.

I'm struck by how short our summer has been. We have only a few weeks to collect all our data, and the birds' short breeding season isn't long enough to address more than a single small part of the puzzle. This year we discovered the nonbreeders, but the swarmers are here so briefly that we didn't have time to do much with them. It will be next summer before we have another chance to study them. Devising a method of scoring plumage will have to wait another year. I sometimes envy my molecular biologist friends who can collect data year round in the comfort of their laboratories.

Mary's and my research does last all year, though. We are just trading data collection for data analysis and writing. Research is never finished until the data are analyzed and the results published. For the next nine months we'll keep thinking about cliff swallows—there's not a waking hour of any day of my life that I don't think of them in some way—but we'll be doing it more abstractly. The birds become numbers and words on a page as we try to convey to others what happened this summer, how they illustrate interesting biological concepts, what they tell us about animal social life. Data analysis also is a process of discovery. What are the patterns in the numbers? What facts do they reveal that one could never have known from simple observation? Learning something new about cliff swallows in the cold darkness of winter is exciting, and I look forward to it even if all it requires is using a computer and interpreting numbers.

Yet nothing can compare with coming to Whitetail, holding a wild cliff swallow, watching three thousand birds swirl above the culvert. Being here in the field is the only reason I do science, and it's a melancholy time when the end comes. I know I'll be back, but right now the next nine months look like an eternity.

I want to fumigate Whitetail and Dunwoody one final time this afternoon. That will be the last official act of the field season. The birds are still picking up bugs and introducing them into the fumigated sites. Among our 110 birds this morning we caught two that had swallow bugs attached to their feet. I can't do anything about whatever is introduced after today. But with most of the remaining birds soon to migrate, I can't believe many more parasites will colonize Whitetail or Dunwoody this season.

When I return from fumigating, Mary takes the blue truck to the car wash in town for a good cleaning before we put it in storage. It still has grime on it from the evening with the aerosol cow poop at Feedlot. While she's gone, I've been instructed to do a final "body count" for the season. All summer we've had a chart hanging on the wall in the lab, listing each colony and the number of captures there on each daily visit. Mary wants to know the total, in part to anticipate how much work lies ahead of her this fall entering the captures in the computer. I get out my calculator and start adding them up: 17,533 total captures for the summer. Most of the birds caught twice on a single day count only once in this tabulation, so it's safe to say that Mary and I and the assistants collectively took cliff swallows out of nets over 18,000 times this summer.

Every entry on the chart brings back a memory as I punch it into the calculator: training the assistants with big nets at Paxton before the river rose; the frustration at CR 6 and Annie's dropping her sunglasses into the canal; the trials of getting the drop net over and trying to surprise the little butt-heads at Prairie Dog; the swarms of black flies at Oshkosh and our relief at avoiding the game warden; the way Judy cleaned up at Bluffs and how Kathy and I did at McDougals; the thrill of doing the new colonies; the big day at Whitetail. The chart is a rough gauge of our effort at each site. We netted at Whitetail on twenty-seven days this summer, a third of the field season. Our total captures for Whitetail are 8,623 birds. Although many of these are residents caught on multiple days, the high number of captures relative to the 3,400 birds that actually lived there gives some indication of the extent to which nonresidents were attracted to that culvert. At the other extreme is the one visit to McDougals that yielded only seven birds—but that represented 87.5 percent of the colony. I doubt we caught that high a percentage of the true residents even at Whitetail.

The 17,533 captures enable us to compare this summer with others. Since 1991, when we started our extensive netting program, our yearly totals have ranged from a high of 21,272 in 1992 to a low of 16,702 last year. This summer ranks fourth among the five years, which is better than I would have guessed. We missed being third by only 349 captures. Considering we did almost nothing during May, the season proved very productive. Had the weather been more "normal" in May, perhaps we could have challenged the all-time record.

But there's no such thing as a "normal" year out here. Every year is different in some way. This is one of the most obvious lessons we've learned from studying cliff swallows in the same place for fourteen years. Last summer, for example, was considered warm because May and the first part of June had none of the cold weather that is typical of most years. Yet the second half of last summer wasn't that much warmer than average, and at no time did we have stretches of 100° heat as we did in mid-July of this year. On paper the cold May and hot July of this year may even out and make this summer look "normal," but it certainly wasn't normal for the birds. It all depends on when the heat or the cold comes and how prolonged it is. Short bursts of cold weather interspersed with warmer conditions have far less impact on the swallows than the same number of cold days concentrated together.

With the cold weather early, the hot weather late, and not much time to get ready for migration, one would guess that fewer birds of all ages will survive to make it back next year. By continuing our research we'll know if that happens, and if it does, who survived and who didn't. How costly was breeding this summer relative to other years, and will the nonbreeders have the ultimate advantage by being more likely to return in 1996? The only thing we can safely predict about next summer is that it will be different in some way.

Tonight I give a slide presentation about our research to John Janovy's parasitology class. Looking at the photos of the birds on the screen, I realize that soon I'll be experiencing the thrill of cliff swallows only indirectly. On paper, through photos, in my mind.

Tomorrow's our last day to be here with the real ones.

July 26

Waking up this morning without a plan to go out to collect data is totally foreign to us after almost eighty days in the field. The warm, sunny weather makes staying in this morning seem even stranger. But I realize I don't need to worry about the weather anymore. Whether it's windy, sunny, cloudy, or rainy doesn't matter now. The only good thing about the field season's being over is that we won't have to battle the elements every day for the next nine months.

By noon the blue truck is loaded and parked in its overwintering spot in the garage, and the *Valdez* is packed with the stuff going back home with us. After lunch our primary task is to clean the apartment, and in an attempt to escape this fate I hike up to the tops of the bluffs overlooking Cedar Point. The highest of these bluffs tower three hundred feet above Keystone Lake and the river floodplain. I climb the rocky hill behind our apartment, a relatively gentle grade interspersed with irregular sandstone outcroppings and juniper trees. The rocky outcroppings here are similar to the cliffs that swallows nest on in Garden County, yet these by the station have never attracted birds. I wonder if the abundance of bridges, culverts, and the like so close to Cedar Point is why the swallows don't use these cliffs.

I sit on a rock at the top of the bluffs. Behind me is a flat pasture that extends to the south as far as I can see—the plateau between the North and South Platte valleys. In front of me, the North Platte valley escarpment drops abruptly, exposing spectacular views of Keystone Lake, the diversion dam, and the Sand Hills. The gently lumpy Sand Hills are much greener than they usually are in late July because of the wet summer. Staring at the Sand Hills, visible for maybe fifteen miles to the horizon, is what I do when I want to experience wilderness. They are desolate, unpopulated, not too changed by humans. And they are vast. I'm intimidated. What a challenge it must have been for the first settlers and ranchers to try to colonize portions—so much so that to this day Arthur County, seven hundred square miles out in the middle of them, has a human population of only 462.

Whenever I gaze at the Sand Hills, I become a little envious of scientists who get to do their research in wild places like that. Our work is not done in romantic or exotic locations: it's done in ditches under the road, on bridges over man-made canals, beside railroad tracks. I fantasize about what it would be like to study our birds out in the middle of the Sand Hills, far from the influence of humans and their trappings.

I always come back to reality after a while. Get real. There are no swallows in the Sand Hills. There's nothing you'd want to study out on those prairies, I tell myself. It's fun to daydream about the Sand Hills, though, pretending they're an impenetrable wilderness full of undiscovered biological secrets and new kinds of swallows.

Sitting here on my rock, I think of an essay John Janovy wrote fifteen years ago in one of his books about Keith County. He said you *need* what you can see from these bluffs, that this very view represents the human need for wilderness. For me the totality of a swallow summer embodies my need for wilderness, which translates into a need for the unpredictable, for excitement, danger, discovery, satisfaction, frustration, wonder. The past eighty days have had all this and a lot more.

After I spend a relaxing hour drinking in this beautiful vista, I figure it's time to climb back down to help Mary with the cleaning. But instead of finding her in the apartment sweeping the floor, I learn that she decided to go sailing. The vertebrate zoology instructor brought his sailboat with him and has been looking for a sailing partner. Mary jumped at the chance.

I get to spend what's left of my afternoon off cleaning by myself.

This evening we visit the Dairy Queen for an ice cream sundae—to toast the eleven-year-olds and to remember how excited the assistants got when we brought them here. It seems like ages ago. The trip to town tonight is officially to get dry ice to pack our dead birds in—the three net casualties, roadkills, and the juveniles the snake killed—for transport back to Tulsa tomorrow. It's also a chance to say good-bye to Ogallala. We feel more at home here than anywhere else we've lived, and we're going away for nine months. Sadness is beginning to overwhelm me, and I expect to get more emotional when we go to Whitetail for a final time tonight.

We drive from town directly to Whitetail. Our last visit until next May. On the way we pass Morning Glory, where several hundred birds are swarming at nests. These are the first cliff swallows we've seen all day. I didn't hear or see any passing overhead while I was up on the bluff. We cross Kingsley Dam, then head back east on the county road to Whitetail. We pull off on the roadside and stop just west of the culvert, far enough back to give us a good view of the birds entering and exiting. Will, the Swainson's hawk, is sitting on the telephone pole near us, watching bird TV again. He has a lot to watch tonight: there must be at least two thousand cliff swallows at Whitetail.

These birds are swarming in and out of the culvert like crazy. It looks like mid-May. I can see that many of them are independent juveniles, going into the middle tunnel, landing at nests, playing house. Hundreds more swallows are sitting on the power lines or foraging nearby. The usual squabbling is happening, with incoming birds trying to knock perched ones off the wire. Even juveniles are doing it. They start early in life being little butts to each other.

This concentration of birds is remarkable, even given Whitetail's tremendous appeal to this species. Maybe this is serving as a staging area; migratory bands are attracted to each other and assemble here for the night, with many of them ready to move on tomorrow and be replaced by others. I start to have doubts about whether we made the right call to stop the fieldwork. *All these birds here!* But I also know that they always concentrate at sites in the evenings, and if we went down there with a net all of them would leave. It's like the crèche in the fallen tree: they don't have to be here now. Still, it's very hard to be leaving tomorrow with this many birds still at Whitetail, even if almost all of them will be gone in a few days.

We just sit in the truck and watch for a while. Mary doesn't say anything because she knows I'm sad about leaving. I enjoy just watching the birds come and go, as we do early in the year before we start netting. It's soothing and peaceful. Soon, though, my mind starts to race in flashbacks to earlier this summer. I remember my first visit when I found so many nests had fallen and wondered whether the birds would rebuild them and whether Whitetail would be large this year. I remember the big day when we caught over seven hundred birds and how zombielike Annie and Kathy were afterward. I remember the abyss. I remember how wonderful it was to net the north side this year. I remember all the other characters who came and went here this summer—Will, Mortimer the muskrat, the predatory grackle, the fraternity-boy fishers, the bull snakes, the kestrel, and all the nonbreeding cliff swallows. God, the summer was short. The season just flew by.

I also start thinking about next year. How many of the birds we're seeing now will return next summer? How big will Whitetail be? What about the abyss—will it alter the creek's flow pattern and affect which tunnels will be preferred next year? Will the newer nests survive the off-season better, with fewer falling between now and next May? And my thoughts jump to other places. What about the new culverts along the railroad tracks? Which new and unused ones, if any, will be chosen next year? Will fumigated Dunwoody start to get bigger than Knight's Culvert? Will the birds be back in that weird tube again? Will the big bridge over the North Platte River just down the road, the site called Keystone, be used next year? It wasn't active this summer for the first time in over a decade. Will CR 4 be the big one next year instead of its neighbor CR 4½? Where will the nonbreeders show up, and what will they be doing?

My intense desire to get those answers is the magnet that will draw me back here.

It's a slow process, doing fieldwork on an animal as complex as the cliff swallow. Each year we take another step forward and uncover new questions and more steps to take. I came to Nebraska to study cliff swallows as a young man, and now I'm almost middle-aged. In between, I've had an exhilarating experience learning things about these birds I love so much. My career, as measured by external criteria—positions held, grants received, professional recognition—has had its ups and downs, but I've been on an ever-ascending high of discovery since the first day John Hoogland suggested I study cliff swallows. The essence of research is that intrinsic thrill and satisfaction of learning something new. No one can take your discoveries away from you. I don't need acclaim or other people's recognition that my research is interesting, although that's nice to have. There are many things *I* still want to learn about cliff swallows, and that's why I'll come back next summer. Whether anyone funds the fingerprinting project for next year is immaterial.

I'll be back.

I'm still surprised by the number of birds here this evening. Almost all the other colonies are deserted, yet a couple of thousand birds are concentrated at Whitetail. This illustrates why I think cliff swallows have so much to tell us about social life. They crave to be near others of their species, even though that crowding is often so costly to them. How can foraging advantages compensate the poor late nesters within a colony whose nests are overrun by parasites moving out of the earlier nests? They can't, because the late nesters lose their eggs and young entirely: the parasites kill them all. Ectoparasitism is the ultimate cost for these birds, and nothing can ameliorate the complete loss of reproductive success. Yet many birds insist on crowding in with others, sometimes well past the point where it can be beneficial. I see all these birds trying to squeeze into the culvert right now, wasting a lot of energy fighting and quarreling over nests to sit in. Go down the road to Keystone, birds. There are hundreds of empty nests there, probably ones that don't have bugs. But everybody's here—the herd mentality at work.

Humans have the herd mentality too. Although I'm not supposed to anthropomorphize my research animals, I can see all manner of parallels between cliff swallow social life and that of people. Take a big colony like Spillway, for instance. It's an avian slum, New York City incarnate among birds. Crime is high; losing property to thieves is always a threat. Someone is constantly out to cheat you or exploit you, maybe by giving you an extra egg to care for. Keep your doors locked—or your nest guarded—at all times. It's a place for roving gangs of hoodlums, adolescents out to steal from you, and especially from your defenseless small children.

So why live in such an environment? The answer depends on who you are. If you're the one who's able to exploit others, maybe you'll do okay with so many potential victims to choose from. But the victims don't seem to gain anything; the late nesters in the big colonies pay the ultimate cost. It's easy to see why well-paid businesspeople or celebrities might live in a New York City, but why do Joe and Jane Average? Wouldn't they be better off in Roscoe, Nebraska? Their opportunities—the "benefits" of their smaller colony—might not be much changed, but the costs would be much less. Why are humans so social at times, and yet why do many of us seem so miserable being around others?

I don't study cliff swallows to shed light on human behavior. I don't care that much about humans. Perhaps someday someone will explore the patterns common to swallow coloniality and that of people. They exist, because some general principles apply across all social organisms. Increased competition for resources in larger groups is inevitable, whether you're talking about cliff swallows in different colonies competing for insect food or humans in different cities competing for precious space to put their garbage. Parasites and disease-causing pathogens spread faster in bigger groups, whether it's parasitic bugs in cliff swallow colonies or a flu virus in human cities.

It's time to say good-bye. Damn, it's hard to drive away from Whitetail. The importance of this little road culvert in my life overwhelms me. I think of all the hours spent here over the past fourteen years, of the thousands of birds caught here, of all the assistants who've been here, of all we've learned about cliff swallows here. Mary understands how difficult it is for me and says she's ready to go back only when I am.

July 27

We said our good-byes yesterday. All that's left now is get in the truck and go home.

We get up at dawn, as we did during the heat wave. Another hot spell is developing, and Diana, Tony, and the others have my sympathy for having to endure 100° heat again. No one else is up this early, and I'm glad there'll be no more farewell scenes. We put the last items in the *Valdez* and drive out the west gate.

The last thing to be loaded was a cardboard box containing all the completed data sheets from this summer. The box weighs fourteen pounds. Our whole lives, everything we've lived for during the past eighty days, are in that box. Its contents are priceless, completely irreplaceable. I'll be paranoid until we get it safely to Tulsa. When we stop for gas and restroom breaks, either Mary or I will always stay with the truck. When we stop for lunch, we'll park so I can watch the truck—and the fourteen pounds of data—out the window of the restaurant.

We grab some donuts in Ogallala for breakfast, and soon we're headed to the interstate and eastward. A few cliff swallows are flying near the Ogallala bridge and at the culvert called McDonald's close to North Platte. Those are the only ones we see this morning. The symmetry of everything is comforting. When we arrived eighty days ago, we saw the first cliff swallows of the year at McDonald's and Ogallala.

We drive along in silence. We're both reflecting on the summer. What I'll miss the most, besides the birds, is the uncertainty of fieldwork. The thrill of the unexpected. Out here something new, something unusual, something not predicted is always happening. The challenge of continually dealing with the unexpected is what I'll miss when we "return to the world." Life back home is regimented, orderly, boring, and only occasionally does something unpredictable happen.

Life back home. Ugh! I cringe at what lies ahead during the next nine months, stuff I could blissfully ignore during the past eighty days. Ahead of me await classrooms where I'll have to try to teach students who don't want to learn, who want to be handed a college degree just for showing up. Ahead of me waits the chore of sitting on committees to evaluate whether some of my colleagues deserve tenure and promotion. Other trials and tribulations of the off-season await: stupid academic politics, the reams of administrative red tape required of any university professor nowadays; fighting about manuscripts with editors and reviewers; wasting time writing grant proposals, most of which have little hope of being funded. But I do these things, as cheerfully as I can, because doing them makes it possible, ultimately, for me to come to Cedar Point for eighty days and study swallows.

I try to redirect my thoughts back to cliff swallows. Who might be able to tell me something about the plumage of nonbreeders? As soon as we return, I need to talk with one of my graduate students who'll also be studying cliff swallows. He wants to go to south-central Arizona—where I first tried to study cliff swallows fifteen years ago—and collect some data on the Mexican cliff swallows to compare with the Nebraska population. In two days he leaves on a scouting trip. We need to discuss what he should look for.

At North Platte we turn south. We've seen the last cliff swallows of the summer. There are none anywhere along our route in Kansas or Oklahoma. The hot and sunny day is in stark contrast to the cool and stormy weather we experienced when we drove this road in May, but it's been such a wet year that the fields are still lush and green. When we stop for lunch in Hays, Kansas, the temperature has already exceeded 100°.

When we arrive in Wichita, we're in more traffic than I've seen in the past eighty days. The frantic, hectic life of a large colony. As honking cars zip around us on the four-lane interstate, it finally hits me that the summer is over. Really over. Nine months to go. Whitetail seems a million miles away, I lament. Mary smiles and tells me to relax. Whitetail's never far away, she says, for it's always there in your heart.

She's right.

Index